T0350300

Turks in the Indian Subcontinent, Central and West Asia

Turks in the Indian Subcontinent, Central and West Asia

The Turkish Presence in the Islamic World

Edited by
Ismail K. Poonawala

OXFORD
UNIVERSITY PRESS

OXFORD
UNIVERSITY PRESS

Oxford University Press is a department of the University of Oxford.
It furthers the University's objective of excellence in research, scholarship,
and education by publishing worldwide. Oxford is a registered trademark of
Oxford University Press in the UK and in certain other countries.

Published in India by
Oxford University Press
YMCA Library Building, 1 Jai Singh Road, New Delhi 110 001, India

© Oxford University Press 2017

The moral rights of the authors have been asserted.

First Edition published in 2017

ISBN-13: 978-0-19-809220-9
ISBN-10: 0-19-809220-2

Typeset in ScalaPro 10/13
by The Graphics Solution, New Delhi 110 092
Printed in India by Replika Press Pvt. Ltd

CONTENTS

FIGURES

NOTE ON TRANSLITERATION

The system of transliteration used in this book for Arabic, Persian, Turkish, and Urdu is essentially the same as that adopted in the second edition of *The Encyclopaedia of Islam*, with a few modifications, namely j for *jīm* instead of dj; q for *qāf* instead of ḳ. Pairs of letters joined by a bar underneath, such as dh, gh, kh, sh, and th are written without the bar.

Well-known place names, such as Mecca, Medina, Baghdad, Damascus, as well as certain terms like imam, imamate, caliph, and caliphate are retained in their accepted English forms as given by the Webster's *Third New International Dictionary of the English Language*.

ABBREVIATIONS FOR PERIODICALS

A	*Anadolu/Anatolia*
AA	*Artibus Asiae*
AARP	*Art and Archaeology Research Papers*
AB	*Art Bulletin*
ABSA	*Annual of the British School, Athens*
AeI	*Athar-e Iran*
AEMA	*Archivum Eurasiae Medii Aeivi*
AI	*Annales Islamologiques*
AIUON	*Annali dell' Istituto Universitario Orientale di Napoli*
Annales	*Histoire, Sciences Sociales (École des Hautes Études en Sciences Sociales, Paris)*
AOASH/AO	*Acta Orientalia Academiae Scientiarum Hungaricae also referred to as Acta Orientalia*
ArOt	*Archivum Ottomanicum*
ArsI	*Ars Islamica*
Belleten	*Belleten of Türk Tarih Kurumu*
BSOAS	*Bulletin of the School of Oriental and African Studies (London)*
BSOS	*Bulletin of the School of Oriental Studies (London)*
CAJ	*Central Asiatic Journal*
CL	*Country Life*
DMBI	*Dā'irat al-macārif-i buzurg-i Islāmī (Tehran)*
EI2	*Encyclopaedia of Islam, 2nd ed.*
EIr	*Encyclopaedia Iranica*
EW	*East and West*
GMS	*Gibb Memorial Series*

IA	ıslam Ansiklopedisi
IC	Islamic Culture
IESHR	Indian Economic and Social History Review
IJMES	International Journal of Middle East Studies
IOS	Israel Oriental Studies
IQ	The Islamic Quarterly
Iran	Iran, Journal of the British Institute of Persian Studies
IrCaucasus	Iran and the Caucasus
IS	Iranian Studies (The Journal of the Society for Iranian Studies)
Islam	Der Islam
JA	Journal Asiatique
JAOS	Journal of the American Oriental Society
JESHO	Journal of the Economic and Social History of the Orient
JIH	Journal of Indian History
JMES	Journal of Middle East Studies
JRAS	Journal of the Royal Asiatic Society
JRASB	Journal of the Royal Asiatic Society of Bengal
JSS	Journal of Semitic Studies
JTL	Journal of Turkish Literature
JWCI	Journal of the Warburg & Courtauld Institutes
JWH	Journal of World History
KCA	Körösi Csoma Archivum
Kdo	Kunst des Orients
Keletkutatas	Hungarian Journal
MAS	Modern Asian Studies
MLI	Mare Luso-Indicum
OA	Oriental Art
PTF	Philologiae Turcicae Fundamenta
RAfr	Revue Africaine
REB	Revue d'études byzantines
REI	Revue des Études Islamiques
RO	Rocznik Orientalistyczny
SA	South Asia
SIH	Studies in History, Journal of the Centre of Historical Studies, Jawaharlal Nehru University, New Delhi
SI	Studia Islamica
South Asia	Journal of South Asian Studies (South Asian Studies Association of Australia)
ST	Sovetskaya Tyurkologiya
STY	Sanat Tarihi Yilliği

Turcica	*Revue d'Études Turques: Peuples, langues, cultures, états (École des Hautes Études en Sciences Sociales, Paris)*
VD	*Vakıflar Dergisi*
ZDMG	*Zeitschrift der Deutschen Morgenländischen Gesellschaft*

PREFACE

The papers collected in this volume were delivered on the occasion of the nineteenth Giorgio Levi Della Vida Award and Conference in Islamic Studies held by the Gustave E. von Grunebaum Center for Near Eastern Studies at the University of California, Los Angeles, on 18–19 May 2010. The Giogio Levi Della Vida Medal was established by the late Gustave von Grunebaum, the founder and first director of the Center, to honour the memory of this illustrious Italian linguist of Semitic languages for his expertise on the history and culture of the Near East and his contributions to the development of Near Eastern Studies in the United States. He was born in Venice in 1886 to a Jewish family and moved with them to Genoa and then to Rome. He studied at the University of Rome with the Hebraist Ignazio Guidi and graduated in 1909. Thereafter he participated in several expeditions to Cairo, Crete, and Athens. In 1911 he returned to Rome and worked with Leone Caetani, historian of the Near East, on the editorial staff of the *Annali dell'Islām* (*Annals of Islam*).[1] From 1914 to 1916, he headed the department of Arabic language and literature at the Eastern University of Naples. During the First World War, he was an army interpreter and then was appointed to the department of Semitic Philology at the University Torino. In 1920 he moved to the University of Rome as a professor of Hebrew and Comparative Semitic Languages. In 1924, he became the president of the National Union of Liberal and Democratic Forces. He was among the twelve Italian university professors who refused to pledge an oath of allegiance to the Fascist leader and regime in 1931. At this time he was assigned by the Vatican Library to catalogue its Arabic manuscripts.

Following the promulgation of the radical laws in Italy in 1939, Giorgio Levi Della Vida fled to the United States. Upon his arrival he was offered a teaching position first at the University of Pennsylvania, Philadelphia, and then at the University of California in San Diego (UCSD). As a token of his appreciation for the support he received from UCSD, he donated his private library to the latter institution.[2] He returned to Italy in 1945 and was reinstated to his position at the University of Rome, where he taught Islamic history and culture until his retirement in 1959. He died in Rome in 1967 after a brief illness.

The award was established in 1967 to encourage research in the field of Islamic Studies and to honour distinguished scholars in the field. The medal is awarded biennially to an outstanding scholar whose work has significantly advanced the study of the Islamic civilization. The scholar is selected by a committee of international scholars appointed by the Chancellor of the University of California, Los Angeles, under the chairmanship of the director of the Gustave von Grunebaum Center for Near Eastern Studies. The award carries with it the obligation to present in person a formal lecture at the University of California, Los Angeles, as part of a conference. The recipient chooses the theme of the conference, and variations on the theme are presented by a group of senior scholars with well-established international reputations selected by the recipient.

The recipient of the 2010 award was Professor Clifford Edmund Bosworth. He selected the theme 'The Turkish Presence in the Islamic World'. He is the author and/or editor of more than twenty books on various topics ranging from the premodern history of the Central and Eastern Islamic lands and of Central Asia, to high Arabic literature. His first book, *The Ghaznavids: Their Empire in Afghanistan and Eastern Iran*, based on his doctoral dissertation and published in 1964, set a high standard of scholarship and research. It was followed by *The History of the Saffarids of Sistan and the Maliks of Nimruz* and *The Later Ghaznavids: Splendour and Decay*. Yet, his other work entitled *The Medieval Islamic Underworld: The Banu Sasan in Arabic Society and Literature* demonstrates his ability to tackle unusual topics through a critical analysis of literary sources. His English edition of W. Barthold's *Historical Geography of Iran* surpasses the prestigious Russian edition. For more than thirty years, he served as an editor for the second edition of *The Encyclopedia of Islam*. He is also a consulting editor for the *Encyclopedia Iranica* and co-editor of *Iran, Journal of the British Institute of Persian Studies*.

Finally, it is my pleasure to thank my student Eric Bordenkircher, who is about to finish his PhD dissertation in Islamic Studies, for his assistance in editing the chapters and his keen eye for details and consistency. Without his help the volume might not have been as readable as it is now.

Ismail K. Poonawala

Notes

1. It is a monumental study of the sources for the life of Muḥammad and his immediate four successors. Caetani gives for each event in the texts, all the versions in chronological order with a detailed critical analysis. Ten volumes, published between 1905 and 1926, cover the early Islamic history until the year 40 of the Hijra.
2. Unfortunately, in the late 1970s the UCSD discontinued Arabic language classes; consequently this collection was disbanded and sent to the UCLA library. The librarian kept the copies they did not have, but sold the remaining items. I was lucky to buy several volumes in Arabic.

INTRODUCTION

Ismail K. Poonawala

The present volume is neither a historical nor a political narrative in the usual sense of the words; rather it is a collection of papers delivered at a conference that explored the emergence of the Turkish peoples and their contribution to the historical development of the Islamic world and its civilization. It is, therefore, a work of collective scholarship where one finds contributions from some of the best scholars on Islamic history. From their respective fields of specialization, these scholars reassess the contribution of the Turks in the shaping of the Islamic civilization. The scope of the book is not restricted to the original homeland of the Turkish people in Central Asia or present-day Turkey but extends far beyond their geographical homeland to the Indian subcontinent where they dominated for several centuries since the establishment of the Delhi Sultanate and culminating in the Mughal Empire.

Although the contributions of the Turkish peoples to the historical development of the Islamic world and its civilization have been overshadowed by the Arabs and the Persians, their role in the further expansion of Islam and its advancement cannot be underestimated. Students of Islamic history know very well that Arabic, Persian, and Turkish are the three major linguistic components for the study of Islam and Islamic culture. Hence, it will not be out of place to cite Marshall Hodgson from his monumental work *The Venture of Islam*. The rise of Persian, he writes, had more than purely literary consequences. It served to carry a new overall cultural orientation within

Islamdom. While Arabic held its own as the primary language of the religious disciplines and even of natural sciences and philosophy, Persian became, an increasingly significant component of Islamdom, the language of polite culture, and even invaded the realm of scholarship. He further observes that more local languages of high culture that later emerged among Muslims, such as Turkish, Urdu, and so on, depended upon Persian as their prime literary inspiration. Henceforth, the Turks also developed nuanced and sophisticated political and cultural traditions. It cannot be ignored that some enduring political and economic institutions introduced in India by the Mughals were developed by the Turks in Central and West Asia.

Turkish rulers and military commanders came to dominate vast stretches of Islamic lands, from Algeria in the West to the Bay of Bengal in the East, from the middle of the Volga region in the North to Yemen in the South, for almost a millennium until the early twentieth century. And their presence was by no means limited to military and governmental aspects; Turkish scholars, theologians, jurists, poets, and other literary figures, all became part of the rich fabric of the Islamic world and its culture. The chapters collected in this volume demonstrate the richness and profoundness of their contribution and how it developed from the emergence of the Turkish people in their Inner Asian homeland to the formation of prominent and powerful states, such as the Qarakhanids, the Seljuqs of Rum, the mighty Ottomans, the rulers of Turkish origin in Iran (the Safavids) and the Mughals of India, and their cultural and literary achievements. The political process in those empires was deeply influenced by the Turkish presence. Their military organization, ethos, and beliefs provide a common thread that runs through the fabric of those empires. In focusing on their social and cultural activities, several of the chapters bring to light some neglected aspects of Islamic culture.

The chapters are organized into five broad sections as follows:

Part I: Cultural changes among the Turks and their emergence in the Islamic world;
Part II: The Seljuqs and their legacy;
Part III: The Turks in the Indian Subcontinent;
Part IV: Turkish achievements in cartography and geography; and
Part V: Turkish connection to the origins of the Safavids.

The first and the foremost theme treated in Part I is the emergence of the Turks in the Islamic world. It should be noted that the history of early Turks, especially the process of their incorporation in the

Islamic world, has been rather neglected by historians. Scholars in this section move beyond conventional frames of reference and investigate issues of identity, consciousness, and historical memory among the Turks once they entered the Islamic fold. These articles address an important lacuna in our knowledge, and enrich our understanding of the early Turks.

The first essay by Peter B. Golden deals with historical memory and notions of history among the early Turkic peoples. Did the Turkic peoples who entered the Islamic orbit bring with them a historicized past? Were there written historical accounts? If not, what was the role of oral tradition? The author notes that the monuments of Old Turkic have not mentioned a word about their history as such. This leads him to examine various extant inscriptions. The most significant in this respect are the historical accounts in Turkic, written in runiform script on royal tomb complexes of the Uyğurs in the eighth century who succeeded the Turks of the eastern empire. Ethnogonic tales, hinted at in the inscriptions, and preserved in Chinese sources, also promoted the miraculous origins of the Ashina royal clan of the Turks, born of a wolf, a theme widespread across Eurasia. According to Ibn Faḍlān, the Khazars, the Ashina-ruled successors of the Turks in the westernmost region of their empire, also built tomb complexes. However, they are yet to be discovered. Khazar-generated historical data of the tenth century mentions their genealogical tree going back to the Biblical figure Togarmah, son of Japheth. In his *Dīwān lughāt al-Turk*, Maḥmūd al-Kāshghrī, dealing with Islamized and Islamizing Turkic groups, he presents their genealogies in accordance with Islamic and Iranian traditions as descended from Turk, the son of Hapheth (Yāfith). Golden concludes his essay by stating that Islam, and Seljuq and Mongol hegemony effaced the older wolf-Ashina Turk traditions and promoted the various Oghuz Khan legends as the starting point of steppe and Turko-Islamic history. Nonetheless, the author notes, the old wolf-Ashina traditions continued among Qipchaq Turkic peoples, especially among those who were relatively latecomers to Islam.

The second essay by Gary Leiser is based on *waqf* (pious endowments) documents dating back to the thirteenth century. He examines those records to demonstrate how the Seljuq Turks of Anatolia used those pious endowments as instruments to speed up the process of the Islamization of Anatolia in the thirteenth century. Leiser's research focuses on Christian properties, including Christian villages that were established as *waqfs* to support various Muslim institutions such as mosques and *madrasas*. The study reveals the extent to which those endowments undermined the economic and social structure of the Christian community and thus played a role in the transformation of Anatolia from a predominantly Christian to a largely Muslim region and, ultimately, its Turkification.

The third chapter in this section by C. E. Bosworth traces the interaction, and the initial inclusion into, of the Turks with the Islamic World. According to Bosworth, the main catalyst for the incorporation of the Turks into the Muslim community was the need for slaves and soldiers during the Abbasid Empire. It was the performance of the Turks in battle that garnered an appreciation among Arab Muslims in the Empire but also the perception that they were uncivilized. As Bosworth argues, it was this barbaric stereotype that slowed their assimilation into the Muslim community and made the Arabs look down on the Turks. Furthermore, he suggests that Arab Muslims attempted to maintain a monopoly on the areas of scholarship and religious leadership to prevent it from being diluted by non-Arabs. It is worth noting that in discussions pertaining to Islamic culture, its distinctive, rich, and profuse character, historians have generally concerned themselves with the Arabs and the Persians, assigning a footnote to the Turks for their military contributions.

Chapters in Part II deal with the Seljuq architecture and educational system. These essays are of great significance for those who are interested in looking at Islamic history as an integrated unity with variations on the theme. The first chapter in this section by Robert Hillenbrand examines the relationship between the Iranian and Anatolian traditions of architecture in the period between 1100 and 1300. He explains how the Iranian architectural tradition, enriched by elements from the neighbouring and cognate culture of contemporary dynasties in Afghanistan and Central Asia, reached maturity at a time when Anatolia was still largely Christian. Politically and culturally, the relationship between the eastern Iranian world and that of the Rum Seljuqs and the other lesser Anatolian dynasties was that of a senior to junior partner. However, it was the Iranian and not the Anatolian world that felt the full annihilating force of the Mongol invasion, and this allowed the Anatolian architectural tradition to develop rapidly and to such effect that briefly it was able to eclipse that of Iran in the thirteenth century. By concentrating on five interlinked topics, namely material, form, scale, structure, and ornament, the chapter identifies how these two sister traditions of Seljuq architecture diverged. It also examines what their distinctive strengths were and what links could be proposed between them.

The second chapter by Carole Hillenbrand discusses the creation of the Nizamiyya colleges under the watchful eye of Nizam al-Mulk, the well-known Seljuq vizier of the Sultan Alp Arslan and Malik Shah. Her study addresses the Nizamiyya in Baghdad, the physical attributes of these centers of learning, their students and the curricula. She argues that the personal involvement of Nizam al-Mulk in the establishment of the Nizamiyyas served as a means to stabilize and unify the various forces within the Seljuq Empire during his lifetime. This chapter has implications that go beyond the Seljuq state. The Nizamiyya education was at the core of the madrasa reforms in Mughal India, where there was a marked shift of emphasis from traditional to rational sciences.

The three chapters in Part III are marked by a sustained reflection on neglected themes in Indian Muslim historiography. The first chapter by Sunil Kumar deals with trans-regional contacts and relationships between Turks, Mongols, and the Delhi Sultanate in the thirteenth and fourteenth centuries. One should bear in mind that the making of the Delhi Sultanate coincided with the sacking of Baghdad in 1258, the seat of the Islamic caliphate, by the Mongols. Thus, in the literary records of the Delhi Sultanate, the Mongols are depicted as the great threat while the Sultanate is regarded as resolutely combating the Mongol menace. As *Dār al-Islām* is destroyed, the court of Delhi is regarded as the 'Sanctuary of Islam' where Islam and Islamic culture flourish. Immigration and regional contacts with the central Islamic lands are, therefore, treated as peripheral to their narratives of Sultanate history. Kumar questions those accounts and interrogates the sources to uncover different kinds of contacts and relations between the Delhi Sultanate and the regions euphemistically described as the 'upper lands' (*iqlīm-i bālā*). Kumar also probes the nature of elisions in the documentation regarding the contact of the Sultanate with the Turks and the Mongols. He poses the questions: What were the nature and extent of those contacts and why do the chroniclers find it difficult to put them at the forefront of their narratives? Their silence, Kumar asserts, is extraordinary when one recognizes that many of the Delhi Sultans were Turks and that the founding dynasts of two Sultanate regimes were at one time Mongol auxiliaries and brought with them a train of retinues that had spent a large part of their career fighting in the Afghan frontier.

The second essay, written by a leading historian of Mughal India, explores emotions and their reflection not only in literary works but the great monuments of architecture of the period. This is, I think, one of the first attempts to employ the methods of emotional history when analysing the Mughal Empire. It is quite correct to state that no early modern Muslim ruling dynasty has left as rich a record of their lives and personal feeling as the great Mughals. This valuable record of royal memoirs, such as *Baburnama, Tuzuk-i Jahangiri*, and correspondence between the emperors and their princes, cover most family relationships and most human emotions. Adopting a somewhat novel approach to this subject in his chapter, Francis Robinson focuses on two types of particularly powerful relationships: father and sons, and husband and wife. The former embraced the whole gamut of paternal and filial emotions, often mixed with personal rivalry, bloody succession struggles, and court intrigues. The latter reveals enduring family traits of respect and often passionate love for their womenfolk. Robinson adds that in some cases it is possible to make connections between the powerful emotions generated in the family and some of the great monuments they built, such as the Taj Mahal.

Historians know very little of the Turkish literature written in the Mughal period. Scholars working on Mughal literary tradition have almost exclusively confined themselves to the Persian works, with occasional references to Arabic and Hindawi works. The Turkish works written in Mughal India have generally been ignored. The third chapter by Benedek Péri brings to light and explores the state of Turkish language and literature in medieval and modern India and tries to answer a number of questions. Did the Turks who settled in India use Turkish? If they did, when, where, how, for what purposes, and for how long? Was the language of their ancestors the only means of communication with their families, or did it serve other purposes? Did the Turkish language gain any special role in India? The readers will be pleasantly surprised as the chapter uncovers several yet to be studied aspects of Turkish language in India.

Part IV deals with the contribution of the Turks in the field of cartography and geography. Leaving aside the early Muslim contributions in this field, in the flux of scholarly works on European overseas trade and discovery, and the subsequent scientific revolution, the contributions of the Turks in map-making and oceanography have been ignored by the Western historians. The two essays based on the accounts of the famous adventurer, Evliya Çelebi and the cartographer, Piri Reis highlight their contributions in the field. In the first chapter of this section Robert Dankoff addresses an entirely new field of investigation and explores Evliya Çelebi's expeditions on the Nile. Evliya Çelebi had spent decades crisscrossing the vast territories of the Ottoman Empire and had recorded his adventures in a

nine-volume work entitled *Seyahatname* (Travelogue). After arriving
in Cairo in 1672 at the age of sixty, he spent the next ten years exploring Egypt and its African hinterland. These explorations, Dankoff
states, resulted in two monumental achievements: first, the tenth
volume of his *Seyahatname*, half of which is devoted to his expeditions on the Nile; and second, a large map of the Nile, preserved in the
Vatican library. Dankoff's contention is that the Nile is the linchpin
of these monumental achievements providing structure and pattern
for a myriad of other extensive notes and comments. Moreover, the
two (the expeditions on the Nile and its map) were conceived and
executed together as the twin culmination of a half century of travel,
exploration and writing.

In the second article, Svat Soucek takes up an entirely new field
of investigation. The topic of his essay is the place of the Ottoman
Empire and Ottoman civilization, during its early period and in
the context of the rise of the contemporaneous West, as perceived
through the cartographic and geographical literature produced by
Turks. Subsequently, the focus of inquiry shifts to the life and work
of Piri Reis and related matters in the sixteenth century. Voyages of
exploration and discovery, overseas trade, scientific revolutions, and
incipient colonization were the hallmarks of the dawn of the modern
era. The great cartographer Piri Reis had focused on one aspect of
those dynamic forces that fuelled the rise of the West. In 1526 Piri
Reis presented an expanded version of the *Kitabi Bahriye* (Book on
Navigation) to Suleyman the Magnificent. He was in an ideal position to launch a most rewarding career. All that he needed was the
Sultan's endorsement to organize an Ottoman counterpart to the
Spanish *Casa de Contratacion* or the Portuguese *Casa da India*. Had
the Sultan supported the plan, a team of gifted and eager adepts using
the remarkable collection of maps, charts, and texts the master Piri
Reis had collected during three decades of sailing and research, he
would have given birth to an outstanding Ottoman school of cartography and oceanography. Since the Sultan did not pay any attention to
this adventurous Ottoman Turk, his work went unnoticed.

The final chapter of the book by Ali Anooshahr stands apart from
other studies; hence it occupies this part by itself. The author re-
examines the rise of the Safavid Sufi order in late fifteenth-century
northwestern Iran that subsequently established one of Iran's most
brilliant dynasties, the Safavids, and exposes the role of the Turks in
the success of their military campaigns. Modern scholars have generally treated the rise and development of the Safavids under Shaykh

Junayd and Shaykh Haydar as a teleology of heterodox religious uprisings reaching its apex under Shah Isma'il, the founder of the Safavid state who projected himself as a millennial saviour figure. Anooshahr contends the prevailing view and with new evidence gleaned from the sources of their origins argues that the father and grandfather of Shah Isma'il were marginal figures in the Sufi order who were pushed to desperate actions due to interference in their religious/Sufi institutions under the Qaraquyunlu dynasty. He further argues that their military (or plundering) campaigns in the Caucasus coincided with certain developments in the Ottoman Empire that allowed for the recruitment of not only newly converted, semi-literate Turkoman pastoral tribes, but also Turkoman soldiers in search of fortune. He concludes that the accusation of heresy was brought up against them only after the death of Shaykh Haydar.

I

CULTURAL CHANGES AMONG THE TURKS AND THEIR EMERGENCE IN THE ISLAMIC WORLD

I

'ETERNAL STONES'
Historical Memory and Notions of History among the Early Turkic Peoples

PETER B. GOLDEN

Medieval chroniclers and annalists, no less than modern historians, chose from 'a spectrum of *memorabilia*'[1] those historical memories that they considered edifying or worthy of note. This was often done with the intention of presenting an ideologized representation of events, trumpeting the virtues, heroic deeds, and victories of rulers and dynasties that legitimated their rule. Controlling the past constituted one of the 'fundamental aspects of power and authority'.[2] Official, written history could also shape collective memory, which became as politicized as official accounts.[3]

Medieval notions of history were closely tied to religion, especially in the Judeo–Christian–Islamic traditions, in which history illuminated the workings of the divine in human affairs. In some societies, not entirely divorced from notions of ancestor worship, history also served as an important guide to precedents, proper practice, and, flowing from that, guidelines for the resolution of political problems. Thus, in China, advisers to the emperor often based their rationale for a particular course of action on documented historical precedents.[4] As is well known, the imperial agrarian civilizations (China, Greater Iran, and subsequently the Caliphate, and more distantly Byzantium) surrounding the Turkic Central Eurasian world were history-oriented. But, what of the pre-Islamic Turkic nomadic peoples to their north, the followers of *Tengri*, the supreme celestial deity of the Turko-Mongolian world[5] and the practitioners of some form of shamanism?[6] Did they keep written historical records? Were written historical precedents summoned to play a role in decision-making? If written records were lacking, what was the role of oral tradition and what distinctions should be made between it, 'history', and 'collective memory'?[7] In short, did the Turkic peoples who entered the Islamic orbit bring with them a historicized past and, if so, what happened to those notions with Islamization and direct contact with the Middle East?

We begin our discussion with the period when Turkic-speaking peoples were first coming into the view of their sedentary neighbours, all of whom possessed writing and time-keeping systems (for example, calendars)—the basic tools needed to produce a written record to be passed on to posterity. The earliest historical record is rather one-sided. Aside from one major monument, from c. 582 (others are now coming to light) and the remarkable eighth-century runiform inscriptions in Mongolia stemming from the Türks and Uyğurs, and those of the Qırğız found in the Yensei region,[8] it is the Turks' sedentary neighbours who record their traditions and tell us much more about the peoples of their 'tribal borderlands' than the latter do about themselves. This is not to say that pre-literate peoples largely relying on oral traditions lack historical consciousness. Modern studies of oral traditions indicate that they most definitely do not.[9]

Unfortunately, we encounter the familiar paucity of sources. There is no doubt that history-relating or history-bearing oral traditions in nomadic Central Eurasia existed—and continue into modern times,[10] for example, the tales of the deeds of *alp eren* ('heroic fighting men'). For the medieval era, Maḥmûd al-Kâṣġarî, writing in c. 1077 in an Islamic milieu, provides us with fragments of poetry and tales that relate to historical events.[11]

Although genealogies, real and fictive, the building blocks of history, constitute an important part of essential knowledge among the nomads of Central Eurasia,[12] early ethnogonic myths have largely been preserved in accounts written down by the neighbours of the Turkic Central Eurasian nomads rather than coming directly from the latter in their own tongues. We will follow the ethnogonic theme in the course of this chapter. The question of language is also interesting. The Türks, the first of the Turkic peoples to write their history, initially recorded events not in Turkic, but in Soġdian, the lingua franca of the Silk Road, which may have functioned as a chancellery language for them. With ongoing archaeological investigations, our current picture is changing. The earliest Türk inscription with historical content is found in the poorly preserved Bugut stele dated to 582 BCE, part of the burial complex[13] for Tatpar Qağan (Chin. 佗鉢 Tuobo/Tabo, [EMC $tā/t^ha pat$] r. 572–81).[14] It contains an inscription in Soğdian as well as twenty lines in Sanskrit. Although fragmentary, it makes reference to some figures that are otherwise barely known or unknown.[15] The stele was mounted on a tortoise, a symbol of longevity borrowed from China or India in the mythologies of which the world rested on the back of a tortoise.[16] It is found as the socle of all the Türk and Uyğur burial steles.[17] Tatpar's Buddhist inclinations should also be taken into account.[18] In addition, the site had balbals, stone statues symbolizing slain foes, a common feature of later Türk grave complexes.[19] The monument in its imagery and symbols shows Buddhist, Indian, Chinese, and Mazdean influences.[20] Clearly, it reflected the syncretism of Türk culture and addressed a wide audience. There are also Soğdian fragments associated with stone statues and Türk royal burials in Xinjiang (for example, that of Nirî Qağan) in the last quarter of the sixth century. The number of these stone statues scattered across the steppes has been placed at 1,000. Some 200 are found in Xinjiang. Work on the inscriptional material is still in its infancy.[21] Perhaps dating to this same period is the inscription of the Huis Tolgoy Memorial complex with the still unread Brâhmî and Kharoṣṭhî inscriptions.[22]

In the early eighth century, the Türks produced written historical records in Turkic: the runiform inscriptions of the Orkhon and surrounding areas.[23] These monuments are similar to Bugut in style[24] and also contain material in Soğdian (and other languages like Chinese). The Turkic runiform script dates from at least the early eighth century and perhaps even as early as the sixth century, and has been found in various forms across Turkic-speaking Eurasia, from Danubian Europe to Mongolia.[25] It is clear from the beauty and poetry of the language that the history recorded therein was preceded by a long oral and history-reciting tradition that continued practices already on display in the Bugut inscriptions.[26] Louis Bazin, writing in 1963, suggested that the Turkic runiform inscriptions appeared 'spontaneously as the natural development of the funeral rite',[27] but the Bugut inscription, was not known when he wrote that. The Orkhon inscriptions had a prehistory. Moreover, these major inscriptions, whether in Soğdian or Turkic, came into being in critical periods. Bugut, although open to a number of variant readings, does have Tatpar Qağan as its central focus. He was the last of the Ashina qağans to rule over a united empire. After his reign, fragmentation, inherent early on, set in and the eastern and western qaǧanates grew apart.[28]

There has also been considerable debate regarding the genre of the inscriptions: history, historical tales, epics, poems, a form of folklore, or some combination of them all?[29] Recently, D.V. Ruxljadev has argued, correctly in my view, that their authors were not 'professional historians' seeking to present a systematic interpretation of the past. Rather, their goals were primarily eulogistic and propagandistic. Like the *rhetors* of old, they sang the praises of the deceased ruler 'in the context of the official ideology', using historical events to shape a point of view for their readers (or listeners)[30] and promoting formulae underscoring the dynasty's divine origins or association with the divine. A certain stylization is certainly present, but 'mythological and poetic (deliberately invented) motifs' are largely absent. As a consequence, the Orkhon inscriptions cannot be termed 'historical tales'. The events described are too concrete with specific details and dates that are usually lacking in epics. While there may be some exaggeration of personal acts of heroism, there is nothing of the 'fantastic' in the accounts. The events are real and anchored in specifically stated times. Although drawing on the same 'raw' material as historical tales and from *memorates* ('blocks of syncretic information' about events), the Orkhon inscriptions with their strong political-ideological message, buttressed by precise historical facts, aim at convincing the audience.[31] History has a lesson; it gives evidence of the workings of the divine in human affairs. The rulers had the mandate of heaven to rule (KT, S9: 'because Heaven/the Celestial God so ordered, because I myself possessed the heavenly good fortune I became [lit. 'sat'] Qaǧan': *täŋri yarlıqaδwqın üčün özüm qutwm bar üčün qaǧan olorDwm*[32]); failure to heed the Qaǧans invariably brings disaster to the Türks and swift punishment to the subject peoples. Türk historical writing was hardly unique in presenting official ideologies, engaging in fulsome praise of rulers and stern warnings to those who disobey.

The authors were not newcomers to the art of historical narration and the documents/monuments are alive with human speech, drama, and action. Interestingly enough, we know the names of the authors who composed the texts and/or oversaw the carving of those texts on the 'eternal stones' (KT, S12, Turk. *beŋü taš*, Soǧdian, Bugut 1: *nwm snk* 'stones of law'). The message was meant to last for eternity. Bilge Qaǧan (r. 716–34, or a relative speaking in his name) composed much of the text for his brother Kül Tegin's[33] inscription (cf. KT, E27, 30, 31, N10 references to *inim kül tegin* 'my younger brother

Kül Tegin'). Kül Tegin (d. 731) was Bilge Qağan's chief adviser and military commander. In his own monument Bilge Qağan 'speaks' in his own voice, enumerating his services to the *Türk boδun*.[34] The memorial complexes were multilingual, some containing Soğdian and Chinese[35] texts alongside Turkic. The Tang emperor Xuanzong (712–56[36]) personally composed a eulogy for Kül Tegin's mausoleum. The complex was decorated with pictures of the deceased engaged in combat.[37] The question of Chinese and other influences on the Orkhon Türk burial complexes and of Türk influences on Tang practices, especially for the tomb of Taizong (626–49), remains to be fully investigated.[38]

The Kül Tegin and Bilge Qağan monuments (KT, SE and BQ, SW) inform us that their nephew,[39] Yolluğ Tegin, wrote—or at the least oversaw the carving of—the inscriptions (KT, SE: *bwnĵa bitig bitigmä köl tegin atısı bitiδim*, KT, SW: *taš bitiδim*, BQ, SW: *bilgä qağan bitigin yollwğ tegin bitiδim*), staying on the site for a month and four days.[40]

Curiously, the Orkhon inscriptions have little to say regarding origin tales, other than a brief formulaic introductory line (see later). Perhaps, the ethnogonic accounts were all too familiar and needed no repetition. As we will see, some of these traditions, even their wording, were maintained orally for over a millennium.

What did the Türks call this writing? There is, as far as I know, no documented Old Turkic term for 'history'. Needless to say, there is one today, mainly based on Arabic *ta'rîkh* ('date, history') used in Turkish, Azeri, Türkmen, Tatar, Bašqort, Qazaq, Qırğız, Qumuq, Uzbek, and Uyğur. This came with Islam.[41] Qaračay-Balqar alongside *tarix* also have *istoriya* (< Russ.), the same is true of the non-Muslim Khakas who use *istoriya* and *tarχın*, the latter clearly deriving from *ta'rîkh*. Similarly, the Orthodox Christian Chuvash, whose language is the only survivor of Oğuric or Oğuro-Bulğaric, use the word *istori* (< Russ. *istorija*). Sharply differentiated from these terms is the Tuvan *töögü*. Whether this is somehow connected with Classical Mongol *teüke(n)* 'historical book(s) or source(s), history, annals, story, tale',[42] [Modern Mong. *tüüχ* < *teüke(n)* < **tegüke(n)*], is unclear.[43] Two Qırğız grave inscriptions, E-31 (Uybat II) from the middle Uybat River zone and E-37 (Tes') from Khakasia, dating perhaps to the mid-ninth century, mention that the deceased was a *čaŋšı*, one meaning of which in Chinese (the source of this title) is 'remembrancer, annalist' (< Chin. 長 史 *zhangshi*: MC *tjaŋ + şi*) or *changshi*.[44] If so, this would denote some official charged with the keeping of annals. The Türko-Soğdian materials, fragmentary though they are, make reference to reigns and the number of years that a Qaǧan ruled. Clearly, some official must have been tasked with this.

A key element in recording history is time and the runiform monuments attempt, with considerable precision, to place events in time as well as in space.[45] In Old Turkic *öd/öδ* denoted 'time, a concrete point in time'[46] and probably is the root underlying the term *ödik/ödig* ('report, record'),[47] perhaps approximating a sense of 'history' or 'notes of things past'. There are, of course, terms for 'year' (*yıl*)[48], the four seasons,[49] but no terms for individual months or days of the week. These are indicated by numbers, as in the Uyǧur inscription of Šine Usu (Eletmiš Qaǧan, Chin. Moyan[50] Čor = Bayan Čor), E3: *törtünč ay toquz yaŋıqa* 'on the ninth day of the fourth month'[51]—*yaŋı*, 'new,' in Uyǧur also denoted 'one of the first ten days of the month'.[52] In some instances, Chinese terms are used, not unexpectedly, as in the Uyǧur translation of the biography of Xuanzang (for example *ikinti ay yiti yaŋı ki toŋguz künkä* 'in the second month on the seventh day, the day of *ji* and of the pig of the new moon').[53] Chinese accounts give contradictory information, implying in some sources that the Türks judged time by the changing of the seasons, but in others indicating that some kind of reckoning system that could determine anniversaries must have been in use.[54] Kâšǧarî remarks that the Turks 'do not have names for the seven days, since the week became known only with Islam. Also, the names of the months, in the cities, are given in Arabic'. Otherwise only the names of the four seasons are used.[55] There is a system, but distinct names for months and days developed well after Islamization.

In the earliest Turkic historical writings, years are denoted according to the twelve-year animal cycle calendar.[56] The origins of this system remain debated.[57] It was used in both the Soǧdian-language Bugut and Turkic runiform inscriptions and can be corroborated with the Chinese sources. The system is very old in the Turkic world. It is found in Oǧuric as preserved in the Bulgarian prince list (written in Oǧuric Bulǧaro-Turkic and Slavic, perhaps first recorded in Greek letters or even a variant of the Turkic runiform script, but preserved in a Cyrillic re-transcription)[58] and in the Čatalar inscription of 822, for Omurtag Khan (r. 815–31), written in Greek letters.[59] The prince list extends only to the ninth century. The Balkan Bulǧars converted to Christianity in 864 and were already in the process of Slavicization.[60] The ancestors of the Bulǧars left Central Eurasia well before this. They were among the Oǧuric peoples pushed westward in migrations, initially touched off by the Xiongnu, spanning a period from the second century BCE to the fifth century CE.[61] Oǧuric tribes were in contact with Constantinople in c. 463.[62] Presumably, the Bulğars, first noted in 480, already had the twelve-year animal cycle calendar, which they preserved.

This system was quite familiar to Kâsğarî, who even provides the dating of his *Dîwân* according to this system together with the Islamic one.[63] Nestorian Christian gravestones in Syriac from fourteenth-century Kyrgyzstan continue to make use of this system alongside the 'Seleucid' year-reckoning.[64] The contemporaneous Volga Bulğar grave inscriptions, written in a mix of Arabic and Bulğaric Turkic, have not preserved traces of the animal cycle calendar,[65] but they were among the earliest Turkic peoples to convert to Islam.

Seemingly, use of this system would contradict the *Zhoushu* (50, 2,v°), which remarks that that the 'Turks know nothing of the passing of the years and reckon only by when the grass becomes green'.[66] The *Suishu* (1, 1,0 r°) states categorically that the calendar was given to the Türks in 586—unless the reference is to some other time-reckoning system. In any event, the Türks were already using the animal cycle calendar in Bugut.[67] Moreover, we are told that the Türks made an annual pilgrimage to their ancestral cave,[68] but we are not told how they computed that. The Kül Tegin and Bilge Qağan inscriptions (KT, E8, BQ, S7) make specific reference to the fifty years during which the Türks were subjects of the Tabğač (China). Indeed, the Kül Tegin inscription states (KT, NE) that he 'died in the year of the Sheep, on the seventeenth day. We held his funeral on the twenty-seventh day of the ninth month'. His tomb complex (*taš barq*) with its pictures and statues was completed in 'the year of the Monkey on the twenty-seventh day of the seventh month'.[69] The Bilge Qağan inscription (BQ, S9) tells us that he served as *Šad* (a rank just below that of Qağan and usually held by an Ashina[70]) for nineteen years and as Qağan for nineteen years, which corresponds closely to what is known from other sources.[71] Clearly, a count was being kept.

Something further should be said about the contents of the Bugut inscription as it is the oldest known (thus far) record from the Türk Empire.[72] Its fragments provide some information on the succession of several Qağans and the years in which they assumed the throne. Thus, we are told (B-1: 3) that the *bğy mğ' t't(p)['r]* 'Lord (or God-like[73]) Mağa Tatpar Qağan' came to power 'in the year of the hare'.[74] Soğdian *bğy* when employed with reference to the qağans, brings to mind the Turkic formula *tengriteg* ('God-like') of the Orkhon inscriptions, a likely continuity in ideological representations. The Qağan, when he dies, 'returns to the gods'. In Bugut (B-1:3–4), Tatpar and his predecessor, Muğan, are described as 'the (two) rulers upon the whole world from the east to the west'. Muğan is also described as having (B-2: 2-5) 'ruled countries ... the seven continents [= the whole world] and fed the people well'.[75] The reference to universal hegemony was common for divinely mandated rulers. In a letter dating perhaps to 595, an unnamed Türk Qağan presents himself to the Byzantine emperor Maurice (582–602), as 'the Chagan, the great lord of seven races and master of seven zones of the world' (ὁ Χαγανός ὁ μέγας δεσπότης ἑπτὰ γενεῶν καὶ κύριος κλιμάτων τῆς οἰκουμένης ἑπτὰ[76]). The Sâsânids also used this image of the 'lord of the seven climes',[77] that is, of the known world, as well as the notion of rule over the peoples of the 'four corners' of the world (see later, for Türk example: BQ, E2, 3).[78] The Qağan is celebrated for his (re)distribution of goods to the people and for his role as an intermediary with *Tengri*. The inscription also lists various titles and officers of the state.[79]

Ethnogonic Tale

The ethnogonic tale of the Türks has parallels in the Iranian world (for example, the Wusun, see later) and in tales found in a larger Eurasian culture zone, extending to Europe. The Ashina, the Türk royal clan, had profound ties with the Iranian Saka and Tokharian regions of East Turkistan.[80] The name Ashina is very likely East Iranian (cf. Khotanese Saka *âşşeina—âşşena* 'blue'). *Ashina* never appears in a Turkic source, but is most probably translated: *kök* 'blue' (cf. the *Kök Türk* [KT, E3, BQ, E4]) perhaps also used here as a geographical colour referent designating the 'East'.[81] The theme of a lupine ancestor and miraculous salvation runs across Eurasia.[82] In the Türk variant, a young boy survives the massacre of his people, is nursed by a wolf, later impregnates the wolf, and the Ashina descend from this union. After leaving the ancestral cave (north or north-west of Gaochang/ Qočo in Eastern Turkistan), they take service with the Rouran as subject metal workers in the Altay. Another account has a variation on this, noted also by the Chinese sources, which adds that whatever the contradictions, all the accounts agree that the Türks derived from a wolf.[83]

This was not simply a topos of Chinese historiography—our only written source. The Bugut inscription, which does not mention the tale (at least in the fragments that have survived), has a bas-relief of a she-wolf sheltering a boy, a theme repeated in the Kül Tegin and Bilge Qağan monuments.[84] The Chinese recorded these tales from the Türks and remark that the latter placed a wolf's head on their banners. The Orkhon inscriptions say nothing of this, but simply recount that 'after the blue heavens above and the brown earth below were created, between the two of them mankind was created [*Üzä kök täŋri asra yağız yer qılıntwqδa ekin ara kiši oğlı qılınmıš*] ... Bumın Qağan and Ištemi Qağan sat as rulers' (KT, E1).[85] Clearly, the tale was too familiar and did not need to be engraved on 'eternal stones'.

The Wolf Theme: The Wusun

The earliest account of lupine origins among Central Eurasian peoples was recorded during the Han era (202 BCE–220 CE) in the *Shiji* of Sima Qian (104–87 BCE) and the *Hanshu* of Ban Gu (32–93 CE), in their discussion of the 烏孫 Wusun (OCM ʔâ sūn, LHan ʔɑ suən, EMC ʔɔ swən, perhaps *Aświn = Aśvin 'the Cavaliers'[86]), most probably an Indo-Iranian, Iranian, or Tokharian-Iranian mix of nomadic peoples, originally located in the Gansu region.[87] They have been identified with the Iranian *Asiani*/Ἄσιοι who invaded Graeco-Bactria in the late second century BCE.[88] The Wusun had been attacked by the Da Yueji (in the *Hanshu* account) or by the Xiongnu (according to Sima Qian) and their king was killed. His recently born son and heir, the *kunmo* 昆莫 (OCM *kûn mâkh*, LHan *kuən ma*[c], EMC *kwən mak*[89]), had been taken away by his guardian. When the latter went to look for food, he left the *kunmo* unguarded in the grass. Upon his return, he saw a she-wolf suckling the child while ravens flew overhead 'with meat in their beaks'. The wolf theme, ancient in Eurasia, probably came to the Turks (and thence to the Mongols) from 'Scythian' peoples.[90] Wolves appear as ancestors or progenitors of ruling houses and states as far west as Rome. Indeed, 'wolf-men' figure prominently in the founding of a number of states in the Indo-European tradition.[91]

A lupine ancestor was not unique to the Türks alone among the Turkic peoples. The Gaoche ('High Cart' people), part of what was later termed the Tiele confederation which included the Uyğurs, claimed a male lupine ancestor.[92] The Uyğurs, like the Türks, had wolf's-head banners.[93] Balkan Bulğar rulers were alleged to be able to morph into wolves (and other animals).[94] The mid-ninth century(?) Syriac *Apocalypse of Baḥira* says of the 'Turks' (*Ṭurkâyê*) that they 'resemble wolves'.[95] Rus' sources describe a Cuman chieftain, Bonyak, as communing with wolves on the eve of battle in order to predict the future.[96] The lupine theme filtered into Firdowsî's *Šah-nâma*. He equates the 'Turanians', originally Iranian nomads, with the Turkic peoples and says that the army of Arjâsp, the descendant of

Tûr as the ruler of China and Turan, bore a standard with the image of a wolf.[97]

The Orkhon Inscriptions

The inscriptions continued an earlier tradition of the public eulogizing of the deceased and a remembrance of his glorious deeds.[98] These were now set on stones for eternity. They can be viewed as a form of ancestor worship, well known in the Turkic steppe world.[99] They differ from these public eulogies only in that the narrative of events and heroic deeds is presented in the voice of the deceased directly addressing the viewer of the inscription. One of the earliest inscriptions[100] (c. 720–6, the dating is disputed[101]) was dedicated to Küli Čor (full title: Išbara Čıqan Küli Čor and most probably a member of the Ashina ruling house[102]), who died at the age of eighty in combat against the Qağanate's foes (KČ, W3, E23). Among his merits was leadership of the Tarduš sub-confederation of the Türk realm and his repeated battles against the subject Qarluq confederation. He was a fearsome warrior and the inscription is largely devoted to his martial deeds. It was authored by a person named Bentir (?), who wrote 'information which [people] do not know, things which I know and remember; I inscribed so many inscriptions about them' (S2–3/ S27–8: *bäntir (?) bänim...bilmäz biligin biltükümün ödükümün bunča bitidim*).[103] This is not so much History as records for History, akin to annalistic literature. The Ongi(n) inscription, dated after 732, perhaps to 740, is similar in character, extolling the martial virtues of Bilge Išbara Tamğan Tarqan, an Ashina, and celebrating the revival of the Türk people. The inscription was composed by his son.[104]

Somewhat different in its modes of address is the Tonyuquq inscription (726), which speaks in the first person to the audience. It sets the historical stage by noting that its hero, an adviser to the Türk Qağans of the second empire from its revival in the late 670s until his death in 725,[105] was born in China while the Türks were still under Chinese rule (W1: *tabğač eliŋä qılındım türk boδwn tabğačqa körür ärdi*). While Elteriš (r. 682–91), the Ashina who revived and was the first ruler of the Second Türk Qağanate, gathered scattered Türks who were living in 'forests and rocky places' (*ıda tašda*) into a fighting force of 700, some of whom were on foot (*yadağ*), it was Tonyuquq, the inscriptions boasts, who brought Elteriš to the Qağanate: 'because Tengri gave me wisdom, I myself [and no other] made [him] qağan [*täŋri bilig berdük üčün özüm ök qağan qısδım*] ... I myself [and no other] was his counselor and chief military commander' (Tonyuquq, W4-7 *bilgesi čaβıšı bän ök ärdim*), 'I myself, Bilge Tonyuquq brought the Tü[rk Qağan] and Türk people to the land of the Ötüken and hearing that the Türks had settled in the Ötüken, the peoples of the south, west, north and east came' (Tonyuquq,S17: *tü...türk boδwnwğ ötükän yerkä özüm bilgä twńwqwq ötükän yerig qonmwš teyin äšidip bäryäki boδwn quryaqı yıryaqı öŋräki boδwn käldi*[106]). He also states (Tonyuquq, II, E51) that he enthroned Elteriš's successor, Qapğan Qağan (r. 691–716), and concludes that if not for him and Elteriš, the Türk people would not exist (Tonyuquq, II, E58–62). The account is filled with details of messages and intelligence reports received, the planning and carrying out of perilous operations through snow and over mountains and the gaining of victory over their foes, the Toquz Oğuz, Qırğız, Chinese, and others. All of this dramatic first-person account is occasionally peppered with proverbs or sayings of the time. The authors take pains to relate the events as accurately as possible.[107]

The Kül Tegin (732) and Bilge Qağan (735) inscriptions were authored or at least overseen by Yolluğ Tegin, their nephew (KT, SE, see above). Indeed, it is not unlikely that Bilge Qağan himself prepared some or much of the text for both inscriptions and the same was probably true of Tonyuquq's inscription.[108] These are presented as first-person accounts in which the 'Heaven-like and Heaven-born [or Heaven-conceived] Türk Bilge Qağan' (KT,S1, BQ, E1: *täŋri-täg täŋridä bolmwš türk bilgä qağan*), eulogizes his brother Kül Tegin, directly addresses his family (the royal Ashina), the Türk people (*türk boδun*), and subject peoples, extolling his own and his brother's many services to the Türk people and the 'important laws' that he established at his accession for the peoples of the 'four corners' of the world (BQ, E2: *törüg tört bulwŋdaqı...[it]δm*),[109] the law and order that their forefathers, Bumın and İštemi, who ruled 'over mankind' (BQ, E3 *kiši oğlınta üzä*), brought not only to the Türks but to the peoples of the 'four corners,' making 'those with heads bow and those with knees kneel'. The Ötüken Yıš[110] is declared the best place for ruling the realm (*el tutswq yer ötükän yıš ärmiš*) and its possession a necessity for Türk qağans. The inscriptions chastise the Türk people for their disobedience which allowed China to dominate them, recount the tale of the foundation of the second Türk Qağanate, and issue stern warnings to their readers, who lost their empire and wealth because they failed to heed their rulers: 'Türk begs and people, harken to this' (KT, S10: *türk bäglär boδwn bwnı äšidiŋ*). 'I have inscribed onto the eternal stones all the words that I have, see [them] and know [them]!'

(KT, S 11: *näŋ näŋ saβım ärsär tašqa urdwm aŋar körü biliŋ.*[111]) There is a dramatic telling of how Elteriš began the revival of Türk fortunes with 17 followers. Their numbers grew to 70. With the favour of Tengri, his warriors were like wolves, their foes like sheep, and his followers grew to 700. Thereafter, the revival of the state is described in specific detail, enumerating the peoples subjugated, titles awarded, campaigns (47) and battles (20) in which he personally took part (KT, E12–15, E34–40), and the age of the deceased when he went on one or another campaign. Even the names of the horses that died in one of Kül Tegin's battles are noted (KT, E32–3), while one hundred arrows struck Kül Tegin's armour. Due to his tireless efforts, he clothed a people who were naked, brought them wealth, increased their numbers, and made them a great power (KT, E29–30). How much of this was taken from memory or from some written accounts is unknown.

The elaborate burial complex, outfitted with 'exceptional grave goods' (*aδınčığ barq*), was built with Chinese assistance and placed in a region of easy access so that people could see the monument and read the words. The inscriptions combine political propaganda with the high drama of the recent history that had revived the Türk state. They also imply a high level of literacy among his people.[112] A brief historical reference is made to the founders of the first Türk state, the Qağans Bumın and İstemi, who, having ascended to power, took control of the realm, and established the law (KT, S1: *bumın qağan ištemi qağan olurmıš olurupan, türk boδunıŋ ilin törüsin tuta birmiš*),[113] one of the first acts of a new state.

Uyğur Inscriptions

With their frequent invocations of their possession of *qut* (heavenly good fortune), closely akin to Iranian *χwarəna/farn(ah)*,[114] and their lists of subjugated peoples, military victories and commands to erect and engrave these monuments, the inscriptions are strongly reminiscent of those of the Achaemenids and their imperial predecessors in the Middle East.[115] The references to *qut* and to the carrying out of Heaven's will give the inscriptions a religious undertone justifying the qağanal dignity of the Ashina, their right to rule and dominate the subject peoples.[116]

The Uyğurs show a keen awareness of their 'ancient' history in the inscriptions they erected to glorify their overthrow of the Ashina Türks and Ashina-led Basmıls, who briefly succeeded the Türks (743–4) as Qağans.[117] History is invoked to legitimate their claim—especially that of their ruling clan, the Yağlaqar[118]—to the supreme Qağanate, a claim that they maintained antedated that of the Ashina. In the inscriptions of Tes (750) and Terχ(in) (c. 753–4 or 762)[119] written in the name of Eletmiš Bilge Qağan (Bayan Čor, r.747–59) and his successor Bögü Qağan (759–79), the Uyğurs proclaimed that their rulers of old 'sat on the throne [olormwš]. For three hundred years they ruled over the realm [el¹²⁰]. Then, their people departed' (Tes, N1–2, in Kljaštornyj, N8: anıŋ el[l]i üč yüz yıl el tutmwš anjıp boδwnı barδı¹²¹). At some point (the inscription is in fragments and there are a variety of readings and interpretations), they 'in the east submitted to China. The Uyğur qağan[s] sat [on the throne] satisfactorily and were [rulers] for seventy years'¹²² (Tes, N5, Kljaštornyj, N, 11). The Terχin inscription (earlier termed 'Tariat,' E1–2) tells of 'Yolluğ Qağan ... Bumın Qağan, three qağans who reigned, for 200 years they reigned', whose state then collapsed due to internecine strife.¹²³ Bumın's reign (552) was, indeed, 200 years earlier. In Terχin, the 'author' is, nominally, the Qağan himself, Eletmiš Bilge Qağan (actually this is his title 'The Wise Qağan who made the realm'). He relates the events, giving precise dates for his victories: (Tes, W4) taqığw yılqa 'in the year of the hen' (Terχin, E7), 'on the fourteenth [day] of the seventh month' (yetinj ay tört yeğirmikä).¹²⁴ This kind of chronological precision again implies some kind of record-keeping.

The earlier chronology going back to pre-Türk dominion is rather murky. For good measure, Bumın, who defeated the Tiele/Toquz Oğuz confederation of which the Uyğurs were members in 546, on behalf of their common Rouran/Asian Avar overlords,¹²⁵ is also invoked. Bumın's name, as that of an empire-founder, was obviously important in establishing a legitimate line of succession. Within the nomadic confederations, the tribal name associated with the ruling house (for example Türk with the Ashina) becomes the political name of the confederation. The actual ethno-linguistic composition of the confederation may not undergo any great changes with the *translatio imperii*—although 'losers' in the contest for power, if they do not fully submit, will migrate away. Thus, the 'Türk' confederation becomes now the Uyğur or Toquz Oğuz confederation with a similar tribal constituency (minus the Qarluqs and some others, see below). The ethnonym *Türk* continues on in a politico-cultural context, used in one or the other context by the Khazars (see later), the post-imperial Uyğurs, the Oğuz, and the Qarakhanids.¹²⁶ The continuing use of *Türk*, even in a more restricted cultural sense, is certainly an element of ongoing historical consciousness. In the Islamic orbit, *Turk* became a generic term for Central Eurasian nomad peoples, well before the Qarakhanid era and was refracted back to Turkic peoples who were not using this name as they entered the Islamic world.[127] The 'author' of the Terχin monument also indicates (Terχin, W 1–3) that, having established his headquarters, he had the text carved onto 'flat stone' (*yası tašqa*). He set his polity in order, using language that is very similar—undoubtedly consciously so—to that of the Türk rulers' inscriptions: *üze kök täŋri yarlıqaδwq üčün asra yağız yer iğid(d)ük üčün elimin törümün etindim*, 'Because the blue heaven above so ordained and the brown earth below nourished [me], I founded my realm and my customary law'.[128] These are not merely funerary monuments, but historical markers meant to make known and glorify the deeds of the early Uyğur rulers in well-known turns of speech and lay blame on those who brought ruin on their earlier *els* (realms, states).

Part of the historical narrative of these early Uyğur inscriptions cannot be retrieved. Somewhat more information is found in the inscription at Šine Usu (759/760), dedicated to Eletmiš Bilge Qağan. It appears to reference the setting up of the Terχin inscription (Šine Usu, E8 *bitigimin yaratıtdım*) located near the Tez [Tes] River and describes in some detail the bitter wars, external and internal, that the Yağlaqar fought to gain and retain power in the years 739–59, sometimes providing information that is not recorded in other (that is Chinese) accounts.[129] The Yağlaqar are noted as ruling over the On Uyğur, and Toquz Oğuz and the 'Türk Qağan sat on the throne (or had reigned) exactly for fifty years' [Šine Usu, N3–4: *suß anda qalmıšı on uyğur toqwz oğwz üzä yüz yıl olorwp s... a/ä orqwn ögüz W... türk qağan äl(i)g yıl olormwš*].[130] The account tells how he captured Ozmıš (or Özmiš) Qağan, the last Ashina Türk ruler and his wife, the Qatun, in 744 and then drove off his erstwhile allies, the Qarluqs in 745 (or 746, Šine Usu, N9–11). Warfare continued with the Qarluqs, Tatars, Basmıls, Türgeš, and others. He describes places where he established stockades, set up his throne (*örgin*) and had the city of Bay Balıq built by Soğdian and Chinese artisans on the Selenge River (Šine Usu, W5).

The partially preserved Sevrey inscription found in the southern Gobi was not part of a grave complex, but appears to have been a triumphal marker of the successful Uyğur campaign concluding in 762, which ended the rebellion touched off against the Tang by An Lushan (755), one consequence of which was the conversion in Luoyang of the Uyğur Qağan Bögü to Manichaeism in 762. A plausible argument can be made to date it to 763.[131]

Inscriptions at Qara Balġasun (810? 821?) were written in Chinese, Soġdian, and Turkic. The Chinese account[132] gives a brief history, with a reference to the Türk Ashina who pacified the 'external and internal lands', and the Basmıl Ashina who changed the 'mandate of heaven', again taking 'our old state'. A brief sketch of the Uyğur qağans up to the early ninth century follows,[133] along with their notable deeds, including the Uyğurs' intervention to save the Tang during the revolt of An Lushan, its stormy aftermath and the conversion of the Uyğur Qağan Bögü to Manichaeism. Added here is the coup by an element of the Uyğur elite that killed Bögü (779) and many of his supporters, including Soġdians, who played the key role in his conversion and were a powerful faction at the court. The new religious orientation also impacted commercial relations with the Tang.[134] Wars with the Qırğız, Tibetans, and internal strife are also noted.

The Soġdian inscription covers some of the same ground, but has a stronger Manichaean flavour and also mentions the Arabs (7b/Fr.9:7/38: *t'z-'yk'n*) and the 'Amîr al-Mu'minîn' [10b: 6/20, 7/21: *t'z-yk'n'y](m)wmyn xm'r*].[135] Much less remains of the runiform text. It (and the earlier reading of the Soġdian inscription[136]) note that the inscription was written 'in commemoration of the god-like Uyğur Tengri Qağan [entitled] Ay Täŋgridä Qut Bulmıš Alp Bilgä' (r. 808–21).[137] The Uyğur Qağan, however, was now seen in a new religio-ideological light. He was a warrior for the Light in the battle against Evil, a spiritual son of Mani (the latter was believed to be of royal descent, connected with the Sâsânids), a just king who offered salvation, a ruler who could bring the 'one true faith' to the world.[138] The religious component of Qara Balġasun takes on far more importance. The Türk and Uyğur inscriptions present a kind of 'national' history. Only the eastern Türks and Uyğurs produced these monumental inscriptions. None have, thus far, been uncovered in the Western Türk realm.

The Old Qırğız Inscriptions

The Qırğız runic monuments, found in the upper Yenisei region in present-day Khakasia and Tuva,[139] are, overall, straightforward epitaphs that give the name/title of the deceased, extol his heroism in warfare and service to the state. Most do not offer much in the way of concrete historical details.[140] However, some connections can be teased out of them. Altın Köl I (E-28, from Khakasia) is dedicated to Elig Bört Opa Bars, a member of the qağanal Bars clan of the Qırğız, who died in combat, perhaps in the Qırğız–Türk wars that marked the reign of Qapğan Qağan (691–716),[141] himself a casualty of them. The hero of Altın Köl II (E-29, from Khakasia), Inančü Alp Saŋun, was the twin brother of Elig Bört Opa Bars, who died while on a diplomatic mission to Tibet in the early eighth century (*tüpüt qanqa yalabač bardım kälmädim*).[142] One of the early Qırğız inscriptions from the beginning of their 'imperial period', following their overthrow of the Uyğur Qağanate in 840, is the 'Süji (Mong. Süüž) Inscription' (840?) that begins 'I [was] appointed in the Uyğur lands of the Yağlaqar khans ... I am a son of the Qırğız, the Boyla Qutluğ judge'.[143] The Uybat VI inscription in Khakasia eulogized Tirig Beg, who was like 'a boar with tusks' (*azığlığ toŋuz*) 'when the land of the Uyğur Qağan was taken',[144] another reference to the conquest of 840. The Begre Inscription (E-11) notes that the deceased, the *İčreki* Tör Apa 'from the age of fifteen went on campaigns against China' (the Tabğač Khan) and acquired 'gold, silver, camels and captives' because of his martial valour.[145] These are interesting fragments, but one cannot reconstruct a narrative of Qırğız history from them, nor does that appear to have been their goal.

While the Qırğız were micro-historical in their monuments, that does not seem to have been the case with the Qitan (Turk. Qitañ, Chin. 契 丹 Qidan = LMC *kʰit tan*[146]), a Mongolic people or 'para-Mongolic-speaking people',[147] who founded a dynasty, the Liao (916–1125), that ruled northern China, Manchuria, and Mongolia. They became the imperial masters of Mongolia around 924. According to their dynastic annals, the *Liaoshi*, in that year when Abaoji (907–26), the Qitan Qağan, came to the old Uyğur capital, he 'ordered that the old stone tablet of Bilgä Khaghan be erased and reinscribed in Ch'itan, Turkic, and Chinese to commemorate his meritorious deeds'.[148] This 'stone tablet' has not been found. What is interesting to note here is that the Qitan, former subjects of the Türk Empire, whose consort clan, the Xiao, was of Uyğur descent,[149] were still aware of the *beŋü taš* tradition. In 1130, as Yelu Dashi, the founder of the Qara Khitai realm in Central Eurasia, the refugee-successor state of the Liao who were overthrown in China by the Jin in 1125, was negotiating his way through Uyğur lands, he reminded the Uyğur ruler, yet another Bilge Qağan, that his ancestor Taizu (Abaoji) had invited the Uyğurs to return to their former abode in Mongolia.[150]

The Khazar–Türk Tradition

The Khazars, another successor state of the Türks, present a different picture. The Tang dynastic annals regularly refer to them as 'Türk

Khazar' (突厥可薩 Tujue Kesa, 突厥曷薩 Tujue Hesa),[151] pointing to their Türk origins. The continuity with Ashina–Türk political traditions is obvious from the largely Arab and Persian accounts we have of the internal workings of the Khazar Qağanate. The Khazars also built substantial grave complexes for their Qağans (described by Ibn Faḍlân[152]). None have yet been found, hence we do not know if they communicated history. Like the Uyğurs, the Khazars converted to a world religion, one that, like Manichaeanism, was without a political base or central see. The Khazars converted to Judaism in a process that may have begun in the eighth century, but one that brought Judaism to the status of the state religion (at least among the bulk of the ruling elite and core tribes) by the early ninth century.[153] In addition to a Hebrew document from (or perhaps to) the Khazar Jewish community in Kiev (Qiyyob) from the tenth century, we have several Khazar accounts (also in Hebrew) from the mid-tenth century, written on the eve of the fall of Khazaria, that recount Khazar history. One composed by an 'unknown Khazar Jew',[154] another coming from the pen of the Khazar ruler Joseph[155] (or more probably his Jewish scribe), in response to enquiries from Ḥasdai b. Šaprûṭ, a Jewish courtier of the Spanish Umayyads in the middle and latter half of the tenth century. Joseph tells his correspondent of Khazar origins, about the rise of the state and its conversion to Judaism and tries to situate these events in a context with which a learned Jew of the Middle Ages would be familiar. Joseph's letter and that of the 'unknown Khazar Jew' contain differing accounts of the Khazar conversion to Judaism, accounts which are, nonetheless, similar thematically to other Central Eurasian Turkic conversion narratives (for example religious debates preceding the conversion of the ruler, 'the complex of mountains, sea and cave').[156] The Khazar conversion is, in its way, a typical product of Central Eurasian religious and cultural syncretism. It brought the Khazars into the 'history' of the Abrahamic religions, 'de-barbarizing' them for a Mediterranean audience. Conversion introduces a significant break with some past cultural practices,[157] but the Khazars, despite their championing of Judaism, continued many of the Ashina royal traditions, producing a unique version of Central Eurasian sacral kingship, including human sacrifices at royal burials.[158]

Joseph calls himself the King of Togarmah (ha-melekh ha-togarmî), 'the Turkic king'. Togarmah is the son of Japheth from whom the Turks derived according to medieval Jewish tradition. The eponymous 'Khazar' is presented as one of the ten sons of Togarmah. (Other sons include Bulġar, Savir, Oġuz, Avar, and other Central Eurasian peoples.)[159] The acceptance of a universal religion required a reorientation of ethnogonic myths and the creation of ties to the larger confessional community. Asked to give a description of his kingdom and its history, Joseph says that he found 'in our genealogical books' the record of their descent from Japheth et al. Unless this was a literary flourish, it seems quite likely that there was some kind of official 'king's list', or books of royal genealogy. Knowledge of one's genealogy remains a well-attested Central Eurasian nomadic tradition.[160] Other comments point towards some kind of historical record keeping. Joseph notes that 'it was written' in earlier times that their numbers were small and they waged war with peoples who were greater in number and more powerful than they. The Khazars, of course, were victorious.[161] Among their defeated foes were the Onoġundur-Bulġars (וננתר, *Wonuntur/Vonuntur*, the Oġuric form of this name by the tenth century[162]). Joseph's letter indicates a clear historical memory of this signal event, which ushered in the era of Khazar domination of the Western Eurasian steppelands. Aside from accounts of martial exploits, Joseph's letter also contains a 'king's list' giving his line of descent from previous rulers, beginning with Obadiah, who strengthened the realm and the faith. The 'letter of the Unknown Khazar Jew', written perhaps by a contemporary of Joseph and only partially preserved, also has rather precise political and military details regarding Khazaria's relations with its neighbours.

Islamo–Turkic Traditions

Islamic sources also formulated an acceptable genealogical tradition adapting, where feasible, ethnogonic tales that were current among the Turkic peoples they encountered.[163] Initially, Muslims did this unilaterally, making use of the rich Iranian traditions of 'Iran' and 'Turan' to properly situate the Turks in the fearsome 'lands of the North'. With Islamization, the Turks, in time, adopted these largely Irano-centric traditions as well. As early as the mid-ninth century, Ibn Khurdâdhbih, a Persian 'Abbâsid official, was deriving the Turks from *Ṭûj (or Ṭûš, son of Afrîdûn).[164] These associations are absent in the essays on the Turks penned by the more Arabo-centric al-Jâḥiẓ (d. 255/870), Ibn Khurdâdhbih's contemporary.[165] Two centuries later, Gardîzî, writing in Persian, considered them axiomatic.[166] His accounts of the Turkic peoples give many examples of a mix of Turkic, Iranian, and Islamic traditions.[167] Among Gardîzî's accounts is the tale that ascribes the sparseness of the Turks' beards to Japheth who had been given wolf's milk (and ant eggs) when he became ill in childhood.[168] The mention of wolf's milk in any connection with Turkic origins immediately brings to mind the ethnogonic accounts of the origins of the Ashina and in this instance may reflect some distant echo of that tale.

Afrâsiyâb (Farâsiyâb) figures prominently in the Muslim genealogies. al-Mas'ûdî, writing in the 930s, reported that the Qarluq ruler was the 'Qağan of Qağans' who united the Turkic tribes. 'From these Qağans was Farâsiyâb the Turk, the victor over the land of Persia.'[169] Gardîzî confirms the passing of the 'paramountcy' of the Western Türks to the Qarluqs, although some details, based perhaps on other traditions, differ.[170] Muslim Turkic intellectuals readily adopted the Afrâsiyâb theme.

It is with Maḥmûd al-Kâšġarî, writing in Baghdad in the 1070s, that we first encounter someone directly from the Turkic world (he may have been a scion of the Qarakhanid ruling house[171]), working in a Turko-Muslim cultural space, who was attempting to explain the Turkic world, which, in the form of the Seljuk Sultans now dominated key regions of the Arabo–Irano–Islamic heartlands to the Arabic-reading Muslim literati of the Middle East. Kâšġarî further expands on already established Middle Eastern, in particular ancient Iranian, linkages. Iranians encompassed much of Central Eurasia, steppe and sown, adjoining the Middle East before the Türk conquest of the mid-sixth century. The Turkic domination of 'Turanian' space offered opportunities for their 'integration' into Irano-Arabic Muslim conceptions of the world.

Kâšġarî drew on both the Japhethic tradition and pre-Islamic Iranian legends. He traced the Turks' twenty tribes 'to Turk, son of Japheth, son of Noah.... Each tribe has branches whose number only God knows'. Citing learned Muslims, with a chain going back to the Prophet Muḥammad, he says that 'Turk' 'is the name given by God', who has 'a host whom I have called *at-Turk* and whom I have set in the East; when I am wroth over any people I will make them sovereign above them'. The Turks possess 'an excellence' that is 'above the rest of created beings'. God named them, 'settled them in the most exalted spot', and 'called them his own army'.[172] As in the Khazar example, he has situated the Turks in world history, wrapped them in genealogies recognizable in the Abrahamic religious tradition, and given them an explicit role in the divine plan. This was linked to the newly gained preeminence of the Seljuks. Kâšġarî says much about the 'Oğuz-Türkmen', from whom the Seljuks derived (from the Qınıq *qabîla* 'tribe/sub-tribe'), 'since people need to know them'.[173] Historical memory in the form of genealogy was very important and genealogical location (real or fictive) still constitutes a significant element of identity in parts of the Turko-nomadic world. Among the Oğuz (and others), two strangers meeting for the first time inquire: *boy kim* (who are your kinsmen, your clan, your people)? They then name their subtribe and still smaller subdivisions. The subtribes bear the names of eponymous ancestors.[174]

Kâšġarî, however, often had only murky notions about some of the not too distant past of the Turkic peoples of whose dialects and culture he claimed exceptional knowledge.[175] Thus, Ötüken, the seat of power for the Türks and Uyğurs—and later for the Mongols—was simply a place-name 'in the deserts of Tatâr near Uighur'.[176] *Khazar*, which is mis-vocalized as *Khuzâr* in his text, is also simply the 'name of a place in the country of the Turks'.[177] Of his contemporaries, the *Qaŋlı*—the eastern branch of the Qıpčaqs—he merely notes that it is the 'name of an important man of Qifčâq'.[178] Islamization may have done much to erase a non-Muslim past. Kâšġarî readjusts lexical elements to meet new needs. Thus, *yalŋuq, yalŋuq kiši*, a term noted already in eighth-century Uyğur texts as denoting 'human being, man', 'humankind',[179] becomes or is translated as 'Adam', 'sons of Adam',[180] bringing the Turks into the Abrahamic genealogical tradition.

Afrâsiyâb, Jamšîd, and Dhu'l-Qarnayn (Alexander the Great) make an appearance as well. Thus, the former title *čaŋšı* (see earlier) is noted as the name of 'an emir of Khotan.... They say that [the name] is changed from Jamšîd'.[181] Kâšġarî's tales of Afrâsiyâb and Dhu'l-Qarnayn, as Dankoff notes, bear little resemblance to those of the Iranian epic traditions and the Alexander romances that circulated widely in the Middle East (and thence Europe).[182] Rather, they reflect 'indigenous Central Asian legends relating to Tonga Alp Är and to King Shu as national heroes of the Turks'.[183] The former was equated with Afrâsiyâb and the latter was depicted as a contemporary and foe of Dhu'l-Qarnayn. Legends about Alexander, especially his founding of cities (an activity in which he was engaged), were already noted in sixth–seventh-century Central Eurasian traditions. The Byzantine historian Theophylactus Simocatta, whose early seventh-century *History* (of the reign of the Emperor Maurice) contains a famous excursus on the land of Ταυγὰστ (= *Tabġač* = northern 'China' and the surrounding region), writes that the cities of Ταυγὰστ and Χουβδὰν (Soğd. Khumdân = Chang'an, the Chinese capital) were founded by

Alexander the Great. As the toponym Khumdân was most probably transmitted by Iranian and then Xiongnu nomads, it is likely that tales and traditions about Alexander were already circulating by the late third–second century BCE among Central Eurasian nomads.[184] The association of the Turkic peoples with Afrâsiyâb (Avest. *Fraŋrasyan*, Middle Pers. *Frâsyâg, Frâsiyâv*[185]), the ruler of Turan and arch foe of Iran in Persian historical legend, may date to as early as the mid-sixth or possibly seventh century, when the Türks became a presence in Transoxiana. Thereafter, it has been suggested, the 'Turks themselves cultivated the legends of Afrâsiyâb as a Turkish hero after they had come into contact with the Iranians'.[186] Ibn Khurdâdhbih in the mid-ninth century already associated the title of 'Tûrânšâh' with the Turks.[187] By the early tenth century, the Afrâsiyâb–Turan–Turk connection was firmly established among Muslim authors such as al-Ṭabarî (d. 923).[188] Kâšġarî derives his 'Khâqânî Turks'[189] (the 'Qarakhanids', an artificial name created by scholars[190]) from Afrâsiyâb, whom he identifies with the legendary Turkic hero Alp Er Toŋa, a linkage that was probably not original with him.[191] Kâšġarî's contemporary, Yûsuf Khâṣṣ Ḥâjib, in his *Qutadğu Bilig* similarly notes Toŋa Alp Er as a Turkic prince of 'outstanding fame and glory... the Iranians call him Afrâsiyâb'.[192] Actually, the Turkic texts never explicitly make this linkage, rather it is our cultured authors who do. Yûsuf Khâṣṣ Ḥâjib hints at his sources: Iranian written tradition, 'The Iranians have written this all down in books—and who could understand it if it were not written down?'[193] As with Afrâsiyâb, there is no substantial evidence that an Alp Er Toŋa ever actually existed.[194]

Variants of the dynastic designation, *al-khâqâniyya, al-khâniyya*, appear in later sources. By the time of Juwainî, Juzjânî, Ibn al-Athîr, and Jamâl Qarshî, thirteenth-century authors, the association of Afrâsiyâb with the Turks, and with the Qarakhanids (Âl-i Afrâsiyâb) in particular, was a long-established part of the Turko-Islamic genealogical tradition.[195] But, it took a number of forms and had a number of claimants. Thus, Juwainî, citing Uyğur 'opinion', reports: 'It is said that Buqu Khan was Afrasiyab.'[196] 'Buqu Khan' was Bögü Qağan who converted to Manichaeism (see earlier). Ibn Ḥassûl (d. 1058), a *wazîr* of the Seljukid Toğrul (d. 1063), linked that dynasty to Afrâsiyâb.[197] Niẓâm al-Mulk (d. 1092), the famous *wazîr* of Alp Arslan and Malikšâh also makes this connection, although only in passing.[198] Abu'l-Ġâzî Bahadur Khan, writing in the seventeenth century, also reports the claim of the Seljuks that they descended from a son of Afrâsiyâb who fled to the Qınıq.[199] This would indicate an internalization of this 'tradition' in later Turkic historical writing. Nonetheless, this notion does not appear to have been part of the Seljuk official ideology and may have taken root later.[200]

Frye and Sayılı have suggested[201] that a cult of lamentation of Afrâsiyâb/Alp Er Toŋa existed among the Türks and is hinted at in the Kül Tegin and Bilge Qağan inscriptions (KT, N7, BQ, E31). According to the inscriptions, following a victory in 714, ten warriors of the Toŋra were killed at the funeral of 'Toŋa Tegin',[202] presumed here to be a reference to Alp Er Toŋa. This seems unlikely. Rather Toŋa Tegin here is most probably a member of the royal house who fell in battle and human sacrifices were made at his funeral. However, in translating the lines of a later poem of lamentation *ulšïp ärän börläyü* ('the men howl like wolves'), Kâšġarî renders it as 'the men howl like wolves (in grief over Afrâsiyâb)'.[203] Afrâsiyâb is nowhere mentioned in the portion of the Turkic text cited by Kâšġarî. His introduction of the name into his translation may point to the existence of such a practice associated with Afrâsiyâb or it may be a means of placing this practice in a context that was more familiar to his Irano-Muslim audience. The same may be said of his citation of a verse 'describing Time in the elegy of King Afrâsiyâb'.[204]

Kâšġarî also associated a number of cities with Afrâsiyâb: Barčuq, a city in inhabited by the Čaruq tribe, in which Afrâsiyâb was said to have imprisoned 'Bîzan, son of Nebuchadnezzar',[205] Marv,[206] and Barsğan, Kâšġarî's father's natal town (he terms its population 'the worst' because they are 'unsociable and miserly').[207] Afrâsiyâb was also associated with Ordu Kend (Kâšġar).[208] Other toponyms are associated with his progeny (for example his daughter Qâz[209]).

Why the eagerness to identify with Afrâsiyâb? Barthold argues that the identification of Turan and the Turkic world was already a part of the Persian-language cultural world, the culture of Firdowsî (d. 1020) and his *Šâhnâma*, a culture which the Qarakhanids, now Muslims and drawn towards the Irano-Muslim world, were happy to accept and into which they were anxious to integrate their own traditions.[210] Bosworth dates the strong influence of the Persian national epic on the Turks to a period 'well before Firdausî's time'.[211] Yarshater (see earlier) makes this influence virtually contemporary with the extension of the Türk empire to Central Eurasia. Frye and Sayılı would date the Turan–Turk connection to 932 when the Qarakhanids assumed power, as a Muslim dynasty in the region.[212] We have some notion as to when Muslim literati made this linkage (already used by Ibn Khurdâdhbih). We can only presume that it came to the

Turkic peoples after sustained contact with the Iranian world and fully blossomed, when Turks, or rather Turkic intellectuals, sought to integrate their 'history', real and imagined, into the Middle Eastern cultural zone. This could only have become meaningful after significant Islamization. The Volga Bulğars were the first Turkic people to convert to Islam on a large scale by the 920s.[213] Although they were peoples of the North, there are no hints of identification with Turan. In 960, '200,000 tents of the Turks' converted to Islam,[214] most probably in the Qarakhanid realm. Around 985, Seljuk (Selčük) had converted, part of a larger process of Islamization amongst the Oğuz and setting the stage for the movement of Oğuz tribesmen into the Middle East.[215] Another mass conversion ('10,000 tents') took place in 1043 among the pagan Turks around Kašğar and Balasağun.[216] In the aftermath of these mass conversions and the Seljuk takeover of substantial parts of the Arabo-Persian Middle East by 1055, the question of finding a 'proper history' for the Turks in the Islamic world became important especially as they were centered in Iran. As Bosworth has noted, this need to 'forge a connection with the glorious traditions of ancient Iran' was relatively brief and 'drew to an end in the eleventh century'.[217] These connections, already part of the Arabo-Persian historico-geographical canon, remained as part of a politico-cultural fund from which Turkic intellectuals could draw, when needed.

Hua poses the question: if Kâšğarî's intention was to explain the world from which the Seljuks sprang to their nominal 'Abbâsid overlords, why did he 'attach the Qarakhanid royal family, rather than that of the Seljuq, to Afrasiyab'?[218] Moreover, he argues, the Seljuk connection with Afrâsiyâb antedated that of the Qarakhanids and the latter were simply mimicking the Seljuks. They both, in turn, may have simply accepted 'a narrative creation' by non-Turkic intellectuals (that is Ibn Ḥassûl).[219] The Turan-Turk linkage, however, was already widely accepted in Muslim circles and most probably long familiar to Kâšğarî and other Turkic intellectuals in Central Eurasia.

The Seljuks and Qarakhanids were not the best of friends in the 1070s. Alp Arslan, marching against the Qarakhanids, had been killed by a Khwârazmian captive in late 465/1072.[220] In 1074, his son and successor Malikšâh (1072–92) forced the Western Qarakhanids (the Qarakhanid realm had divided into eastern and western realms by the mid-eleventh century) to accept Seljuk overlordship. Subsequent campaigns would confirm Seljuk hegemony and extend their orbit to the eastern Qarakhanids as well.[221] Of Seljuk ties to Afrâsiyâb, Kâšğarî says nothing. Perhaps he knew nothing of them. Perhaps he did not want to acknowledge such claims. Working in Baghdad, he had to tread cautiously. He does, however, underscore the distinction between the Oğuz dialect and that of the 'Khâqânî,' that is Qarakhanids, which he considers the most elegant.[222] We return to the question: why did Kâšġarî and others accept the linkage of Turan with the Turkic world? Why the connection of the mythical hero Alp Er Toŋa with Afrâsiyâb, the representative of an age-old nemesis of Iran? This was hardly an inviting entrée for the Turks into the Irano-Muslim world. Was Kâšġarî blindly following an already established fictional genealogy, familiar to his Muslim audience? Or did Turan's martial prowess and geographical location make them suitable 'ancestors'? Hua suggests that Qarakhanid intellectuals were influenced by the Seljuks,[223] although we are none too sure when the latter, on their own, began to invoke the Afrâsiyâb connection. Evoking legendary martial peoples as ancestors was hardly new. The Romans, in declaring their Trojan origins, did something similar. Although stating that his goal was to better aquaint the Middle East with their new, Turkic masters, Kâšġarî, who was not inattentive to things Oğuz, has much more to say about the larger Turkic world and is not shy about elevating his Qarakhanids. He put a Turkic stamp not only on nomadic Central Eurasia, but its urban regions as well. He claims that *kend* (city) is a Turkic word (it is clearly a borrowing from Iranian *kand* or *qand*[224]) and cites its presence in the toponyms Baykend, Taškend, Özkend, and Tüzkend as evidence that 'all of Transoxania', east of Baykend 'is part of the Turk lands.'[225] The Turks, thus, are not merely nomads, but cultured city-folk as well. At the same time, he was wary of cities and those whose contacts were too close with the Iranian world, criticizing their poor elocution. He explicitly chides the Oğuz (and hence the Seljuks) as having forgotten 'many Turkic words' because they 'mixed with the Persians ... and used Persian instead'.[226] He even provides Turkic origins for Persian words; for example he claims that Persian *diz* (castle) was borrowed from Turkic *tez* (any high place).[227] Kâšġarî cites the proverb, *tatsız türk bolmas baššız börk bolmas* ('there is no Turk without a Tat [just as] there is no hat without a head' ['Tat' is a term for non-Turks, in particular Iranians[228]]), which implies a certain dependency of the Turks on the Iranians. In translating the proverb, however, he offers two versions: 'a Turk is never without a Persian [just as] a cap is never without a head' and 'there is no Persian except in the company of a Turk [just as] there is no cap unless there is a head to put it on',[229] placing the Persians in the inferior position. He reinforces this with another proverb, playing on the homonym, *tat* ('rust'): *qılıč tatıqsa iš yunčır är tatıqsa ät tınčır* ('when rust overtakes a sword the condition [of the warrior] suffers, [just as] when a Turk assumes the morals of a Persian his flesh begins to stink'). This is coined to advise a person to be steadfast and to live among his own kind.[230] There is ambivalence at work here.

Kâšġarî also invokes the wars and interactions between Dhu'l-Qarnayn (Alexander the Great) and the Turkic peoples in some distant past, when 'the people were then nomads'.[231] 'King Šu' was the leader of the twenty-two Oġuz sub-groupings (*boy*) in these contests. He is credited with building Sûyâb and the nearby Balasaġun. In the course of these wars, Dhu'l-Qarnayn gave names to the Qalač (Khalaj) Turks and Türkmen with appropriate folk etymologies based on Turkic and Persian.[232] In these tales of Turkic wars with Dhu'l-Qarnayn, Alexander the Great usually speaks in Persian.[233] Kâšġarî attributes to him a Persian etymology for the ethnonym *Uyġur: xudxur* (< *înân xudh xurand* 'these are independent in feeding themselves'), later changed to *Udχur*. He presents it as a 'principality composed of five cities'.[234] This is certainly a reference to Bešbalıq (lit. 'Five Cities'), one of the principal Uyġur cities. They are 'the strongest of the infidels'.[235] According to Kâšġarî, Alexander also bestowed Persian-based names on the Čigil (one of the leading tribal sub-confederations of the Qarakhanid union) and Türkmen.[236] Some of this information was transmitted to Kâšġarî orally, as he notes. These Alexander tales, markedly different from Persian and Arabic versions of the Alexander romance, as Dankoff suggests, posit 'a long-established Alexander tradition among the Turks', although its ultimate origin among and mode of transmission to them is not known.[237]

In light of the not overly veiled hostility or at least ambiguity of Turko-Persian and more broadly Turko-Iranian relations noted earlier, the willing association of the ancient mythical hero of the Turks with the ancient mythical leader of Turan, Iran's age-old nemesis, takes on a different connotation. Kâšġarî and other Turkic intellectuals are implying that in the millennia-old Iran–Turan conflict, the Turks—whether the Qarakhanids ruling in old Iranian cities such as Bukhara and Samarqand or the Seljuks ruling in Iran-Iraq and adjoining regions—now have the upper hand. The Afrâsiyâb connection gave the Turks a status of parity, indeed, of antiquity, in the traditions of the Irano-Muslim Middle East, while at the same time clearly distinguishing them. Kâšġarî and his cohorts are making use of Iranian historical traditions and spinning them for their own ideological purposes. He is anxious to show that the Turks are the equals (if not superiors) of their Byzantine, Armenian, Georgian, Arab, and Iranian subjects. Before leaving Kâšġarî mention must be made of the examples of heroic poetry he cites, the building blocks of historical epics, which recount the wars of the Qarakhanids with pagan Turkic peoples.[238] Kâšġarî also takes note of the very un-Islamic twelve-year animal cycle calendar employed by the Turks. He comments that it is used to mark 'dates of birth and battle'. Its origin is shrouded in the past when 'one of their kings once required information about a battle'. Because the answers were confused, they decided to adopt this system. Each animal was associated with an omen.[239]

A Brief Note on the Later Japhethic Tradition

The Turk–Japhethic connections are later fully elaborated in Rashîd al-Dîn (d. 1318), who used Turko-Mongolian sources. He records that the 'the prophet Noah' divided the earth, between his sons Ḥâm, Sâm, and Yâfith 'who is the father of the Turks' and was sent to the east. According to him, Mongol and Turk traditions 'say the same thing', but the Turks called Yâfith Abulja Xân, and do not hold for certain if this Abulja Khân was the son of Noah or his grandson; however, they are in agreement that he was of his progeny (*nasl*) and close to him in time. All of the Mongols and the tribes (*aṣnâf*) of the Turks and the steppe-dwellers are of his progeny as was Abulja Xân. The latter had a son named Dîb Yâqûy who surpassed his father in power and royal virtues. He had four sons, who were named Qarâ Khan, Or Khan, Küz Khan, and Kür Xân. The whole of these peoples (*aqwâm*) were unbelievers (*kâfir*). Oğuz Khan was a son of Qara Khan. This is an early variant of the *Oğuznâma*, the Oğuz Khan tale, which appears to have supplanted other ethnogonic sagas in the Mongol era. Oğuz Khan is credited with giving names to the various Turkic peoples.[240] In one variant, dealing with the origins of the Nöküz and Derlekin Mongols, the eponymous ancestors of these tribes/clans, stem from their joining with a wolf in the Ergene Qon valley where they had taken refuge.[241] Although Qazwînî (c. 1340) who reports this legend considers it 'weak' (*ẓa'îf*), it nonetheless points to the continuation of the lupine ancestral account, which had its own variant among the Chinggisid Mongols. In this variant as well, the Oğuz Khan tale is also projected back to Iranian–Turanian antiquity, as well as intertwined with the Mongols.

Survival of the Ashina Tradition

What of the Ashina wolf tale, so integral a part of the early Türk ethnogonic tradition? Did it disappear? What is quite extraordinary is its preservation among the Qaračay-Balqar, ample evidence of the strength of the oral tradition. The Qaračay-Balqar are a small Qıpčaq-speaking people (perhaps 250,000 worldwide), who are the only Turkic grouping in the Caucasus to have adopted the mountaineer culture of the North Caucasus. They have incorporated this tale into the Nart Sagas, now the common cultural property of a number of peoples in the North Caucasus. They form a cycle of heroic warrior tales that have roots in the ancient Iranian (Alanic) world.[242] There is a strong Alanic substratum in Qaračay-Balqar culture,[243] the presumed immediate source/inspiration for the Qaračay Nart tales. In the tale of the birth of the *Nart* hero Örüzmek (< Osetian: Uruzmag/ Uryzmæg, Circassian: Warzameg, Wezyrmej[244]), we are told that Debet, a Nart blacksmith (the protector of all smiths, born from the union of Heaven and Earth: 'the God of the heavens [*kök teyrisi*] married the goddess of the Earth [*jer teyrisi*], the heavens thundered and the Earth became pregnant [*kök kükürep, bu Jer buwaz bolğandı*]), was out one night, while seeking ore. He was in a cave when an 'amazing blue light'[245] streaked across the heavens and crashed to earth. He went to investigate and saw in the middle of a very big deep hole a great blue rock that had split in two (*eki jarılğan kök tašnı*). Inside it was a young hero (*wa bir tulpar jašıq*). This little child (*sabiyčik*), having firmly seized a huge wolf by the neck was suckling from her. All the birds (*qanatlıları* 'winged creatures') and animals of the district gathered and stood there looking at this amazing sight. He picked him up and as they went the child grew. 'The Narts called him Wolf Suckling [*Börü Emček*]. Later, when he grew up and became a true Nart, they called him Örüzmek.'[246] The Osetin and Circassian tales of Warazmeg/Warzameg's origins are completely different. The wolf theme is clearly a preservation of the ancient ethnogenetic myth of the Türks (and Wusun) still recited today. The wolf held a position of profound reverence in traditional (pagan) Qaračay-Balqar beliefs. Wolf hair and bones were used in amulets to effect cures of various ailments. The wolf was considered the strongest enemy of all evil spirits that were harmful to humankind. The wolf was able to see demonic creatures and could eat their children. There was also a belief in *obur*s, changelings/werewolves (who could also take the shape of other animals) and were believed to possess clairvoyance.[247]

Among the Qaračay Nart songs is one dedicated to the Old Türk goddess of fertility, Umay,[248] called here Umay-Biyče also known as the 'Daughter of Teŋri' (*teyrini*[249] *qızı*). In it, the sons of the Narts are described as having a wolf-mother.[250] According to another Qaračay legend, spiders, which ate plants, animals, and humans, attacked and decimated a large tribe, which lived in swamplands. A snake, Čıntı Jılan and its seven offspring, helped the survivors, who settled on an island in the swamp. They then had a falling out with the snake, which cursed them. All the humans died from the curse except for a young boy who was saved from starvation by a wolf-like creature. The child, originally called Dewet (cf. Debet), was now named Totorxun by the snake (Totur was the pagan god of hunters and protector of wolves[251]). When Toturxun reached maturity, the she-wolf married him and gave birth to ten sons. Of these, only Tüyürman survived. He became a great smith (*gürbeji*). Once again, the Old Türk Ashina tale, blended with local traditions and names, is apparent.[252]

Interestingly, the opening lines of the tale of the 'Gods and Narts' (*teyrile bla nartla*) is strongly reminiscent of the origin myth recorded in the Orkhon inscriptions and is unique among the Nart Tales: 'After Heaven and Earth were created, mankind was created in between the two of them' (*kök bla jer jaratılğandan sora ekisini ortasında adam ulu jaratılğandı*);[253] Orkhon: 'After the blue heavens above and the brown earth below were created, between the two of them mankind was created' (*Üze kök tengri asra yağız yer qılıntuqda ekin ara kiši oğlı qılınmıš* KT, E1).[254] Here we have evidence of the strength of oral tradition.

In essence, the early Turks were working with three traditions: (*a*) the native oral tradition, (*b*) a probable annalistic written tradition, which included the twelve-year animal cycle system of dating notable events, and (*c*) traditions adapted to the world religions (and associated imperial cultures) that they adopted. Islam, in particular, increasingly overshadowed the 'native' tradition. The fact that the Qaračay-Balqars were relative latecomers to Islam (seventeenth–eighteenth century) may have aided the preservation of the lupine myth, now in Nart form.

The process could be very swift. The Mongols, as far as we can tell, had no writing system prior to the early thriteenth century, but maintained, presumably, an oral tradition. Literacy, using the Uyğur script, was introduced by Tatar Tuŋa, an Uyğur 'seal-keeper' previously in the service of the Naiman Tayang Qan. He joined the Chinggisid enterprise with the defeat of the Naiman and provided the technical 'infrastructure' for the production of the *Secret History of the Mongols* c. 1228 (between the death of Činggis Khan in August 227 and July–August 1229), one of the richest historical sources from Central Eurasia.[255]

Notes

1. Patrick J. Geary, *Phantoms of Remembrance: Memory and Oblivion at the End of the First Millennium* (Princeton: Princeton University Press, 1994), p. 9.
2. Geary, *Phantoms of Remembrance*, pp. 7, 9.
3. Geary, *Phantoms of Remembrance*, p. 12.
4. See the correspondence of Li Deyu on the Tang dynasty's handling of the crisis that followed the fall of the Uyğur Qağanate to the Qırğız in 840; see Michael R. Drompp, *Tang China and the Collapse of the Uighur Empire: A Documentary History* (Leiden: Brill, 2005). On Niẓâm al-Mulk's use of Türkmen-Seljuk history, see Ali Anooshahr, *The Ghazi Sultans and the Frontiers of Islam* (Abingdon, UK and New York: Routledge, 2009), p. 104.
5. András Róna-Tas, 'Materialien zur alten Religion der Türken', in *Synkretismus in den Religionen Zentralasiens*, eds. Walter Heissig, Hans-Joachim Klimkeit, *Studies in Oriental Religions*, vol. 13 (Wiesbaden, 1987): p. 34; see also Bruce G. Privratsky, *Muslim Turkistan: Kazak Religion and Collective Memory* (Richmond, Surrey: Curzon, 2001), p. 112n2, influenced perhaps by monotheistic ideas.
6. On early Turko-Mongolian religious ideas, see Jean-Paul Roux, *La religion des Turcs et des Mongols* (Paris: Payot 1984). Robert Dankoff, 'Kâšğarî on the Beliefs and Superstitions of the Turks', in *From Mahmud Kaşgari to Evliya Çelebi*, by Robert Dankoff (Istanbul: Isis Press, 2008), pp. 92–3, suggests that the Turkic *qam* was more 'diviner, soothsayer, conjurer, witch-doctor, magician or the like' than the shamans of Mircea Eliade's *Shamanism: An Archaic Technique of Ecstasy* (Princeton: Princeton University Press, 1994).
7. Geary, *Phantoms of Remembrance*, pp. 10–11: 'historians and anthropologists have overstressed the distinction between oral and written remembering' and his discussion, in medieval western writings, of the blending of 'individual' and 'collective memory,' of 'written and oral memory' in the shaping of texts.
8. Sergej G. Kljaštornyj, 'Drevnetjurkskie Pamjatniki: Novye Perspektivy Istoriografičeskogo Izučenija', in *Turcica et Ottomanica. Sbornik statej v čest' 79-letija M.S. Mejera*, eds. I.V. Zajceva, S.F. Oreškova (Moskva: Vostočnaja literatura RAN, 2006), pp. 64–70.
9. Indeed, in the ancient and medieval Near East, with low levels of literacy, the oral preservation of 'cultural lore', historical data, and historico-legal precedents was all-important. Written works were 'mainly used to support an oral performance', Karel van der Toorn, *Scribal Culture*

and the Making of the Hebrew Bible (Cambridge, Massachusetts: Harvard University Press, 2007), pp. 10–14. The Qur'ân, the 'revealed texts' of which were written down during the Prophet Muḥammad's lifetime, was 'transmitted orally', and oral tradition regarding proper recitation played an important role. Indeed the written text, codified in the caliphate of 'Uthmân (644–56), 'became more than an aide memoire for its recitation' only through 'the activities of Ibn Mujâhid' (859–956), see F. Leemhuis, 'From Palm Leaves to the Internet', in *The Cambridge Companion to the Qur'ân*, ed. J.D. McAuliffe (Cambridge: Cambridge University Press, 2006), pp. 145–9. On medieval Western Europe, see Geary *Phantoms of Remembrance*, pp. 15–16, on *memoria*. The account of the rise of the Xiongnu state (whatever its ethno-linguistic affiliations may have been) preserved in the Chinese histories [Sima Qian, *Records of the Grand Historian: Han Dynasty*, trans. B. Watson, rev. ed. (Hong Kong and New York, 1993), vol. 2, p. 134] detailing Modun's murderous rise to power probably came from a Xiongnu source preserved as an oral tradition, see Nicola Di Cosmo, 'Ethnography of the Nomads and "Barbarian Identity" in Han China', in *Intentional History: Spinning Time in Ancient Greece*, eds. L. Foxhall, H-J. Gehrke, N. Luraghi (Stuttgart: Franz Steiner, 2010), pp. 307–11.

10. See Nora K. Chadwick, and Victor Zhirmunsky, *Oral Epics of Central Asia* (London: Cambridge University Press, 1969); Fuzuli Bayat, *Oğuz Destan Dünyası* (Istanbul: Ötüken, 2006); see A. Nurmanova, 'La tradition historique orale des Kazakhs', *La mémoire et ses supports en Asie Centrale* in *Cahiers d'Asie Centrale* 8 (2000): pp. 93–100 for a brief overview of the different genres of Kazakh oral historical narratives. They were first written down in Kazakh in Arabic script in the late nineteenth–early twentieth century. Study of these manuscripts began in the 1920s. For examples and discussion of epic and historical tales among other Turkic peoples, see Muharrem Ergin, ed., *Dede Korkut Kitabı* (Ankara; Ankara Üniversitesi Basımevi, 1964); and Vasilij .V. Bartol'd, Viktor M. Žirmunskij and Andrej N. Kononov, eds. and trans, *Dede Korkut, Kniga moego deda Korkuta. Oguzskij geroičeskij epos* (Moskva-Leningrad: Izdatel'stvo Akademii Nauk, SSSR, 1962); X. Korogly, *Oguzskij geroičeskij epos* (Moskva: Nauka, 1976); Arthur T. Hatto, ed. and trans., *The Memorial Feast for Kökötöy-Khan (Kökötöydün Aši): A Kirghiz Epic Poem* (Oxford: Oxford University Press, 1977); Ja. S. Axmetgaleeva, *Issledovanie tjurkojazyčnogo pamjatnika "Kisekbaš kitaby"* (Moskva: Nauka, 1979); *İdegäy. Tatar xalıq dastanı* (Qazan: Tatarstan kitap naşriyatı, 1997); L. Ibrahimova, *Törki xalıqlar ijatında "Čura batır" dastanı* (Qazan: Fiker, 2002). M.Č. Džurtubaev, *Karačaevo-balkarskij geroičeskij epos* (Moskva: Pomatur, 2004).

11. Robert Dankoff, 'Three Turkic Verse Cycles Relating to Inner Asian Warfare', in *From Mahmud Kaşgari to Evliya Çelebi*, by Robert Dankoff (Istanbul: Isis Press, 2008), pp. 27–39. On the dating of his *Dîwân*

Luġât-at-Turk, see Maḥmūd al-Kāšġarī, *The Compendium of the Turkic Dialects: Dīwān Luyat at-Turk*, ed. trans. Robert Dankoff in collaboration with James Kelly, *Sources of Oriental Languages and Literatures*, 7, 3 vols (Duxbury Massachusetts: Harvard University Press, 1982–5) (henceforth Kâšġarî/Dankoff, 1982–5), vol. 1, pp. 1, 6–7. The manuscript was part of the caliphal library, which appears to have made its way to Mamlûk Cairo after the fall of Baghdad in 1258. Here it was copied in 664/1266 and brought to the Sultanal library in Istanbul after the Ottoman conquest of the Mamlûk realm 1516–17, see discussion in the new Russian translation of the work done in Kazakhstan: *Maxmūd al-Kāšġarī, Dīvān Luġāt at-Turk*, Z-A. M. Auézova, ed. and trans. in Russian (Almaty: Daik-Press, 2005), pp. 13–14. Reşat Genç, *Kaşgarlı Mahmud'a Göre XI. Yüzyılda Türk Dünyası*, Türk Kültürünü Araştırma Enstitüsü 147 (Ankara: Ankara Üniversitesi Basımevi, 1997): pp. 6, 12–13, argues that Kâšġarî began work on the *Dîwân* in 1072 and completed it in 1074 (the date of the colophon, which Dankoff and Kelly believe to be an error).

12. Cf. the Kazakh saying *žeti atasın bilmegen žetesiz* ('one who does not know his seven forefathers is despicable/ senseless'), see Nurmanova, 'La tradition historique', p. 97; Privratsky, *Muslim Turkistan*, pp. 61–2, 116–17. See also the comments of Veniamin P. Judin, 'Ordy: belaja, sinjaja, seraja, zolotaja...' in Utemiš-xadži, *Čingiz-name*, ed. and trans. V.P. Judin, commentary by Meruert X. Abuseitova (Alma-Ata: Gılım, 1992), p. 19, who considers genealogical myths to be the basis of Turko-Mongolian religion and the 'picture of the world'.

13. Cengiz Alyılmaz, 'The Bugut Inscription and Mausoleum Complex', in *Ērān ud Anērān: Webfestschrift Marshak 2003*, available at http://www. transoxiana.org/Eran/Articles/alyilmaz.html, notes that the 'Bugut mausoleum complex' was 10 km west of Bugut Mountain 'in the region of the Bayn Tsagaan Gol (Sacred White Lake), Arhangay Aymag'. It was a sacred zone before, during, and after the Türk era.

14. Previously often reconstructed as *Taspar. See Edwin Pulleyblank, *Lexicon of Reconstructed Pronunciation in Early Middle Chinese, Late Middle Chinese, and Early Mandarin* (Vancouver, B.C.: UBC Press, 1991), pp. 313 佗 (tuo), 40 鉢 (bo) [EMC (= Early Middle Chinese, c. 601)]. The Bugut inscription was first published by Sergej G. Kljaštornyj, and Vladimir A. Livšic, 'Sogdijskaja nadpis' iz Buguta', *Stranyi narody Vostoka* 10 (1971): pp. 121–46 and Sergej G. Kljaštornyj and Vladimir A. Livšic, 'The Sogdian Inscription of Bugut Revised', *Acta Orientalia Academiae Scientiarum Hungaricae* 21 (1972): pp. 69–102. The most recent reading is by Yutaka Yoshida and Takao Moriyasu in *Provisional Report of Researches on Historical Sites and Inscriptions in Mongolia from 1996 to 1998*, eds. Takao Moriyasu and Ayudai Ochir (Osaka: Society of Central Eurasian Studies, 1999), pp. 122–5. The readings and interpretations vary, in part, probably because of erosion over the last decades. On the context of the Bugut inscription, see Sergej G. Kljaštornyj, and

Vladimir A. Livšic, 'Otkrytie i izučenie drevnetjurkskix i sogdijskix épigrafičeskix pamjatnikov Central'noj Azii', in *Arxeologija i étnografija Mongolii*, ed. A.P. Okladnikov (Novosibirsk: Nauka, 1978), pp. 52–8. The use of Soġdian in this Türkic milieu was not limited to Bugut; the Türgiš, who dominated the Western Türk realm for a time in the eighth century, used Soġdian on their coinage. There are also Soġdian inscriptions from the Qırğız lands and later from the Qarakhanid realm, see Kljaštornyj and Livšic, The Sogdian Inscription, p. 82.

15. Kljaštornyj and Livšic, The Sogdian Inscription, pp. 75, 85–6, read 'Mahantegin', a younger brother, in their interpretation, of Muhan Qağan (d. 570 or 571), who 'was a regent or co-ruler' of Tatpar. Yoshida in Moriyasu and Ochir, *Provisional Report of Researches*, pp. 123–4 (B-1-1,2,3,4,5) has 'Muqan Qaghan' and mentions (B-2, 7-9) 'Magha Umna Qaghan'.

16. Bahaeddin Ögel, *Türk Mitolojisi* (Ankara: Türk Tarih Kurumu, 1971, 1995), vol. 1, p. 442.

17. Roux, *La religion des Turcs*, p. 102; Kljaštornyj and Livšic, 'The Sogdian Inscription', pp. 70–1, probably indicating that the deceased was a member of the ruling dynasty.

18. Wolfgang E. Scharlipp, *Die frühen Türken in Zentralasien* (Darmstadt: Wissenschaftliche Buchgesellschaft, 1992), pp. 20–1.

19. Leonid R. Kyzlasov, 'O značenii termina *balbal* drevnetjurkskix nadpisej', in *Tjurkologičeskij sbornik 1966* (Moskva: Nauka, 1966), pp. 206–8. Sir Gerard Clauson, *An Etymological Dictionary of Pre-Thirteenth Century Turkish* (Oxford: Clarendon Press, 1972), p. 333; Roux, *La religion des Turcs*, p. 277; on the Turkic *balbal* tradition see Roux, *La religion des Turcs*, pp. 260–2, 277–80, and with regard to its continuation as such among later Turkic peoples, see Jaroslav. R. Daškevič and Edward Tryjarski, *Kamennye baby pričernomorskix stepej* (Wrocław-Warszawa-Kraków: Wydawnictwo Polskiej Akademii Nauk, 1982), pp. 18–26; Edward Tryjarski, *Zwyczaje pogrzebowe ludów tureckich na tle ich wierzeń* (Warszawa: Wydawnictwo naukowe PWN, 1991), pp. 36–7, 302–5. Kül Tegin [East E24–25, Árpád Berta, *Szavaimat jól halljátok... A türk és ujgur rovásírásos emlékek kritikai kiadása* (Szeged: JatePress, 2004), pp. 154–5, on the referencing of the runic inscriptions see note 32 later] says that he had a *balbal* of the Qırğız Qağan erected for his uncle (Qapağan Qağan, r. 691–716), who died fighting the Qırğız.

20. Roux, *La religion des Turcs*, pp. 25–6

21. Takashi Ôsawa, 'Aspects of the relationship between the ancient Turks and Sogdians—Based on a stone statue with Sogdian inscription in Xinjiang', in *Ērān ud Anērān: Studies Presented to Boris Il'ič Maršak*, by Matteo Di Compareti, Paola Raffetta, and Gianroberto Scarcia (Venice: Libraria Editrice Cafoscarina, 2006), pp. 471–504, also in *Ērān ud Anērān Webfestschrift Marshak 2003*, available at http://www.transoxiana.org/Eran/Articles/osawa.html; Lin Meicun, 'A survey of the Turkic cemetery in Little Khonakhaï', in *L'islamisation de l'Asie centrale*, ed.

Étienne de la Vaissière, *Studia Iranica* 39 (Paris, 2008): pp. 377–96; Sören Stark, *Die Alttürkenzeit in Mittel-und Zentralasien: Archäeologische und historische Studien* (Wiesbaden: Dr Ludwig Reichert Verlag, 2008), pp. 73–5; Étienne de la Vaissière, 'Maurice et le Qaghan: à propos de la disgression de Théophylacte Simocatta sur les Turcs', *Revue d'études byzantines* 68 (2010): pp. 219–24.

22. See Türik Bitig, available at http://irq.kaznpu.kz/?mod=1&tid=1&oid=3&lang=e, found near the Bulgan aimag in Mongolia.

23. The Čöyren inscription was earlier dated to c. 688–91, see Kljaštornyj and Livšic, 'Otkrytie i izučenie', p. 48, but is now viewed as eighth–ninth century, see Béla Kempf, 'Old Turkic runiform inscriptions in Mongolia: An Overview', *Turkic Languages* 8, no. 1 (2004): p. 44.

24. Kljaštornyj, 'Drevnetjurkskie Pamjatniki', p. 65. Cengiz Alyılmaz ['Bugut Yazıtı ve Anıt Mezar Külliyesi Üzerine', *Selçuk Üniversitesi, Türkiyat Araştırmaları Dergisi* 13 (Bahar, 2003): p. 13], notes that Bugut has a 'biographical and didactic' quality that relates historical events. In content and form it served as a model for the later Orxon inscriptions.

25. Igor' L. Kyzlasov, *Runičeskie pis'mennosti evrazijskix stepej* (Moskva: Vostočnaja Literatura RAN, 1994), Igor' V. Kormušin, *Tjurkskie enisejskie épitafii. Teksty i issledovanija* (Moskva: Nauka, 1997); Aleksandr M. Ščerbak, *Tjurkskaja runika. Proisxoždenie drevnejšej pis'mennosti tjurok* (Sankt Peterburg: Nauka, 2001), esp. pp. 33ff. A derivation from Aramaic script systems (via Iranian), indigenous *tamğas* ('brands') and other sources have been suggested. Viktor G. Guzev and Sergej G. Kljaštornyj, 'Drevnjaja pis'mennost Velikoj Stepi', in *Tjurkologičeskij Sbornik 2007–2008* (Moskva: Nauka, 2009), pp. 170–2, argue that it is an 'autochthonous' system that developed from signs and pictograms that were widespred in the Turko-Eurasian world. Under the influence and in imitation of neighbouring writing systems in China and the Irano-Semitic Middle East, these were developed or evolved into a full-fledged writing system. Throughout Central Eurasia there are numerous runiform inscriptions that remain to be deciphered and a goodly number that may not be in Turkic, see Semih Tezcan, 'Dağlık Altay'da Uluslararası Türkoloji Sempozyumu', *Kanat. Bilkent Üniversitesi Türk Edebiyatı Merkezi Bülteni*, sayı 31 (Güz, 2009): pp. 4–5.

26. Kljaštornyj and Livšic, *The Sogdian Inscription*, pp. 80–1.

27. Louis Bazin, 'Man and the Concept of History in Turkish Central Asia during the Eighth Century', *Diogenes* 42 (1963): p. 83.

28. See discussion in P.B. Golden, *An Introduction to the History of the Turkic Peoples*, Turcologica, 9 (Wiesbaden: Harrasswitz, 1992): pp. 130–1; Scharlipp *Die frühen Türken*, pp. 21–2; Ôsawa, 'Relationship between the ancient Turks and Sogdians'; Stark, *Die Alttürkenzeit in Mittel-und Zentralasien*, pp. 17, 72n320, 305–7.

29. See Sergej G. Kljaštornyj, 'Mifologičeskie sjužety v drevnetjurkskix pamjatnikax', in his *Istorija Central'noj Azii i pamjatniki runičeskogo pis'ma*

(Sankt-Peterburg: Filologičeskij fakul'tet Sankt-Peterburgskogo gosudarstvennogo universiteta, 2003), pp. 319–39 and Sergej G. Kljaštornyj, 'Épičeskie sjužety v drevnetjurkskix pamjatnikax', in Kljaštornyj, *Istorija Central'noj Azii*, pp. 339–58.

30. Dmitrij V. Ruxljadev, 'Drevnetjurkskie runičeskie pamjatniki i žanr istoričeskogo skazanija', *Altaica* XI (2006): pp. 85–97.

31. Lev N. Gumilëv, *Drevnie tjurki* (Moskva: Nauka, 1967), pp. 332–3; Ruxljadev, 'Drevnetjurkskie runičeskie pamjatniki', pp. 90–5. Bazin, 'Man and the Concept of History', pp. 84–5 argues that they are 'true historical syntheses' using a 'funeral eulogy' to create a 'historical synthesis of the whole period' of the man's life.

32. Berta, *Szavaimat jól halljátok*, p. 131. References to the texts are cited mainly in abbreviated form: BQ (Bilge Qağan), KT (Kül Tegin) with indications of direction, North (N), South (S), East (E) West (W) and line number. There are numerous editions of the runiform texts, often with somewhat or very different readings of some passages and employing different transcription systems. I have indicated the texts and the lines (noting, as needed, when a different numbering is used) and employed a somewhat simplified transcription system while retaining some of the specificities of the system being cited. The most extensive corpus can be found in Hüseyin N. Orkun, *Eski Türk Yazıtları*, 4 vols (Istanbul: Devlet Basımevi, Alâeddin Kıral Basımevi, 1936–41), reprinted (Ankara: Türk Dil Kurumu, 1987), which contains the fullest range of texts (but not the most recent readings), while others focus on the major monuments of the eighth century: S.E. Malov, *Pamjatniki drevnetjurkskoj pis'mennosti* (Moskva-Leningrad: Izdatel'stvo Akademii Nauk SSSR, 1951); Talat Tekin, *A Grammar of Orkhon Turkic*, Uralic and Altaic Series, 69 (Bloomington, Indiana; Indiana University Publications – Mouton: The Hague, 1968), Gubajdulla Ajdarov, *Jazyk orxonskix pamjatnikov drevnetjurkskoj pis'mennosti VIII veka* (Almaty: Nauka, 1971), Moriyasu and Ochir, *Provisional Report of Researches*, Berta, *Szavaimat jól halljátok*, Talat Tekin, *Orhon Yazıtları* (Ankara: Türk Dil Kurumu, 2006). I have simplified some of Berta's elaborate transcription system, replaced his ï with ı, ý with g, ẅ with ö or ü, but retained his w, which may stand for o or u. For a brief bibliography of the inscriptions, see Kempf, 'Old Turkic runiform inscriptions in Mongolia', pp. 41–52. A reference to a particular edition indicates that I view that reading as preferable.

33. Some editions, including Berta, *Szavaimat jól halljátok*, prefer to render the name as *Köl Tegin*, but see Clauson, *An Etymological Dictionary*, p. 715, who notes that the 'vowel is uncertain', and in light of the Chinese 'k'üe' (闕 Pinyin: *que* EMC [= c. 601] k^h*uat*, LMC [Late Middle Chinese, seventh–eighth centuries], k^h*yat*, see Pulleyblank, *Lexicon of Reconstructed Pronunciation*, p. 263) opts for *ü*. *Kül/Köl* may well be a title.

34. Boδun is the collective plural of boδ 'clan, lineage' meaning in this context 'an organized tribal community, a people, in the sense of a community ruled by a particular ruler,' Clauson, *An Etymological Dictionary*, pp. 296–7, 306. The Türk boδun consisted of 30 tribes, see Mihály Dobrovits, 'The Thirty Tribes of the Turks', *Acta Orientalia Academiae Scientiarum Hungaricae* 57, no. 3 (2004): pp. 257–62.

35. G. Schlegel, *Die chinesische Inschrift auf dem uighurischen Denkmal in Kara Balgassun*, in *Mémoires de la Société Finno-Ougrienne* IX (Helsingfors, 1896), James R. Hamilton, 'L'inscription trilingue de Qara Balgasun d'après ls estampages de Bouillane de Lacoste', in *Documents et archives provenant de l'Asie Centrale*, ed. A. Haneda (Kyoto, 1990), pp. 125–33.

36. This was during a period of relative peace (717–40) between the Tang and the Türks, marked by trade and discussion of marital ties, see Pan Yihong, *Son of Heaven and Heavenly Qaghan. Sui-Tang China and its Neighbors*, Studies on East Asia 5, no. 20 (Bellingham, Washington: Center for East Asian Studies, Western Washington University, 1997), pp. 276–8. This was also a means of subtlely extending the mantle of Tang authority. Chinese emperors had the tradition of 'composing panegyrics' and 'even ... personally providing the calligraphy' for the grave inscriptions as 'permanent testimony of imperial regard', see H.J. Wechsler, *Offerings of Jade and Silk* (New Haven-London: Yale University Press, 1985), p. 143.

37. Liu Mau-tsai, *Die chinesischen Nachrichten zur Geschichte der Osttürken (T'u-küe)* (Wiesbaden: Harrassowitz, 1958), vol. 1, p. 179; vol. 2, pp. 613–14n953, 620n994 (the *Jiu Tang shu* mistakenly gives the date as 732); Roux, *La religion des Turcs*, p. 276–7.

38. Wechsler *Offerings of Jade and Silk*, p. 153: Taizong ordered the placing of statues of 'barbarian' chieftains who had been subjected to Tang rule within the tomb complex. Despite claims of the antiquity of this practice, in this instance it seems to have been taken from the Türks.

39. Osman F. Sertkaya, *Göktürk Tarihinin Meseleleri* (Ankara: Türk Kültürünü Araştırma Enstitüsü, 1995), p. 14, while noting that Yol(l)uğ Tegin has, 'with caution', been identified as the son of Bilge Qağan, the precise meaning of *qağan atısı* and the blood relationship expressed here is unclear.

40. The text is poorly preserved, see the readings in Berta, *Szavaimat jól halljátok*, pp. 178, 187. Yolluğ Tegin refers to his work simply as *bitig* 'anything written, inscription book, letter, document' < *biti-* 'to write' Clauson, *An Etymological Dictionary*, pp. 299–300, 303.

41. Mamlûk Qıpčaq (late fourteenth–early fifteenth century): *ta'rîkh* 'date, day,' but not 'history', Recep Toparlı, H. Vural, R. Karaatlı, *Kıpçak Türkçesi Sözlüğü* (Ankara: Türk Dil Kurumu, 2003), p. 263.

42. Ferdinand D. Lessing, et al., *Mongolian-English Dictionary*, 3rd ed. (Bloomington, Indiana: The Mongolia Society, 1995), p. 808.

43. Édgem R. Tenišev, et al., *Sravnitel'no-istoričeskaja grammatika tjurkskix jazykov*, 2nd, rev. ed. (Leksika, 2001), p. 69, see a 'reliable parallel' between Mong. **tew(e)-*, *teüke* and Turkic **teb*, cf. Čaǧatay *tewlük*, Tatar *täwlək*, Qazaq *täwlük* etc. 'full span of 24 hours, full span of time' but the Turkic evidence is late (fifteenth century). Cf. Tunguso - Manchu **tiv-*, Evenk. *tiva:n* 'to live, be (of a person)', and so on. For larger Altaic questions, *see* Sergei Starostin, A. Dybo, O. Mudrak, *Etymological Dictionary of the Altaic Languages* (Leiden-Boston: Brill, 2003), vol. 2, p. 1408: **t'eba* 'time' Mong. **tewke* 'history' Turk. **teb* 'time, day and night', Jpn. **támpi* 'time'. The existence of an Altaic language family, whether related genetically or the result of convergence/areal phenomena, remains hotly contested, see Christopher I. Beckwith, *Koguryo: The Language of Japan's Continental Relatives* (Leiden: Brill, 2004), pp. 184–94; Alexander Vovin, 'The End of the Altaic Controversy', *Central Asiatic Journal* 49, no. 1 (2005): pp. 71–132; Jerry Norman, 'A New Look at Altaic', *American Orientaly Society* 129, no. 1 (2009): pp. 83–9.

44. Kormušin, *Tjurkskie enisejskie épitafii*, pp. 96–9, 123–7; Igor' V. Kormušin, *Tjurkskie enisejskie épitafii. Grammatika, tektstologija* (Moskva: Nauka, 2008), pp. 123–4, 127–8, translates *čaŋšı* as 'annalist' (letopisec); Clauson, *An Etymological Dictionary*, p. 426; see Axel Schuessler, *Minimal Old Chinese and Later Han Chinese* (Honolulu: University of Hawai'i Press, 2009), p. 82 (3–35), 103 (4–52), whose Middle Chinese form for *zhang* seems to be a closer reconstruction than that of Pulleyblank, *Lexicon of Reconstructed Pronunciation*, 長 pp. 50 (*chang* EMC *driaŋ*[h], LMC *trhiaŋ*), 398 (*zhang* EMC *triaŋ'*, LMC *triaŋ'*), 283 (*shi* EMC *ṣi'/ṣi*, LMC *ṣr̩*). See Charles O. Hucker, *A Dictionary of Official Titles in Imperial China* (Stanford: Stanford University Press, 1985), #185: *chǎng-shih* [*zhangshi*] 'senior scribe.' See also there for other titles that are homonyms. Paul Pelliot and Louis Hambis, *Histoire des campagnes de Gengis Khan* (Leiden: Brill, 1951), vol. 1, p. 80: an official in charge of neighbouring vassal states.

45. On early Turkic temporal notions, see Sergej G. Kljaštornyj, 'Predstavlenie o vremeni i prostranstve v drevnetjurkskix pamjatnikax' in Kljaštornyj, *Istorija Central'noj Azii*, pp. 237–42. On calendars and chronology, see Louis Bazin, *Les systèmes chronologiques dans le monde turc ancient* (Budapest-Paris: Akadémiai Kiadó, Editions du CNRS, 1991).

46. Cf. *ödüš* 'a period of 24 hours' (Clauson, *An Etymological Dictionary*, p. 72), *öδleg* 'times and seasons' see Starostin, Dybo, Mudrak, *Etymological Dictionary*, vol. 2, p. 1042, Clauson, *An Etymological Dictionary*, p. 866, Tenišev, *Sravnitel'no-istoričeskaja grammatika*, 68–9, Érvand V. Sevortjan, et al., *Étimologičeskij slovar' tjurkskix jazykov* (Moskva: Nauka, 1975-ongoing), vol. 1, pp. 516–17. Cf. also post-840 Uyǧur *ödün* 'time', *Maytrısimit*. *Burkancıların Mehdîsî Maitreya ile Buluşma Uygurca İptidaî Bir Dram*, ed. Şinasi Tekin (Ankara: Sevinç Matbaası, 1976), p. 66 (18.50), probably

dating to the ninth century, see Alessio B Bombaci, *La Letteratura Turca* (Firenze-Milano: Sansoni-Accademia, 1969), p. 39; Nurettin Demir and Emine Yılmaz, 'Uygur Edebiyatı (VIII-XIV. Yüzyıl). 2. Nesir' in *Türk Edebeiyatı Tarihi*, ed. Talât Halman, 2nd ed. (Istanbul: TC Kültür ve Turizm Bakanlığı Yayınları), vol. 1, p. 163, places the Uyğur translation between the eighth and eleventh centuries. By the Qarakhanid era (cf. Kâşğarî) it also came to denote 'Fate,' Dankoff, *From Mahmud Kaşgari to Evliya Çelebi*, p. 77. Öd/Öδ may also have denoted a 'god of time', Sergej G. Kljaštornyj, 'Predstavlenie o vremeni i prostranstve v drevnetjurkskix pamjatnikax', in Kljaštornyj, *Istorija Central'noj Azii*, p. 239; Roux, *La religion des Turcs*, p. 123. The word existed in Oğuric as *ödek*. It has not survived in Chuvash but has in Hungarian, *idő* ('time') where it was borrowed from Oğuric, Lajos Ligeti, *A Magyar nyelv török kapcsolatai a honfoglalâs előtt és az Árpád-korban* (Budapest: Akadémiai Kiadó, 1986), pp. 28-9.

47. *Ujgurskaja versija biografii Sjuan'-czana*, ed. and trans. L. Ju. Tuguševa (Moskva: Nauka, 1991), p. 121: VI. 30, lines 2-5: *tükäl käziklig qılu täginip baštınqı atın tayto χan ödin täki kirügi illär ödigi tip uru tägindim(i)z...* 'arranging everything in a sequential fashion, we gave it the initial name of Report on the Western Countries in the Time of the Great Tang (*tayto*) Emperor...' cf. also Kahar Barat, ed. and trans., *The Uygur-Turkic Biography of the Seventh-Century Chinese Buddhist Pilgrim Xuanzang. Ninth and Tenth Chapters*, Indiana University Uralic and Altaic Series, 166 (Bloomington, Ind.: Indiana University Research Institute for Inner Asian Studies, 2000), p. 204: X: 11b, 9–10*: *ädgü qılınčlar ötigin bitigil* 'write down ... the record of my meritorious deeds'. It might derive from ö—'to think, remember', see Clauson, *An Etymological Dictionary*, pp. 2–3, or perhaps related to öt—with the idea of 'movement through or over' when used intransitively 'almost always with "time"'. Cf. *ötüg* 'request, memorial to a superior' (Clauson, *An Etymological Dictionary*, p. 51 views it as 'etymolgically obscure'), see also Sevortjan, *Étimologičeskij slovar' tjurkskix jazykov*, pp. 556–8 (öt—'povestvovat', rasskazyvat'), *ötiklä*—'to record, mention, remember one by one' (M. Erdal, *Old Turkic Word Formation: A Functional Approach to the Lexicon* [Wiesbaden: Harrassowitz Verlag, 1991], 2 vols, p. 443). The Uyğur translation of Xuanzang by Šıŋqo Šeli Tutuŋ dates to the tenth or early eleventh century, see discussion in Barat, *The Uygur-Turkic Biography*, pp. iii, xii–xiii.

48. Tenišev, *Sravnitel'no-istoričeskaja grammatika*, pp. 71–2. Turkic largely distinguishes between 'year in the age of a person' (*yaš*) and 'year in the calendar' (*yıl*). Tuvan again has an interesting exception, using *xar* (lit. 'snow') for *yaš*: *kaš xarlıg sän* 'how old are you?' (lit. 'how many snows are you?'), cf. Turkish *kaç yaşındasın?* Volga Bulğar of the thirteenth–fourteenth century monuments, Chuvash, its descendant, and Qaračay-Balqar have also not retained the distinction between 'year' (in

reference to a person's age) and calendrical year, see Bazin, *Les systèmes chronologiques*, pp. 55ff.

49. For example, *yar/yaz originally 'spring' ('summer,' in many Turkic languages, e.g. Osm. yaz), *yay 'summer', *gür/güz/küz 'autumn,' *qıl'/qıš 'winter,' Tenišev, *Sravnitel'no-istoričeskaja grammatika*, p. 72–6.

50. 磨延 EMC *ma jian*, LMC *mua jian*, Pulleyblank, *Lexicon of Reconstructed Pronunciation*, pp. 217, 356, probably *Bayan Čor, see Hamilton, *Les Ouïghours à l'époque*, pp. 4, 139.

51. Erhan Aydın, *Şine Usu Yazıtı* (Çorum: KaraM, 2007), p. 38; Berta, *Szavaimat jól halljátok*, p. 286.

52. Clauson, *An Etymological Dictionary*, p. 943.

53. Tuguševa, *Ujgurskaja versija biografii Sjuan'-czana*, p. 103 = VI, 8.4–5, cf. p. 144: VIII, 12.3: 144: *küz yitinč ay ki yılan künka* 'Autumn, in the seventh month on the day of *ji* and the Snake.' 巳 *Ji* (Pulleyblank, *Lexicon of Reconstructed Pronunciation*, p. 140, EMC *ki/ kiˀ*, LMC *kiˀ*, Yuan era *kiˋ*) is a Chinese calendrical marker, the 'sixth Heavenly Stem').

54. Liu, *Die chinesischen Nachrichten*, vol. 1, p. 463. On early Turkic time-reckoning, see Bazin, *Les systèmes chronologiques*, pp. 35ff.

55. Kâšġarî/Dankoff (1982–5), vol. 1, p. I: 272, see also P.B. Golden, 'The Days of the Week in Turkic: Notes on the Cumano-Qıčpaq Pattern', *Acta Orientalia Hungarica* 47, no. 3 (1995): pp. 363–75. The mid-fourteenth century Rasûlid Hexaglot's Turkic calendrical entries still note *yaz evveli* ('first month of spring'), *ikinč ay* ('second month [of spring]'), *üčünč* ('third [month of spring]'), and so on, see *The King's Dictionary. The Rasûlid Hexaglot: Fourteenth-Century Vocabularies in Arabic, Persian, Turkic, Greek, Armenian and Mongolian*, edited with an introduction and commentary by P.B. Golden, trans. Tibor Halasi-Kun, P.B. Golden, L. Ligeti, E. Schütz, with essays by P.B. Golden and T.Th. Allsen (Leiden-Boston: Brill Publishers, 2000), pp. 238–40.

56. Peter A. Boodberg, 'Marginalia to the Histories of the Northern Dynasties', in his *Selected Works of Peter A. Boodberg*, ed. A.P. Cohen (Berkeley-Los Angeles-London: University of California Press, 1979), pp. 285–9, deduces that the animal cycle calendar was in use among the nomadic peoples of the northern Chinese borderlands in the early sixth century.

57. In Turkic some of the animal names (*ud* 'ox, *luu* 'dragon, *yund* 'horse' *laġzın* 'pig' alongside *toŋuz*) are borrowings from a still undetermined language, perhaps Rouran, as is suggested by Alexander Vovin, 'Some Thoughts on the Origins of the Old Turkic 120 year Animal Cycle', *Central Asiatic Journal* 48, no. 1 (2004): pp. 118–32. Starostin, Dybo, Mudrak, *Etymological Dictionary*, vol. 2, p. 1484, suggests *udV* 'ox, buffalo' as an Altaic root for Turk *ud* 'ox, bull,' Mong. *odu-s* 'wild yak, buffalo'. *Lu* would appear to stem from Chin. *lung* (Clauson, *An Etymological Dictionary*, p. 762), *laġzin* (Clauson, *An Etymological Dictionary*, p. 764, 'probably Tocharian'). Clauson, *An Etymological Dictionary*, p. 946, considered *yunt/yund* 'a

generic term for 'horse'. See Denis Sinor, 'Altaic Equine Terminology', in *Essays in Comparative Altaic Linguistics* (Richmond, Surrey, UK: Curzon, 1997), #XIII, pp. 309–12, Denis Sinor, 'The Present State of Uralic and Altaic Studies' in *Essays in Comparative Altaic Linguistics* (Richmond, Surrey, UK: Curzon, 1997), *III, pp. 117–47, and Denis Sinor, 'Samoyed and Ugric Elements in Old Turkic' in *Essays in Comparative Altaic Linguistics* (Richmond, Surrey, UK: Curzon, 1997), #XIX, p. 771, for associations with Samoyedic. Starostin, Dybo, Mudrak, *Etymological Dictionary*, vol. 2, p. 1523, proffered an Altaic origin (*žūnti 'young animal,' Turk. *junt 'horse, mare') and discounted Sinor's Samoyed borrowing. Turkic also had *ebren, evren 'snake, dragon,' see Starostin, Dybo, Mudrak, *Etymological Dictionary*, vol. 1, p. 491 and Clauson, *An Etymological Dictionary*, p. 13–14 evren 'something which revolves' < evir-, hence 'the firmament', dome-shaped oven, Qıpčaq ewren 'adder', and so on.

58. See Rašo Rašev, *Bŭlgarskata ezičeskakultura VII-IXvek*(Sofija: Nasledstvo, 2008), pp. 239–41. On the Old Bulğaro-Turkic month names, see Mosko Moskov, *Imennik na bŭlgarskite xanove (Novo tlŭkuvane)* (Sofija: Dŭržavno izdatelstvo 'D-r Petŭr Beron,' 1988), pp. 80–101.

59. Cf.: σιγορελεμ: *šegor älem* 'Year of the Cow/Ox', Talat Tekin, *Tuna Bulgarları ve Dilleri* (Ankara: Türk Dil Kurumu, 1987), pp. 60–1, Omeljan Pritsak, *Die bulgarische Fürstenliste und die Sprache der Protobulgaren* (Wiesbaden: Harrassowitz, 1955), p. 34 *et passim*, Bazin, *Les systèmes chronologiques*, pp. 452ff. Pritsak, *Die bulgarische Fürstenliste*, pp. 42,48, suggests that the materials stem from two 'Prince Lists', one completed in the last quarter of the seventh century and the other sometime after 777, but before 814. For theories on this calendar, Moskov, *Imennik na bŭlgarskite xanove*, pp. 127–42.

60. Vasil Zlatarski, *Istorija na bŭlgarskata dŭržava prez srednite vekove* (Sofija: Dŭržavna Pečatnica, 1918–40) reprint (Sofija: Akademičesko izdatelstvo 'Prof. Marin Drinov' 1994–2002), vol. 1, pp. 332ff.; vol. 2, pp. 1ff.; John A. Fine, Jr., *The Early Medieval Balkans: A Critical Survey from the Sixth to the Late Twelfth Century* (Ann Arbor: University of Michigan Press, 1983), pp. 112ff.

61. Golden, *History of the Turkic Peoples*, pp. 92–5.

62. Priscus in *The Fragmentary Classicizing Historians of the Later Roman Empire, Eunapius, Olympiodorus, Priscus and Malchus*, ed. and trans. R.C. Blockley, (Liverpool: Francis Cairns, 1981, 1983), vol . 2, pp. 352–5.

63. Kâšǧarî/Dankoff (1982–5), vol. 1, pp. 271–2.

64. Wassilios Klein, *Das nestorianische Christentum an den Handelswegen durch Kyrgyzstan bis zum 14. Jh.* Silk Road Studies III (Turnhout, Belgium: Brepols, 2000), pp. 161–3, 166, 168–76.

65. Talât Tekin, *Volga Bulgar Kitabeleri ve Volga Bulgarcası* (Ankara: Türk Dil Kurumu, 1988), pp. 52ff.; Marcel Erdal, *Die Sprache der wolgabolgarischen Inschriften*, Turcologica, Bd. 13 (Wiesbaden: Harrassowitz Verlag, 1993, pp. 32–42.

66. Liu, *Die chinesischen Nachrichten*, vol. 1, p. 10; Bazin, *Les systèmes chronologiques*, p. 118.

67. Bazin, *Les systèmes chronologiques*, pp. 118–19, who argues that the two systems were complementary, but the traditional Turkic system did not 'satisfy the scientific spirit of the Chinese annalists' for whom only astronomy-based reckoning could serve as the basis for time-reckoning systems.

68. Liu, *Die chinesischen Nachrichten*, vol. 1, p. 10; vol. 2, pp. 500–1.

69. Kül Tegin died in February 731; the funeral rites were performed in November of that year; the grave complex was completed in 732, see, René Giraud, *L'empire des turcs célestes* (Paris: Librairie d'Amerique et d'Orient Adrien-Maisonneuve, 1960), p. 55; Liu, *Die chinesischen Nachrichten*, vol. 2, p. 620n994, Roux, *La religion des Turcs*, p. 277; Saadettin Gömeç, *Kök Türk Tarihi*, 2nd printing (Ankara: AkÇağ, 1999), pp. 3–5.

70. Clauson, *An Etymological Dictionary*, p. 866; Giraud, *L'empire des turcs célestes*, p. 73.

71. Giraud, *L'empire des turcs célestes*, p. 38. Bilge Qağan was poisoned by rivals, an event which the *Jiu Tangshu* mistakenly places in 732, see Liu, *Die chinesischen Nachrichten*, vol. 1, pp. 179, 260 (correctly in 734); vol. 2, p. 620n998.

72. Bugut, B1 has the forms *tr'wkt* ('Turks'), *trwkc* ('Turkish' as in *trwkc bģy* 'the Turkish lord'), Soğd *trwk* = *Truk* as read by Kljaštornyj and Livšic, 'The Sogdian Inscription of Bugut Revised', pp. 85, 87–8, is similar to Khotanese Saka *ttrûka*. On Khotanese Saka *ttrûka*, see Sir Harold Bailey, *Khotanese Texts VII* (Cambridge: Cambridge University Press, 1985), pp. 101–3. On the complexity of these transcriptions (including Chinese 突 厥 *Tūjué*, pronounced in the Chinese of that era something like EMC **duətkuat*, LMC *thutkyat*, or *thwət kwət, thot kwət*, on the Early Middle Chinese reconstruction, see Pulleyblank, *Lexicon of Reconstructed Pronunciation*, pp. 311 (tū), 168 (jué), Schuessler, *Minimal Old Chinese*, pp. 313 (31–12a), MC *tʰwət*, 240 (22–2c). MC *kjwet*, see C.I. Beckwith, 'The Chinese Names of the Tibetans, Tabghatch, and Turks', *Archivum Eurasiae Medii Aevi* 14 (2005): pp. 13–20. Yoshida reads Bugut, B1 as: *tr'wkt 'shy-n's* as **Turkit/*Turukit /*Trukit* Ashinas, which is not without problems, exacerbated by the poor preservation of the monument. Indeed, Sergej Kljaštornyj, who saw the monument in 1968, did not read the opening line as containing the name *'shy-n's*/Ashinas, see Kljaštornyj and Livšic, 'The Sogdian Inscription of Bugut Revised', pp. 85, 87–8, with no mention of the Ashinas. Beckwith, 'The Chinese Names of the Tibetans, pp. 15–17, finds the reading and interpretation 'extremely problematic at best'. He argues that *tr'wkt* is not **turkît ~*turkit* and that such a form does not exist in Soğdian, concluding that the meaning of *tr'wkt* in the Bugut inscription is 'unknown'. Kljaštornyj and Livšic, 'The Sogdian Inscription of Bugut Revised', pp. 87–8, explain this form on the basis of changes in Soğdian.

73. Soġdian bġy (*baġe/baġi) may be rendered as 'lord', cf. bġ [baġ]) 'God, Lord, king, sir, excellency', bġ'nyk [baġânik] 'divine,' bġy 'ġšywny [baġe/i axšêwanê 'His Majesty,' see B. Gharib, Sogdian Dictionary (Tehran: Farhangan Publications, 2004), pp. 100–01, 103.] Kljaštornyj and Livšic, 'The Sogdian Inscription of Bugut Revised', p. 80, render it as 'lord', or 'the lord', but Yoshida translates it as 'God (like)', see Moriyasu and Ochir, Provisional Report of Researches, p. 123.

74. The translations are based on Yoshida's recent readings in Moriyasu and Ochir, Provisional Report of Researches, pp. 123–4 with reference to the earlier edition of Kljaštornyj and Livšic, 'The Sogdian Inscription of Bugut Revised', pp. 85, with extensive commentaries.

75. Moriyasu and Ochir, Provisional Report of Researches, pp. 123–4.

76. Theophylactus Simocatta, Historiae, ed. C. de Boor (Stuttgart: Teubner, 1887), reprint (1972), p. 257, The History of Theophylact Simocatta, trans. Michael and Mary Whitby (Oxford: The Clarendon Press, 1986), p. 188. Étienne de la Vaissière, 'Maurice et le Qaghan: à propos de la digression de Théophylacte Simocatta sur les Turcs', Revue d'études byzantines 68 (2010): pp. 219–24, dates the letter to 595. On the basis of a Soġdian inscription, he identifies the Qaġan with Niri Qaġan (588–604), one of the Ashina contestants for power in the Türk realm.

77. Geo Widengren, 'The Sacral Kingship of Iran', in The Sacral Kingship/ La Regalitá Sacra (Leiden: Brill, 1959), pp. 245–50; Jamsheed Choksy, 'Sacral Kingship in Sasanian Iran', Bulletin of the Asia Institute N.S. 2 (1988): pp. 37, 42–5, 48.

78. Said A. Arjomand, 'Evolution of the Persianate Polity and Its Transmission to India', Journal of Persianate Studies 2 (2009): p. 115. This was a notion that went back to ancient Middle Eastern idealogies of kinghsip, see Henri Frankfort, Kingship and the Gods (Chicago: University of Chicago Press, 1948), reprint (1978), p. 228; Francis Dvornik, Early Christian and Byzantine Political Philosophy: Origins and Background (Washington, D.C., Dumbarton Oaks, 1966), vol. 1, pp. 31, 35.

79. Kljaštornyj and Livšic, 'The Sogdian Inscription of Bugut Revised', p. 77.

80. The Suishu derives them from 'mixed Hu,' see Liu, Die chinesischen Nachrichten, vol. 1, p. 40; Ahmet Taşağıl, Gök-Türkler (Ankara: Türk Tarih Kurumu, 1995–2004), vol. 1, pp. 12–13, 95, 110–11; N. Yamada, 'The Original Turkish Homeland', Journal of Turkish Studie, 9 (1985): pp. 243–6. Chin. 胡 Hu, at this time, denoted Iranian peoples, in particular Soġdians, Liu, Die chinesischen Nachrichten, vol. 1, p. 40 (on 'mixed Hu barbarians'). The term Hu had a range of meanings: 'Northern Barbarian', 'Western Barbarian', and 'Soġdian,' see Anatolij G. Maljavkin, Tanskie Xroniki o Gosudarstvax Central'noj Azii (Novosibirsk: Nauka, 1989), p. 111n21; İsenbike Togan et al., Çin Kaynaklarında Türkler. Eski T'ang Tarihi (Ankara, 2006), p. 154. For a plausible reconstruction of early Ashina-Türk movements, see Sergej G. Kljaštornyj, 'Xunny i tjurki v Vostočnom Turkestane', in Kljaštornyj, Istorija Central'noj Azii,

pp. 420–6 and Sergej G. Kljaštornyj and Dmitrij G. Savinov, *Stepnye imperii drevnej Evrazii* (Sankt-Peterburg: Filologičeskij fakul'tet Cankt-Peterburgskogo gosudarstvennogo universiteta, 2005), pp. 77–9. Turmoil in the Xiongnu state in the first century CE brought many 'Xiongnu' to the shelter of the (future) Great Wall. In 265, Kljaštornyj posits a mass movement here of 'Huns', including Ashina, anxious to accept Chinese overlordship and protection. In the early fifth century, some of these groupings fled to Gaochang and in 460 were brought under Rouran rule. In these regions they absorbed non-Hunnic peoples. They adopted the name *Türk* after their migration to the Altay and retained the name Ashina as name of their ruling clan. In this reconstruction there are two stages: Gansu-Gaochang (265–460) and Altaian (460–553) in the formation of the Türks.

81. See the most recent discussion in Sergei G. Kljaštornyj, 'The Royal Clan of the Turks and the Problem of Early Turkic-Iranian Contacts', in Kljaštornyj, *Istorija Central'noj Azii*, pp. 446–9 and Sergei G. Kljaštornyj, 'The Royal Clan of the Turks and the Problem of its Designation', in *Post-Soviet Central Asia*, eds. Touraj Atabaki and John O'Kane (London-New York: Tauris, 1998), pp. 366–9, Kljaštornyj, Savinov, *Stepnye imperii drevnej Evrazii*, pp. 79–81. A derivation from the Tokharian **aršila* (cf. the Tokharian title *âršilâñči*) as suggested by C.I. Beckwith, *The Tibetan Empire in Central Asia* (Princeton, Princeton University Press, 1987), pp. 206–8, is a possible explanation for Ἀροίλας 'the senior ruler of the Turks' noted in Menander, *The History of Menander the Guardsman*, ed. and trans. R.C. Blockley (Liverpool: Francis Cairns, 1985), pp. 172–3. However, if the reading *Ašinas* in the Bugut inscription is correct, such an explanation would be unlikely.

82. Evgenij I. Kyčanov, *Kočevye gosudarstva ot gunnov do man'čžurov* (Moskva: Vostočnaja Literatura, 1997), pp. 250ff.; Roux, *La religion des Turcs*, pp. 188–93.

83. See Liu, *Die chinesischen Nachrichten*, vol. 1, pp. 5, 40–1; Denis Sinor, 'The Legendary Origins of the Türks', in *Folklorica: Festschrift for Felix J. Oinas*, eds. E.V. Zygas, P. Voorheis (Bloomington, Indiana, 1982), pp. 223–57.

84. Alyılmaz, 'Bugut Yazıtı'. See also Kljaštornyj and Livšic, 'Otkrytie i izučenie drevnetjurkskix', p. 57 and Kljaštornyj and Livšic, 'The Sogdian Inscription of Bugut Revised', p. 71.

85. Berta, *Szavaimat jól hallják ok*, p. 139; Tekin, *Orhon Yazıtları*, p. 24. Traces of this famous passage may, perhaps, be found in the *Qutaδğu Bilig* written by Yûsuf Xaṣṣ Ḥâjib in 1069 [Yûsuf Khâṣṣ Ḥâjib, *Kutadgu Bilig*, ed. Reşit R. Arat, 2nd ed. (Ankara: Türk Dil Kurumu, 1979, p. 197, verse 1800]: cf. *yağız yir yašıl kök* 'brown earth, light-blue sky', see also comments of Edward Tryjarski, 'Origin of Royal Sovereignty and Doctrinal Legitimacy of the Ruler According to Yûsuf Khâṣṣ Ḥâjib of Balasagun', in *Acta Berolinensia: The Concept of Sovereignty in the Altaic World*.

Permanent International Altaistic Conference, 34th Meeting, Berlin 21–6 July 1991, ed. Barabara Kellner-Heinkele, Asiatische Forschungen, Bd. 126 (Wiesbaden: Harrassowitz, 1993), pp. 289–90, 292n14. Bazin, 'Man and the Concept of History', p. 85, suggests that the inscriptions are equating them with the 'contemporaries of the first men,' an interpretation not sustained by the texts.

86. OCM = Minimal Old Chinese (before 200 BCE), LHan = Later Han (first-second centuries CE, see Schuessler, Minimal Old Chinese, p. 51 (#1–28), 339 (#34–28E); Pulleyblank, Lexicon of Reconstructed Pronunciation, pp. 325, 297 wu 'crow, black' sun 'grandson'. On the rendering of this name as Aśvin, see C.I. Beckwith, Empires of the Silk Road (Princeton: Princeton University Press, 2009), p. 376, who suggests that they 'could well have been Old Indic speakers'. The Chinese characters used to transcribe this ethnonym fit in with the ancestor tale.

87. Sima Qian, Records of the Grand Historian, vol. 2, pp. 156, 233–4, 237–43 and the Hanshu in A.F.P. Hulsewé, China in Central Asia. The Early Stage: 125 B.C.–A.D. 23 (Leiden: Brill, 1979), pp. 142–62, 214–15, both based on the report of Zhang Qian, a second century BCE Han diplomat-intelligence agent. See Edwin Pulleyblank, 'The Wu-sun and Sakas and the Yüeh-chih Migrations', Bulletin of the School of Oriental and African Studies 33, no. 1 (1970): pp. 155–7. Ljudmila A. Borovkova, Carstva 'zapadnogo kraja', (Moskva: Intitut Vostokovedenija, 2001), p. 107 and Ljudmila A. Borovkova, Kušanskoe carstvo po drevnim kitajskim istočnikam (Moskva: Institut Vostokovedenija 2005), pp. 42ff. place them in the Gansu corridor, near the Yuezhi and west of the Xiongnu and argue that the Yuezhi and Wusun were ethno-linguistically closely related Europoid peoples, probably Tokharians and Iranians, see B.A. Litvinskij, ed., Vostočnyj Turkestan v drevnosti i rannem srednevekov'e. Étnos, jazyki, religii (Moskva: Nauka, 1992), p. 17; J.P. Mallory, In Search of the Indo-Europeans (London: Thames & Hudson, 1989), pp. 59–60. Richard N. Frye, 'Ossete-Central Asian Connections', Studia Iranica et Alanica. Festschrift for Vasilij Ivanovič Abaev (Roma: Istituto italiano per l'Africa e l'Oriente, Istituto universitario orientale, Dipartimento di Studi Asiatici, 1988), p. 82. The identifications are not without problems, see Augusti Alemany, Sources on the Alans. A Critical Compilation (Leiden: Brill, 2000), pp. 399, 401. Bahaeddin Ögel, Büyük Hun İmparatorluğu Tarihi (Ankara: Kültür Bakanlığı, 1981), vol. 1, p. 490, citing the Hanshu, locates their early homeland to the east of Qilian mountains and west of Dunhuang, to the southeast of the Tianshan. Alemany, Sources on the Alans, p. 397, puts them alongside the Yuezhi 'between Dunhuang and Qilian mountains', whence they were driven westward by the Xiongnu. See C.B. Wakeman, 'Hsi Jung (the Western Barbarians): An Annotated Translation of the Five Chapters of the T'ung Tien on the Peoples and Countries of Pre-Islamic Central Asia' (unpublished PhD diss., University of California-Los Angeles, 1990), pp. 513–30, for discussion of the Wusun data.

88. The *Hanshu* reports that the *kunmo* and his people moved west, with the permission of the Xiongnu, to take revenge against the 'Great' (Da) Yuezhi, who, in the meantime, had driven out the Se (Saka). The Wusun then occupied the Ili valley. Borovkova, *Carstva 'zapadnogo kraja'*, pp. 107–13, 245–52, places the Yuezhi defeat of the 'small' Wusun polity in 182 BCE. This was followed, in turn by the Xiongnu conquest of both the Yuezhi and Wusun in 177. In 167, the Xiongnu drove out the Yuezhi from the Gansu corridor. They went to the Ili region where the Wusun, acting, at least in principle, as agents of the Xiongnu, attacked them in 163. The Yuezhi were driven further westward while the Wusun fully established themselves in the Ili valley c. 161–160. The Han tried to draw them into conflict with the Xiongnu, but the Wusun maneuvered skillfully between the two.

89. Schuessler, *Minimal Old Chinese*, pp. 74 (#2–40), 33 (#43–1); Pulleyblank, *Lexicon of Reconstructed Pronunciation*, pp. 179, 218. The language and hence etymology of this term/title remains unclear. Beckwith, *Empires of the Silk Road*, pp. 376–7, renders the Middle Chinese form as *kwənmɔ or *kwənmak, following Pulleyblank, but prefers the form found in the *Han shu*: 昆彌, *kunmi* MC *kwənmji and suggests that this represents kʷin, or kʷil, kʷir, kʷēr, rendering a foreign kin/kēn or similar forms with a final –l or –r + Late Old Chinese *ñ(r)ek ~ *mīk < Early Old Chin. *mē(r)(e)k, producing a *kin/*kēn (etc.)*mē or *bē, perhaps to be sought in Old Indic. Jurij A. Zuev, *Raniie tjurki: očerki istorii i ideologii* (Almaty: Dajk-Press, 2002), p. 26, reconstructs these characters as ġuən-mâk = Iran. *hvar-baġ 'Sun-God'.

90. Jean-Paul Roux, *Le sang* (Paris, 1988), pp. 42–3, 52. Pole-axes of chieftains decorated with a wolf's head are found in the Kama region and date to the sixth–fourth centuries BCE, see Rima D. Goldina, E.M. Chernykh, 'Forest and Steppe: A Dialogue of Cultures', *Acta Orientalia Academiae Scientiarum Hungaricae* 58, no. 1 (2005): p. 42.

91. András Alföldi, *Die Struktur des voretruskischen Römerstaates* (Heidelberg: C. Winter, 1974); Kris Kershaw, *The One-Eyed God: Odin and the (Indo-) Germanic Männerbünde*, in *Journal of Indo-European Studies*, Monograph series no. 36 (Washington, D.C., 2000), pp. 27, 59, 61 ('the warrior as wolf is Indo-European'), 2000: 134ff. and D.G. White, *Myths of the Dog-Man* (Chicago, 1991), p. 28. Vatic powers were associated with them as were warrior cults, whose members were caught up in 'wolfish rage', Bruce Lincoln, *Death, War, and Sacrifice* (Chicago: University of Chicago Press, 1991), pp. 131–7; see also M. Speidel, 'Berserks: A History of Indo-European "Mad Warriors"', *Journal of World History* 13, no. 2 (2002): pp. 280–1, 285, and those who lived outside of the traditional social-legal systems, Thomas V. Gamkrelidze, and Vjačeslav V. Ivanov, *Indo-European and the Indo-Europeans*, trans. J. Nichols (Berlin: Mouton-de Gruyter, 1995), vol. 1, 413ff.; Kershaw, *The One-Eyed God*, pp. 118–19.

92. See Ögel, *Türk Mitolojisi*, vol. 1, pp. 17–18, V.S. Taskin, *Materialy po istorii drevnix kočevyx narodov gruppy dunxu* (Moskva: Nauka, 1984), p. 401; Kyčanov, *Kočevye gosudarstva*, pp. 253–4, based on the *Weishu* account. See also Edwin Pulleyblank, 'The High Carts', *Asia Major* 3, no. 1 (1990): pp. 21–6; Zaurbek K. Gabuev, *Étnogoničeskie predstavlenija drevnix kočevnikov Velikoj Stepi. Irancy i tjurki* (Mosvka: Nauka, 2002), 39–40; Mihály M. Dobrovits, 'Maidens, Towers and Beasts', in *The Role of Women in the Altaic World*, Permanent International Altaistic Conference 44th Meeting, Walberberg, 26–31 August 2001, ed. Veronika Veit, Asiatische Forschungen Bd. 152, (Wiesbaden: Harrassowitz, 2007), p. 50.

93. Colin Mackerras, *The Uighur Empire According to the T'ang Dynastic Histories* (Canberra: Australian National University Press, 1972), p. 17; Drompp, *Tang China and the Collapse of the Uighur Empire*, p. 173.

94. Liudprand, *Die Werke Liudprands von Cremona*, ed. J. Becker, 3rd ed., *Scriptores rerum germanicarum*, vol. 41 (Hanover-Leipzig:Hahnsche Buchhandlung, 1915), p. 88.

95. M. Dickens, 'The Sons of Magog: The Turks in Michael's *Chronicle*', *Parole de l'Orient* 31 (2006): p. 436n17 and his 'Turkâyê: Turkic Peoples in Syriac Literature Prior to the Seljüks', PhD diss., University of Cambridge, 2008, pp. 120–5.

96. *Polnoe sobranie russkix letopisej* (henceforth *PSRL*), ed. Arxeografičeskaja Komissija (Moskva-Sankt Peterburg/ Petrograd/ Leningrad:1846–1921), reprint (Moskva: Jazyki russkoj kul'tury, 1997–ongoing), vol. 1, cc. 270–1.

97. Tadeusz Kowalski, 'Les Turcs dans le Šâh-Nâma', *Rocznik Orientalistyczny* XV (1939–49): p. 96, reprinted/ translated in *The Turks in the Early Islamic World*, ed. C.E. Bosworth (Aldershot: Ashgate/Variorum, 2007), p. 131.

98. Bazin, 'Man and the Concept of History', pp. 81–3.

99. P.B. Golden, 'Religion among the Qıpčaqs of Medieval Eurasia', *Central Asiatic Journal* 42, no. 2 (1998): pp 194–6. On the Kazakh 'domestic cult of ancestor-spirits', Privratsky, *Muslim Turkistan*, pp. 17–9, 114–53.

100. Some scholars view the Čoyren Inscription as the oldest, dating it to c. 687–92, see Kljaštornyj and Livšic, 'Otkrytie i izučenie drevnetjurkskix', p. 48 (c. 688–91) and Guzev and Kljaštornyj, 'Drevnjaja pis'mennost Velikoj Stepi', p. 148 (c. 688–91); Sertkaya, *Göktürk Tarihinin Meseleleri*, p. 318 (687–92). But, Kempf, 'Old Turkic runiform inscriptions in Mongolia', p. 44 places it in the eighth-ninth centuries.

101. On the dating: Kempf, 'Old Turkic runiform inscriptions in Mongolia', p. 45. Stark, *Die Alttürkenzeit in Mittel-und Zentralasien*, p. 79, suggests: 'auf jeden Fall nach 714, vielleicht sogar nach 732'. M. Dobrovič (Mihály Dobrovits), 'K voprosu ličnosti glavnogo geroja pamjatnika Kuli-Čoru', in *Central'naja Azia ot axemenidov do timuridov. Arxeologija, istorija, étnologija, kul'tura*, ed. Valerij P. Nikonorov (Sankt-Peterburg: Institut istorii material'noj kul'tury RAN, Gosudsarstvennyj Érmitaž, Vostočnyj fakul'tet Sank-Peterburgskogo gosudarstvennogo universiteta, 2005), pp. 86–8, places his death after 732 and hence, the monument is older

than those of Tonyuquq and Kül Tegin. The monument has direct ties with that of the latter.

102. Gömeç, *Kök Türk Tarihi*, p. 43, reads the name/title as Köl İč Čor and identifies him with the *qağan inisi el čwr tegin* ('younger brother of the Qağan [probably Bilg Qağan] El Čor,'(KČ, E24, Berta, *Szavaimat jól halljátok*, p. 17). According to Dobrovič, 'K voprosu ličnosti glavnogo' he was a nephew of Elteriš and may have had ties to the Ašide as well.

103. Moriyasu and Ochir, *Provisional Report of Researches*, pp. 151–3, Berta, *Szavaimat jól halljátok*, p. 17 *(bntrbnm: *bäntäz bän ?, bäntir (?) bänim ? etc.)*; see also text in Sir Gerard Clauson and Edward Tryjarski, 'The Inscription at *Ikhe-khushotu*', *Rocznik Orientalistyczny* 34 (1971): pp 7–33, Ajdarov, *Jazyk orxonskix pamjatnikov*, pp. 334–8. On the proper reading of his name/title, see Sir Gerard Clauson, *Studies in Turkic and Mongolic Linguistics* (1962), reprint (London-New York: Routledge Curzon, 2002), pp. 88–9.

104. See Mihály Dobrovits, 'Ongin Yazıtını Tahlile Bir Deneme', *Türk Dili Araştırmaları Yıllığı-Belleten 2000*, (Ankara: Türk Dil Kurumu, 2001), pp. 147–50, Moriyasu and Ochir, *Provisional Report of Researches*, pp. 132–4.

105. Giraud, *L'empire des turcs célestes*, pp. 28ff., 59–65; Liu, *Die chinesischen Nachrichten*, vol. 2, p: 594–7n846; Sergej G. Kljaštornyj, 'Tonjukuk-Ašide Juan'čžén' *Tjurkologičeskij sbornik 1966* (Moskva: Nauka), pp. 202–5.

106. Berta, *Szavaimat jól halljátok*, p. 54.

107. Bazin, 'Man and the Concept of History', pp. 88–90.

108. Bazin, 'Man and the Concept of History', pp. 89, 91; Stark, *Die Alttürkenzeit in Mittel-und Zentralasien*, pp. 76–7 on dating.

109. In KT, E2: surrounding foes: *tört bulwŋ qop yağı ärmiš* 'there were enemies [in] all four quarters.'

110. Clauson, *An Etymological Dictionary*, p. 976: *yïš* '"mountain forest", the upper parts of a mountain covered with forest, but also containing treeless grassy valleys'. *Ötüken* may derive from Proto-Turkic *ötü 'old, old abandoned house, everything old, name of the homeland of the Turks ('old country')', ' Turk > Bur[yat] *ütügen* 'shaman word for earth', see Starostin, Dybo, Mudrak, *Etymological Dictionary*, vol. 2, p. 1068.

111. Similar wording in BQ, N15 *on oq oğlıŋa tatıŋa tägi bwnı körü biliŋ bäŋü taš toqıtδım* 'as far as the progeny of the On Oq (= Western Türk realm) and of the *Tat* (term for Iranian subjects), I had this eternal stone engraved so that seeing it you should know!'

112. On the wide range of objects, including implements of daily life, on which runic inscriptions are found, see Kyzlasov, *Runičeskie pis'mennosti evrazijskix stepej*; Cengiz Alyılmaz, *(Kök) Türk Harfli Yazıtların İzinde* (Ankara: KaraM, 2007); Törbat et al. 'A Rock Tomb of the Ancient Turkic Period in the Zhargdont Khairkhan Mountains, Khovd Aimag with the Oldest Preserved Horse-head Fiddle in Mongolia—A Preliminary Report', in *Bonn Contributions to Asian Archaeology*, 4 (2009): pp. 373–4 have found a runic inscription on the neck of a fiddle in a Türk-era rock tomb

in the Nüxen Xad mountain in the Žargalant Xairχan mountain range in Xovd aimag, Mongolia. Sergej G. Kljaštornyj, 'Xazarskie zametki', in *Tjurkologičeskij Sbornik 200–2004* (Moskva: Vostočnaja Literatura, 2005), pp. 95–102 and Kljaštornyj, 'Drevnetjurkskie Pamjatniki', p. 66, argues that literacy in the Türk Qağanate surpassed that of early Medieval Europe.

113. Tekin, *Orhon Yazıtları*, p. 24, Berta, *Szavaimat jól halljátok*, pp. 139–40 (KT,E1/BQ E2).

114. É.A. Grantovskij, *Ranjaja istorija iranskix plemën Perednej Azii* (Moskva; Vostočnaja Literatura RAN, 2007), pp. 177ff., Gherardo Gnoli, 'Farr(ah)' *Encyclopaedia Iranica* (London-Boston: Routledge, New York: Bibliotheca Persica, Press, 1982-ongoing), vol. 9, pp. 312–19, available at http://www.iranica.com/newsite/, Richard N. Frye, 'Central Asian Concepts of Rule', in *Ecology and Empire: Nomads in the Cultural Evolution of the Old World*, ed. Gary Seaman, Ethnographics Monographs (Los Angeles: Center for Visual Anthropology, University of Southern California, 1989), pp. 135–40.

115. For the texts with translation: R.G. Kent, *Old Persian: Grammar, Texts, Lexicon*, 2nd rev. ed., American Oriental Series, vol. 33 (New Haven: American Oriental Society, 1953), pp. 116ff.; A. Kuhrt, *The Persian Empire: A Corpus of Sources from the Achaemenid Period* (Abingdon-New York: Routledge, 2007), pp. 22ff.

116. Bazin, 'Man and the Concept of History', p. 97, views the 'essential function' of these inscriptions as 'religious'.

117. Denis Sinor, 'The Uighur Empire of Mongolia', in *History of the Turkic Peoples in the Pre-Islamic Period*, ed. Hans R. Roemer, in *Philologiae et Historiae Turcicae Fundamenta*, vol. 1, *Philologiae Turcicae Fundamenta*, vol. 3 (Berlin: Klaus Schwarz Verlag, 2000), pp. 188–9, 203–4, who argues, correctly in my view, that the Uyğur rise to power was a 'revolt' followed by a continuation of essentially the same elements that had constituted the Türk Empire, but now under a different ruling house and dominant confederation.

118. The Yağlaqar led the revolt that toppled the Ashina-led Basmıl in 744, in alliance with the Uyğurs and Qarluqs. They also killed last of the Ashina Türk rulers, Ozmıš (or Özmiš) Qağan and sent his head to the Tang, Liu, *Die chinesischen Nachrichten*, vol. 1, pp. 180, 230–1; vol. 2, p. 630n1006 on the confusing events; Mackerras, *The Uighur Empire*, pp. 54–5, 126n1; Taşağıl, *Gök-Türkler*, vol. 3, pp. 54–9; Golden, *History of the Turkic Peoples*, pp. 138, 156, 158. For a reconstruction of the early history of the Uyğurs, see Kljaštornyj, Savinov, *Stepnye imperii drevnej Evrazii*, pp. 110–11 and Ablet K. Kamalov, *Drevnie ujgury VIII-IX vv.* (Almaty: Naš Dom, 2001), pp. 58–60.

119. For editions see S.G. Kljaštornyj, 'The Tes Inscription of the Uighur Bögü Qaghan', in Sergej G. Kljaštornyj, *Pamjatniki drevnetjurkskoj pis'mennosti i étnokul'turnaja istorija Central'noj Azii* (SPb.: Nauka, 2006), pp. 143–64; Sergei G., Kljaštornyj, 'The Terkhin Inscription',

in Kljaštornyj, 'The Tes Inscription', pp. 128–43; Moriyasu and Ochir, *Provisional Report of Researches*, pp. 158–67, 168–76, Berta, *Szavaimat jól halljátok*, pp. 227–40, 241–6.

120. Clauson, *An Etymological Dictionary*, pp. 121–2: 'A political unit organized and ruled by an independent ruler... realm.' The *el* was composed of *boδs*, collective plural *boδun* (see earlier). Giraud, *L'empire des turcs célestes*, pp. 25–6, would translate *el* as 'empire', which fits the Türk and Uyğur contexts.

121. Berta, *Szavaimat jól halljátok*, pp. 234, 238; Kljaštornyj, 'The Tes Inscription', pp. 143–64, see esp. pp. 157,159: *biŋ eli üč yüz yıl el tutmıš ančıp bodunı b[ar]rdı* 'they sat on the throne. For three hundred years they ruled over many (lit thousand) *els*. Then, their people perished.'

122. See Berta, *Szavaimat jól halljátok*, p. 235: *öŋrä taβğačqa bazlanmıš uyğur qağan toq olormwš yetmiš yıl är[miš]*. Rather different versions can be found in Kljaštornyj, 'The Tes Inscription', pp. 157–9; Moriyasu and Ochir, *Provisional Report of Researches*, pp. 159–61.

123. Berta, *Szavaimat jól halljátok*, p. 248 (*...yol(l)wğ qağan...bwmın qağan üč qağan olormwš eki yüz yıl olormwš...aqıza barmıš učuz kölkä atlığın tökä barmıš*, ' *...**poured, poured their cavalry into the Učuz Lake'257; Kljaštornyj, 'The Tes Inscription', pp. 135, 138, reads it, (as E16), with perhaps greater certainty: *yolığ qağan* (10 signs are damaged) *...bumın qağan üč qağan olurmıš* (73 signs are damaged) *[bodu]nı qıza barmıš see* :135,138: 'Yolığ –qağan...Bumın-qağan, (these) three qaghans have sat on the throne. They have sat on the throne for two hundred years ... their peoples, having become enraged, perished....' The passage is open to a variety of readings.

124. Berta, *Szavaimat jól halljátok*, pp. 234, 248–9.

125. Liu, *Die chinesischen Nachrichten*, vol. 1, p. 7; Taşağıl, *Gök-Türkler*, vol. 1: 17, 96; M.R. Drompp, 'Imperial State Formation in Inner Asia: The Early Turkic Empires (Sixth to Ninth Centuries)', *Acta Orientalia Academiae Scientiarum Hungaricae* 58, no. 1 (2005): pp. 103–4.

126. P.B. Golden, *Ethnicity and State Formation in Pre-Činggisid Turkic Eurasia*, The Central Eurasian Lectures, vol. 1 (Bloomington, Indiana: Department of Central Eurasian Studies, 2001), pp. 13–19.

127. Vasilij V. Bartol'd, *Dvenadcat' leksij po istorii tureckix narodov Srednej Azii*, in V.V. Bartol'd, *Sočinenija* (Moskva: Izdatel'stvo Vostočnoj Literatury, 1963–1977), vol. 5 (1968), pp. 39–40.

128. Berta, *Szavaimat jól halljátok*, p. 252. Kljaštornyj, 'The Tes Inscription', pp. 134, 136–7 has: *etinti* 'were founded' or 'organized' instead of *etindim* 'I organized': 'As the blue sky above was merciful (to me) and the brown earth below nourished me, my realm and customary law were founded.'

129. A.K. Kamalov, 'The Moghon Shine Usu Inscription as the Earliest Uighur Historical Annals', *Central Asiatic Journal* 47, no. 1 (2003): pp. 77–90.

130. Berta, *Szavaimat jól halljátok*, p. 282, (Hung. trans.) 301 ('the river [water], there [then] the people who remained ruled over the Ten Uyğur and Nine Oğuz for one hundred years ... The Orkhon river ... the Türk Qağan ruled exactly fifty years'), Moriyasu and Ochir, *Provisional Report of Researches*, pp. 178, (Eng.) 182 '(some Yağlaqar noble) men who had remained (or survived) at *** [were ruling?] over the people of the On Uyğur and Toquz Oğuz for a hundred years ... the river Orqun ... I heard that the Türük *qağans* had sat on the throne (or had reigned)) exactly for fifty years.' See the earlier reading in Ajdarov, *Jazyk orxonskix pamjatnikov*, pp. 343–4: *anta qalmısı on uyğur toquz oğuz üze yüz olurup ... türk qıbčaq elig yıl olurmıs* 'the people that remained there ruled over the ten (tribes) of the Uyğurs amd over the nine tribes of the Oğuz for one hundred years ... the Türks-Qıpčaqs resided for fifty years.' See also Aydın, *Şine Usu Yazıtı*, p. 33.

131. Sergej G. Kljaštornyj and Vladimir A. Livšic, 'Sévréjskaja kamen', *Sovetskaja Tjurkologija*, no. 3 (1971): pp. 106–12.

132. See translation in Kamalov, *Drevnie ujgury VIII-IX vv.*, pp. 194–7.

133. The Chinese names and their Turkic equivalents are given in, James R. Hamilton, *Les Ouïghours à l'époque des cinq dynasties d'après les documents chinois* (Paris: Imprimerie nationale – Presses universitaires de France, 1955), pp. 139–41.

134. On these issues, see Kamalov, *Drevnie ujgury VIII-IX vv.*, pp. 137–60.

135. Moriyasu and Ochir, *Provisional Report of Researches*, pp. 215–19.

136. O. Hansen, *Zur soghdischen Inschrift auf dem dreisprachigen Denkmal von Karabalgasun* (Helsinki: Suomalais-Ugrilainen Seura/Finno-Ugrian Society, 1930), pp. 14, 23–5.

137. Moriyasu and Ochir, *Provisional Report of Researches*, pp. 219–23; Hamilton, *Les Ouïghours à l'époque*, p. 141.

138. A. Van Tongerloo, 'Manichaen Religion and the Concept of Sovereignty among the Uighurs', in Kellner-Heinkele, *Concept of Sovereignty in the Altaic World*, pp. 276–7, 280–1.

139. Bazin, 'Man and the Concept of History', pp. 82–3. Not all monuments found here are necessarily Qırğız, cf. the Znamenka find dated sometime between 700 and 766 (Stark, *Die Alttürkenzeit in Mittel-und Zentralasien*, p. 78).

140. For example, E-10 (Elegest-1), on the left bank of the Yenisei, of its twelve lines only line 8 refers to a specific event: 'in the battle at Čilbilig alone, in which I personally entered the fray, I captured eight enemy warriors' *čilbiligdä bir tägimdä säkiz är sürdim*, see Kormušin, *Tjurkskie enisejskie épitafii*, pp. 236–7 and comments, p. 241. Ruxljadev, 'Drevnetjurkskie runičeskie pamjatniki', pp. 95–6, among others, argues that the lack of ideological content, so typical of the Türk and Uyğur inscriptions, reflected a society of diffused power-holders, who did not need a 'national' history.

141. Kormušin, *Tjurkskie enisejskie épitafii*, pp. 117–20, E-68, from El-Bažı in Tuva, (Kormušin, *Tjurkskie enisejskie épitafii*, pp. 152–4, is dedicated

to Qara Bars Inanču Čigši, who, given his Bars name and high titles, may also have been of the royal Bars clan). Sergej G. Kljaštornyj, 'Stely Zolotogo ozera (k datirovke enisejskix runičeskix pamjatnikov'), in Kljaštornyj, 'The Tes Inscription', pp. 335–40, argues that the Bars of Altın Köl I is the Bars-beg Qağan of the Qırğız killed by the Türks (in a campaign by the then *šad* but later Bilge Qağan) in the winter of 710–11.

142. 'I went to the Khan of Tibet as a emissary. I did not come (home)', Kormušin, *Tjurkskie enisejskie épitafii*, pp. 120–2. Kljaštornyj, 'The Tes Inscription', pp. 336, 341–2, reads it differently and identifies Inanču Alp Saŋun as the throne name of Bars-beg Qağan and suggests this was the embassy sent by the Qırğız to Tibet in 711.

143. Kormušin, *Tjurkskie enisejskie épitafii*, pp. 76–7: *uyğur yirintä yağlaqar qan-ta käl... qırğız oğlı män boyla qutluğ yarğan*, Igor' V. Kormušin, 'Tamgovye analogii naskal'nyx nadpisej iz doliny Alaš (Zapadnaja Tuva) iz stely iz Sudži (Severnaja Mongolija) ili eščё raz k voprosu o kyrgyzskom xaraktere Sudžinskoj nadpisi', *Tjurkologičeskij Sbornik 2007–2008* (Moskva: Vostočnaja Literatura RAN, 2009), pp. 182–4; see also S.E. Malov, *Pamjatniki drevnetjurkskoj pis'mennosti* (Moskva-Leningrad: Izdatel'stvo Akademii Nauk SSSR, 1951), pp. 76–7 and Sertkaya, *Göktürk Tarihinin Meseleleri*, p. 212: *uyğur yirintä yağlaqar qan ata käl[dim]*. Berta, *Szavaimat jól halljátok*, pp. 320–3, translates it as: 'From the Uyğur land I came Yağlaqar Qan Ata, I am a son of the Qırğız people, I am Boyla Qutluğ Yarğan', but Yağlaqar Qan Ata, must refer to the Uyğurs, although the Yağlaqar hold on power had been shaken by internal strife in the decades before the fall of the Empire, see Golden, *History of the Turkic Peoples*, pp. 162–3. *Boyla* is a 'high title', *qutluğ* 'enjoying the favor of heaven, fortunate, happy, blessed' (Clauson, *An Etymological Dictionary*, pp. 385, 601).

144. Kormušin, *Tjurkskie enisejskie épitafii*, p. 158: *uyğur qan yärin alduqda azığlığ toŋuz täg tirig bäg*.

145. Kormušin, *Tjurkskie enisejskie épitafii*, pp. 272–4: *bäš yägirmi yašımda tabğač qanğa bardım-a är ärdämim üčün alpun altun kümišig ägritäbä eldä qazğandım-a*.

146. Pulleyblank, *Lexicon of Reconstructed Pronunciation*, p. 248 契 (qì), p. 70 丹(dān)

147. Juha Janhunen, *Manchuria: An Ethnic History*, Mémoires de la Société Finno-Ougrienne 222 (Helsinki: The Finno-Ugrian Society, 1996), 139–49 and Juha Janhunen, 'Para-Mongolic', in *The Mongolic Languages*, ed. Juha Janhunen (London-New York: Routledge, 2003), pp. 391–402 and Daniel Kane, *The Kitan Language and Script*, Handbook of Oriental Studies, Section 8, Central Asia (Leiden-Boston: Brill, 2009). Their language has been preserved in two Chinese-like writing systems.

148. Karl A. Wittfogel and Fêng Chia-shêng, *History of Chinese Society: Liao (907–1125)*, in *Transactions of the American Philosophical Society*, n.s. 36 (Philadelphia: The American Philosophical Society, 1949), p. 576.

149. Wittfogel and Fêng, *History of Chinese Society*, p. 23.

150. Emil Bretschneider, *Mediaeval Researches from Eastern Asiatic Sources* (London: Trubner, 1888), reprint (New York: Barnes & Noble, 1967), vol. 1, p. 214 (who has it dated to 1121); Wittfogel and Fêng, *History of Chinese Society*, pp. 635–6, who gives a truncated version of the letter, dates it to 1130 as does Michal Biran, *The Empire of the Qara Khitai in Eurasian History* (Cambridge: Cambridge University Press, 2005), p. 36.

151. Sun Shirota, 'The Chinese Chroniclers of the Khazars: Notes on Khazaria in Tang Period Texts', *Archivum Eurasiae Medii Aevi* 14 (2005): pp. 231–61.

152. Ahmed Z. V. Togan, ed. and trans., *Ibn Faḍlân's Reisebericht, Abhandlungen für die Kunde des Morgenlandes*, XXIV, no. 3 (Leipzig: Deutsche Morgenländische Gesellschaft, 1939): pp. 44 (Arabic), 99–100 (German).

153. See discussion of the dating in P.B. Golden, 'The Conversion of the Khazars to Judaism', in *The World of the Khazars: New Perspectives*, eds. P.B. Golden, H. Ben-Shammai, A. Róna-Tas (Leiden-Boston: Brill, 2007), pp. 151–6.

154. The 'Schechter' or 'Cambridge Document,' Norman Golb and Omeljan Pritsak, *Khazarian Hebrew Documents of the Tenth Century* (Ithaca: Cornell University Press, 1982); A.N. Torpusman, 'Antroponimija i etničeskie kontakty narodov Vostočnoj Evropy v srednie veka', in *Imja–étnos – istorija*, ed. M. Členov (Moskva, 1989), pp. 48–53;V. Orel, 'O slavjanskix imenax v evrejsko-xazarskom pis'me iz Kieva', *Palaeoslavica* 5 (1997): pp. 335–8.

155. Joseph's letter has survived in a long and a short version; the former in a manuscript in St Petersburg, which may date to the thirteenth century, and the latter in a manuscript, at Oxford, dating from the sixteenth century. The Kievan letter and the 'Letter of the Unknown Khazar Jew' were preserved in the Cairo Geniza and are now housed in Cambridge University. The fundamental publication is that of Pavel, K. Kokovcov, *Evrejsko-xazarskaja perepiska v X veke* (Leningrad: Izdatel'stvo Akademii Nauk SSSR, 1932).

156. See Devin DeWeese, *Islamization and Native Religion in the Golden Horde* (University Park, Pennsylvania, 1994), pp. 170–2, 300–8 and Golb and Pritsak, *Khazarian Hebrew Documents*, pp. 106–13.

157. Jerry Bentley, *Old World Encounters: Cross-Cultural Contacts and Exchanges in Pre-Modern Times* (Oxford-New York: Oxford University Press, 1993), p. 5.

158. P.B. Golden, 'The Khazar Sacral Kingship-Revisited', *Acta Orientalia Academiae Scientiarum Hungaricae* 60, no. 2 (2007): pp. 161–94.

159. Kokovcov, *Evrejsko-xazarskaja perepiska v X veke*, pp. Heb. 20, 28, Russ. 74, 91.

160. For example, Qazaqs are expected to know their *žeti ata* 'seven forefathers', see Privratsky, *Muslim Turkistan*, pp. 116–17; Adrienne L. Edgar,

Tribal Nation: The Making of Soviet Turkmenistan (Princeton: Princeton University Press, 2004), pp. 24–5.

161. Kokovcov, *Evrejsko-xazarskaja perepiska v X veke*, pp. Heb. 20–1/Russ. 74–5.

162. P.B. Golden, 'Khazarica: Notes on some Khazar terms', *Turkic Languages* 9, no. 2: pp. 216–17. The Bulğar union was defeated in the latter half of the seventh century and one grouping under Asperuχ crossed the Danube in 679 and entered the Balkans giving rise to the Balkan Bulğar state, see Veselin Beševliev, *Die protobulgarische Periode der bulgarischen Geschichte* (Amsterdam: Hakkert, 1980), pp. 145–90 and the articles in *Bŭlgari i Xazari prez rannoto srednovekovie*, ed. Cvetelin Stepanov (Sofija: Centŭr za Izsledvanija na Bŭlgarite, 2003).

163. I.G. Konovalova, 'Tjurki i slavjane v étnogenealogijax srednevekovyx arabo-persidskix avtorov'. *Tjurkologičeskij Sbornik 2002* (Moskva: Vostočnaja literatura RAN, 2003), p. 286.

164. Ibn Khurdâdhbih, *Kitâb Masâlik wa'l-Mamâlik*, ed. M.J. De Goeje (Leiden: Brill, 1889), p. 15. Afrîdûn/Ferêdûn, Avest. Θraêtaona, Middle Pers. Frêdôn is a mythical Iranian hero, see Ol'ga M. Čunakova, *Pexlevijskij slovar' zoroastrijskix terminov, mifičeskix personažej i mifologičeskix simvolov* (Moskva: Vostočnaja literatura RAN, 2004), p. 235. Of his three sons, Salm, Êriz (Îraj) and Tôz/Tûr (Pazend. Tûr, Pehl. Tws, Avest. Tūra, Čunakova, *Pexlevijskij slovar' zoroastrijskix terminov*, p. 224), he gave Turkistan and China to Tûr [A. Tafażżolî, 'Ferêdûn' in *Encyclopaedia Iranica*, ed. Ehsan Yarshater, 1982–ongoing, sub: 'Ferêdûn', available at http://www.iranicaonline.org/articles/feredu- and I. Rak, *Mify drevnego Irana* (Ekaterinburg: U-Faktorija, 2006), pp. 143–5]; Tôz/Tur is Tûj.

165. Ramazan Şeşen, ed. and trans., *Hilâfet Ordusunun Menkıbeleri ve Türkler'in Fazîletleri* (Ankara: Türk Kültürünü Araştırma Enstitüsü, 1967).

166. Gardîzî, *Ta'rîkh-i Gardîzî*, ed. 'Abd al-Ḥayy Ḥabîbî, (Tehran: Dunyâ-i Kitâb, 1363/1984), pp. 545–6: the Turks spring from the *Čîniyân*, but this is probably an error, as noted by Arsenio P. Martinez, 'Gardîzî on the Turks', *Archivum Eurasiae Medii Aevi* 2 (1982): pp. 116–17; see also Hansgerd Göckenjan, and István Zimonyi, *Orientalische Berichte über die Völker Osteuropas und Zentralasiens im Mittelalter* (Veröffentlichungen der Societas Uralo-Altaica, Bd. 54, Weisbaden: Harrassowitz, 2001), p. 95, who retain *Čîniyân*, but note (111) the tradition associated with Tûj in Ibn Khurdâdhbih and others.

167. Much of his material comes from earlier authors, in particular from the Jaihânî 'school' and the data collected in the now lost *Kitâb al-Masâlik wa'l-Mamâlik* compiled by Abu 'Abdallâh Muḥammad b. Aḥmad al-Jaihânî. The Jaihânî family, of probable Khwârazmian origin, served the Sâmânids in the tenth century. Károly Czeglédy, 'Gardîzî on the History of Central Asia (746–780 A.D.)', *Acta Orientalia Academiae Scientiarum*

Hungaricae 27, no. 3 (1973): pp. 257–67; Zuev, *Raniie tjurki*, pp. 129–30; Göckenjan and Zimonyi, *Orientalische Berichte*, pp. 1–22.

168. Gardîzî, *Ta'rîkh-i Gardîzî*, p. 547, Martinez, 'Gardîzî on the Turks', p. 118.

169. Al-Mas'ûdî, *Murûj adh-Dhahab wa Ma'âdin al-Jawhar*, ed. Charles Pellat (Beirut: Publications de l'Université Libanaise, 1966–79), vol. 1, p. 155. Qarluq paramountcy was also noted by Yâqût, *Mu'jam al-Buldân* (Beirut: Dâr Ṣâdir, 1955), vol. 2, p. 24. See discussion in Golden, *History of the Turkic Peoples*, pp. 196–9. Al-Mas'ûdî has contradictory notices on Farâsiyâb, saying that since he was born in the land of the Turks, historians err in claiming that he was a Turk, but elsewhere giving his genealogy as 'Farâsiyâb b. Bašank b. Zây Arsan b. Turk, and this Turk was the forefather of the rest of the Turks', see al-Mas'ûdî, *Murûj adh-Dhahab*, vol. 1, pp. 266, 274.

170. Gardîzî, *Ta'rîkh-i Gardîzî*, pp. 548–9, Martinez, 'Gardîzî on the Turks', pp. 118–20.

171. Omeljan Pritsak, 'Mahmud Kâşgarî Kimdir', *Türkiyat Mecmuası* X (1953): pp. 243–6; Kâšġarî/Dankoff (1982–5), vol. 2, p. 364 (who notes that he was born in Barsğan, near Issıq Köl in modern Kyrgyzstan and not far from Kâšġar). Genç, *Kaşgarlı Mahmud'a Göre XI*, pp. 1–4, raises some doubts about his royal pedigree.

172. Kâšġarî/Dankoff (1982–5), vol. 1, pp. 273–4.

173. Kâšġarî/Dankoff (1982–5), vol. 1, pp. 4, 82.

174. Kâšġarî/Dankoff (1982–5), vol. 2, p. 219, cites, as an example, a response from an Oğuz Salğur: 'My kinsmen (*raht*) are the subtribe (*qabîla*) Salğur' or else he mentions one of the other branches '(*butûn*)... They are the proper names of the ancestors of the subtribes'. Elsewhere, Kâšġarî/Dankoff, (1982–5), vol. 1, p. 102, comments that the Oğuz 'consist of twenty-two branches (*batn*) ...' and then having listed them remarks: 'These are the principle subtribes (*qabâ'il*). Then each subtribe is composed of branches and sub-branches (*furû*'), which I have omitted for the sake of brevity. The names of these subtribes are the names of their ancestors who gave birth to them in olden times. They trace their ancestry back to them, just as among the Arabs one says 'Banu Salim' or 'Banu Khafâja'.'

175. Kâšġarî/Dankoff (1982–5), vol. 1, p. 70.

176. Kâšġarî/Dankoff (1982–5), vol. 1, p. 159. The location of the Ötüken remains uncertain. See the brief overview in Stark, *Die Alttürkenzeit in Mittel-und Zentralasien*, p. 141n733. Most scholars place it in the Khangai Mountains around the upper course of the Orkhon river, see Sergej G. Kljaštornyj, *Drevnetjurkskie runičeskie pamjatniki kak istočnik po istorii Srednej Azii* (Moskva: Nauka 1964), p. 34 (in the forested zone of eastern Khangai); Geng Shimin, 'Die alttürkischen Steppenreiche (552–745)', in *History of the Turkic Peoples in the Pre-Islamic Period*, ed. Hans R. Roemer, in *Philologiae et Historiae Turcicae Fundamenta*, vol. 1, *Philologiae Turcicae Fundamenta*, vol. 3 (Berlin Klaus Schwarz Verlag, 2000), p. 105.

177. Kâšġarî/Dankoff (1982–5), vol. 1, p. 312.
178. Kâšġarî/Dankoff (1982–5), vol. 2, p. 343.
179. Clauson, *An Etymological Dictionary*, p. 930.
180. Kâšġarî/Dankoff (1982–5), vol. 1, p. 94.
181. Kâšġarî/Dankoff (1982–5), vol. 2, p. 343.
182. Károly Czeglédy, 'A szír Nagy Sándor-Legenda', *Az MTA I. Osztályának Közleményei* XIII (1958): pp. 3–20. These legends developed in late Hellenistic circles in the 3rd century CE.
183. Robert Dankoff,, 'Qarakhanid Literature and the Beginnings of Turco-Islamic Culture', in *Central Asian Monuments*, ed. Hasan B. Paksoy (Istanbul: Isis, 1992), p. 76.
184. Theophylactus Simocatta, *Historiae*, p. 266; Étienne de la Vaissière, *Sogdian Traders: A History*, trans. James Ward (Leiden-Boston: Brill, 2005), pp. 22–4.
185. He is a descendant of Afrîdûn and Tûj (Tûr). Ferdinand Justi, *Iranisches Namenbuch* (Marburg: 1895), reprint (Hildesheim: Georg Olms Verlagbuchhandlung, 1963), p. 103; Čunakova, *Pexlevijskij slovar' zoroastrijskix terminov*, p. 233–4; Ehsan Yarshater, 'Afrâsîâb', *Encyclopaedia Iranica* (London-Boston: Routledge, New York: Bibliotheca Persica, Press, 1982–ongoing), available at http://www.iranicaonline.org/. See also the brief synopsis of Frâsiyâb's lineage in Al-Bîrûnî, *Athâr al-Baqiyya 'an Qurûn al-Khâliyya. Chronologie orientalischer Völker*, ed. Eduard Sachau (Leipzig: Otto Harrassowitz, 1923), pp. 103–4: a descendant of 'Turk' and 'Tuž'.
186. Yarshater, 'Afrâsîâb'; Bartol'd, *Sočinenija* , vol. 5, p. 79.
187. Ibn Khurdâdhbih, *Kitâb Masâlik wa'l-Mamâlik*, p. 17.
188. Al-Ṭabarî, *Annales*, I–III (I–XVI), eds. M.J. De Goeje, et al. (Leiden: Brill, 1879–1901), vol. 1, p. 433–6, Al-Ṭabarî, *Ta'rîkh al-Ṭabarî. Ta'rîkh al-Rasul wa'l-Mulûk*, ed. Muḥammad Abu'l-Faḍl Ibrâhîm (Cairo: Dâr al-Ma'ârif bi-Miṣr, 1967–9), vol. 1, pp. 379–80, Al-Ṭabarî, *The History of al-Ṭabarî*, ed. Ehsan Yarshater, vol. 3, *The Children of Israel*, trans. W.M. Brinner (Bibliotheca Persica, Albany: State Universsity of New York Press, 1991), pp. 22–4, describing the event in which 'Farâsiyâb' and 'Manûšihr' [Manôčihr] determined the borders between Iran and Turan/the Turks; Richard N. Frye, and Aydın M. Sayılı, 'Turks in the Middle East Before the Saljuqs', *Journal of the American Oriental Society* LXIII (1943): p. 202. al-Mas'ûdî, *Murûj adh-Dhahab*, vol. 1, p. 266, in one section questioned it, commenting that because 'Farâsiyâb', a great-grandson of Tûrak (not 'Turk') was 'born in the land of the Turks', historians have been mistaken in thinking that he was a Turk. Elsewhere, he makes the link without comment, see endnote 169 earlier.
189. Kâšġarî/Dankoff (1982–5), vol. 1, pp. 75, 84 ('Khâqânî kings' who speak 'the most elegant' Turkic). On the names of the Qarakhanids, see the thorough discussion in Ekber N. Necef, *Karahanlılar* (Istanbul: Selenge, 2005), pp. 128–38. On titulature: Kâšġarî/Dankoff (1982–5), vol. 1, p. 302 defines *tärim* as the 'title by which one addresses princes (*takâkîn*) and

those princesses (*xawâtîn*), and others, great or small, who descend from Afrâsiyâb'. It was reserved for the 'sons of the Khâqânî kings' (vol. 1, p. 314), *begler bagi* (vol. 2, p. 79 'emir of emirs' [as if to say Afrasiyâb']), *χan* [Kâšġarî/Dankoff (1982–5), vol. 2, p. 229] the title of the supreme ruler, the Khâqân ('This name is given to those who are descendants of Afrâsiyâb. He is the Khâqân.'). The princesses were called *altun tärim* ('golden royal lady', Clauson, *An Etymological Dictionary*, p. 549). *Qatun* (*xatun* 'wife of the lord or ruler', Clauson, *An Etymological Dictionary*, pp. 602–3) is defined as 'the name of all female descendants of Afrâsiyâb' [Kâšġarî/Dankoff (1982–5), vol. 1, p. 311].

190. C.E. Bosworth, 'The Heritage of Rulership in Early Islamic Iran and the Search for Dynastic Connections with the Past', *Iran* XI (1973): p. 62. See also discussion in Tao Hua, 'The Muslim Qarakhanids and Their Invented Ethnicity', in *L'islamisation de l'Asie centrale*, ed. Étienne de la Vaissière, *Studia Iranica*, vol. 39 (Paris: Association pour l'avancement des études iraniennes, 2008), pp. 342–3.

191. Kâšġarî/Dankoff (1982–5), vol. 1, p. 92 (*alp är toŋa öldi mü* ['has Alp Er Toŋa died?'] rendered as 'Has King Afrâsiyâb died?'), vol. 2, p. 225 ('*Toŋa alp är – who is Afrâsiyâb'*), vol. 2, p. 337: 'King Afrâsiyâb, chief of the Turks had the title *toŋa alp är* meaning 'a man, a warrrior (as strong as) a tiger'.' A.Z. Validi (A.Z.V. Togan), 'On Mubarakshah Ghurî', *Bulletin of the School of Oriental Studies* 6, no. 4 (1932): pp. 852ff. argues that Kâšġarî's linkage of Alp Er Toŋa with Afrâsiyâb points to a longer 'Turkish epic poem on Afrasiyab-Tunga Alp', see also A. Zeki Veledi Togan, *Umumî Türk Tarihine Giriş*, 2nd ed. (Istanbul: Edebiyat Fakültesi Basımevi, 1970), pp. 18, 19, 36, 49, 108–10, 167–8.

192 Yûsuf Khâṣṣ Ḥâjib, *Kutadgu Bilig*, p. 43 (ll. 277–82), English translation *Wisdom of Royal Glory (Kutadgu Bilig) A Turko-Islamic Mirror for Princes*, trans. Robert Dankoff (Chicago and London: University of Chicago Press, 1983), p. 48. He also quotes his sayings (Ḥâjib, *Kutadgu Bilig*, p. 581 [l.5861], Dankoff, *Wisdom of Royal Glory*, p. 230), without mentioning Afrâsiyâb.

193. Ḥâjib, *Kutadgu Bilig*, p. 43, Dankoff, *Wisdom of Royal Glory*, p. 48.

194. The name means 'Brave Warrior Hero'/'Hero Brave Warrior'. Kâšġarî's claim that *toŋa* means 'tiger' is not confirmed elsewhere, see Clauson, *An Etymological Dictionary*, p. 515, who renders it 'hero, outstanding warrior,' Ögel, *Türk Mitolojisi*, vol. 2, pp. 60–1. In the thirteenth century (?) '*Atabetü'l-Ḥaqayıq* the *toŋa är* is equated with 'Alî, see Edib Ahmed b. Mahmud Yükneki, *Atebetü'l-Hakayık*, ed. Reşit R. Arat (Istanbul: Ateş Basımevi, 1951), p. 44 (l. 34).

195. See Omeljan Pritsak, 'Die Karachaniden', *Der Islam* 31 (1953–4): p. 20; Necef, *Karahanlılar*, p. 128; 'Alâ'ud-Dîn 'Aṭâ Malik Juwainî, *Ta'rîkh-i Jahân-Gushâ*, ed. Muḥammad Qazwînî (Leiden: Brill-London: Luzac, 1912, 1916, 1937), vol. 2, p. 88, English translation 'Alâ-ad-Din 'Ata-Malik Juvaini, *The History of the World-Conqueror*, trans. John A.

Boyle (Cambridge, Massachusetts: Harvard University Press, 1958), p. 355; al-Juzjânî, *Ṭabaqât-i Nâṣirî*, ed. 'Abd al-Ḥay Ḥabîbî (Tehran: Dunyâ-yi Kitâb, 1363/1984), vol. 1, pp. 140, 245; Ibn al-Athîr, *Al-Kâmil fi'l-Ta'rîkh*, ed. Carl J. Tornberg (Beirut: Dâr Ṣâdir, 1965–6; reprint of the Leiden: Brill edition of 1851–76 with different pagination), vol. 11, p. 82; Jamâl Qaršî, *Mulḥaqât al-Ṣurâḥ*, in Vasilij V. Bartol'd, *Turkestan v époxu mongol'skago našestvija* (St Peterburg: Tipografija Imperatorskoj Akademii Nauk, 1900), č. 1, *Teksty*, p. 130, see also Tao Hua, 'The Muslim Qarakhanids', p. 345–6, who argues that Jamâl Qaršî based his account on a now lost *Ta'rîkh Kâšgar* by al-Alma'î, written probably in 'the late 1070s–early 1080s', i.e. a contemporary of Maḥmûd al-Kâšġarî.

196. Juwainî, *Ta'rîkh-i Jahân-Gushâ*, vol. 1, pp. 39–40, Juvaini, *The History of the World-Conqueror*, vol. 1, p. 54.

197. C.E. Bosworth, 'The Saldjuḳids II. Origins and Early History', *Encyclopaedia of Islam* (Leiden: Brill, 1954–2009), vol. 8, p. 937; Tao Hua, 'The Muslim Qarakhanids', p. 347.

198. Niẓâm al-Mulk, *Siaset-namé. Kniga o pravlenii vazira XI stoletija Nizma al-Mul'ka*, trans. commentary Boris N. Zaxoder (Moskva-Leningrad: Izdatel'stvo Akademii Nauk SSSR, 1949), p. 12.

199. Bartol'd, *Sočinenija*, vol. 5, pp. 93–4, notes that 'a legend about their descent from Afrâsiyâb was composed and accepted, as it was for the Qarakhanids', which accompanied their claims of descent from the Qınıq subgrouping of the Oğuz. Abu'l-Ġâzî [see Ebulgazi Bahadır Han, *Şecere-i Terâkime*, ed. Zuhal Karga Ölmez (Ankara: Simurg, 1996), p. 206], comments that the Seljuks, before becoming 'pâdišâhs' said that they were Türkmen and that the latter were their 'brothers'. After becoming rulers of a state, however, 'they claimed that they descended from a son of Afrâsiyâb who fled from Kaykhosrow and came to the Qınıq, grew up among them, but maintained that they were the thirtieth generation descended from Afrâsiyâb. Later tradition, thus, seems to accuse the Seljuks of manipulating genealogies and hence history. Abu'l-Ġâzî remarks that the Seljuks brought no use to the people (*ilge ve xalqġa faydası tigmedi*).

200. Ögel, *Türk Mitolojisi*, vol. 2, pp. 58–9.

201. Frye and Sayılı, 'Turks in the Middle East', p. 202.

202. Chinese accounts (*Tungdian*) merely note that 'Tung-e Tegin' was captured and killed in internal Türk strife, see Taşağıl, *Gök-Türkler*, vol. 3, pp. 34, 39, 41, 69, who conflates Toŋra Tegin and Toŋa Tegin. See also doubts expressed by Necef, *Karahanlılar*, pp. 129–30n11 on this identification.

203. Kâšġarî/Dankoff (1982–5), vol. 1, p. 189.

204. Kâšġarî/Dankoff (1982–5), vol. 1, p. 173. Ögel, *Türk Mitolojisi*, vol. 2, pp. 59–60 is inclined to view it as a lamentation.

205. Kâšġarî/Dankoff (1982–5), vol. 1, p. 292.

206. Kâšġarî/Dankoff (1982–5), vol. 2, p. 225: '*toŋa alp är* – who is Afrâsiyâb – built the city of Marv.'

207. Kâšġarî/Dankoff (1982–5), vol. 1, p. 331, vol. 2, p. 364. The anonymous 12th century (c. 1126) *Mujmal at-Tawârîkh wa'l-Qiṣaṣ*, ed. Muḥammad Bahar (Tehran: Khâwar, 1318/1939), reprint, ed. Muḥammad Ramażânî (Tehran: Kalâlah-i Khâwar, n.d.), p. 100, derives the 'Barsxân' grouping from an eponymous 'Barsxân' a son of 'Turk'.

208. Kâšġarî/Dankoff (1982–5), vol. 1, p. 270; Bartol'd, *Sočinenija*, vol. 5, p. 79, Kâšġar was viewed as the capital of Afrâsiyâb.

209. Kâšġarî/Dankoff (1982–5), vol. 2, p. 225: Qaz Oynı, Qaz Suwı, also vol. 2, p. 337: Yuŋu river near 'town of Bârmân', named after the son of Afrâsiyâb who had allegedly built it.

210. Bartol'd, *Sočinenija*, vol. 5, p. 79, Vasilij V. Bartol'd, 'Obzor istorii tjurkskix narodov', in Bartol'd, *Sočinenija*, vol. 5, pp. 433, and Vasilij V. Bartol'd, 'Sostojanie i zadači izučenija istorii tureckix narodnostej', in Bartol'd, *Sočinenija*, vol. 5, pp. 460–1.

211. C.E. Bosworth, 'The Development of Persian Culture under the Early Ghaznavids', *Iran* VI (1968): pp. 33–44, 44.

212. Frye and Sayılı, 'Turks in the Middle East', p. 202.

213. F.Š. Xuzin, *Volžskaja Bulgarija v domongol'skoe vremja (X -načalo XIII vekov)* (Kazan': Fest, 1997), pp. 110–14.

214. Ibn Miskawaih, *Tajârub al-Umam. Eclipse of the 'Abbasid Caliphate*, ed. Henry F. Amedroz, trans. D.S. Margoliouth (Oxford: Blackwell, 1920–1), reprint of Arabic text (Baghdad: Maktabat al-Mutannâ', n.d.), Arabic text, vol. 2, p. 181; Ibn al-Athîr, *Al-Kâmil fi'l-Ta'rîkh*, vol. 8, p. 532.

215. Golden, *History of the Turkic Peoples*, pp. 216–18

216. Ibn al-Athîr, *Al-Kâmil fi'l-Ta'rîkh*, vol. 9, p. 520.

217. Bosworth, 'The Heritage of Rulership in Early Islamic Iran', p. 62; See also Tao Hua, 'The Muslim Qarakhanids', pp. 341–2.

218. Tao Hua, 'The Muslim Qarakhanids', p. 346.

219. Tao Hua, 'The Muslim Qarakhanids', pp. 347–8.

220. Ibn al-Athîr, *Al-Kâmil fi'l-Ta'rîkh*, vol. 10, p. 73.

221. Sergej A. Agadžanov, *Gosudarstvo sel'džukidov i Srednjaja Azija v XI-XII vv.* (Moskva: Nauka, 1991), pp. 93–5, Ibrahim Kafesoğlu, *Sultan Melikşah Devrinde Büyük Selçuklu İmparatorluğu* (Istanbul: Osman Yalçın Matbaası, 1953), pp. 19–20, 119–23; Golden, *History of the Turkic Peoples*, p. 222; B.D. Kotchnev, 'La chronologie et la généalogie des Karakhanides du point de vue de la numismatique', in *Études karakhanides*, eds. V. Fourniau, et al., in *Cahiers d'Asie Centrale*, vol. 9 (Tachkent-Aix-en-Provence: Édisud, 2001), p. 50.

222. Kâšġarî/Dankoff (1982–5), vol. 1, pp. 76, 84.

223. Tao Hua, 'The Muslim Qarakhanids', pp. 343–4, finds no evidence for the earlier date.

224. Gharib (1995), p. 190: *knδ(h)*, kand/t, kanθ, (qnθ, knδ), Khotanese *kanthâ* 'city'; Édgem R. Tenišev and A.V. Dybo, *Sravnitel'no-istoričeskaja grammatika tjurkskix jazykov. Pratjurkskij jazyk-osnova. Kartina mira pratjurkskogo étnosa po dannym jazyka* (Moskva: Nauka, 2006), pp. 796–7.

225. Kâšġarî/Dankoff (1982–5), vol. 2, p. 225. He also cites Taškän as another name of Taškend/Šâš (vol. 1, p. 333).
226. Kâšġarî/Dankoff (1982–5), vol. 1, p. 115.
227. Kâšġarî/Dankoff (1982–5), vol. 2, p. 211; but Clauson, *An Etymological Dictionary*, p. 570, reads it as *tiz* and views it as a borrowing from Persian *diz*.
228. Clauson, *An Etymological Dictionary*, p. 449: 'alien, prob. A subject, but in any case inferior'. Kâšġarî/Dankoff (1982–5), vol. 1, p. 88 also uses it to denote 'an Uighur infidel'.
229. Kâšġarî/Dankoff (1982–5), vol. 1, p. 273; vol. 2, p. 103.
230. Kâšġarî/Dankoff (1982–5), vol. 2, p. 103.
231. Kâšġarî/Dankoff (1982–5), vol. 1, p. 362.
232. Kâšġarî/Dankoff (1982–5), vol. 2, pp. 362–3. *Qalač* < *qal ač* literally 'remain hungry' Kâšġarî/ renders as 'stay, remain, abide'. *Türkmen* he derives from Pers. *Turk-mânand* 'they resemble Turks' [Kâšġarî/Dankoff (1982–5), vol. 2, p. 624: 'These look like Turks.'] See al-Bîrûnî, *Kitâb al-Jamâhir fî Ma'rifat al-Jawâhir* (Haidarâbâd: Matba'at Jam'î yat Dâ'irat al-Ma'ârif al-'Uthmâniyya, 1355/1936), p. 205; Fadlallâh Rašîd ad-Dîn, *Jâmi' at-Tawârîkh*, eds. Muhammad Rowšan, and Mustafâ Mûsawî (Tehran: Nashr-i Alburz, 1373/1994), vol. 1, p. 55. See Faruk Sümer, *Oğuzlar*, 3rd ed. (Istanbul: Milli Eğitim Basımevi, 1980), pp. 51–2. The tale of the origin of the Turks and Türkmen is recorded by Badr ad-Dîn 'Aynî, (855/1451), a Mamlûk official and historian [Kâšġarî/Dankoff (1982–5), vol. 1, p. 19–21]; Robert Dankoff, 'Qarakhanid Literature and the Beginnings of Turco-Islamic Culture', in *Central Asian Monuments*, ed. Hasan B. Paksoy (Istanbul: The Isis Press, 1992), p. 76. On the basis of 'congruity of narrative alone', Dankoff ['The Alexander Romance' in the Diwan Lughat at-Turk' in Dankoff, 'Beliefs and Superstitions of the Turks', pp. 108–9] tentatively profers an identification with the Türgeš-Western Türk ruler, noted as Sulu 蘇 祿 (EMC *sɔ ləwk*, LMC *suǎ ləwk* (Pulleyblank, *Lexicon of Reconstructed Pronunciation*, pp. 201, 29) in the Chinese sources (Liu, *Die chinesischen Nachrichten*, vol. 1, pp. 171, 223, 429; vol. 2, p. 891) for *Suluq/Soluq? Sülük? (Clauson, An Etymological Dictionary*, p. 827: *sülük* 'army horses' (?), probably not 'leech'etc.? Šu, in this light, would be problematic. Du'l-Qarnayn's role in dispensing names to Turkic peoples is not unlike that of Oğuz Khan in the later cycle of Oğuz legends reported by Rašîd ad-Dîn.
233. Kâšġarî/Dankoff (1982–5), vol. 1, pp. 124–5, 139, 301.
234. Kâšġarî/Dankoff (1982–5), vol. 1, pp. 139–40.
235. Kâšġarî/Dankoff (1982–5), vol. 1, p. 140 lists the other cities: Sulmi (built by Du'l-Qarnayn), Qočo, Janbalıq and Yaŋı Balıq. See also Dankoff, 'Beliefs and Superstitions of the Turks', p. 104.
236. Kâšġarî/Dankoff (1982–5), vol. 1, pp. 301; vol. 2, p: 362–3, and Dankoff, 'Beliefs and Superstitions of the Turks', pp. 100–2.
237. Dankoff, 'Beliefs and Superstitions of the Turks', p. 107.

238. Kâşgarî/Dankoff (1982–5), vol. 1, p. 163, 249, 250, 327, 344, 353; vol. 2, pp. 7, 137, 356.

239. Kâşgarî/Dankoff (1982–5), vol. 1, p. 271–2.

240. 'Oğuz Khanism' has been compared to 'Činggisidism', its rival, which supplanted it in Central Eurasia [Judin, 'Ordy: belaja, sinjaja', pp. 20–1]. Rašîd ad-Dîn, *Jâmi' at-Tawârîkh*, vol. 1, pp. 47–53, which also relates how he brought the Oğuz to Islam. See also, Mihály Dobrovits, 'The Turco-Mongolian Tradition of Common Origin and the Historiography in Fifteenth Century Central Asia', *Acta Orientalia Academiae Scientiarum Hungaricae* 47, no. 3 (1994): pp. 270ff. on the various subsequent Persian and Turkic versions of the Oğuz Tale. The variant of Abu'l-Ġâzî Bahadur Khan (Ebulgazi Bahadır Han, *Şecere-i Terâkime*, pp. 116–17) differs in some respects from the one given in Rašîd ad-Dîn. Japheth is here sent to the north. Moreover, there is uncertainty as to whether he was a 'prophet' or not. He was ordered by this father to settle on the banks of the Volga and Ural rivers (*Atıl ve Yayıq suyının yaqasığa*) where he lived for 250 years. His sons were Türk, Khazar, Saqlâb, Rûs, Miŋ, Čîn, Kimârî and Târikh (?). Japheth designated his eldest son, Türk, as his successor. His son Tütek is credited with being a contemporary of Gayomars, the first king of Iran (Gaya-marətan, Gayômart, etc. the 'first man' and subsequently the first ruler of Iranian tradition; Justi, *Iranisches Namenbuch*, pp. 108–9; Čunakova, *Pexlevijskij slovar' zoroastrijskix terminov*, pp. 81–2, al-Mas'ûdî, *Murûj adh-Dhahab*, vol. 1, p. 260 on 'Kayûmarth'). He was succeeded, 240 years later, by his son Amulja Khan and then his son Baquy Dib Khan (Ebulgazi Bahadır Han, *Şecere-i Terâkime*, pp. 117–20), and so on. Thereafter follows one of the variants of the Oğuz Khan tale. Amulja Khan is clearly the same name as Abulja Khan, but now set in a different genealogical order. Amulja probably derives from *amul* 'quiet, peaceful,' see László Rásonyi and Imre Baski, *Onomasticon Turcicum. Turkic Personal Names*, Indiana University Uralic and Altaic Series, vol. 172 (1–2) (Bloomington: Denis Sinor Institute for Inner Asian Studies, 2007), vol. 1, p. 64 and Clauson, *An Etymological Dictionary*, p. 160–2 (*amul* 'quiet, mild, equable, peaceful, even-tempered'). On the *Oğuznâma*, known in Uyğur and Oğuz Turkic variants since the late thirteenth-fourteenth century, see Bombaci, *La Letteratura Turca*, p: 127–8; Sir Gerard Clauson, 'Turks and Wolves', *Studia Orientalia* 28, no. 2 (1964): pp. 16–18, Korogly, *Oguzskij Geroičeskij Epos*; Semih Tezcan, 'Oğuznameler', in *Türk Edebiyatı Tarihi*, ed. Talât Halman, 2nd ed. (Istanbul: TC Kültür ve Turizm Bakanlığı Yayınları, 2007), pp. 621–34. Cf. an early Ottoman variant: Ali Yazıcızâde, *Tevârîh-i Âl-i Selçuk*, ed. A. Bakır (Istanbul: Çamlıca, 2009), pp. 5ff. who mentions an *Oğuz-nâme* written in Uyğur script.

241. Hamdallâh Qazwînî, *Târîx-i Guzîdah*, ed. 'A. Navâ'î (Tehran: Amîr Kabîr), 3rd printing, (1364/1985), pp. 562–3 (see also Dobrovits, 'The Turco-Mongolian Tradition of Common Origin', pp. 171–4), c. 1340: 'it

happened that their origin stemmed from the progeny of Yâfith, son of Nûḥ and the Muġûls call Yâfith Abunja Khan. From his sons is Turk, forefather of the Turks ... the forefather of the Muġûls, whom the Muġûls call Dîb Yâqû Khan...' Qara Khan is one of his sons and one of his sons is Oğuz Khan, 'whom the Muġûls call Oğuz Ata', he became the ruler of this people (*qaum*). 'After Oğuz Khan, rulership remained in the seed of Oğuz Khan for close to one thousand years. In the time of Frîdûn, his son Tûr led a great army against them.' From the ensuing disaster two individuals of Oğuz Khan's people survived, Nöküz and Qiyan. They and their wives and growing progeny settled in the valley of Ergene Qon. Their descendants are ancestral to the Mongols, see Rašîd ad-Dîn, *Jâmi' at-Tawârîkh*, vol. 1, p. 148.

242. C.S. Littleton, and L.A. Malcor, *From Scythia to Camelot* (NewYork: Routledge, 2000), argue that they are the source for the Arthurian legends.

243. Vladimir A. Kuznecov, *Očerki istorii Alan* (Ordžonikidze: IR, 1984), pp. 29–30, notes that some Qaračay-Balqars were still bilingual in Osetic and Turkic in the eighteenth century.

244. See *Narty. Adygejskij geroičeskij epos*, trans. A.I. Alieva (Moskva: Vostočnaja Literatura, 1974), p. 352, sub 'Sosruko', n1.

245. On the frequency of the color 'blue' (Turkic *kök*, also the term for 'sky', heavens'), see Ögel, *Türk Mitolojisi*, vol. 1, pp. 42–3, 67.

246. *Narty. Geroičeskij épos balkarcev i karačaevcev*, ed. A.I. Alieva (Moskva: Vostočnaja Literatura, 1994), Qaračay text: 74, Russ. trans. 308–9; *Karačaevo-balkarskie mify.Qaračay-malqar mifle*, ed. M.Č. Džurtubaev, (Nal'čik: El'brus, 2007), pp. 462–3 (Qaračay text).

247. Maxti Č. Džurtubaev, *Duxovnaja kul'tura Karačaevo-balkarskogo naroda*, in *As-Alan*, ed. B. Lajpanov (Moskva: 'Mir Domu Tvoemu', 1998), vol. 1: pp. 114, 126.

248. Leonid Potapov, 'Umaj-Božestvo drevnix tjurkov v svete étnografičeskix dannyx', *Tjurkologičeskij Sbornik 1972* (Moskva: Nauka, 1973), pp. 265–86.

249. *Teyri< tengri* 'God, Heaven'. The shift of *ng/ŋ > γ* is sporadic in a number of Turkic languages, see Édgem R. Tenišev et al., *Sravnitel'no-istoričeskaja grammatika tjurkskix jazykov. Fonetika* (Moskva, 1984), pp. 242–3.

250. Alieva, *Geroičeskij épos balkarcev i karačaevcev*, Qaračay text, p. 283/Russ. trans. p. 582; Džurtubaev, *Karačaevo-balkarskie mify.Qaračay-malqar mifle*, p. 210: *öz anaları – qančıq börüdü* 'their own mother is a she-wolf'.

251. Alieva, *Geroičeskij épos balkarcev i karačaevcev*, glossary, p. 647. In the Ossetic tradition, however, Tutyr is the god that protects sheep from wolves. Gabuev, *Étnogoničeskie predstavlenija*, p. 48. V.I. Abaev, in 'The Pre-Christian Religion of the Alans' (XXV International Congress of Orientalists, Papers Presented by the USSR Delegation, Moscow, p. 14), however, notes him as 'the patron of wolves'.

252. Gabuev, *Étnogoničeskie predstavlenija*, pp. 47–8. The snake and the wolf still function in Tuvinian shamanism as protectors, Sevjan I. Vajnštajn,

Mir kočevnikov Centra Azii (Moskva: Nauka, 1991), p. 242: *čilan eeren* and *börü eeren*. Tuv. *eeren* < *ee* 'spirit-master'. The *eeren* are good spirits, also termed *ongon* (Vajnštajn, *Mir kočevnikov Centra Azii*, pp. 240–1).

253. The Qaračay texts are found in Alieva, *Geroičeskij épos balkarcev i karačaevcev*, Qaračay, p. 68/Russ. trans., p. 302.

254. Tekin, *Orhon Yazıtları*, p. 24.

255. Igor de Rachewiltz in *The Secret History of the Mongols. A Mongolian Epic Chronicle of the Thirteenth Century*, ed. and trans. Igor de Rachewiltz (Leiden-Boston: Brill, 2004), vol. 1, pp. xxxv–xxxvi, and his 'The Dating of the Secret History of the Mongols—A Re-interpretation', *Ural-Altaische Jahrbücher*, N.F. 22 (2008): pp. 150–84, argues that the *Secret History* was unique in that it was not written 'primarily for historical reasons, nor for mere entertainment. There is no counterpart for this genre of literature in the oral and written literature of the nomadic peoples in Asia or elsewhere' (de Rachewiltz, Dating of the Secret History of the Mongols, p. 159). It is an 'epic chronicle rather than a heroic epic', which aimed at the 'glorification of the conqueror's clan for the sake of posterity' (de Rachewiltz, Dating of the Secret History of the Mongols, p. 162).

2

THE *WAQF* AS AN INSTRUMENT OF CULTURAL TRANSFORMATION IN SELJUQ ANATOLIA

Gary Leiser

Between the Battle of Manzikert in 463/1071, in which the Seljuq sultan Alp Arslan defeated the Byzantine emperor Romanus IV Diogenes, and the final collapse of the Seljuq Sultanate of Anatolia in 707/1307 under the Mongols, Turkish tribes, primarily those of the Seljuqs, expanded west across Anatolia, or Rum as it was then called, to the Aegean. Only a few strips of territory—the Empire of Trebizond, Cilician Armenia, and the shores of the straits—were outside their control. Thus, within little more than two centuries most of Anatolia became politically part of the *Dār al-Islām*, the Abode of Islam. One of the most important contributions of the Turks to Medieval Islamic civilization was to bring most of Anatolia within the political sway of Islam and begin its gradual transformation from a predominantly Christian into a predominantly Muslim region.

Despite two centuries of expanding Turkish political control and the advancement of the Islamization and Turkification of the Anatolian peninsula, by the end of the Seljuq period the majority of the population of Anatolia was still Christian, largely Greek, and to a lesser degree Armenian. These indigenous Christians were predominantly Greek speaking, of course, and sedentary.[1] To be sure, the invasion of Anatolia by Turkish tribes, as with tribal invasions elsewhere, caused much destruction and many of the natives fled.

But neither the countryside nor the cities were wholly abandoned by the Christians. And although some Turks who were not nomads did enter Anatolia, they founded no new cities. Therefore, under the Seljuqs, Anatolia long remained an anomaly as a mostly Christian region under the political control of Islam. For students of the history of Seljuq Anatolia, a major challenge is to explain how, during this time, the Turks went about the process of bringing the native Christian population into the Muslim fold.

Under the Seljuqs, conversion to Islam, no matter how superficial, came about in various ways throughout their realm. It occurred through political or economic expediency, intermarriage, proselytizing by Sufis, and the establishment of Muslim religious institutions, chiefly mosques, *madrasas* (colleges of Islamic law), and *zāwiyas* (hospices or Sufi lodges).[2] One aspect of conversion, which has not been fully investigated, was the Turks' use of the *waqf* (pious endowment), to undermine the economic viability of the Church by employing Christian economic assets and Christians themselves to maintain, support, and spread Muslim institutions.[3] In this chapter we shall examine how the Seljuqs used the *waqf* to impoverish Christianity and strengthen Islam in Anatolia. This process added to the pressure to convert to Islam. In other words, the *waqf* was used as a mechanism whereby Christians were compelled to contribute to their own religious and cultural transformation.

First, a few words are in order about the nature of *waqfs*.[4] In classical Islamic law there were two kinds of *waqfs*, those for the public good (pious or charitable) and those for the benefit of one's family (especially the preservation of family wealth). In both cases the endowment usually consisted of various kinds of property. The revenue that it generated was to be used in perpetuity for a specific purpose.[5] In this chapter we shall be concerned above all with pious or charitable *waqfs*.

It is important to mention here that the Greek Orthodox Church also had an institution of pious endowment. This endowment, called *piae causa* in Byzantine law (also called *moira* and *ousia*), was widespread in Anatolia and continued to function, at least to some extent initially, under Turkish rule. George Ostrogorsky, a renowned scholar of Byzantium, writes that closely related to the philanthropic activity of the Church and the monasteries 'were the charitable institutions, extraordinarily numerous in Byzantium: orphanages, homes for the aged, free hostels for travelers, hospitals, and so on. They enjoyed the most munificent support of the devout Byzantine emperors and were richly endowed with landed property'.[6] Furthermore, apart from endowments established by the Church or emperors, there were charitable foundations established by private individuals that were retained for personal administration, independent of the public authorities of the Church and state. Many of these had similar Muslim counterparts.[7]

There has been some discussion on the origin of the *waqf* and the extent to which the Byzantine practice may have shaped it. In the early twentieth century, such scholars as Carl Becker and Joseph Schacht argued in favour of Byzantine influence on this institution. But Claude Cahen believed their evidence was not convincing. According to Cahen,

> In replacing ecclesiastical authority, for which in Islam there is none, by administrators approved by the *qāḍī* [judge], one has in effect here the equivalent of what would be a *waqf* in favor of a given hospital, etc. But under Muslim domination, what were the forms of charitable giving in use in the Christian community? The books of Oriental cannon law do not appear to envision for the Church anything but donations. Khaṣṣāf [a ninth-century jurist who wrote an authoritative treatise on *waqf*] for his part touches briefly on what he calls the *waqf* of the *dhimmīs* [Christians]: he authorizes gifts to churches but not *waqfs* in their favor; on the other hand, he considers *waqfs* of *dhimmīs* for their poor just as valid as those of the Muslims for their poor, but without entering into the question of their administration. In any case, upon this point, of which we cannot insist here, one cannot take from this similarity the conclusions advanced by some. Of course, with their gradual conversion to Islam, the natives might have been tempted to assist their new religion with charitable acts that they would have conceived somewhat after the pattern of those that they would have known or practiced in previous times; to be inclined in this way they could have used the nascent institution of the *waqf*, but to see in this example the origin of the *waqf* would be to ignore the existence of the ancient *waqf* in Arabia outside of any influence, and misunderstand that the ancient *waqf* is much less a public *waqf* than a private one.[8]

Today the matter is essentially where Cahen left it. He clearly did not dispute, however, the similarity between the Byzantine charitable endowment and the *waqf*. He even suggested that Christian converts would have found it familiar and perhaps used it to assist their new religion. We shall see, in fact, that this occurred in Seljuq Anatolia.

Furthermore, several Byzantine endowed charitable institutions, such as hospitals and hospices, had very close Muslim equivalents. Demetrios Constantelos has pointed out that the hospices or *xenons* were similar to Muslim *zāwiyas* in important respects. Both provided free lodging, food, clothing, and medications to visitors. They even provided monetary assistance. Around 1331 Ibn Baṭṭūṭa described the functions of a *zāwiya* located between Kastamonu and Sinop that was built soon after the area was conquered by the Turks. Constantelos states that, as described by Ibn Baṭṭūṭa, it performed the same functions as a *xenon*.[9] For our purposes, it is sufficient to state at this point that both the concept of the Muslim *waqf* as a private pious endowment and many of the institutions that it supported would have been familiar to Christians living under Turkish rule in Anatolia.

Some forty years ago, upon examining three of the oldest surviving *waqf* documents, or *waqfiyyas*, from Seljuq Anatolia, Speros Vryonis, Jr. was the first to realize that the Turks often used the *waqf* to harness Christian, land, manpower, and revenue to support Islamic institutions at the expense of Christianity. He noted that in 598/1202 Shams al-Dīn Altun-Aba, a Seljuq *amīr* (commander or military governor), established a *waqf* for a *madrasa* and a caravanserai that included Christian villages. In 669/1271 a *waqf* consisting of part of a Christian village was created in the name of Mubāriz al-Dīn Er-Tokush, a leading Seljuq state official of slave origin who died around 625/1228, to support a *madrasa*, a caravanserai, and a mosque. And between 645/1247 and 651/1253, the Seljuq *amīr* Jalāl al-Dīn Karatay, a Greek slave by origin, established *waqfs* for a caravanserai, a *dār al-ṣulaḥā'* ('house of the devout', probably another term for *zāwiya*), and a *madrasa*, the income for which came chiefly from Christian villages.[10] In his assessment of *waqfs*, Vryonis also included the one that Nūr al-Dīn Ibn Jājā, the Seljuq *amīr* of Kırşehir, created in 670/1272 for numerous institutions, including mosques and *madrasas*, in several cities. The lands and villages of Greeks, Armenians, and converts were included in this *waqf*.[11]

While the importance of *waqf* documents for the study of economic and social history has been widely recognized, their significance for the process of Islamization has been neglected. Osman Turan, who published the documents cited by Vryonis, went to great pains to provide the historical context for these documents, often straying far from the subject, but he provided remarkably little analysis, only mentioning the presence of Christian properties in *waqfs* in passing. Several decades later, Mehmet Altay Köymen, in an essay on *waqfiyyas* as primary sources, outlined the kinds of information that can be extracted from *waqf* documents—ethnic, religious, and social relations, toponomy, onomastic, and economic development. With regard to our subject, he only says, citing an unpublished *waqfiyya*, that sometimes a mosque or other institution had only one village as an endowment; and he mentions that for the 'Alā' al-Dīn mosque (begun by Kılıch Arslan II, r. 551–88/1156–92, and completed around 617/1220) and the *dār al-shifā'* (hospital) in Konya, the *jizya* (poll tax on dhimmīs, that is, non-Muslims) on the village of Sille near Konya sufficed. It was about 4,000 dirhams per year. He adds that it can be inferred that the poll tax was collected from Christian villages for the *waqfs*.[12] In any case, the initial assessment of Vryonis has not been fully explored. Meantime, additional endowment documents from Seljuq Anatolia have been published. We shall, therefore, take a closer look at the *waqfs* mentioned by Vryonis and also survey some of the more recently published documents in order to gauge more accurately the extent to which the Seljuqs used *waqfs* as an instrument of cultural change.[13]

All *waqf* documents usually contain the same kind of information and often follow the same format. They begin with honorifics concerning the founder, followed by the purpose of the endowment, a delineation of its properties (but without exact measurements or well-defined locations), an explanation of the function of the endowed institution, a description of the staff, services provided, salaries and expenses, oversight and its relationship to the founder's family, and finally the signatures of those who witnessed the document.

One of the oldest surviving *waqfiyyas* from Seljuq Anatolia is, as mentioned above, that of Shams al-Dīn Altun-Aba. A military commander during the reigns of sultans Kılıch Arslan II and his son Rukn al-Dīn Sulaymān Shah (r. 593–601/1192–1204), he died in 634 or 635/between 1236 and 1238. He had no children, so he may have been of slave origin. His *waqf*, dated 598/1202, was for a *madrasa*, a caravanserai, and for the burial of the poor and the needs of converts to Islam. The *madrasa* was located outside Konya at a place called the 'New Market'. The caravanserai was at Arkit between İlgin and Akşehir. The endowment document initially states that two villages were included in the *waqf*. A third village was added later. The villages included their inhabitants, most of whom were Christians. The villages were K(G)andāqufs,[14] outside Konya, and Sarājik, in a district administratively attached to Konya. The third village, Kadā Kala, was west of Konya. Among the lands bordering Kandāqufs were the villages of Jibrā'īl, Dayr (Monastery of) Būtmūn, Arbājman, and Batāmnā, all of which were probably also Christian. The lands bordering the village of Kadā Kala included those of the Kilīsa (the Church) and the village of Baqāyās.[15] Among the other properties in the *waqf* was a *khān* (caravanserai, warehouse, or multi-roomed building) outside Konya which contained eighteen residences (*maskan*) and was surrounded by properties of Greek Christians. Other properties were more than forty-six shops and even a vegetable garden (*bustān*) in the Konya plain. The latter bordered on the woods of ... the son of Baṭrīq Liyānūs (these two names might be one) al-Rūmī (the Greek) and on the lands of Mīkhā'īl the son of Mārūs al-Qūnawī al-Rūmī.[16] Ottoman *waqf* registers show that Altun-Aba's endowment was still active in the sixteenth century.[17]

As mentioned, this Seljuq *waqfiyya* makes provisions for the needs of converts. So far, no other document is known to contain such provisions. But presumably there were others. This is clear evidence that, at least on the part of some founders, *waqfs* were used as part of a deliberate policy of Islamization. This document states that one-fifth of the income from the *khān* was to be used to meet the expenses of 'those who distance themselves [that is, convert] from groups of infidels and abandon groups who have deviated and fallen into error, be they strangers or people from these regions, and disassociate themselves from worshipping idols and desist from *al-inkāf* [being haughty] with regard to adoration [of images] and images [sic] and crosses, and free themselves from following dogmatic vanities [namely, those who were] Majūs, Christians, and Jews, and be above associating with them in *biya'* [churches, synagogues] and in *kanā'is* [churches, synagogues] and *ṣawāmi'* [monks' cells]'. Majūs was the Arabic name for Zoroastrians, but Turan argues that it was a term for pagans, that is, shamanistic Turks.[18] The funds were to pay for food, clothing, shoes, circumcision, instruction in learning the Koran, and even in learning how to pray.[19]

Next we have the endowment of Mubāriz al-Dīn Er-Tokush. He was originally a slave of Sultan Ghiyāth al-Dīn Kay Khusrau I (r. 588–93/1192–7, 601–8/1205–11). He served as a military commander and governor of Antalya for this sultan and his successors, 'Izz al-Dīn Kay Kā'ūs I (r. 608–16/1211–20) and 'Alā' al-Dīn Kay Qubād I (616–34/1220–37). Er-Tokush died childless around 625/1228, but the *waqfiyya* in his name was not drawn up until 669/1271. The endowed property consisted of one-fifth of the village of Aghrūs (meaning 'field' in Greek), which belonged to the town of Borlu, which was attached administratively to Isparta. It was meant to support a *madrasa* in the village of Aghrūs, a caravanserai in the village of Dhādhīl, which was also attached to Borlu, and a Friday mosque in Antalya. The *madrasa* bears a date of 621/1224. At the beginning of the seventh/thirteenth century, Kılıch Arslan III (r. 600–01/1204–5) once and for all seized from Byzantium the area around Isparta, including Aghrūs. It was certainly a Christian village. Moreover, it was so well known that, as the *waqfiyya* states, no delineation of its borders was necessary. It is likely that one of the sultans granted it to Er-Tokush in return for military service, if he did not actually conquer it.[20]

More extensive than either of these preceding endowments were those of Jalāl al-Dīn Karatay who died in 652/1254. Originally a Greek slave, and trained in the service of 'Alā' al-Dīn Kay Qubād, he rose to become an important Seljuq statesman. Indeed, he oversaw the government during the critical time after the Mongol defeat of Sultan Ghiyāth al-Dīn Kay Khusraw II in 641/1243. He had two brothers who also served the Seljuq state and he was a friend of Jalāl al-Dīn al-Rūmī.[21]

In 645/1247, he first established a *waqf* composed of many properties for a caravanserai east of Kayseri. This endowment included the lands of the Christian village of Sarākhūr, which was on the road to Elbistan, and the lands of the neighbouring village of Līkandūn,[22] which was probably also Christian. Līkandūn bordered the property of the monastery called 'Manastirīz'.[23] From sixteenth-century Ottoman *waqf* registers, Turan lists the names of some of the inhabitants of these and nearby villages: Kaya son of Sarkis, Arslan son of Hachuk, Budak son of Migirdich, and Sarkis son of Bal-Yemez. The Armenian names are obvious. These two Christian villages maintained their existence until the early twentieth century.[24]

Furthermore, the *waqf* included a *khān* outside Kayseri in the butchers' market next to the Door of Ayāwāsil (St Basil), and contiguous with the 'church', the property of Thrayānī, and the property of the cloth merchant Yānil. Also part of the endowment was a house (*dār*) in Kayseri next to the properties of Sarkis al-Qass (the priest), Mīnās, and Sīmāqūn. There was also a meadow outside Kayseri bordering on the properties of Mikhā'īl and Rūmānī. The funds from the endowment properties supported not only the caravanserai of Karatay but also provided funds, food, shoes, and medications (like a *xenon*) for Muslims and infidels (*kāfirs*) who stayed there. In addition, they provided an annual stipend and grains for any of the founder's relatives or freed slaves, Muslims or infidels, who were incapable of earning a living and took refuge there. More properties outside Kayseri were added to this *waqf* in 646/1248, which included lands bordering on the properties of Istibānūs (Stephen), Agūb (Hagop), Thrayānī, Mīnās, and Shusūk.[25]

The *waqfiyya* for the *dār al-ṣulaḥā'* in Antalya was prepared in 646/1247, shortly before it was built in 648/1250–1. Its properties consisted of two shops outside Konya next to the properties of the heirs of Lūsunk and Ḥalūl son of Barṣawmā,[26] a house outside Konya next to the property of Maryam the daughter of ʿAbd Allāh, a shop next to the village of Yuḥannā, an oven, parcel of land, and the village of Sizma, which was probably Christian.[27] It should be mentioned that in contemporary documents, it was customary to give the name ʿAbd Allāh' to the father of someone who had converted. So-and-so the son of ʿAbd Allāh is frequently found among the names of the witnesses who signed *waqfiyyas*. Even Karatay's name is given as Karatay son of ʿAbd Allāh.[28]

As for Karatay's *madrasa*, it was built in 649/1251 and Rūmī attended its opening ceremonies. Its endowment deed was later drawn up in 651/1253. The *waqf* lands included the village of Ḥurnāwul, which was attached administratively to Divriği. It bordered on the monastery of Shārāykūn and was probably Christian. A number of villages that were connected to each other, Kūmasa, Kūralma (the reading of this name is conjectural), and Makar, were added to the endowment in 652/1254. They were probably Christian as well and bordered on the villages of Sunkur Kilise and Kirfard.[29]

In 655/1257, a contemporary of Karatay, the Rifāʿī Shaykh Sayyid Nūr al-Dīn Alp Arslan built and endowed a *zāwiya* in the village of Zadwī in what is today the province of Amasya. The endowment properties consisted of a large number of villages. Many had non-Turkish names, such as Falānbīl and Takālūza, and were certainly Christian. Even some that had Turkish names were probably Christian, such as Alaca Kilise, Guz Kilise, and Firenkhisarı (the Frankish, that is Byzantine, fortress).

Virtually everything in these villages and on their agricultural lands was included in the *waqf*. These things are listed and are fairly standard for such endowments: gardens, mills, houses, residences, towers, fortresses, canals, springs, trees, wells, rivers, public baths, bridges, vegetable gardens, lakes, ponds, pastures, plains, buildings, hills, mountains, and sheep folds. This *waqf* even included the rubbish dumps and 'places where men gathered', 'places where children played', and 'places where women wept.' Clearly, everything on these properties, which must have generated considerable wealth, was to support the *zāwiya*, which was for the benefit of 'all Muslims, men and women'.[30]

An approximate contemporary of this Rifāʿī Shaykh was the Seljuq official Atabak Arslandoğmuş. He served in several capacities, such as Master of the Horse (an official title) and as a military commander, primarily under Mongol domination. He is mentioned by Rūmī and last appears in sources from 656/1258. He built a law school, the Atabekiyya *Madrasa*, in Konya sometime after 654/1256 and endowed it with a village on the island of Kāsī in Lake Beyşehir. This island had been a monastic centre.[31]

Like Karatay, another Seljuq vizier who served under Mongol hegemony, was Ṣāḥib Ata Fakhr al-Dīn 'Alī (d. 687/1288). He too established charitable endowments and even had the title Abū' l-Khayrāt (Father of Charitable Deeds).[32] He established *waqfs* for two institutions: an *imāra* (*imaret*) or soup kitchen (often used synonymously with *zāwiya*) in Konya and the great Gök *Madrasa* in Sivas.

The *waqfiyya* for the *imāra* was drawn up in 663/1264 and was supplemented twice in the following two years. Again, included in its endowment were properties with non-Turkish names, such as half the village of Azazraz near Konya and all of the village of Shīghūn near Kırşehir, which were probably Christian. The village of Kilisecik (Little Church) was also part of the endowment as were all the lands 'known as the lands of Badr al-Dīn Yaḥyā the son of Zakariyyā' the translator from Konya', who was perhaps a convert.[33]

As for the endowment of the Gök *Madrasa*, which included a nearby *dār al-ẓiyāfa* (guest house or hospice), its document was drawn up in 679/1280 and was supplemented in 694/1295. At the beginning of the document the founder states that one of the reasons he decided to build this *madrasa* was that the cities which were within territory controlled by the Seljuqs were in a state of decay and scholars had begun to desert even such great cities as Sivas. Here the term 'infidels' certainly referred to the Mongols. This ultimately was a very rich *waqf* that provided many comforts for the institution. The numerous properties in it included half the shop in the butchers' market in Sivas next to the property of the heirs of Yahūdī Maḥmūd, a convert, and the Jewish houses. Another was the shop in the cooks' market in Sivas next to the 'church *waqf*'. Outside this city were such endowment properties as the Greek village of Lakarcı,[34] which was attached administratively to Divriği and was surrounded by other Greek villages, and the Greek village of Kasrik, subject administratively to Dutlu. The latter was so well known that, again, there was no need to demarcate its boundaries. Among the other villages were Ekodefteros (or Ekutfetros) and all its lands. Also mentioned are seven of twelve shares of the property purchased from 'Erfil' (which could also be read as 'Ermeni,' that is, 'the Armenian'). Thus, here too, lands inhabited by Christians were incorporated in a *waqf*.[35] This *waqf* continued to function into the late Ottoman period.

Another Seljuq official of slave origin who established an endowment was Sayf al-Dīn Turumtay. He was Master of the Horse for Sultan ʿAlāʾ al-Dīn Kay Qubād I and warden of the fortress of Amasya during the reign of Sultan Ghiyāth al-Dīn Kay Khusraw II. He went on to play an important role in the Seljuq government under the Mongols. When he died in 679/1280, he was governor of Amasya. There he built and endowed the Gök *Madrasa* (not to be confused with the one in Sivas). The *waqfiyya*, which was brief, was drawn up in 665/1266; and the college was probably built shortly beforehand. The endowment consisted of six villages in a district that was administratively attached to Amasya. They were probably clustered together, if not contiguous. One had the non-Turkish name of Raza. Other non-Turkish place names are mentioned when describing the borders of these villages: Arghūmā, Mandarān, and Rankūk.[36] Again it is reasonable to assume that one or more of the six villages were Christian.

Finally, let us turn to the last Seljuq-era *waqf* mentioned by Vryonis, that of Nūr al-Dīn Ibn Jājā. It is the richest and most extensive endowment known to us, thus far, from the Seljuq period. Indeed, it also surpasses all of the other *waqf*s with respect to the number of institutions that it supported. Surprisingly little is known of the founder. He first appears in history as the *amīr* of Sultanyüği (Eskişehir). Then, in 596/1261, he was appointed *amīr* of Kırşehir. As a military commander he suppressed several uprisings against the Seljuqs. He also played a role in the struggle for control of the Seljuq state while it was under Mongol domination. Ibn Jājā was on good terms with Rūmī, who mentions him, but apparently he was cool toward Ḥājjī Bektash. In 675/1277, the Egyptian Mamlūk Sultan Baybars invaded Anatolia in anticipation of an uprising there against the Mongols. He defeated the Mongols and their Seljuq allies near Elbistan and captured Ibn Jājā and his brother, which means that Ibn Jājā was obviously collaborating with the Mongols. Shortly thereafter, he was released in Syria with other prisoners and returned to Anatolia. He last appears in sources in 667/1278.[37]

Ibn Jājā's endowment was recorded in three complementary documents, dated 670/1272. The endowment is remarkable not only for its scale, as we shall see, but also because two of the three endowment documents were recorded in Mongolian as well as Arabic, which would also tend to confirm Ibn Jājā's close association with Mongol hegemony. No other *waqfiyya*s in Mongolian are known.

In Kırşehir the endowment properties funded the construction of a *madrasa*, a tomb (*türbe*) for the founder, and a tomb for his sister. They also supported a mosque next to the *madrasa*, a *khānqāh* (dervish convent), *zāwiya*, *maktab* (school), and *dār al-ṣulaḥā'*. In Kayseri they supported a Friday mosque.[38] In İskilib they supported a *madrasa*. In Talımegini they funded the construction of a *madrasa* and a mosque. In Sultanyüği they funded the construction of a mosque, the repair of seventeen other mosques, the repair of a *zāwiya*, and the construction of a *khān* and a mosque attached to it. The properties were located mainly in and around Kırşehir, İskilib, Kuşhisar (Koçhisar), and Sultanyüği, and to a lesser degree in the regions of Ankara, Konya, and Aksaray.[39] Ibn Jājā was certainly a very wealthy man.

The endowment properties included a kebab house and a shop in the Armenian bazaar in Kırşehir;[40] the village of Sarkis A'lā (perhaps Aghilī) outside Ankara;[41] all of the place called 'Dūlāt' (perhaps Dūlāb) next to the Armenian cemetery outside Konya;[42] half the common shares of the village of Taş Pınar in the region (*nāḥiya*) of Arman (the Armenians) and all the houses called 'Arman Khān' located next to the public bath built by the sultan outside the Laranda gate of Konya and bordering the property of Ḥārūq;[43] half the irrigated land (*al-arḍ al-saqiyya*) at the place called 'Ayūstafānūs' (St Stephen) outside Kırşehir;[44] all the agricultural land outside İskilib known as the land of 'Alā' al-Dīn 'Alī belonging to the *amīr* Quṣtanṭīn, all the land in the same region known by the name Jalāl bordering on the property of the *dhimmī* (that is, Christian) Isāsūs, all the land in the same region known by the name Quṣtanṭīn the Deaf;[45] the mill known by the name of Quṣtanṭīn outside İskilib and bordering on the land of Quṣtanṭīn;[46] all of the house used as a hospital in İskilib bordering on the property of Jacob who converted to Islam, all of the land known by the name 'Karbād' and bordering the vineyard of the *dhimmī* Kālanij, all of the vineyard at the place called 'Kara Kaya' bordering the vineyard of the *dhimmī* Kālanij and the vineyard of 'the Priest' (*al-qass*), all of the vineyard called . . . [the text here is obscure] bordering on the vineyard of Barṣawmā, all of the place called 'the Priest' in the *dhimmī* village and bordering the road of the *dhimmī* village, all of the land of the *dhimmī* village called 'Kanāk' bordering the road going to the *dhimmī* village and the property of the *dhimmī* Kūmī; all of the land called 'Būkā' [the reading of this place name is conjectural] bordering the threshing place called the 'Armenians' and the vineyard of the Priest;[47] two irrigated lands, apparently near Kırşehir, called 'the vineyards of the infidels' and three vineyards at the same place.[48] Altogether there is no doubt that Christians occupied many of Ibn Jājā's properties and contributed to his charitable foundations.

It should be self-evident, therefore, that Christian villages and lands were included in *waqf*s to support Muslim religious and other institutions. In some cases these documents specifically state that a village or land was Christian. In other cases we can infer this because of their non-Turkish names or because they were surrounded wholly or in part by Christian properties. And even a Turkish name did not guarantee that a village was completely Muslim, especially since so many Turks were still nomadic.

Furthermore, we should not overlook the fact that Christians could also directly or indirectly support Muslim institutions by renting or patronizing properties or establishments that were part of *waqf*s. The endowment of Ibn Jājā, for example, included a cloth merchants' warehouse in the cloth market, a shop in the grocers' market, a shop in the Armenian market, a painter's shop, a shop in the butchers' market, three shops in the shoe market, four shops in the carpenters' market, a shop in the second-hand market, three shops in the fullers' market, a shop in the *halva* market, a vise-maker's market, a harness-maker's shop, and even a pigeon roost. All of these places were in or outside Kırşehir.[49] Almost all endowments included 'shops', whose functions are unknown. In addition, various endowments, as noted above, included such things as ovens, mills, houses, residences, public baths, vegetable gardens, pastures, buildings, and sheep folds. Christians must have rented or done business at many of these places.

Unfortunately, the *waqfiyyas* do not state how the founders of the endowments acquired their properties. Some were purchased, but others were certainly obtained by conquest or as grants. Some of the founders were military commanders who conquered Byzantine territory and, as was customary, kept part of the spoils. In other cases the sultans granted them conquered land. The sultans made similar grants to leading government officials and family members.

Many of the Christian villages and lands that appear in the *waqf*s described above may have originally been endowment properties belonging to the Church that were seized and then 'recycled' to support Muslim institutions. We know that this process occurred outside Anatolia in some regions that Muslims conquered from Christians. It is noteworthy, for example, that when Saladin captured Jerusalem from the Crusaders in 1187, he turned the Church of St Anne into a *madrasa* and used the endowment of that church, which included a village outside the city, to support the *madrasa*. This village was presumably inhabited by Christians.[50]

It is impossible to estimate the full magnitude of the wealth derived from Christians that was funneled through *waqfs* to support Muslim institutions, especially those central to the faith. In light of even the few *waqfiyyas* that we have examined above, however, it must have been enormous. Many of the mosques and *madrasas* that were supported were large buildings. They also had a large staff[51] and provided many services that required considerable income. Moreover, the endowments were intended to function in perpetuity as permanent sources of revenue for the Muslim institutions. We know that the *waqfs* of Altun-Aba, Karatay, and Ṣāḥib Ata continued to function in the sixteenth century. Thus, in this way, over the centuries, the Turks directed incalculable amounts of Christian wealth towards Muslim institutions. The spread of these institutions throughout Anatolia had at least two general effects. First, they anchored the Muslim community. Mosques and *madrasas* in particular served as centres for instruction in Islamic rituals and the inculcation of Islamic law, which were the essence of religious identity, of course, for Muslims. Islamic law made a Muslim a proper Muslim. This was an important element for those Turks whose conversion up to this point was rather superficial. Second, as these institutions spread throughout Anatolia, they served to proselytize Islam and inevitably put pressure on Christians to convert.

At the same time, the cumulative economic consequences, over two centuries, of incorporating more and more Christian lands into *waqfs* deprived the Church of funds and undermined its ability to function in Anatolia. By the fourteenth century the pauperization of the Church in that region was readily apparent. This is revealed in two important Byzantine sources, the *acta*, documents recording decisions of patriarchal synods, which included administrative affairs, and the *notitiae episcopatuum*, lists of metropolitanates in order of their rank. A synodal act of 1368, for example, states, with regard to including the metropolitanate of Pyrgion under the administration of Ephesus, that 'all of its properties were removed [having been captured by the barbarians] and it was not able to provide for the necessities of its metropolitan. And this also happened in other churches, the archbishoprics being joined to the metropolitanates, as they were not able to exist by themselves, because of the poverty'.[52] In another act, of 1387, the metropolitan of Antalya and Perge complains that the 'ruling foreigners' (the Turks) had seized all the property of his church. Thirty years earlier, its metropolitan had stated bluntly, 'without these villages there is no church'.[53] As for the *notitiae*, they show that by the fourteenth century numerous metropolitanates in Anatolia had fallen in rank compared to those in Europe and some had disappeared, above all as the result of impoverishment. Therefore, the administrative structure of the Church in Anatolia was in a state of crisis. This was also true of the Christian community. The wealth that the Church needed to maintain its structure was also needed to maintain important social services for its community. As this wealth eroded and Christian charitable institutions declined or disappeared, so too did a sense of Christian identity. Under these circumstances, many Christians may, in fact, have turned to Muslim institutions, such as caravanserais, hospitals, *imāra*s, or even *zāwiya*s, for assistance.

Finally, it should be mentioned that the Ottomans continued the Seljuq practice of including Christian villages and properties in their charitable endowments. As early as 1942, in a pioneering study of *zāwiya*s, Ömer Lutfi Barkan mentioned two villages around Konya called 'Karye-i Kilisâ' and 'Karye-i Zimmiye' (*qarya* means village in Arabic) that were included in a *waqf* for a *zāwiya* during the reign of Süleyman the Magnificent (r. 1520–66).[54] More recently Vryonis, citing M. Tayyib Gökbilgin, referred to four major *waqf*s in Trabizond in the same century that supported a mosque, an *imāra*, and the provincial military structure (*timar*s). Their money came from many Christian villages and even monasteries.[55] The mathematician and geographer Ebu Bekr b. Behram el-Dımaşki (d. 1691), in his supplement to Kâtib Chelebi's great description of the world, *Kitâb-ı Cihânnümâ*, describes the town of Honaz as follows: 'A town in the Denizli Valley and at the northern foot of a large snow-capped mountain. It has a fortress carved into [here the word in the Turkish text is a bit obscure] a rock cliff that is difficult of access, also vineyards, gardens, and streams. Most of the people are Greek [Rūm] *dhimmi*s. It is a pious endowment [*waqf*] of Sultan Süleyman.'[56] Later he describes Mount Olympus near Bursa and the mountain opposite it, and says, 'The area between these two mountains is the area between Bursa and Kita. This is a low mountain [opposite Mt Olympus] . . . . The village called "Eşkel", which is opposite Eski Kaplıca and is a pious foundation (*waqf*), is located at a high place on this mountain. This is a village of *dhimmi*s.'[57]

William Griswold published five *waqfiyya*s that describe a single group of properties that was transferred from the sixteenth century to the twentieth century to the descendants of the original donor. Griswold characterized this as a 'mundane' family *waqf.* It was established prior to 975/1567 by a certain Molla İsa Bey, the title *molla* meaning that he held an official position as a Muslim judge. The property in question was located in and around the small western Anatolian city of Lefke, today known as Osmaneli, about 25 kilometres east of İznik. All of the quarters of Lefke were Christian except one, which was mixed. The villages around Lefke, in which endowed properties were located, were also probably Christian despite their Turkish names. The properties included taxable dwellings; and the names of Christians (Greeks) who were responsible for paying the taxes. Other taxes are also specified. Indeed, this document is a kind of tax assessment describing the responsibilities of the inhabitants of the properties to the family of the donor. In short, taxes paid by the inhabitants were regarded as income from the *waqf.* For our purposes these documents demonstrate the use of properties and lands inhabited by Christians to support the *waqf* of an important Muslim religious official.[58]

***

The *waqf* documents that we have examined clearly reveal that during the Seljuq period, the properties of Muslim pious endowments included Christian villages and lands that generated funds to support Muslim institutions, especially religious institutions. By contributing monetarily to these institutions, Christians thus contributed, albeit involuntarily, to their own cultural transformation, that is, Islamization. They also did so by renting or patronizing various shops or establishments that were included in the *waqf*s. The inclusion of Christian villages and lands in *waqf*s must have been common practice. It is unlikely that the publication of additional *waqfiyya*s will change this general assessment.

Most of the founders of the endowments that we examined were important Seljuq military leaders or officials. They certainly understood the consequences of their actions. In other words, harnessing Christians and Christian lands to the benefit of Islam must have been a deliberate policy. The Seljuq rulers, as some of their titles indicate—'the Might of the Brilliant Religious Community, Helper of the Shining Nation of Islam, the Manifestation of the Word of God Most High, the Guardian of the Religious Community and This World'—certainly felt an obligation to spread the faith.[59] Given that the great majority of the people in the countryside were Christian, in many cases recently conquered, the institution of the *waqf* would have been seen as an efficient and effective means of spreading Islam at their expense. It would have allowed for the building and support of many mosques, *madrasas*, and *zāwiyas* throughout Anatolia at little cost to the 'state' while depriving the Church of great wealth.

Finally, some of the endowments offered direct enticements to convert. The endowment of Altun-Aba provided generously for the needs of converts. That of Karatay provided, as we have seen, funds, food, shoes, and medications for Muslims and infidels who stayed in his caravanserai and an annual stipend and grain for any of his relatives or freed slaves, Muslims and infidels, who were incapable of earning a living and took refuge there. In this case Karatay, who was probably of Greek origin, provided assistance to infidels in general and to his Muslim and non-Muslim, that is, Christian, relatives in particular. By not distinguishing between Muslims and non-Muslims, especially among his relatives, he blurred the line between the faiths and made the transition to Islam easier. It should also be mentioned that infidels could, and did, benefit not only from caravanserais, hospitals, and *imāras* but also from various public works such as bridges, fountains, and irrigation systems that were also supported by *waqfs*. For many Christians this further obscured the difference between the nature of Christian pious endowments and those of Muslims and, again, contributed to the 'merging' of practices and traditions in Anatolia that facilitated conversion from Christianity to Islam. There is some irony, perhaps, in the fact that many converts signed their names as witnesses to various *waqfiyyas*.

Therefore, the Seljuqs of Anatolia deliberately and effectively employed the *waqf* as an instrument to exploit Christian economic resources in Anatolia for the benefit of Islam and, at the same time, reduce the wealth of the Church and its ability to function. This was an important means by which they helped bring about the gradual cultural transformation of Anatolia. This transformation, which synthesized a wide range of customs, practices, beliefs, and art forms from different peoples, eventually resulted in its own distinct version of Islamic civilization. Politically it created a new base for the expansion of Islam into Europe with innumerable consequences for the Christian and Muslim worlds.

Notes

1. This was the view of Claude Cahen, the leading Western authority on the Seljuqs of Anatolia. He states, 'However numerous the Turkish

population may have been, it is clear that there were still many non-Muslims, who were probably the majority almost everywhere—in the proportion of ten to one, according to William of Rubruck [d. c. 1293], 'La Turquie Pré-Ottomane', trans. P.M. Holt as *The Formation of Turkey* (Harrow, England: Longman, 2001), p. 123. Apart from William of Rubruck, another contemporary Christian source says, for example, that the majority of the subjects of the Seljuq Sultan Kılıch Arslan b. Mas'ūd (r. 551–88/1156–92) were Greeks, Gary Leiser, 'The *History of the Patriarchs of the Egyptian Church* as a Source for the History of the Seljuqs of Anatolia', *Living Islamic History: Studies in Honour of Professor Carole Hillenbrand*, ed. Yasir Suleiman (Edinburgh: Edinburgh University Press, 2010), p. 114. It seems to me that perhaps the main reason that there are so few Muslim literary sources for the history of the Seljuqs of Anatolia is that the Muslim population was too small and nomadic to justify many such works. Moreover, most Muslims were Turks for whom Turkish was not yet a literary language. Persian literature was the domain of only a few at the court. There was no audience for Arabic literature, although Arabic was the language of the faith and official documents.

2. One of the most recent overviews of this subject is by V.L. Ménage, 'The Islamization of Anatolia', ed. Nehemia Levtzion *Conversion to Islam* (New York: Homes and Meier, 1979), to which add Gary Leiser, 'The Madrasah and the Islamization of Anatolia before the Ottomans', eds. Joseph Lowry et al. *Law and Education in Medieval Islam* (Chippenham, England: Gibb Memorial Trust, 2004).

3. Halim Baki Kunter, 'Türk vakıfları ve vakfiyeleri uzerine mücmel bir etüd', *VD* 1 (1938): pp. 110–11, lists the many Muslim institutions, in addition to mosques, *madrasas*, and *zāwiyas*, that were supported by *waqfs*. Cf. the list of institutions in M. Zeki Oral, 'Aksaray'in tarihî önemi ve vakıfları', *VD* 5 (1996): p. 239, that were supported by 211 *waqfs* in Aksaray alone.

4. The plural of *waqf* is *awqāf*, however, following the English pattern, I have used *waqfs* throughout this chapter.

5. For the general history and evolution of the *waqf*, see R. Peters, et al. 'Wakf', *EI2*. 11: pp. 59–78.

6. Cited in Demetrios J. Constantelos, *Poverty, Society and Philanthropy in the Late Mediaeval Greek World* (New Rochelle, New York: Aristide D. Caratzas, 1992), p. 117.

7. John Philip Thomas, *Private Religious Foundations in the Byzantine Empire* (Washington: Dumbarton Oaks, 1987), pp. 2–3. Byzantine private religious foundations have their origins in the late Roman Empire and predated *waqfs*. They continued until the end of the Byzantine Empire. Indeed, Greek private religious foundations continued under Ottoman administration.

8. This is my English translation of the relevant passage in Claude Cahen, *Les Peuples Musulmans dans l'Histoire Medieval* (Damascus:

Institut Français de Damas, 1977), p. 302. For a recent summary of the status of this issue see Peter C. Hennigan, *The Birth of a Legal Institution: The Formation of the Waqf in Third-Century A.H. Ḥanafī Legal Discourse* (Leiden: Brill, 2004), pp. 50–7. This subject is certainly not closed. For some suggestive ideas on the continuation of Christian pious endowments under Islam and their possible influence on the origin of the *waqf*, see Johannes Pahlitzsch, 'Christliche Stiftungen in Syrien und im Irak im 7. und 8. Jahrhundert als ein Element der Kontinuität Zwischen Spätantike und Frühislam', in *Islamische Stiftungen Zwischen Juristischer Norm und Sozialer Praxis*, eds. Astrid Meier, et al. (Berlin: Academie Verlag, 2009), pp. 39–54.

9. Constantelos, *Poverty, Society and Philanthropy*, p. 120. H.A.R. Gibb, believed this was a *madrasa*. See his translation of Ibn Baṭṭūṭā, *The Travels of Ibn Baṭṭūṭa* (London: Cambridge University Press, 1958–62), vol. 2, p. 464n186, although Ibn Baṭṭūṭa calls it a *zāwiya*, see the Arabic text Ibn Baṭṭūṭa, *Riḥlat Ibn Baṭṭūṭa* (Beirut: Dār Ṣādir, 1964), p. 318.

10. Speros Vryonis, Jr., *The Decline of Medieval Hellenism in Asia Minor and the Process of Islamization from the Eleventh through the Fifteenth Century* (Berkeley: University of California Press, 1971), pp. 352–4. Vryonis cites the documents for these *waqf*s that were published, respectively by Osman Turan, 'Selçuk devri vakfiyeleri: I. Şemseddin Altun-Aba, vakfiyesi ve hayatı', *Belleten* 11 (1947): pp. 197–235; Turan, 'Selçuk devri vakfiyeleri: II. Mübarizeddin Er-Tokuş ve vakfiyesi', *Belleten* 11 (1947): pp. 415–29; Turan, 'Selçuk devri vakfiyeleri: III. Celâleddin Karatay, vakıfları ve vakfiyeleri', *Belleten* 12 (1948): pp. 17–158.

11. Vryonis, *The Decline of Medieval Hellenism in Asia Minor*, p. 354. The documents for this endowment were published by Ahmet Temir, *Kırşehir Emiri Caca Oğlu Nur El-Din'in 1272 tarihli Arapça-Moğolca vakfiyesi* [1959] (Ankara: Türk Tarih Kurumu, 1989).

12. Mehmet Köymen, 'Selçuklu devri kaynakları olarak vakfiyeler', in *Studi Preottomani e Ottomani*, ed. Aldo Gallotta (Naples: Istituto Universitario Orientale, 1976), p. 163. The fact that the poll tax could be included in *waqf* income suggests that Christian villages might have been especially lucrative properties to have in *waqf*s. The endowment collected both a percentage of income from a Christian village and a tax, which would not have been the case with Muslim villages. See another example later. This matter requires further investigation.

13. Most Seljuq *waqf* documents remain unpublished. As indicated in the previous note, Köymen examined forty-nine that he found in various places, mostly in the Vakıflar Genel Müdürlüğü in Ankara, Başbakanlık Arşivi Genel Müdürlüğü, Topkapı Sarayı Müzesi Arşivi, and Ankara Etnoğrafya Müzesi. Furthermore, some were in private hands. A few *waqf* documents from the thirteenth century survive as inscriptions on the buildings that they supported. See, Ét. Combe et al., eds, *Répertoire Chronologique d'Épigraphie Arabe* (Cairo: Institut Français d'Archéologie

Orientale, 1931–64), vol. 10, pp. 10–11; vol. 12, pp. 51–5; vol. 13, pp. 111–12. They are all Artuqid inscriptions in Mardin. A corpus of these texts, edited and translated, would constitute the most important source for the economic and social history, in its widest sense, of Seljuq Anatolia. This history, in fact, cannot be written without them. We should add that *waqf* documents from the immediate post-Seljuq period, the fourteenth century, can also shed light on the Seljuq period and even help clarify the texts of Seljuq documents. Nicolas Trépanier, 'Food as a Window into Daily Life in Fourteenth-Century Anatolia' (Ph.D. diss. Harvard University, 2008), analyzed approximately 35 *waqf* documents dated 700–95/1300–93. Much of what he says is relevant to the thirteenth century.

14. The pronunciation of native village names written in Arabic, such as this one, can be somewhat conjectural. In the sixteenth-century, Kandāqufs was apparently the village of Arkit between Akşehir and İlgin; Turan, 'Selçuk devri vakfiyeleri: I': p. 205.

15. The reading of this place name might be Papaz Kayası. Turan, 'Selçuk devri vakifiyeleri: I': p. 205.

16. Turan, 'Selçuk devri vakifiyeleri: I': pp. 225–7. Around the same time, al-Malik al-Manṣūr Artuq Arslan, the ruler of the Turkish Artuqid state that bordered southeastern Anatolia, established a *waqf* for the Khātūniyya Madrasa in Mardin. Inscribed on the building and dated 602/1206, its *waqfiyya* states that the endowment included the places known as Dayr (the Monastery of) Mar Ḥassās within Mardin. This monastery no doubt belonged to the Syrian Jacobite Christians who made up a large part of the population of Mardin. See Combe, *Répertoire Chronologique d'épigraphie Arabe*, vol. 10, pp. 10–11. In the early thirteenth century the Artuqids were, for a while, subjects of the Seljuqs of Anatolia.

17. Turan, 'Selçuk devri vakfiyeleri: I': p. 203.

18. Turan, 'Selçuk devri vakfiyeleri: I': pp. 216–20. There were certainly shamanistic or superficially Islamized Turks then in Anatolia. However, Majūs was also a term for Norsemen, see A. Melvinger, 'al-Madjūs', *EI2* 5: pp. 1118–21. We know that Norsemen had long served in the Byzantine army, especially in the celebrated Varangian Guard. We also know that 'Frankish' (European) mercenaries served in the Seljuq army. See for instance, A. Yaşar Ocak, *La Revolte de Baba Resul ou la Formation de l'Heterodoxie Musulmane en Anatolia au XIIIe Siècle* (Ankara: Türk Tarih Kurumu, 1989), pp. 71–2. It is possible that Norsemen were among the 'Franks'.

19. Turan, 'Selçuk devri vakfiyeleri: I': p. 233.

20. Turan, 'Selçuk devri vakfiyeleri: II': pp. 415–20, 428. Turan discusses the curiously late date of the *waqfiyya* and says it might be an error, pp. 419–20, 423. Based on later records, he notes that Aghrūs had a Christian quarter well into the sixteenth century.

21. On his life see Turan, 'Selçuk devri vakfiyeleri: III': pp. 17–49.

22. Perhaps the ancient Lykandos.

23. Turan, 'Selçuk devri vakfiyeleri: III': p. 111.

24. Turan, 'Selçuk devri vakfiyeleri: III': p. 68. The name 'Bal-Yemez' is somewhat enigmatic here. This was the name of a large calibre gun used by the Ottomans. It was also a nickname of Turkish military commanders.

25. Turan, 'Selçuk devri vakfiyeleri: III': pp. 112–15, 122–6.

26. Bar Ṣāwmā is a Syriac name. The Monastery of Mār Bar Ṣāwmā, near Malatya, was the seat of the Jacobite patriarchate.

27. Turan, 'Selçuk devri vakfiyeleri: III': pp. 156–7.

28. Turan, 'Selçuk devri vakfiyeleri: III': p. 19.

29. Turan, 'Selçuk devri vakfiyeleri: III': pp. 141, 147.

30. Sadi Bayram, 'Amasya-Taşova-Alparslan Beldesi Seyyid Nureddin Alparslan Er-Rufa'inin 655 H./1257 M. tarihli Arapça vakfiyesi tercümesi ile 996 H./1588 M. tarihli Seyyid Fettah Velî silsile-namesi', VD 23 (1994): pp. 31–2, 40–1 (p. 69 of facsimile).

31. İbrahim Hakkı Konyalı, 'Bir Hüccetiki vakfiye: Konya'da Atabekiye medresesi hücceti, Karamanoğlu Alâeddin Beyin vakfiyesi, Melek Hatun'un Karaman'daki Hatuniye medresesinin ve türbesinin vakfiyesi', VD 7 (1968): pp. 97–101.

32. His career has been described by Turan, 'Selçuk devri vakfiyeleri: III': pp. 532–96.

33. Sadi Bayram and Ahmet Hamdi Karabacak, 'Sahib Ata Fahrü'd-Dîn Ali'nin Konya, imaret ve Sivas Gök medrese vakfiyeleri', VD i, 13 (1981): p. 40. Azazraz, in modern Turkish orthography, is difficult to make out in the facsimile of the waqfiyya, see p. 46, photo 10.

34. This village name and those given below are given in modern Turkish orthography. The facsimile of the waqfiyya is mostly unreadable.

35. Bayram and Karabacak, 'Sahib Ata Fahrü'd-Dîn Ali'nin ... vakfiyeleri': pp. 53–4, 56–7, 59.

36. İsmet Kayaoğlu, 'Turumtay vakfiyesi', VD 12 (1978): pp. 91–3, 102–7.

37. Temir, Kırşehir Emiri Caca , pp. 201–5.

38. A Friday or cathedral mosque (jāmi') was where communal prayer was held weekly. The smaller neighbourhood mosque (masjid) was not used for this purpose.

39. Temir, Kırşehir Emiri Caca, pp. 10–11.

40. Temir, Kırşehir Emiri Caca, p. 110.

41. Temir, Kırşehir Emiri Caca, p. 114.

42. Temir, Kırşehir Emiri Caca, p. 115.

43. Temir, Kırşehir Emiri Caca, p. 116.

44. Temir, Kırşehir Emiri Caca, p. 117.

45. Temir, Kırşehir Emiri Caca, p. 123.

46. Temir, Kırşehir Emiri Caca, p. 124.

47. Temir, Kırşehir Emiri Caca, p. 125.

48. Temir, Kırşehir Emiri Caca, p. 145.

49. Temir, *Kırşehir Emiri Caca*, pp. 106, 109–15, 118. It is possible that, as described above in the same endowment, 'all the houses called Arman Khān located next to the public bath built by the sultan outside the Laranda gate of Konya' were a brothel.

50. Johannes Pahlitzsch, 'The Transformation of Latin Religious Institutions into Islamic Endowments by Saladin in Jerusalem', in *Governing the Holy City: The Interaction of Social Groups in Jerusalem between the Fatimid and the Ottoman Period*, eds. Pahlitzsch et al. (Wiesbaden: Reichert Verlag, 2004), especially pp. 53–4.

51. See Kunter, 'Türk vakıfları', pp. 111–15, on the professions of the many people employed by funds from *waqfs*.

52. Vryonis, *The Decline of Medieval Hellenism in Asia Minor*, p. 316.

53. Vryonis, *The Decline of Medieval Hellenism in Asia Minor*, p. 314. Prof. Vryonis has greatly expanded his analysis of the *acta* and *notitiae* in the revised version of his *The Decline of Hellenism*, which is in preparation. He kindly loaned me the proofs of the relevant section.

54. Ömer Lutfi Barkan, 'Osmanlı imparatorluğunda bir iskân ve kolonizasyon metodu olarak vakıflar ve temlikler: I İstilâ devirlerinin kolonizatör Türk dervişleri ve zâviyeler', *VD* 2 (1942): pp. 310–11.

55. Vryonis, *The Decline of Medieval Hellenism in Asia Minor*, pp. 354–5.

56. Published at the end of İbrahim Müteferrika's edition in 1732 of *Kitâb-ı Cihânnümâ*, facsimile reprint (Istanbul: Istanbul Büyükşehir Belediyesi, 2008), p. 643. An English translation of this combined work is in preparation under the editorship of Gottfried Hagen.

57. Müteferrika, *Kitâb-ı Cihânnümâ*, p. 660.

58. William Griswold, 'A Sixteenth Century Ottoman Pious Foundation', *JESHO* 27 (1984), pp. 173–98.

59. These were among the titles of 'Izz al-Dīn Kay-Ka'ūs I. See Scott Redford and Gary Leiser, *Victory Inscribed: The Seljuq Fetiḥnāme on the Citadel Walls of Antalya, Turkey* (Antalya: Suna & İnan Kıraç Research Institute on Mediterranean Civilization, 2008), p. 111.

3

THE APPEARANCE OF THE TURKS IN THE ISLAMIC WORLD

Clifford Edmund Bosworth

At a time when the number of independent Turkish states has suddenly, since 1991, swollen considerably, it is not surprising that these young states and their peoples should seek roots in the past, often the very distant past. The theorists in the infant Turkish Republic of Atatürk latched on to such peoples as the Sumerians and Hittites as their proto-Turkic predecessors in Anatolia and the northern parts of the Fertile Crescent, even though, as we all know, the Turks are first recognized millennia later in the region of what is now Mongolia, and the Hittites have in any case been known since the early years of the twentieth century as undoubted speakers of an Indo-European language. Admittedly, Sumerian is, so far as is known, an isolated language, but the mere facts of geography—Mesopotamia is very remote from northern Inner Asia—make a connection highly improbable. The name 'Turk' has been detected, by those whom one can only call the nationalistically credulous, in names appearing in the Old Testament, in the Assyrian annals, in ancient India, and so forth. Hence, Professor Peter Golden did not completely surprise me when he informed me recently that the new Central Asian Turkish Republics have now appropriated the Scythians as their forerunners in Inner Asia. He has indicated in his paper about the Turkish Karachays of the Northwest Caucasus who are making similar claims (with admittedly a certain modicum of plausibility, in that the Karachays may have an Alanic, hence Indo-European, substratum).[1] And there are still a few Asian languages of unknown connections, like that of Elamitic and the Indus Valley civilization amongst dead ones, and the vestigial Palaeo-Siberian ones of northeastern-most Siberia, and Burushaski in the Pamirs, amongst living ones, which remain a mystery.

Passing from the realms of fantasy of Turkish nationalist linguistic theorists, the best attested early mentions of the Turks come from classical authors of early Christian times. Pomponius Mela, in the mid-first century AD, mentions *Turcae* in the forests north of the Sea of Azov (which must have been a long way north of the Sea, given the intervening steppe lands), and in this same century Pliny the Elder lists the *Tyrcae* amongst the peoples of the lands north of the Black Sea. But it is only in the later sixth century that we have hard evidence about the early Turks; the Chinese annals mention the T'u-Chue and Byzantine historians describe diplomatic exchanges between their emperors and such rulers of the first Turkish Qaghanate like Bumin Qaghan and his uncle Ishtemi. The Byzantines were at this time hoping to establish links with the Turkish Empire and thereby facilitate a northerly trade route across the steppes and deserts of Inner Asia, thus bypassing the Iranian Sasanids and their control of more southerly land and sea routes to the Far East. Hence a Turkish embassy appeared at Constantinople in 563 from 'Askel, king of the Kermikhions'. Then, more importantly, there arrived one in 568, led by the Sogdian Maniakh and from a ruler—called by the Byzantine historian Menander Protector, Silziboulos—bringing Chinese silks as a gift and letters in what are described as *gramma skythikon* 'Scythian writing' (probably, in fact, in Sogdian, the then *lingua franca* of trade across Inner Asia to China). Around this same time, the Turks appear as the T'u-chue in Chinese dynastic annals, with exchanges of embassies, and with various branches of the Turks noted in the annals, accompanied by fanciful, folkloric tales about their origins; but the Turks had probably been known to the Chinese long before this time as a likely element in the Hsiung-nu peoples who had dominated much of Inner Eurasia from at least the fourth century BC.[2]

The Turkish encounter with Islam dates back to two or three generations after the birth of the new faith itself. Western scholars have long dismissed as apocryphal the *hadith*s or traditions attributed to the Prophet Muhammad like 'Leave the Turks alone as long as they leave you alone', with a play on the name 'Turk' and the verb *taraka*, 'to leave'. Information about the steppe peoples can hardly have reached the isolated towns of the Hijaz at the opening of the seventh century, and these traditions about the Turks do not appear earlier than the collections of Abu Dawud and al-Bukhari (mid-ninth century).[3] The Polish scholar Tadeusz Kowalski interpreted the occasional use of the phrase *al-Turk wa-Kabul* in early Arabic poetry (assuming this poetry is genuine anyway) as a familiar expression of the times for somewhere remote and unknown, an *Ultima Thule*, rather than knowledge of a real geographical location of the Turks. Nor can we assume, wrote Kowalski elsewhere, that the Persian national epic, as known to us in the later shape of Firdawsi's *Shah-nama*, gives us first-hand information about the Turks when it places the heroes of the land of Iran in opposition to those of Turan, that is, the lands beyond the Oxus ruled by the Iranians' arch-enemy Afrasiyab, king of Turan.[4] The Turanians of Sasanid times, when the national epic was probably put together, must have been members of steppe confederations of pre-Christian times, like the Scythians and Massagetae, and those of early Christian ones like the Kushans and Hephthalites, whose ranks may admittedly have contained some ethnic Turks but whose leading strata were probably mainly Indo-Europeans, at a time when Indo-European peoples still dominated the western Eurasian steppe lands as far east as the Tarim basin. Firdawsi, living as he did in early Ghaznavid times, had obviously heard of Turkish tribal names like the Oghuz, Qarluq, and Chigil, and introduced them into his poetic narrative to give what he thought would be historical verisimilitude.

As early as the caliphate of 'Umar, Arab raiders pushed through the eastern Caucasus along the western shores of the Caspian and through the so-called 'Caspian Gates', the Bab al-Abwab of the Arab geographers, the later Derbend, and encountered the Khazars. The Khazars were probably a confederation of various Hunnish and Turkic elements rather than a distinct tribe, their name not being known as a constituent people of the early Turks. The century or so from 642 to 737 was filled with Arab–Khazar warfare, with the Arabs at times raiding as far as the Khazar capital Atil near the mouth of the Volga. When in 737 the Umayyad prince, later Caliph, Marwan b. Muhammad defeated the Qaghan of the Khazars, the latter was obliged temporarily to accept Islam, but as is well known, Islam was subsequently just one of the three great monotheistic faiths contending for the souls of the Khazars, many of whom, probably the greater part, must have retained their ancestral animist beliefs anyway.[5] Warfare subsided, and until the Khazar Qaghanate declined in the tenth century, there followed some two centuries of generally peaceful relations between the Khazars and the Muslims, with a significant commerce developing across the Khazar lands, thus linking the caliphate in Baghdad with the basins of the Volga and Don River systems and, ultimately, eastern Europe and the Baltic lands. The legacy of the Khazar lands to the Muslims was principally a human one, for the Khazars acted as intermediaries in the slave traffic from the eastern Eurasian steppes, including South Russia, and this may have included Turks, Ugrians, and Slavs; all these slaves, military and domestic, were, however, lumped together by the undiscerning and uninterested Muslims and given the all-embracing *nisba* 'al-Khazari'.[6]

On what became the northeastern frontiers of the Islamic world, the Arabs found themselves, once they had overthrown the Sassanids, on the banks of the Oxus River facing the Iranian kingdom of Khwarazm and the city states of Sogdia and Transoxania as far as the Syr Darya basin. It was here that the Arabs encountered Turks, now mentioned as such, as with the Khazars, by Arab historians like al-Baladhuri, al-Ya'qubi, al-Dinawari, Ibn A'tham al-Kufi, and al-Tabari. The repulse in the mid-sixth century of the Hephthalites from Iran's northwestern frontier as the result of a temporary alliance of the Sassanid Emperor Khusraw Anushirwan with the Western Turkish Qaghanate apparently allowed some ethnic Turkish elements—perhaps formerly part of the Hephthalite conferedation—to infiltrate the upper Oxus provinces, what is now Tajikistan and northern Afghanistan, and to achieve some local power there. The sources mention the Jabbuyas (whose title must reflect the Orkhon Turkish office of Yabghu) and their Oghuz and Qarluq followers as opponents of the Arab general Qutayba b. Muslim when he campaigned in northeastern Khurasan and across the Oxus during the opening years of the eighth century; and these Jabbuyas were amongst the local rulers of Transoxania, comprising Iranians and Turks, who appealed to the Chinese emperors, who claimed a distant suzerainty over the Central Asian lands, for help against the Arabs, resulting eventually in the Chinese expedition right across the heart of Asia in 751 under the Korean commander Kao Hsien-chi, defeated, however, at Talas by the Arab general Ziyad b. Salih, thus ending Chinese ambitions in the western lands beyond the Ala Tagh and Tien Shan mountains.[7]

Another group of Turks, the Khalaj (but the Arabic consonant ductus could be read as Khallukh, that is Qarluq) is mentioned as nomadizing on the plateaux of eastern Afghanistan between Kabul and Bust. In the later tenth and early eleventh centuries, these Khalaj were a thorn in the flesh of the Ghaznavids, though Mahmud of Ghazna attempted to solve this problem by recruiting them into his multi-ethnic army. These Khalaj of the farthest fringes of the Islamic world were later to have a bright future in Indo-Muslim history as part of the Muslim forces of the Ghurids overrunning northwestern India, eventually forming the Khalji line of sultans in Delhi, which briefly reigned from 1290 to 1320.[8]

An intriguing piece of evidence that may indicate some early Turkish presence in northern Afghanistan has recently turned up in the shape of the so-called 'Bactrian documents', emanating from the classical region of Bactria and the Islamic provinces of Tukharistan and Guzgan. These documents apparently appeared on the art and antiques market, perhaps via somewhere like the Peshawar bazaar, in the 1990s and were acquired by the London-based art connoisseur Nasser al-Khalili. They mostly comprise an archive, extending in date from the fourth to the tenth century AD, in the Middle Iranian Bactrian language (as a result of which we now know much more about what was previously a shadowy tongue, attested only by one inscription and some coin legends), and these have been deciphered and edited by Professor Nicholas Sims-Williams. But there is also a smaller, but still significant number of legal and administrative parchment documents in Arabic stemming from the third quarter of the eighth century, that is, the early 'Abbasid period, mainly from the district of Rub, modern Ruy, south of Samangan and just north of the Paropamisus range; these have been read and edited by Professor Geoffrey Khan. Of interest to us is the fact that Turkish titles like *beg*, *khaqan*, and *tarkhan* appear in them, as parts of names of persons ostensibly Iranian; the solution of this conundrum is unclear, but it would seem that these Turkish terms were at least known in the region.[9]

Items of information like this would seem to indicate that there was a Turkish presence on the fringes of Transoxania and the north-eastern part of Khurasan in early 'Abbasid times, perhaps a presence of at least semi-sedentary confederation, since by the tenth century we have mention by historians and geographers like al-Mas'udi and Ibn Hawqal of essentially Turkish towns on the lower Syr Darya to the southeast of the Aral Sea. These included the 'new town' of Yengi-kent. Dih-i naw, or al-Qarya al-haditha, in the Soviet archaeologist S.P. Tolstov's view, was a re-founding of an ancient Hunnic–Turkish settlement; secondly, there was Jand, which appears in the later tenth and early eleventh centuries as the winter residence of the Yabghu of the Oghuz, later at odds with the Seljuq family of the Qiniq clan of the Oghuz, who also claimed this ancient Turkic title for their own branch of the tribe; and thirdly, Khuwara. There were undoubtedly Muslim traders there, and the local Turks were mainly Oghuz, described as both nomads and sedentaries (*bawadi wa-hadar*). Further up the Syr Darya were other Turkish towns, including Sawran and Sighnaq, and this middle stretch of the river between Jand and Utrar was strongly Turkish, whose people long remained unassimilated to Perso-Islamic civilization; till the end of the twelfth century, it was considered *dar al-kufr*, the home of pagan Qipchaq, against whom the Khwarazm Shahs were to lead raids.[10] Barthold surmised that these towns were founded by emigrants from Transoxania as entrepôts for trade with the steppe lands, but this seems a gratuitous assumption. There is no reason to assume that Turks were not capable of founding settlements, since regions like the Chu Valley of what is now the northernmost part of the Kirghiz Republic, and the adjacent fringe of Kazakhstan, the Semirechye or Yeti Su 'land of the seven rivers', and the Orkhon and Selenga valleys in Mongolia had for long had some familiarity with agriculture and agricultural settlement, precarious though this often was. The late tenth-century anonymous Persian geography, the *Hudud al-'alam*, describes the towns along the northern fringes of Transoxania and middle Syr Darya as having sedentarized Turks who were in a treaty relationship with the Muslims, *turkan-i ashti*, many of whom had themselves become Muslims.[11]

The items of commerce between the eastern Islamic lands and those of the Turks are described in considerable detail by the geographer al-Maqdisi. From the Muslim-settled lands were exported all sorts of textiles, woollen and cotton; rugs and carpets; dressed furs; foodstuff like melons and dried fruits and dried fish; copper vessels; saddles and other accoutrements for horses; weapons, including bows; paper; and so forth. In return, there came from the steppe lands dairy products, meat, hides, and horses. Only a few Muslim travellers and traders made long-distance forays through the steppes and deserts. Tamim b. Bahr al-Mutawwi'i, probably a Khurasanian Arab, must have crossed the mountain barriers of the Tien Shan and then the deserts of what became Eastern Turkestan when in c. 821 he travelled to the capital of what he calls the Toghuzoghuz 'Nine Oghuz', which Minorsky plausibly identified with the capital of the Uyghurs, Qara Balaghasun, on the Orkhon river in Mongolia.[12] A century later, in 921–2, the Arab envoy Ahmad b. Fadlan was part of a mission on behalf of the 'Abbasid caliph al-Muqtadir to the recently converted Muslim king of Bulghar on the middle Volga. He journeyed from Khwarazm through the steppes where the Oghuz nomadized.[13] But none are known to have gone yet further northwards and entered the forest zones of northern Russia and Siberia, dimly known to the Arabs as the *ard al-zulumat* 'land of darkness' and haunt of what must have been Finno-Ugrian peoples like the Wisu and Yura. In the western steppe lands, the people of Bulghar, and further east the Turkish Kirghiz and Kimek tribesmen, obtained by barter furs of sable, marten, silver fox, and so on, and an exotic product like fossil ivory, presumably obtained from the tusks of mammoths preserved in the permafrost of the lower Yenissei and Lena basins, this ivory being highly prized not only as a material for artistic purposes but also ground-up as a medicament and aphrodisiac. Owen Lattimore recorded that in the 1940s when he was writing, the extreme north of Yakutia and the Arctic coastlands yielded 25 tons of mammoth ivory a year. All these items of merchandise were easily transportable and gave a comparatively high financial return for their bulk.[14]

Moreover, the northern lands of Inner Asia, like those of the steppes to the north of the Caucasus and of South Russia, were important to the Islamic world as a source of slaves, pre-eminently Turkish ones. In a slave-holding society like the premodern Islamic one, a constant supply of slaves was necessary, so that the slave markets of Khazaria, Transoxania, and Khwarazm were always busy. Slaves were gained from war captives as soon as the Arabs pressed beyond the Oxus. Governors of Khurasan, such as the Tahirids in the ninth century, regularly included Turkish slaves as part of their annual tribute sent back to Baghdad and Samarra, some gained from Muslim incursions into the steppes but most of them brought in by Turkish intermediaries themselves as a result of Turkish intertribal fighting. We know from his *Pand-nama*, ostensible advice to his son Mahmud of Ghazna, that the founder of the Ghaznavid dynasty, Sebuktegin, whose tribe was probably affiliated with a component of the Qarluq group, hailed from Barskhan on the shores of the Issik-Kol in what is now the Kirghiz Republic, having been made prisoner in tribal conflict and sold as a slave at Chach in Samanid Transoxania. Much of the prosperity of the Samanids in the ninth and tenth centuries must have been founded on the slave trade in their lands. al-Maqdisi quotes from what he calls 'a certain book' which he had seen that the stipulated revenue from Khurasan to the caliphs (this must refer to pre-Samanid, probably Tahirid, times since there is no record that the Samanids, in practice independent, sovereign rulers, ever sent tribute to Baghdad) included 12,000 Turkish slaves per annum. He further mentions that the Samanid administration in Bukhara controlled the export of slaves in transit across Transoxania, charging a fee of 70 to

100 dirhams for each Turkish slave at the Oxus crossing points like Tirmidh and Amul-Shatt and requiring, in addition to this, a licence (*jawaz*) for each slave boy. From information in Ibn Khurradadhbih, Barthold calculated that the average price of a Turkish slave in Tahirid times was 300 dirhams.[15]

Demand for domestic slaves swallowed up a great part of this importation of slaves, although this fact is not well documented. An 'Abbasid military slave commander of the ninth century, Itākh, started off as a cook's boy before taking to the military life, hence the *nisba* or gentillic, by which he was at times known, of al-Tabbakh 'the cook'. When in 1055 the Seljuq leader Toghril Beg entered Baghdad, he found there, according to Barhebraeus, Turkish families of long standing, performing lowly tasks such as stoking baths, baking, and vegetable selling. Many slave girls found their way into harems, some at the very apex of this system; the mother of the caliph al-Muktafi, born in 878, was called Jijak, obviously Turkish *chichek* for 'flower'.[16]

The part which the Turks were to play as slave soldiers (*ghilman*) under the 'Abbasids and their successor states had been anticipated by the situation in Transoxania and Khurasan during pre-'Abbasid times. It is likely that the Turks of the borderlands, already mentioned, were recruited as mercenaries by local rulers, Transoxania, because since pre-Arab conquest times it had been politically fragmented, with the Sogdian city states and the rural areas ruled by *dihqans* often engaged in internecine warfare, so that there were frequent opportunities for employment.

The mass of Muslims within the central and eastern lands of the caliphate became from the early ninth century familiar with Turkish *ghulams*, at a time when new demands for troops in caliphal service had arisen. The old levée en masse of the Arab *muqatila*, the backbone of the armies involved in the first conquests, was already becoming obsolete by the end of the Umayyad period, and the 'Abbasid rose to power in 746–50 with the backing of their Khurasanian guards, ethnically both Arabs and Iranians, the so-called *Abna' al-Dawla*, 'Sons of the Dynasty', and these were still the backbone of al-Ma'mun's forces in the struggle of 810–13 for the caliphate with his brother al-Amin. But even these were beginning to acquire sectional interests; those settled in the Harbiyya quarter, to the north of al-Mansur's Round City at Baghdad, supported the rival claimant Ibrahim b. al-Mahdi whilst al-Ma'mun remained still in distant Khurasan. What were needed were troops brought in from outside, untrammelled by local ties and able to give an unequivocal single-minded loyalty to their masters. Al-Ma'mun latterly, and then his brother and successor al-Mu'tasim, thought that they had found such troops by recruiting free Iranian soldiers from Transoxania, like Afshin Haydar, local prince of Ushrusana south of the middle Syr Darya; Arabs from the deserts adjoining the Nile delta in Egypt, the Maghariba or 'Westerners'; and, above all, Turkish slave troops.[17] The ability now of the caliphs to finance all these reflects the rising prosperity of the caliphal lands at this time, yielding funds with which the caliphs and their provincial governors could for the first time organize and pay for professional, standing armies. No doubt there were hopes, too, for such paymasters that such forces could be used to further the causes of state centralization and the elevation of rulers, caliphs, amirs, or sultans above the level of the general, taxpaying populations, the ra'aya.

At Samarra in northern Iraq, seat of the caliphate in the middle and late decades of the ninth century, adjacent blocks of land were granted out as qata'i', grants of estates, to the various national groups, Turks, Khurasanians, and Maghariba. The allocation of these estates to professional soldiers undoubtedly gave an impetus to the spread of this system of iqta's or land grants in the central Islamic lands, at the outset in Iraq and western Iran, even though the system can be traced back to the second caliph 'Umar's policy in Iraq just after the conquests there. But whereas such earlier grants had been for limited periods only and had not included the right of the muqta' or grantee to collect the kharaj or land-tax himself, the new iqta's evolved into virtually hereditary concessions, usually involving immunity from state officials entering the estates, and which paid a fixed sum only to the central treasury. As the power of the 'Abbasid caliphs waned, grant-holders, secure in their estates, began to usurp for themselves the granting out of protection, talji'a and himaya to weaker parties, corresponding to the commendatio of mediaeval Western European feudalism. The spread of a network of these iqta's injected an element of instability into affairs, since despite the trend towards hereditary possession, confiscations and redistributions could take place as a result of changes in the state at the top. The culmination of such processes was to come later in the Mamluk sultanate of Egypt and Syria, with the periodic distributions by incoming sultans, the rawks. But one of the reasons for al-Mutawakkil's murder in 861 is said to have been the caliph's intention of confiscating the iqta's in Jibal, western Persia, and at Isfahan, of the Turkish general Wasif, and of re-allocating them to his favourite al-Fath b. Khaqan.[18]

Amongst the new troops of this period, Turkish slaves had a particularly high profile. Contemporary Muslim authors of *adab* works, 'Mirrors for Princes', and manuals of war praised Turks as the military race *par excellence* being old horsemen, inured from their steppe background to hardship. Brought from pagan darkness into the clear light of Islam and reared in its faith and culture, it was believed that they would give unalloyed fidelity to their new masters (though the reality was more often than not very different; no fewer than five 'Abbasid caliphs and many other holders of power were killed in conspiracies involving their own slave troops). Al-Jahiz, in his famous epistle on the excellences of the Turks and the rest of the caliphal troops, *Risala fi manaqib al-atrak wa-'ammat jund al-khilafa*, written for al-Fath b. Khaqan, attributes to them some of the virtues of the noble savage— magnanimity, freedom from hypocrisy and intrigue, disregard of flattery, and racial pride—but had to concede their propensities for violence and plundering.[19] Two centuries later, the former Ghaznavid official Ibn Hassul wrote a propaganda tract for his new master, the Seljuq Toghril Beg, called 'The Superiority of the Turks over the Rest of the Troops', *Tafdil al-atrak 'ala sa'ir al-ajnad*, emphasizing their lion-like qualities, their rejection of menial, non-military tasks, and their eagerness for military command. The Persian 'Mirrors for Princes' of that same period, by Kay Kawus and Nizam al-Mulk, emphasize the value of Turkish slave troops for buttressing the power of would-be despotic rulers.[20] A few authors showed a certain interest in the physical anthropology of the Turks, but tended to derive their material from classical Greek sources (which were, of course, referring to peoples of Inner Eurasia like the Scythians, Sarmatians, and Huns, who were almost certainly not Turks at all) rather than to rely on direct observation. Thus, authors like al-Mas'udi and Sharaf al-Zaman Tahir Marwazi simply cite Hippocrates and Galen on the effects of the cold and damp steppe climate on the Turks' balances of humours, their constitutions, and their libidos. In all these cases, attitudes to Turks involved a racial stereotyping, and the existence of cowardly or unmilitary Turks were exceptions that only proved the rule.[21]

As for convincing detail on the tribal affiliations of the Turks brought in as military slaves, we have virtually no information for the earlier period. The *nisbas* given to them like al-Khazari, al-Bukhari, al-Isfijabi, and so on simply refer to the slave markets through which they had passed when brought from the steppes into the Islamic lands.[22] The information of al-Maqrizi Ahmad b. Tulun, whose father is said to have been a *mawla* of the Samanids in Transoxania

and who became governor of Egypt for the 'Abbasids in 868, founding a short-lived line in Egypt and Syria, which came from the Toghuz
Oghuz, is exceptional; and given the time-gap of over five centuries
between the Tulunids and the Mamluk historian's time, must be
treated with reserve. Various tribes of the Turks and other peoples
of the outer steppe lands as far as Mongolia had been known to the
Arabic and Persian geographers. But it is only with the appearance on
the Islamic scene at the end of the tenth century and the opening of
the eleventh one of the Qarakhanids and the Seljuqs that these tribal
divisions become significant for events actually within the Islamic
lands. That these were now of interest to some individuals at least
seems to be indicated by the composition at Baghdad in the last quarter of the eleventh century of Mahmud al-Kashghari's Turkish-Arabic
dictionary, the *Diwan lughat al-turk*, which went into such detail as
listing the twenty-two component clans of the Oghuz.[23]

The caliphs' Turkish troops were highly unpopular with the local
people in Iraq due to their violence and their role as king-makers in
the dynastic squabbles concerning succession to the throne. Arabic
sources of the later ninth and tenth centuries unanimously regard
the Turks as barbarians, *'uluj*, a maleficent influence in the state, and
a contributory factor in the decadence and growing impotence of the
caliphate; thus the tenth-century Baghdad poet Ibn Langak stigma-
tizes them as 'apes on saddleback' (*qurudan rakibin 'ala 'l-suruj*). It is
now that the anti-Turkish *hadiths* that were mentioned at the outset
come into circulation. Some held that the Turks could be the twenty-
fourth tribe of the people of Gog and Magog; the one tribe whom
Dhu'l-Qarnayn, Alexander the Great, had been unable to contain
behind the barrier which he erected against them in Inner Asia, and
an eschatological role was ascribed to them as a people who had to
be combatted before the end of the world and the Day of Judgement.

In general, the Turks were kept apart from the Arab and Persian
masses by their domineering behaviour and by a linguistic barrier (though we have mention of Turks who acted as interpreters
and something like liaison officers with the general population),
it is nevertheless possible to discern that not all the Turkish soldiers were unlettered barbarians. Something of the Arab–Persian
cultural heritage does seem to have rubbed off on certain individuals. Al-Fath b. Khaqan was clearly a man of culture in addition to
his military prowess; he was a member of al-Mutawakkil's literary
circle, patronized al-Jahiz and the poet al-Buhturi, assembled a valuable library at Samarra, with an emphasis on philosophical works,

much consulted by scholars, and was himself a poet and writer in Arabic. Bechkem, a powerful figure in Iraq in the 930s as aide of the *Amir al-Umara'* Ibn Ra'iq, knew Arabic and enjoyed the company of such scholars as the *adib* and chess-player Abu Bakr Muhammad al-Suli and the physician Sinan b. Thabit b. Qurra, to whom he gave generous pensions.[24]

Nevertheless, over the subsequent centuries it was hard for the Turks within the central and eastern Islamic lands to live down their reputation solely for excellence in warfare, equestrian skills (*furusiyya*), and martial arts, a judgement which speedily became a stereotype amongst the Arab and Persian religious and literary classes. By the eleventh century, with the establishment of Turkish ruling powers, whether of servile origin like the Ghaznavids or of free, tribal origin like the Qarakhanids and Seljuqs, Turks were controlling a vast swathe of territory from northern Syria to northwestern India, with only the Fatimids of southern Syria and Egypt and minor lines in the Arabian peninsula being actually Arab in ethnos. Some two centuries later, with the rise to power of the Mamluks in Egypt and Syria and the ejection of the Byzantines from Anatolia, Turkish rule was even more extensive: in addition to the Mamluks, there were now in Anatolia the Rum Seljuqs and other Turkmen beyliks, amongst them the nascent Ottomans; powerful Turkmen lines in Iraq and Persia, paving the way for the later triumph of the Safavids there; and Turco-Mongol powers in Transoxania, one sprig of which became implanted in Northern India as the Mughals. Thus virtually the whole of the central and eastern lands became one vast *dawla turkiyya*, only petering out with the establishment of the British in India, the demise of the Ottoman Empire after the First World War, Reza Shah's replacement of the Qajars in Iran, and the almost unnoticed end of Muhammad 'Ali's line in 1953 with the Egyptian Revolution. Bernard Lewis has rightly commented that in these earlier times, a non-Turk in authority was regarded as an oddity.[25]

But in Arab minds, Turks, of whatever tribal or territorial affiliation, were lumped together as a single ethnic group. Hence when the Mamluks came to include amongst their personnel palpably non-Turkish races like the Oyrat Mongols, Kurds, Khwarazmians, and others who came as Wafidiyya, 'those arriving in delegations', to swell the ranks of the Qipchaq Bahris, whilst the Burjis were recruited very largely from the Circassians and Abkhaz of the northwestern Caucasus and adjacent steppes, all these groups were still for the Arabs undifferentiated 'Turks', to be considered as uncouth, unlettered intruders

into the world of the 'turban-wearers', *muta'ammimun*, those pre-
eminent in scholarship, theology, and polite literature—the Arabs.[26]
This process was somewhat analogous to Western attitudes of the
later mediaeval and early modern periods, which described all the
Muslims they encountered, from Morocco to Syria, as 'Moors'.

The one sector of Arab life and culture that the Arabs of 'Abbasid
times could jealously guard was their primacy in scholarship and religious leadership, defence of the pure faith, with the ulema as heirs of
the Prophet and guardians of his heritage. Yet even this now began
to be eroded. When the Great Seljuqs instituted the sultanate at the
side of the 'Abbasid caliphate, there passed *de facto* to the sultans the
caliphs' original functions as military leaders, defenders of the borders
of Islam, so that already in the middle years of the eleventh century
Ibn Hassul could praise his master Toghril Beg as 'the salvation of the
Muslims', *ghiyath al-muslimin*. Then the claim of the Arab religious
institution to sole guardianship of the faith crumbled in the thirteenth
century in face of the onslaught of infidel Mongols. The hordes of
Hulegü and his Il-Khanid successors extinguished the moribund
'Abbasid caliphate and their westwards advance was only halted in
1260 at 'Ayn Jalut in Palestine and then at Damascus fifty years later
by the Turkish Mamluks, whom the Arabs regarded as ethnically similar to the Mongols, both races coming as they did from the remote,
mysterious Inner Eurasian steppes. The surprise of the contemporary
Syrian Arab historian Abu Shama has been often quoted: 'It is truly
remarkable that the Tatars were broken and destroyed by their own
kinsmen, the Turks.' Moreover, the Turkish Mamluks were at this time
dislodging the Frankish Crusaders (regarded by the Muslims as allies
of the Mongols) from their last footholds on the Levant coast, with
Acre falling in 1291, and they went on to reduce to tributary status the
Christian kingdom of Little Armenia, an achievement important to the
Mamluks because the Rupenid kingdom lay across the route from the
Black Sea shores by means of which came slave replenishments for
the ruling and military Mamluk institution. The fall of Acre was hailed
by an Arabic poet cited by the historian Ibn al-Furat: 'Praise be to God,
the nation of the Cross has fallen; through the Turks the religion of the
Arab Chosen One has triumphed!'[27] Such victories for the faith raised
the status of the Mamluk sultans in the eyes of their Arab subjects
at large, seen in their approbation of the sultans in Arabic folk epic
literature like the *Sirat al-Malik al-Zahir Baybars*.

Despite this, approbation by the Arab ulema was slow in coming and distinctly grudging. They found the decline of their own

previously unchallenged prestige as sole guardians of Islamic orthodoxy hard to bear. The late Ulrich Haarmann examined their attitudes
and noted that, for example, in certain attested cases, Mamluks and
their retainers were forbidden to enter some madrasas, let alone to
study in them.[28] The rich religious, literary, and philological culture
of the Mamluk court, in all three languages of Turkish, Arabic, and
Persian, was ignored by Arabic historians of the time. (One may note
that this period is especially notable for the production of several
grammars and vocabularies of Qipchaq Turkish, such as the 'Book of
Comprehending the Turkish Language', *Kitab al-Idrak li-lisan al-atrak*,
by the fourteenth-century Granadan author, writing in Cairo, Abu
Hayyan, amongst at least three other works of his on Turkish philology
no longer extant; also, several works in Turkish on *fiqh* are known.[29])
The sons of Mamluk amirs, the second-generation *awlad al-nas*, now
cut off from their Mamluk past by their free status and birth into
the Islamic faith, and Arabic rather than Turkish-speaking, played
a decisive role as intermediaries between the Qipchaq Turkish and
Circassian military élite and the Arabic-speaking ulema and *udaba'*.
Yet they seem to have been far from welcome in Arab literary and
scholarly circles unless they renounced totally their Turkish heritage.
Haarmann again noted that the historian Ibn Aybak al-Dawadari, a
member of the religious élite but proud of his Turco-Mongol heritage,
was given the cold shoulder, as it were, by the compilers of biographical dictionaries who accorded him little mention; Ibn Taghribirdi
attracted criticism for his Turkishness from local Arab–Egyptian
scholars like al-Sakhawi (who was admittedly a distinctly critical character); and when a late fifteenth-century Arab scholar like Abu Hamid
al-Qudsi, in a history which he wrote and dedicated to a Mamluk amir,
lauded his Turkish rulers as the saviours of Islamic faith and protectors of the Muslim masses, this was rather a perverse reflection of a
violent personal feud with his legal and scholarly colleagues.[30]

Only a restricted number of Arab authors were sympathetic enough
to give the Mamluks and other Turks their due. One of them was
Ibn Khaldun, a Maghribi, hence a detached observer of the Egyptian
and Syrian scene, who had a more generous and wide-reaching view
of the evolution of Islamic faith and society. He saw Turkish rule
as something like an inevitable stage of this process, even a natural development in the history of the Arab people. It had come after
the comparatively short domination of the Arabs within Islam, and
from their likewise tribal background and mores, *akhlaq badawiyya*,
the Mamluks and other Turks had brought a new intensity of feeling

and a renewed religious faith involving the determined vigour of true believers ('aza'im *imaniyya*); their ascendancy was a proof of God's continuing concern for His Muslim people and the welfare of the Islamic lands. He saw the Turks as still at the height of their authority and vigour, and their domination as a phase of Islam that would endure and would move the centre of gravity of the Islamic world further north than it had originally been, with its origins in Arabia.[31]

However, Ibn Khaldun's voice here was a distinctly lone one. The subsequent inclusion of much of the central Arab lands within the Ottoman Turkish Empire exacerbated the situation, leading to the still fairly general modern Arab view that all the ills of Islam have stemmed first from the Mongol invasions and then from the continued domination of the Turks. But that is another story.

Notes

1. P.B. Golden, this volume.
2. Denis Sinor, 'Diplomatic Practices in Medieval Inner Asia', in *Essays in Honor of Bernard Lewis: The Islamic World from Classical to Modern Times*, eds. C.E. Bosworth et al. (Princeton: Darwin Press, 1989), pp. 341–2; Denis Sinor, 'The Establishment and Dissolution of the Türk Empire', in *The Cambridge History of Inner Asia*, ed. Denis Sinor (Cambridge: Cambridge University Press, 1990), pp. 301–5; P.B. Golden, 'The Turks: Origins and Expansion', in *Turks and Khazars: Origins, Institutions, and Interactions in Pre-Mongol Eurasia*, Ashgate Variorum Collected Studies Series, no. 1 (Farnham: Ashgate Publishing, 2010), pp. 6ff.
3. Ignaz Goldziher, 'Excursus VI: Traditions about the Turks', in *Muslim Studies*, trans. C.M. Barber and S.M. Stern (London: Allen & Unwin, 1967–71), vol. 1, pp. 245–6.
4. T. Kowalski, 'Die altesten Erwahnungen der Turken in der arabischen Literatur', *KCsA* 2 (1926–32): pp. 38–41; T. Kowalski, 'Les turcs dans le Sah-nama', *RO* 15 (1939–52): pp. 84–99.
5. D.M. Dunlop, *The History of the Jewish Khazars* (Princeton: Princeton University Press, 1954), pp. 41–87.
6. P.B. Golden, 'Khazar Turkic Ghulams in Caliphal Service', *JA* 292 (2004): pp. 297–308, repr. in P.B. Golden, *Turks and Khazars*, no. 7 (study with book).
7. H.A.R. Gibb, *Arab Conquests in Central Asia* (London: Royal Asiatic Society, 1923), pp. 29ff.; W. Barthold, *Turkestan down to the Mongol Invasion* [3rd ed. C.E. Bosworth], 2nd ed. GMS, N.S. vol. V (London: Luzac, 1968), pp. 182ff.; C.E. Bosworth, 'Jabguya, ii' in Islamic Sources', *EIr* 14: pp. 316–17.
8. C.E. Bosworth, 'Khaladj, i. History', *EI2* 4: pp. 917–18.

9. Geoffrey Khan, *Arabic Documents from Early Islamic Khurasan, Studies in the Khalili Collection*, vol. 5 (London: The Noor Foundation in Association with the Azimuth Press, 2007).

10. R.N. Frye, and Aydin M. Sayili, 'Turks in the Middle East before the Saljuqs', *JAOS* 63 (1943): pp. 194–207; C.E. Bosworth, *The Ghaznavids, their Empire in Afghanistan and Eastern Iran 99–1040* (Edinburgh: Edinburgh University Press, 1963), pp. 206–26.

11. Anonymous, *Hudud al-'alam*, trans. V. Minorsky, GMS, N.S. 11 (London: Luzac, 1937): pp. 118–19, commentary, p. 357.

12. V. Minorsky, 'Tamim ibn Bahr's Journey to the Uyghurs', *BSOAS* 12 (1947–8): pp. 275–305.

13. Amongst the extensive literature on this author and his journey, see the summary in C.E. Bosworth, 'Ahmad b. Fazlan', *EIr*. 1: p. 640, to which Bibliography should now be added the recent *Ibn Fadlan's Journey to Russia, A Tenth-Century Traveler from Baghdad to the Volga River*, trans. R.N. Frye (Princeton: Markus Wiener, 2005).

14. O. Lattimore, 'Yakutia and the Future of the North', in *Studies in Frontier History: Collected Papers 1928–1958* (London: Oxford University Press, 1962), p. 459.

15. Barthold, *Turkestan*, pp. 227–8, 239–40; Bosworth, *The Ghaznavids*, pp. 39–41, 99–100; C.E. Bosworth, 'The Turks in the Islamic Lands up to the Mid-Eleventh Century', in a separate fascicule of *PTF, Tomum tertium* [*Historia*], ed. Cl. Cahen (Wiesbaden: Franz Steiner, 1970), pp. 4–5.

16. Bosworth, 'The Turks in the Islamic Lands', p. 6.

17. Daniel Pipes, *Slave Soldiers and Islam: The Genesis of a Military System* (New Haven: Yale University Press, 1981), pp. 153–7.

18. Osman S.A. Ismail, 'Mu'tasim and the Turks', *BSOAS* 29 (1966): pp. 12–24; Osman S.A. Ismail, 'The Founding of a New Capital: Samarra', *BSOAS* 31 (1968): pp. 1–13; Bosworth, 'The Turks in the Islamic Lands', pp. 7–8; Matthew S. Gordon, *The Breaking of a Thousand Swords: A History of the Turkish Military of Samarra (A.H. 200–275/815–89 C.E.)* (Albany: State University of New York Press, 2001).

19. See for a translation of Jahiz's epistle, C.T. Harley Walker, 'Jahiz of Basra to al-Fath b. Khaqan on the 'Exploits of the Turks and the Army of the Khalifate in General', *JRAS* (1915): pp. 633–97.

20. On the general topic of the Turkish slave element in Islamic armies at this time see, Bosworth, *The Ghaznavids*, pp. 98–9; Bosworth, 'The Turks in the Islamic Lands', pp. 6–7; C.E. Bosworth, 'Barbarian Incursions: The Coming of the Turks into the Islamic World', in *Islamic Civilisation 950–1150*, ed. D.S. Richards (Oxford: Bruno Cassirer, 1973), pp. 6–7; Pipes, *Slave Soldiers and Islam*, pp. 78–93.

21. al-Mas'udi, *Muruj al-dhahab*, ed. and trans. A.C. Barbier de Meynard and Pavet de Courteille (Paris: Societe Asiatique, 1861–77), vol. 4, pp. 9–10, 32–3; Marwazi, in V. Minorsky, *Sharaf al-Zaman Tahir Marvazi*

on China, the Turks and India (London: Royal Asiatic Society, 1942), pp. 36–8, commentary, pp. 120–2.

22. For what can be deduced about Khazar slave soldiers in caliphal service and their origins, see P.B. Golden, 'Khazar Turkic Ghulams in Caliphal Service: Onomastic Notes', *AEMA* 12 (2001): pp. 15–27, represented in Golden, *Turks and Khazars*, no. IX.

23. Mahmud al-Kashghari, *Compendium of the Turkic Dialects (Diwan Lugat at-Turk)*, trans. Robert Dankoff and James Kelly (Cambridge, Massachusetts: Harvard University Press, 1982–4), vol. 1, pp. 101–2.

24. M. Ben Cheneb, and Ch. Pellat, 'al-Fath b. Khakan', *EI2* 2: p. 838; M. Canard, 'Badjkam', *EI2* 1: pp. 866–7.

25. B. Lewis, 'The Mongols, the Turks and the Muslim Polity', in *Islam in History: Ideas, Men and Events in the Middle East* (London: Alcove Press, 1973), pp. 179–98; Carter V. Findley, *The Turks in World History* (New York: Oxford University Press, 2005), pp. 66–92.

26. For the various Wafidiyya, see David Ayalon, 'The Wafidiyya in the Mamluk Kingdom', *IC* 25 (1951): pp. 82–104. See also Ulrich Haarmann, 'Ideology and History. Identity and Alterity: The Arab Image of the Turk from the Abbasids to Modern Egypt', *IJMES* 20 (1988): pp. 175–96. On the topic in general, and especially in pp. 176–7, on the ethnic clichés and stereotypes of the Mamluk period.

27. Lewis, 'The Mongols, the Turks and the Muslim Polity', pp. 186–7.

28. Ulrich Haarmann, '*Rather the Injustice of the Turks than the Righteousness of the Arabs*—Changing "*Ulama*" Attitudes towards Mamluk Rule in the Late Fifteenth Century', *SI* 68 (1988): p. 76.

29. See Omeljan Pritsak, 'Mamluk-Kiptschakisch', in *PTF, Tomum primum. Philologie*, eds. J. Deny et al. (Wiesbaden: Steiner, 1959), pp. 75–7; Janos Eckmann, 'Die mamluk-kiptschakische Literatur', in *PTF, Tomum secundum. Literatur* (Wiesbaden: Steiner, 1964), pp. 298–302; Ulrich Haarmann, 'Arabic in Speech, Turkish in Lineage: Mamluks and their Sons in the Intellectual Life of Fourteenth-Century Egypt and Syria', *JSS* 33 (1988): pp. 90–1.

30. Haarmann, 'Arabic in Speech, Turkish in Lineage', pp. 103ff; Haarmann, 'Changing "*Ulama*" Attitudes towards Mamluk Rule', pp. 69ff.

31. Lewis, 'The Mongols, the Turks and the Muslim Polity', p. 194; David Ayalon, 'The Mamluks and Ibn Xaldun', *IOS* 10 (1980): pp. 11–13.

II

THE SELJUQS AND THEIR LEGACY

4

BRICK VERSUS STONE
Seljuq Architecture in Iran and Anatolia

ROBERT HILLENBRAND*

The symposium of which this volume is the record focused on cross-cultural encounters, and the briefest glance at a map indicates why that should be a natural way of coming to terms with the culture of medieval Anatolia in the twelfth and thirteenth centuries. It makes sense that the Seljuqs of Rum would have had to look west to Byzantium and, beyond that, to the Mediterranean world; to the south, to Iraq, Syria and Egypt, the lands of the Zengids, Ayyubids, and Mamluks; and to the east, to the world of Iran and Central Asia where their ancestral homelands lay. Politically the least important and most impermeable frontier was to the north, where the Black Sea interposed a major natural barrier to easy communication—although it was from the north that much of the wealth of the Rum Seljuqs came. There, in what is now Ukraine, lay the slave markets that supplied the *mamluks* so coveted by the militarized states of the Near East. The Rum Seljuqs were the middlemen in this lucrative trade.[1]

Geography, then, made Seljuq Anatolia not an island but a bridge, indeed a natural locus of interchange. In the field of the visual arts, the very same geography dictated that forms, ideas, and motifs from

* I would like to express my deep gratitude to Sheila Blair, Jonathan Bloom, David Gye, Leonard Harrow, and Yuka Kadoi for having generously given me permission to use their images in this article. Every effort has been made to trace the copyright holders of Figures 4.10 and 4.27. The publisher would be pleased to hear from the copyright owner so that proper acknowledgement can be made in future editions.

various neighbouring territories, and even cultures, would exert an influence on what was produced in Anatolia. Nor is this all. The presence of numerically important Christian minorities—Greek Orthodox, Jacobites, Armenians, and Georgians—all with their own artistic traditions that had very little to do with those of the Seljuq Turks, enriched this cultural mix with a crucial further dimension. Seljuq Anatolian architecture is the medium in which these non-Muslim elements feature most prominently. Motifs derived from Armenian architecture[2] and book illumination have been identified in the sculptured portals of Divriği (see Figure 4.1),[3] while conversely, Islamic *muqarnas* ornament is found in eleventh-century work at the Armenian capital of Ani (see Figure 4.2),[4] and at numerous other sites thereafter.[5] Some scholars have gone so far as to attribute some of the major buildings of Seljuq Anatolia, such as the portal of the Ince Minare *Madrasa* in Konya,[6] to Armenian architects.[7]

Important as this topic is, however, it is not the primary focus of this chapter. Instead, this chapter will explore in detail one particular subset of these continuous cross-cultural encounters, namely the interplay between the architecture of Seljuq Anatolia and that of Seljuq Iran. The subject is surprisingly neglected given the obvious political, ethnic, and geographical links between these two states.[8]

Figure 4.1   Divriği, Ulu Cami, north portal, detail
Source: David Gye.

Figure 4.2   Ani, Church of the Holy Apostles, narthex
Source: David Gye.

Nevertheless, the increasing specialization in Islamic art militates against such attempts to take the broad view. Over the last generation or so, moreover, the architecture of Seljuq Anatolia has become a virtual preserve of Turkish scholars, and these specialists, however well they know Seljuq buildings in Turkey, rarely have direct experience of cognate Iranian monuments.[9] The present chapter, then, is a preliminary attempt to fill this gap. It is entitled 'Brick versus stone' in the belief that the difference in building material is the defining distinction between these two traditions, though numerous other differences quickly suggest themselves. What follows is essentially an overview that can hope to do no more than tilt at a complex subject.

To put the discussion into proper perspective, it is necessary to begin by pointing out that the architecture of the Seljuqs, in common with that of the smaller Anatolian principalities of the time, began in Iran, not in Anatolia. At a time when Anatolia was still largely Christian, Iranian architects working for Seljuq patrons (and here it is natural to include work done for the Khwarizmshahs in Central Asia[10] and for the Ghaznavids and Ghurids in Afghanistan,[11] since all these areas were culturally part of an Iranian *koine*) were developing classical forms for mosques and *madrasas*, mausolea and caravanserais; refining their techniques for building vaults (see Figure 4.3)

Figure 4.3   Isfahan, Friday Mosque, vaulting
Source: Jonathan Bloom.

and domes; and devising a huge range of decorative motifs and techniques. The architecture that resulted from these experiments, and
that reached maturity long before the Seljuqs of Rum had built their
first major monument, spread from Central Asia[12] and Afghanistan
in the east to the borders of Syria in the west. The empire of the Great
Seljuqs, moreover, was the prime political entity of the eastern Islamic
world. It was greater by several degrees of magnitude than that of the
Seljuqs of Rum, and disposed of correspondingly greater revenues.
The relationship between the two, not only politically but also in the
visual arts, is that of a senior and junior partner. This relationship
must be borne in mind as a corrective to the tendency to make exag-
gerated claims for the art of the Rum Seljuqs. On the other hand, it
was the Iranian and not the Anatolian world that suffered the full
annihilating force of the Mongol onslaught from 1220 onwards. As a
result, the thirteenth century is almost completely void of important
buildings in Iran,[13] Afghanistan, and Central Asia; while in Anatolia,
where Mongol rule involved much less destruction, it was a golden
age for architecture, with scores of major buildings being put up.[14] All
this has tended to skew the picture and obscure the true relationship
between the two architectural traditions.

So much for preliminaries. In what follows, to keep the discussion within manageable bounds, this chapter will concentrate on five

interrelated topics: material, form, scale, structure, and decoration. Under each of these headings the aim will be to identify how these two traditions of Seljuq architecture diverged—what their distinctive strengths are, and what links can be proposed between them. But of course these categories overlap, and besides, many Anatolian buildings of the thirteenth century are Iranian in spirit and are indeed built of brick, decorated with glazed tilework (see Figure 4.4), and some are signed by Iranian masters. In much the same way, but with an extra time lag, a group of early fourteenth-century buildings in Cairo bear the signatures of Iranian craftsmen: in this case, specialists in tile mosaic.[15]

Material

It will be convenient to begin with material, since that effectively determines everything else. The architecture of the Seljuqs of Rum is overwhelmingly, though not exclusively, of stone, with a steady emphasis on the use of dressed stone for surfaces. This stone is given a high degree of finish (see Figure 4.5). Since so much of Byzantine architecture in Anatolia, especially in the centuries after Justinian, was of brick, there was no inherent local reason for the choice of stone.

Figure 4.4   Malatya, Ulu Cami, main dome chamber
Source: David Gye.

Figure 4.5   Aksaray Han, stonework detail
Source: David Gye.

It is worth pointing out, however, that the public buildings of Syria to the south and the Armenian[16] and Georgian churches in eastern Anatolia[17] strongly favoured stone, and the latter agency may have been decisive—though the impact of Syrian architecture is clearly visible at Mardin[18] and Urfa,[19] and in many a caravanserai (see Figure 4.6).[20]

Whatever the reasons behind the preponderance of stone, its implications were manifold. Stone has to be quarried, sometimes at a considerable distance from the building operations themselves, unlike earth—the raw material for baked brick—which can be dug up at the spot. From the outset, then, it is more costly, and it is also much slower to work with, especially when fine ashlar masonry is the aim. This has its own distinctive beauty as a wall surface but it requires skilled, time-intensive labour. Moreover, Rum Seljuq architects tended to favour decoration at the expense of structural innovation; and it follows almost logically that this predisposed them to conservatism. It was their marked lack of enthusiasm for spatial experiment that may conversely account for the emphasis that Rum Seljuq architects accorded the principal façade, making it the cynosure of the entire building. Hence the series of grand, imposing portals, proudly salient from the curtain walls on either side, which are the glory of Rum Seljuq architecture (see Figure 4.7).

Figure 4.6 Alay Han, *girikh* ornament
Source: David Gye.

Figure 4.7   Sultan Han, Aksaray, main façade
Source: David Gye.

Dramatic *muqarnas* hoods and richly applied ornament single out such portals even more assertively (see Figure 4.8).

These draw the eye, of course, as their architects no doubt fully intended; and this leads almost logically to a corresponding lack of emphasis on the plain surfaces of the rest of the principal façade, apart perhaps from a succession of widely spaced buttresses (see Figure 4.9).

And the use of carefully dressed stone for the subsidiary façades, which almost follows from its use on the main façade, has aesthetic implications: it argues a desire to achieve a consistent visual effect, and indicates too that Anatolian Seljuq architects saw the building as a whole, however much attention they lavished on the centrepiece of its principal façade. On the other hand, it is possible to argue that the use of baked brick throughout a building lends it a greater integrity and sense of content (see Figure 4.10) than can be achieved by the use of rubble with ashlar facing.

That said, in many Rum Seljuq monuments, the masons create a variegated wall surface by the use of spolia,[21] windows,[22] coursing in bands of uneven width,[23] and marble—sometimes bi-coloured—for grace notes (see Figure 4.11).[24] Nevertheless, the differences between

Figure 4.8 Sivas, Burujirdi *Madrasa*, portal
Source: David Gye.

Figure 4.9   Sa'd al-Din Han, façade
Source: David Gye.

Figure 4.10   Kerkhi, Turkmenistan, Alemberdar mausoleum, now destroyed
Source: V.Pilyavski, *Pamyatniki Arkhitekturi Turkmenistana* (Leningrad, 1974).

Figure 4.11 Sa'd al-Din Han, marble ornament, detail
Source: David Gye.

baked brick and worked stone are such that even the same form, for example the tomb tower, changes its nature in some elusive way along with the change in material. The gain in precision entails, it seems, a corresponding loss of mass.

Form

As already noted, Rum Seljuq buildings—such as those of Erzurum,[25] Sivas,[26] Kayseri,[27] and Konya[28]—are much more focused on facades than their earlier counterparts in the Iranian world. This may reflect the impact of slightly earlier stone buildings in Syria,[29] and indeed Redford explicitly states, 'It was not, then, the exuberance of Iranian stucco work translated into stone, nor Iranian Seljuq styles in tile and brickwork that were chosen by the Rum Seljuqs. Instead, the pious architecture of Sunni Syria served as the model for this style.'[30] One may note a concomitant lack of interest in lateral facades, which are very much lower and kept plain. But it is in the development of the interior space of the mosques (and for that matter, *madrasas*, though here the scarcity of Iranian examples inhibits the discussion[31]) that the distinctive character of Anatolian Seljuq architecture asserts itself, and it is here too that its differences from Iranian precedents are plainest. With the disappearance of the courtyard, or its reduction to a mere well sunk into the middle of the roof—a modification imposed by the Turkish climate—came a critical diminution of ventilation, lighting, and, above all, space. These interiors are low, dark, and cramped. Their piers are massive but stumpy, their vaults too low to suggest aspiration (see Figure 4.12).

Figure 4.12   Malatya, Ulu Cami, interior
Source: David Gye.

The hypostyle plan is common, but—unlike the version so preva-
lent in the Arab lands—lacks the contrast between closed and open
space and the sheer scale, which together create the characteristic
amplitude of that type with its sense of endless space. Even when the
dome over the *mihrab* is introduced, as at Dunaysir,[32] Mayyafariqin,[33]
and elsewhere,[34] it is robbed of much of its potential effect because it
is too small (covering only a single bay), or is repeated (pairs or trios
of domes were a common feature), or lacks an *iwan* to single it out
and to create a sense of expectancy. In the case of mausolea, the lack
of formal variety is all the more marked, given that over 160 of these
buildings survive.[35] Numerous Iranian types—such as many of the
subdivisions of tombs with triangular flanges or engaged columns,[36]
or those with developed galleries[37]—are not known in Anatolia. The
common octagonal type tends to an exclusive focus on one side, where
not only the doorway but also the principal ornament and inscriptions
are to be found.[38] This solution, too, simplifies the Iranian model.
Yet there are also other elements at work; the high drums and conical roofs of Anatolian Seljuq tomb towers perhaps owe something to
Armenian churches,[39] and it is surely significant that these forms do
not occur in the Iranian world. These mausolea, no less than the dome
chambers of Rum Seljuq mosques,[40] insistently pose the question of
how well brick forms translate into stone. It is precisely because so

much gets lost in the transfer from one material to another that Rum Seljuq architects gradually developed an idiom that dispensed with Iranian precedent and, as one can see with hindsight, foreshadowed Ottoman modes. They gloried in stone just as their Iranian counterparts gloried in baked brick (see Figure 4.13).

In many cases the stone of Seljuq mausolea, which is beautifully cut and beautifully weathered, is itself the principal ornament.[41] Architectonic articulation is not only intrinsically more sparingly used than in Iran, but also has a much more limited vocabulary. The deep or shallow, broad or narrow, lofty or low niches and reveals that animate so many Iranian portals (see Figure 4.14) give way to densely carved overall ornament in a single plane.

All this can be seen clearly enough by comparing a typical Anatolian portal[42] with an Iranian version of the same general form.[43] The same exercise can be carried out in an even more telling way with the zone of transition. The result is that the visual interest shifts from the articulation of space (see Figure 4.15)[44] to the patterning of surface (see Figure 4.16).[45]

Notwithstanding this trend, the proximity of Seljuq Anatolia to the classical world predisposed its architects to deploy a range of classical forms such as columns, capitals, mouldings, and the like, to the extent that the courtyard façade of the Friday mosque of Diyarbakr looks more like a Roman *scenae frons* than an Islamic building.[46]

Figure 4.13   Bukhara, mausoleum of the Samanids
Source: Jonathan Bloom.

Figure 4.14 Ashtarjan, Friday Mosque, portal
Source: David Gye.

Scale

This element requires only a brief discussion here. The basic fact is that most Iranian forms undergo some degree of reduction in the process of transfer to Seljuq Anatolia, and naturally this makes them less monumental. This is true of virtually every form—mosque, *madrasa*,

Figure 4.15 Isfahan, Friday Mosque, north dome, interior
Source: David Gye.

Figure 4.16 Konya, Alaeddin Cami, *mihrab* and Turkish triangles
Source: David Gye.

caravanserai, minaret, and mausoleum. In the case of the first three of these building types, the absence of a courtyard, or its presence on a much-diminished scale, is a key factor. In a single stroke it greatly reduces the options for lateral expansion. Thus there is no parallel in Seljuq Anatolia for the great double-courtyard caravanserais of the eastern Iranian world, like Ribat-i Sharaf (see Figure 4.17),[47] Akcha-Qal'a,[48] and Ribat-i Malik.[49]

The two principal surviving pre-Mongol *madrasa*s in the eastern Islamic world, namely Zuzan and Shah-i Mashhad,[50] are on a scale unmatched by any of the dozens of Anatolian *madrasa*s built during the thirteenth century. Nor does Seljuq Anatolia have any mosques, not even the great Artuqid domes of Mayyafariqin and Dunaysir,[51] whose raw dimensions challenge the great Seljuq mosques like Qazvin[52] or Isfahan.[53] The *qibla* domes of these two mosques have a diameter of 15 metres,[54] which is more than 50 per cent larger than the dome of the major dynastic mosque of the Rum Seljuqs, that of Alaeddin in Konya.[55] The surface area of that mosque is also significantly less than that of these two Iranian buildings, as is the height of the dome over the *mihrab*. Indeed, that dome is, so to speak, elbowed out of prominence by the pointed roof of the mausoleum of 'Ala al-Din Kayqubad himself, which is the principal accent of the mosque's skyline as seen from afar. The imposing height of so many Seljuq tomb towers in Iran is scaled down dramatically in the Turkish examples of this building type; the average Anatolian tomb tower is

Figure 4.17   Ribat-i Sharaf, second court, portal
Source: Jonathan Bloom.

no more than 15 metres high, whereas many Iranian examples are more than double that height, as demonstrated by the examples at Rayy and Radkan West (see Figure 4.18).

It is the same story with minarets: one has only to compare not just three-tiered Iranian minarets like those of Jam[56] and Ziyar[57] but also single shafts like those at Khusraugird (see Figure 4.19) and Damghan[58] with their Anatolian counterparts to be struck by the degree of downsizing that occurs.

Most of these Seljuq Turkish minarets have thicker shafts than Iranian minarets, which tends to make them look stumpy, and the cusps on these minarets visually slow them down, so to speak, thereby reducing their apparent height. Yet that very feature of cusps identifies them in form as proto-Ottoman, and it is interesting to note that the lesson was learned by later architects, who (while continuing to make the cusped balcony a major feature of their design) substantially reduced their diameter and increased their height, thereby transforming them in the process. The minaret of the Ince Minare *Madrasa*, largely toppled by a lightning strike in 1901,[59] and the Yivli Minare at Antalya (see Figure 4.20)[60] do, however, stress absolute height, and extend it illusionistically with slender engaged columns and a conical lantern.

But these are exceptions. The lesson to be learned from these striking disparities of scale is not that the ambitions—or perhaps even the resources—of patrons in Seljuq Anatolia were less than those of the Great Seljuqs, but rather that brick was not only very much cheaper and quicker to produce than stone but also more flexible and ductile as a building material—easier to work with—and much more apt to encourage experiment. Moreover, certain devices of symmetry, balance, massing, and rhythm depend on the use of large spaces to be fully effective. The same goes for proportional ratios, and the alternation of open and closed spaces, of solids and voids. The modest scale of so many thirteenth-century Anatolian buildings discouraged such experiments. To take a single example, the sheer weight of architectonic articulation deployed over an extensive surface changes the impact of a building. If that surface is too small, such articulation can swamp it, making it seem uncomfortably busy. These reflections may also help to explain the pre-eminent role of the portal in so many Anatolian buildings, the way it seems to gather to itself the lion's share of the available decoration, and the corresponding relative neglect of the rest of the outer walls.

Figure 4.18 Radkan West, tomb tower
Source: Leonard Harrow.

Figure 4.19   Khusraugird, minaret
Source: Jonathan Bloom.

Structure

The differences between stone and brick that have just been mentioned were of crucial importance here. Seljuq architecture in Iran owes its spatial diversity to the adoption of a relatively light and thus easily portable brick, 25 centimetres square and 4 centimetres thick.

Figure 4.20   Antalya, Yivli minaret
Source: David Gye.

Pre-Seljuq bricks were often much larger than this—for example, 35 centimetres square by 7 centimetres thick—and were thus cumbersome to use. In Sasanian architecture in Central Asia, mud bricks of 40 centimetres square by 8 cm thick could weigh 24 kilogrammes. It is easy to conceive how liberating it was to use the lighter brick, especially in conjunction with quick-setting lime mortar that enabled the mason to dispense with centring and to create vaults often only one or two bricks thick. This new technology enabled the architect to work by eye. Hence the well-nigh incredible variety of Seljuq vaulting in Iran, with scores of innovative types, each of them deriving extra impact from the others around it. Hence too the cumulative impact of such vaulted interiors, whether in mosques like the Isfahan *jami*[61] or caravanserais like Ribat-i Sharaf.[62] Huge domes with spans of unusual width were now constructed—half a dozen of them in the Isfahan oasis alone. As Lutyens said, 'Do not speak of Persian brickwork; but rather of Persian brick magic.'[63] The inspiring combination of wider spans, thinner vaults, faster work, cheaper material, and no centring encouraged architects to be more adventurous, for failure was much less costly than in the case of stone-built structures. Meanwhile, in Anatolia some architects still followed a vogue for trabeate architecture, including wooden mosques (see Figure 4.21).

Figure 4.21   Beyşehir, Eşrefoğlu Cami, interior
Source: David Gye.

And even in the medium of stone, theirs is not the architecture of daring vaults, dangerously wide spans, lofty domes, and novel bridging solutions in the transition zone between the square chamber below and the dome on a circular collar above. Not for them the ever thinner bearing walls pierced by large openings. Indeed, many of their structures can fairly be described as over-built, with broad, squat piers set too close together, relatively low vaults and walls that are much thicker than they need to be. And the architects had to use wooden centring to put up such vaults. To be fair, they did evolve their own distinctive solution to the problems posed by the zone of transition, developing the system of so-called 'Turkish triangles' that ironed out the contrasting planes in that zone (see Figure 4.22).

But this solution—reducing as it did the plastic, curvilinear, and volumetric quality of the pendentive to a flat, smoothly bevelled surface—quickly became standard issue and generated few variants. Where Iranian architects built complex *muqarnas* domes, as at Sin,[64] their colleagues in Anatolia sometimes used the much more primitive corbelling technique for the same effect, as at the Friday Mosque of Erzurum, whose original construction dates to 1179.[65] The *muqarnas* in Anatolian buildings are usually confined to intrinsically safer places than domes; the favoured location is a

Figure 4.22   Konya, Ince Minare *Madrasa*, interior
Source: David Gye.

semi-dome in a portal, as a solid infill to the upper part of the great entrance arch. This use of the *muqarnas* is scarcely inventive, and there are dozens of examples of it in thirteenth-century Anatolia (see Figure 4.23).[66]

Ornament

Here the picture is much more complicated. Stone has properties denied to baked brick. It allows extra crispness and curvilinearity, and hence a fuller range of motifs than brick and even terracotta. It was, therefore, better suited for exterior ornament, and was enthusiastically developed for this purpose. That said, the carved stone ornament of Seljuq Anatolian architecture draws on a curiously limited pool of motifs in which vegetal elements of all kinds, including the arabesque, are far outnumbered by rectilinear geometrical patterns, especially knotted and polygonal designs of various kinds. These tend to be built up in superposed blocks, each bearing the same pattern, almost like a vertical grid (see Figure 4.24). That tends to look monotonous, for there is no overall articulating framework to act as a counterweight to, and to organize, the dense decorative infill. Thus this kind of carved ornament, for all its virtuoso execution and its undeniably sculptural

Figure 4.23   Sivas, Gök *Madrasa*, portal, detail of *muqarnas*
Source: David Gye.

Figure 4.24   Ağzikara Han, *muqarnas*
Source: David Gye.

quality, operates essentially as all-over decoration, rather than being carefully calibrated to correspond to the principal accents of the architecture that it embellishes.[67]

It would, however, be mistaken to give the impression that Rum Seljuq architectural ornament essentially consists of stone carving, even though that form of decoration accounts for most of what survives. There is also no lack of glazed brick used for inscriptions[68] and for brick patterns in a thoroughly Persian idiom,[69] and numerous examples of tile mosaic or glazed terracotta, especially for *mihrabs*,[70] and glazed inscriptions against a plaster ground.[71] Often enough these compositions are the work of Persian craftsmen, as their *nisbas* attest: al-Tusi, al-Arrani, al-Maraghi, al-Marandi, and so on.[72] These men were probably refugees from the Mongol invasions.[73] Some of their work can be slotted quite precisely into the evolution of colour accents in Persian architecture insofar as surviving buildings allow that development to be traced (see Figure 4.25).

For instance, the work of al-Tusi—a craftsman who had travelled some 1,500 miles west of his home town—in the Sirçalı *Madrasa* in Konya dated 640/1242 (see Figure 4.26),[74] takes up the story of glazed tilework just at the point reached in the immediately pre-Mongol *madrasa* of Zuzan, dated 619/1218.[75]

Figure 4.25   Sivas, Şifa'iye *Madrasa* and Hospital interior
Source: David Gye.

Figure 4.26   Konya, Sirçali *Madrasa*, tilework
Source: David Gye.

Al-Tusi—and indeed Konya as a whole, for it was after all the capital city— is an exception[76] in that this recognizably Persian work is, on the whole, confined to eastern Anatolia, and thus those parts of the plateau that are closest to Iran. It would, therefore, not be far wrong to place the western border of this encroachment of Iranian modes of glazed ornament in the thirteenth century around the region of Kayseri.[77] Perhaps the earliest recorded example of this spread of Persian modes into the architecture of Anatolia is the Friday mosque of Van,[78] probably of the early to mid-twelfth century and thus outside the time-frame of the Anatolian material discussed in this chapter. It was in many ways a sister building to some of the great Friday mosques of Seljuq Iran; from its *muqarnas* squinches echoing those of Gulpaygan[79] to its stucco inscriptions set within a serpentine band undulating along the walls of the dome chamber, as at Qazvin.[80] No examples of glazed ornament were found in the excavations carried out at the site in the 1960s.[81]

Despite the obvious strength of these links with Iranian practice, it is important to remember that in some uses of tilework, especially those found in secular contexts such as the Seljuq palaces at Kubadabad and elsewhere,[82] the Rum Seljuq achievement outperforms that of Seljuq Iran. These underglaze-painted, *mina'i* and lustre tiles—square, hexagonal, or star-shaped—present a remarkable range of motifs: inscriptions, courtly figures including musicians and huntsmen,[83] fish,[84] birds, and animals galore such as bulls,[85] dogs, gazelles, and elephants—also including creatures of fantasy such as phoenixes, dragons,[86] and double-headed eagles (see Figure 4.27).

They evoke a rich iconographical heritage whose symbolic resonances echo those of the huge corpus of such themes found on mosques, *madrasas*, caravanserais, and, above all, mausolea

Figure 4.27　Diyarbakr palace, tile with eagle design
Source: Aslanapa, *Türkische Fliesen und Keramik in Anatolien* (Istanbul: Baha Matbaasi, 1965).

throughout the thirteenth century.[87] This repertoire was by no means confined to the Seljuqs of Rum but was widespread among the many lesser principalities of the time—Artuqids, Mengujukids, Danishmendids, the Shah-i Arman, and others. It is also found on the coinage of most of these dynasties, which underlines its close connection with royal iconography.[88] The expansion of this pictorial tradition to architectural sculpture makes such carvings perhaps the most distinctive defining feature of the architecture of Anatolia in the thirteenth century, and it deserves more detailed examination here.[89]

Some of these themes, like the striding lion with a sun-face partially glimpsed behind its body, or the lion–bull combat,[90] or the raptor with its prey, have a history stretching back for millennia, a history closely linked to royal power and sometimes also to astrology. Other themes have apotropaic significance or serve as quasi-heraldic royal identifiers; yet others have mythical, celestial,[91] planetary, paradisal, or zodiacal significance. Yet more remain at best partially explained—winged horses, griffins, sphinxes, unicorns, sirens, or harpies, (see Figure 4.28) and even more monstrous combinations like winged dog-headed felines.

They draw inspiration from multiple sources[92]—Rome, Byzantium, Sasanian Iran, and even China; but above all they evoke the preoccupations of the immemorial nomadic world of the Eurasian steppe. The

Figure 4.28 Niğde, tomb of Khudavend Khatun, sirens
Source: David Gye.

atmosphere of that world, and its Turkish character—uninflected by Islamic norms and forms—come across far more distinctly in these carvings, for which stone is the more natural medium, than in the architectural decoration, or indeed even the art, produced by the Great Seljuqs in Iran. The reason for this may well be that the bulk of the patronage that was responsible for twelfth-century Seljuq art in Iran was Persian rather than Turkish. That balance seems to have reversed itself in Anatolia in the following century. Stucco rather than stone answered the Iranian urge for sculpture, and the repertoire of the stucco-worker by and large excluded representational art. Conversely, the general neglect of stucco-work in favour of stone-carving even for interiors is a defining marker of Rum Seljuq architecture.

One must concede that the application of this figural or animal sculpture, which as already noted flies in the face of well-established Islamic custom, was not always well-judged and indeed, as the façade of the Çifte *Madrasa* in Erzurum (among many other examples) shows with its bulky so-called 'Tree of Life',[93] could be downright crass.[94] Moreover, the fact that the neighbouring Christian cultures of Georgia and Armenia also used stone rather than brick, and also developed a wide repertoire of figural and animal sculpture (see Figure 4.29), including many hybrids and other creatures of fantasy,

Figure 4.29   Ani cathedral, eagle
Source: David Gye.

also helps to explain the settled popularity of these themes in Anatolia in this period.

The same kind of interchange helps to explain the fashion for chequerboard polychrome masonry, shallow blind arcades, scalloped tympana, torus mouldings, window frames, and a marked preference for relief ornament.[95] In spite of this rich heritage of applied sculptural ornament, thirteenth-century Anatolia presents a very different achievement from that of twelfth-century Iran, where patterned brickwork, carved terracotta, highlights of blue glaze, and colourful stucco in huge compositions gave craftsmen an *embarrass de choix*.

This architectural sculpture in stone required extreme precision in its rendering and, therefore, Iranian brick and even terracotta ornament simply could not match it. And stucco, the preferred medium for the sculptural urges of Iranian craftsmen charged with decorating architecture, was too fragile a medium to be suitable for use on external façades. On the other hand, stone-carving was more impressive up close rather than at a distance, for the relief was usually not high enough to cast a strong shadow. It was also small in scale. In this respect the decorative brickwork of Iran had a more dramatic impact. And for all the intensity of ornament on the portals[96] or *mihrabs*[97] of thirteenth-century Anatolia, there is much less acreage

Figure 4.30   Tim, Arab-Ata mausoleum, stucco panels above doorway
Source: Yuka Kadoi.

of decoration, inside and out, than in the buildings of Seljuq Iran; one has only to contrast the ornament in caravanserais like Ribat-i Sharaf, Ribat-i Mahi,[98] and Daya Khatun[99] with the plainness of their Seljuq Anatolian counterparts. That larger surface area compelled Iranian architects to plan their decorative ensembles on a larger scale than those of their Anatolian colleagues, and this in turn favoured the intensive development of articulating schemes that were essentially architectonic. Such articulation enlivened entire façades in a way that dense, small-scale, carved ornament could never achieve (see Figure 4.30). In short, the differences between Anatolian and Iranian Seljuq architecture boil down to differences in scale, whether in form, structure, or even decoration. And it was the use of brick rather than stone as the basic building material that underpinned all these differences.

Notes

1. On the southern coast of the Black Sea, Sinope was probably the major emporium for this trade. On the Aegean, the corresponding port was Alanya/Ala'iyya. The town still preserves its docking facilities that date back to the thirteenth century and are unique in the Islamic world. They comprise a monumental sequence of five deep adjoining vaulted bays, with skylights to allow for the easy loading and unloading of ships. See David T. Rice, *Islamic Art* (London: Thames & Hudson, 1965), p. 164 and pl. 161.

2. Dorothy Lamb, 'Notes on the Seljouk Buildings at Konia', *Annual of the British School at Athens* XXI (1914–16): pp. 52–4; J. Michael Rogers, *Patronage in Seljuk Anatolia 1200–1300* (University of Oxford: unpublished D.Phil. thesis, 1972), pp. 138–43, 145–9; Barbara Brend, 'The Patronage of Fahr ad-Din, 'Ali ibn al-Husain and the Work of Kaluk ibn 'Abd Allah in the Development of the Decoration of Portals in Thirteenth Century Anatolia', *Kunst des Orients* (*KdO*) 10, no. 1–2 (1975): pp. 173–5.

3. J. Michael Rogers, 'Recent work on Seljuq Anatolia', *KdO* 6 (1969): pp. 153–61, especially pp. 156–60.

4. Paolo Cuneo, *Architettura armena: dal quarto al diciannovesimo secolo ... con testi e contributi di Tommaso Breccia Fratadocchi ... [et al.]*, vol. 2 (Rome: De Luca, 1988), p. 797, no. 5 and Paolo Cuneo, *L'architettura della scuola regionale di Ani nell'Armenia medievale* (Rome: Accademia Nazionale dei Lincei, Quaderno N. 235, 1977), pls Xa, XIVa, and LXIVa, d, and e.

5. Cuneo, *Architettura armena*, vol. 2, p. 797, nos. 1–4 and 6–9.

6. Julius H. Löytved, *Konia: Inschriften der seldschukischen Bauten* (Berlin: Julius Springer, 1907), pp. 69–71, with the reading Kelul b. 'Abdallah for the name of the architect (p. 70); Rogers, *Patronage in Seljuk Anatolia*, pp. 174–7.

7. Rogers, 'Recent work', p. 155; Brend, 'Patronage of Fahr ad-Din', pp. 171–7.

8. For a preliminary statement of the problem, see Rogers, 'Recent work', pp. 138–46. See also Howard Crane, 'Anatolian Saljuq architecture and its links to Saljuq Iran', in *The Art of the Saljuqs in Iran and Anatolia – Proceedings of a Symposium Held in Edinburgh in 1982*, ed. Robert Hillenbrand (Costa Mesa, California: Mazda Publishers, 1994), pp. 263–8. More recently, see Richard P. McClary, 'From Nakhchivan to Kemah: The western extent of brick Persianate funerary architecture in the sixth/twelfth century AD', *Iran* 52 (2015): pp. 119–42 and Richard P. McClary, 'Brick Muqarnas on Rum Saljuq Buildings—The Introduction of an Iranian Decorative Technique into the Architecture of Anatolia', *Funun/Kunsttexte.de* 3 (2014): pp. 1–11. See also Carl F. Riter, 'Persian and Turkish Architectural Decoration: The Interchange of Techniques: 11th through 14th Centuries', *OA*, New Series 15 (1969): pp. 96–104, and Yolande Crowe, 'The Façade of the Hospital at Divrigi', *AARP* 2 (1972): pp. 107–8.

9. An obvious and distinguished exception here is Professor Gönül Öney.

10. Vladimir Piliavsky, ed., *Pamyatniki Arkhitekturi Turkmenistana* (Leningrad: Obshchestvo okhrani pamyatnikov istorii i kul'turi Turkmenskoi CCR, 1974), pp. 158–229.

11. This topic has been transformed in recent years by the numerous publications of Finbarr B. Flood, culminating in his recent prize-winning book *Objects of Translation: Material Culture and Medieval "Hindu-Muslim" Encounter* (Princeton and Oxford: Princeton University Press, 2009). The bibliography for that book lists on p. 327 some of his key articles on Ghurid art.

12. Galina A. Pugachenkova, *Puti razvitiya arkhitektury yuzhnogo Turkmenistana pory rabovladeniya i feodalizma*, (Moscow: Izdatel'niya, 1958), pp. 162–350.

13. Donald N. Wilber, *The Architecture of Islamic Iran: The Il-Khanid Period* (Princeton: Princeton University Press, 1955), pp. 104–26.

14. Derek Hill and Oleg Grabar, *Islamic Architecture and Its Decoration A.D. 800–1500: A Photographic Survey*, 2nd ed. (London: Faber and Faber, 1967), pls. 328–514. See Patricia Blessing, *Rebuilding Anatolia after the Mongol Conquest. Islamic Architecture in the Lands of Rum, 1240–1330* (Farnham and Burlington: Ashgate Publishing Company, 2014), pp. 25–9, 39–121.

15. Claude Prost, *Revêtements Céramiques dans les Monuments Musulmans de l'Égypte*, Mémoires publiés par les membres de l'Institut Français d'Archéologie Orientale du Caire, XL (Cairo: l'Institut Français d'Archéologie Orientale du Caire, 1917), pp. 1–48; Michael Meinecke, 'Die Mamlukischen Faiencemosaikdekorationen: Eine Werkstätte aus Tabriz in Kairo (1330–1350)', *KdO* 11 (1976–7): pp. 85–144.

16. Walter Bachmann, *Kirchen und Moscheen in Armenien und Kurdistan* (Leipzig: J.C. Hinrichs'sche Buchhandlung, 1913).

17. David Winfield, 'Some Early Medieval Figure Sculpture from North-East Turkey', *JWCI* 31 (1968): pp. 33–72.

18. Deniz Beyazit, *Le décor architectural artuqide en pierre de Mardin placé dans son contexte regional*, 2 vols (unpublished Ph.D diss., Département d'Art et d'Archéologie, Université de Paris I Panthéon-Sorbonne, 2009); Albert Gabriel and Jean Sauvaget, *Voyages Archéologiques dans la Turquie Orientale*, vol. 1 (Paris: E. de Boccard, 1940), pp. 11–44.

19. Gabriel and Sauvaget, *Voyages Archéologiques*, vol. 1, pp. 279–86.

20. Hakkı Acun, *Anadolu Selçuklu Dönemi Kervansarayları* (Ankara: İŞ Bankası, 2007) pp. 194–235 (Sa'd al-Din Han and Sari Han near Avanos), 274–303 (Susuz Han and Ak Han), and 453 (Sultan Han near Aksaray).

21. Kurt Erdmann, *Das anatolische Karavansaray des 13. Jahrhunderts*, vol. 3 (*Istanbuler Forschungen*, Bd. 21 and 31) (Berlin: Verlag Gebr. Mann, 1961–76), pp. 89–92.

22. Erdmann, *Karavansaray*, vol. 1, Abb. 142 (Sultan Han near Kayseri).

23. Erdmann, *Karavansaray*, vol. 1, p. 197 (Zazadin Han/Sa'd al-Din Han).

24. Erdmann, *Karavansaray*, vol. 1, p. 194 (Zazadin Han/Sa'd al-Din Han).

25. Rahmi H. Ünal, *Les Monuments Islamiques Anciens de la Ville d'Erzurum et de sa Région* (Paris: A. Maisonneuve, 1968); Blessing, *Rebuilding Anatolia*, pp. 130–42, with references to earlier bibliography.

26. Albert Gabriel, *Monuments Turcs d'Anatolie*, vol. 2 (Paris: E. de Boccard, 1931–34), pls XXXIV–LX; Blessing, *Rebuilding Anatolia*, pp. 69–121, with references to earlier bibliography and R.P. McClary, *The Rum Saljuq Architecture of Anatolia 1170–1220* (unpublished PhD diss., University of Edinburgh, 2015), pp. 127–47 and 274–380.

27. Gabriel, *Monuments Turcs*, vol. 1, pp. 19–100.

28. Löytved, *Konia*, pp. 29–36, 42, 45, 47, 50, 52, 69–70. See also Blessing, *Rebuilding Anatolia*, pp. 21–67, with references to earlier bibliography.

29. Keppel A. C. Creswell, *The Muslim Architecture of Egypt*, vol. 2, *Ayyubids and Early Bahrite Mamluks A.D. 1171–1326* (Oxford: Oxford University Press, 1959), pp. 106–23 and figs 47, 51, 55, 61 and 63; see, too, for the particular case of Aleppo, Yasser Tabbaa, *Constructions of Power and Piety in Medieval Aleppo* (University Park, Pennsylvania: Pennsylvania State University Press, 1997); and, more generally, Yasser Tabbaa, *The Transformation of Islamic Art during the Sunni Revival* (Seattle and London: University of Washington Press, 2001), especially Chapter 6 (pp. 137–62) and pls 74–84.

30. Scott Redford, 'The Alaeddin Mosque in Konya', *AA* 51, no. 1–2 (1991): p. 71.

31. The major examples whose identification as *madrasas* is uncontested are those of Zuzan and Shah-i Mashhad. For the first, see Sheila S. Blair, 'The Madrasa at Zuzan: Islamic Architecture in Eastern Iran on the Eve of the Mongol Invasions', *Muqarnas* 3 (1985): pp. 75–91. For the second, see Michael J. Casimir and Bernt Glatzer, 'Šah-i Mašhad: A Recently Discovered Madrasah of the Ghurid Period in Gharghistan (Afghanistan)', *EW*, n. s. 21, nos 1–2 (1971): pp. 53–68.

32. Gabriel and Sauvaget, *Voyages*, vol. 1, pp. 45–51 and vol. 2, pls XXVI–XXXII.

33. Gertrude Bell, *Palace and Mosque at Ukhaidir: A Study in Early Mohammadan Architecture* (Oxford: Clarendon Press, 1914), pp. 159–60 and pls 84, figs 3, 92, and 93, fig. 2; Gabriel and Sauvaget, *Voyages*, vol. 1, 221–8 and vol. 2, pls LXXVII–LXXIX; Tom Sinclair, 'Early Artuqid Mosque Architecture', in *The Art of Syria and the Jazira 1100–1250*, ed. Julian Raby, Oxford Studies in Islamic Art, vol. 1 (Oxford: Oxford University Press, 1985), pp. 49–68.

34. For example, Harput and Siirt/Is'ird (Robert Hillenbrand, *Islamic Architecture: Form, Function, and Meaning*, 2nd ed. [Edinburgh: Edinburgh University Press, 2000], figs 2.201 and 2.205).

35. Ülkü Ü. Bates, *Anatolian Mausoleums of the Twelfth, Thirteenth and Fourteenth Centuries* (PhD diss., University of Michigan, 1970), vol. 1, pp. 22–371, lists 163; the second volume of her thesis (pp. 372–494) gives an overview. See also Ülkü Ü. Bates, 'The Development of the Mausoleum in Seljuk Anatolia', *Belleten* 34, no. 133, 1970; and Ülkü Ü. Bates, 'An Introduction to the Study of the Anatolian Türbe and Its Inscriptions as Historical Documents', *STY* 4 (1970–1): pp. 73–84.

36. Robert Hillenbrand, *The Tomb Towers of Iran to 1550* (unpublished D.Phil thesis, University of Oxford, 1974), vol.1, pp. 265 and 267.

37. For example, Bukhara, Sangbast, and Merv; see Arthur Pope U. Pope, *Persian Architecture* (London and New York: Thames & Hudson, 1965), figs 77–9, 104, and 149.

38. For example, Oktay Aslanapa, *Turkish Art and Architecture*, trans. from Turkish by Aidan Mill (New York: Prager, 1971), pls 61 and 127 (Divriği, mausoleum of Sitte Melik and Karaman, mausoleum of 'Ala' al-Din Bek).

39. Cuneo, *Architettura armena*, vol. 2, pp. 752–60.

40. For examples, see Aslanapa, *Turkish Art*, pls 3, 4, and 83 (Mayyafariqin, Dunaysir, and Beyşehir).

41. This is best appreciated in colour: see Sonia P. Seherr-Thoss and Hans C. Seherr-Thoss, *Design and Color in Islamic Architecture: Afghanistan, Iran, Turkey* (Washington, D.C.: Smithsonian Institution Press, 1968), pls 100–2 and 115 (Erzurum and Kayseri); and Markus Hattstein and Peter Delius, eds, *Islam: Art and Architecture* (Cologne: Könemann, 2000), p. 375 (Kayseri and Niğde).

42. Such as that of Muzaffar Burujirdi at Sivas, see Gabriel, *Monuments Turcs*, vol. 2, pl. XLVII.

43. For example, the Buyid façade of the Jurjir mosque in Isfahan, see Hill and Grabar, *Islamic Architecture*, pl. 312; or the Haruniya at Tus, see Pope, *Persian Architecture*, pl. 250. Both of these are good examples of how to exploit shadow lines. Alternatively, to choose a more lavishly decorated example, Ashtarjan, see Seherr-Thoss and Seherr-Thoss, *Design and Color in Islamic Architecture*, pl. 52. Seljuq three-dimensional

stone ornament in Anatolia operates within a much more constricted register. See, for example, Seherr-Thoss and Seherr-Thoss, *Design and Color in Islamic Architecture*, pls 109 and 111 (Sultan Han near Kayseri).

44. As in the north dome of the Isfahan *jami'*, see Seherr-Thoss and Seherr-Thoss, *Design and Color in Islamic Architecture*, pl. 10.

45. As in the Karatay *madrasa* in Konya, see Seherr-Thoss and Seherr-Thoss, *Design and Color in Islamic Architecture*, pl. 117.

46. As noted a century ago by Josef Strzygowski; see Max van Berchem and Josef Strzygowski, *Amida* (Heidelberg: Carl Winter's Universitätsbuchhandlung and Paris: Ernest Leroux, 1910), pp. 207–12; for a colour plate, see Hattstein and Delius, *Islam*, p. 380.

47. Muhammad Y. Kiyani, *Discoveries from Robat-e Sharaf* (Tehran: National Organization for the Preservation of Historical Monuments, 1981), pp. 13–14; André Godard, 'Ribat-i Sharaf', *Athar-e Iran (AeI)* 4, no. 1 (1949): pp. 7–43.

48. Pugachenkova, *Puti*, pp. 227–9.

49. Nina B. Nemtseva, 'Rabat-i Malik', in *Khudozhestvennaya Kul'tura Srednei Azii IX–XIII Vekov*, ed. I. Lazar Rempel (Tashkent: Izdatel'stvo Literaturi i Iskusstva Imeni Gafura Gulyama, 1983), pp. 112–42.

50. See endnote 31.

51. Sinclair, 'Artuqid Mosque Architecture', pp. 50–65.

52. Donald N. Wilber and Janine Sourdel-Thomine, *Monuments Seljoukides de Qazwin en Iran, REI Hors-Série* 8 (Paris, 1973): p. 218.

53. Oleg Grabar, *The Great Mosque of Isfahan* (New York: New York University Press, 1990).

54. Robert Hillenbrand, 'Seljuq Dome Chambers in North-West Iran', *Iran* 14 (1976): p. 96 for a table of Seljuq domes; repr. in Robert Hillenbrand, *Studies in Medieval Islamic Architecture*, vol. 2 (Collected Articles) (London: Pindar Press, 2006), p. 347; Redford, 'Alaeddin Mosque', p. 61; Wilber and Sourdel-Thomine, *Qazwin*, p. 26.

55. Redford, 'Alaeddin Mosque', p. 72.

56. See now Janine Sourdel-Thomine, *Le Minaret Ghouride de Jam: Un Chef d'Oeuvre du XII. Siècle* (Paris: Académie des inscriptions et belles-lettres, 2004).

57. Myron B. Smith, 'The Manars of Isfahan', *AeI* 1, no. 2 (1936): pp. 341–6. The other minarets presented in this pioneering article show that Ziyar, though the highest in the whole group, has several parallels whose height is only slightly less.

58. For these minarets, and a general discussion of Iranian minarets of the period, see Jonathan M. Bloom, *The Minaret* (Edinburgh: Edinburgh University Press, 2013), pp. 242–72 and figs 10.18 and 10.19.

59. Löytved, *Konia*, p. 69, with a plate of how it looked before this disaster.

60. Aslanapa, *Turkish Art*, pl. 120.

61. Eugenio Galdieri, *Esfahan: Masğid-i Ğum'a 3: Research and Restoration Activities 1973–1978, New Observations 1979–1982* (Rome: ISMEO, 1984),

pp. 120–1, figs 41–2, 129, figs 54 and 149, fig. 87; Arthur U. Pope and Phyllis Ackerman, eds, *A Survey of Persian Art from Prehistoric Times to the Present* (London and New York: Oxford University Press, 1938–9), reprint (Tehran: Soroush Press, 1977), drawings by Ugo Monneret de Villard on pp. 959–61 and 1032–3; André Godard, 'Voûtes Iraniennes', *AeI* 4, no. 2 (1949): figs 241–2 and 290; and Seherr-Thoss and Seherr-Thoss, *Design and Color in Islamic Architecture*, pls 12–16.

62. Godard, 'Ribat-i Sharaf', figs 2, 21, 34, and 39–41 and Godard, 'Voûtes Iraniennes', fig. 236.

63. Edwin Lutyens, 'Persian Brickwork', *CL* (February 1933): p. 118.

64. Myron B. Smith, 'Material for a Corpus of Early Iranian Islamic Architecture. III. Two Dated Monuments at Sin (Isfahan)', *ArsI* 6 (1939): pp. 1–11.

65. Carl F. Riter, 'A Wooden Dome in Turkey', *OA*, n.s. 15 (1969): pp. 113–15.

66. Aslanapa, *Turkish Art*, pls 10, 21, 30, 35, 41, 44, 50, 54–6, 60–2, 69, 81, 84–6 and 89.

67. Hill and Grabar, *Islamic Architecture*, pls 331, 339, 368, 420, 425, and 454; Gabriel, *Monuments Turcs d'Anatolie*, vol. 2, pls VIII, XI, XIV, XV, XXII(1), and XXV(2) (limiting the examples to Amasya and Tokat; the list could be multiplied indefinitely).

68. See Michael Meinecke, *Fayencedekorationen Seldschukischer Sakralbauten in Kleinasien*, vol. 2 (Tübingen: Verlag Ernst Wasmuth, 1976), pls 2(1), 9(1), 22(2), 42(3-4), 43(3-4), 46(2), 47(1), and 48(1).

69. As at the Ulu Cami of Malatya; see Seherr-Thoss and Seherr-Thoss, *Design and Color in Islamic Architecture*, pls 107–8.

70. Ömür Bakirer, *Onüç ve Ondördüncü Yüzyillarda Anadolu Mihrabları* (Ankara: Türk Tarih Kurumu Basimevi, 2000), pls XXII (figs 45–7), XXV (fig. 54), XXXIX (fig. 85), XLV–XLVI (figs 100–3), XLVIII–XLIX (figs 107–9), L (figs 111–3), LII (figs 116–18), LIII (fig. 120), LIV (fig 122), LV–LVI (figs 124–7), LIX (figs 132–4), LXI–LXII (figs 138–40), LXV (figs 146–8), LXVII (figs 151–2), LXXXIX (figs 201–2), XC (fig. 204) and XCI (fig. 206).

71. For example, the Sirçali *Madrasa* in Konya: Aslanapa, *Turkish Art*, pl. 1. For a good range of colour illustrations showing how varied the element of glazed colour was in medieval Turkish architecture, see Gönül Öney, *Türk Çini Sanatı: Turkish Tile Art* (Istanbul: Binbirdirek Matbaacılık Sanayii A.Ş. Yayınları, 1976), pp. 8–48.

72. Meinecke, *Fayencedekorationen*, vol. 1, pp. 187–9 and Douglas G. Pickett, *Early Persian Tilework: The Medieval Flowering of Kashi* (Madison/Teaneck: Fairleigh Dickinson University Press, 1997), p. 37, where he lists nine craftsmen whose *nisbas* suggest that they were Persians. There is even a Hisnkayfi architect who signed his work in the remote Deccani town of Firuzabad in Central India, though this was in the fourteenth century: George Michell and Richard Eaton, *Firuzabad: Palace City of the Deccan*, Oxford Studies in Islamic Art, vol. 12 (Oxford: Oxford University Press, 1992), p. 34.

73. Meinecke, *Fayencedekorationen*, vol. 1, p. 18; Pickett, *Tilework*, pp. 35–9.
74. Meinecke, *Fayencedekorationen*, vol. 2, pp. 256–76.
75. Blair, 'The Madrasa at Zuzan'; Pickett, *Tilework*, pp. 24–31 and pls 3–4.
76. Though not the only one—see, for example, the Eşrefoğlu Süleyman Bey Cami at Beyşehir, Meinecke, *Fayencedekorationen*, vol. 2, pp. 83–91.
77. Meinecke, *Fayencedekorationen*, vol. 2, pp. 177–86.
78. Bachmann, *Kirchen und Moscheen*, pp. 69–74 and pls 59–63. There is no mention of glaze.
79. Pope and Ackerman, *Survey of Persian Art*, pl. 309.
80. Pope and Ackerman, *Survey of Persian Art*, pl. 305; Wilber and Sourdel-Thomine, *Qazwin*, pls I–VIII.
81. Oktay Aslanapa, '1970 temmuz Van Ulu Camii kazısı', *STY* 4 (1970–1): pp. 1–15.
82. Öney, *Türk Çini Sanatı*, pp. 36–47.
83. Gönül Öney, 'Elements from Ancient Civilizations in Anatolian Turkish Art', *Anadolu/Anatolia* 12 (1970): pp. 27–38.
84. Gönül Öney, 'The fish motif in Anatolian Seljuk Art', *STY* 2 (1966–8): pp. 160–8.
85. Gönül Öney, 'Bull Reliefs in Anatolian Seljuk art', *Belleten* 34, no. 133 (1970): pp. 101–20.
86. Gönül Öney, 'Dragon figures in Anatolian Seljuk art', *Belleten* 33, no. 130 (1969): pp. 193–216.
87. An outstanding example is the tomb of Hudavend Khatun in Niğde, though this was built as late as 1312: Gönül Öney, 'Die Figurenreliefs an der Hudavent Hatun Türbe in Niğde', *Belleten* 31, no. 122 (1967): pp. 155–67.
88. Nicholas Lowick, 'The Religious, The Royal and the Popular in the Figural Coinage of the Jazira', *The Art of Syria and the Jazira 1100–1250*, Oxford Studies in Islamic Art, vol. 1, ed. Julian Raby (Oxford: Oxford University Press, 1985), pp. 159–74; Helen W. Mitchell, 'Some Reflections on the Figured Coinage of the Artuqids and Zengids', in *Near Eastern Numismatics, Iconography, Epigraphy and History: Studies in Honor of George C. Miles*, ed. Dikran Kouymjian (Beirut: American University in Beirut, 1974), 353–8; and William F. Spengler and Wayne G. Sayles, *Turkoman Figural Bronze Coins and Their Iconography*, vol. 1, *The Artuqids* (Lodi, Wisc.: Clio's Cabinet, 1992).
89. For a comprehensive overview of this material, see Joachim Gierlichs, *Mittelalterliche Tierreliefs in Anatolien und Mesopotamien* (Tübingen: Ernst Wasmuth, 1996).
90. Willy Hartner and Richard Ettinghausen, 'The Conquering Lion: The Life Cycle of a Symbol', *Oriens* 17 (1964): pp. 161–71.
91. Gönül Öney, 'Sun and Moon Rosettes in the Shape of Human Heads in Anatolian Seljuk Art', *Anadolu* 3 (1969–70): pp. 195–203.
92. Gönül Öney, 'Mounted Hunting Scenes of Anatolian Seljuks in Comparison to Iranian Seljuks', *Anadolu* 2 (1967): pp. 139–59.

93. For a general treatment of this theme in Anataolian art of the thirteenth century, see Gönül Öney, 'Das Lebensbaum Motiv in der seldschukischer Kunst in Anatolien', *Belleten* 32, no. 1225 (1968): pp. 37–50; cf. Gönül Öney, 'Über eine ortukidische Lebensbaum Darstellung', *VaDe* 7 (1968): pp. 121–5.

94. Ünal, *Les Monuments Islamiques*, pls XXIII and XXV.

95. Every single one of these features occurs on the mausoleum of the Amir Saltuk in Erzurum (Seherr-Thoss and Seherr-Thoss, *Design and Color in Islamic Architecture*, pls 100–1).

96. Rahmi H. Ünal, *L'étude du portail dans l'architecture pré-ottomane* (*Bibliothèque archéologique et historique de l'Institut français d'archéologie d'Istanbul*, 22) (Izmir: T. Matbaacak, 1982). See also McClary, *Rum Saljuq Architecture*, 38–95.

97. Bakirer, *Mihrabları*.

98. Hill and Grabar, *Islamic Architecture*, pls 538–41.

99. Anna M. Pribytkova, *Pamyatniki Arkhitekturi XI Veka v Turkmenii* (Moscow: Gosudarstvennoe Izdatel'stvo Literaturi po Stroitel'stvu i Arkhitekture, 1955), pp. 39–64.

5

THE NIZAMIYYA *MADRASAS*

CAROLE HILLENBRAND

The most famous of all Seljuq viziers, Nizam al-Mulk, had a remarkable career. He held the office of the vizierate for a considerable time—more than twenty-nine years—and used it to fashion the Seljuq state, masterminding the turbulent transition of the Turkish nomads from steppe warlords to Perso-Islamic rulers.[1] He ruled an enormous empire in the name of Alp Arslan (ruled 455–64/1063–72), and even longer in the name of Malikshah (465–85/1072–92), the second and third of the great Seljuq sultans of Iran. Nizam al-Mulk controlled the Seljuq state with his iron determination, his Mafioso ruthlessness, his vast wealth, and the tentacles of his family connections. He was murdered in 485/1092 in his high seventies.[2]

In this chapter one major facet of the rule of Nizam al-Mulk will be discussed—his project of building the Nizamiyya *madrasas*. It will deal with the origins of these *madrasas* and the supervision that Nizam al-Mulk exercised over them. The core of the chapter, namely the great Nizamiyya in Baghdad, will then be discussed. A few words will be devoted to the topic of the students in the *madrasas* and the curricula which they followed. The chapter concludes with an attempt to answer a fundamental question, namely, why were the Nizamiyyas built?

The Origins of the Nizamiyya *Madrasa*[3]

The institution of the *madrasa* has long been associated with the name of Nizam al-Mulk. He came from Khurasan whose patrician families in Nishapur have been analysed so very ably by Bulliet.[4] This milieu was of great assistance to Nizam al-Mulk in his grand enterprise of building up the Seljuq state. Nizam al-Mulk knew the ethos of the patricians of Khurasan and how to enlist their support. He also knew how to balance the two rival legal factions, the Hanafis and Shafi'is, within the Khurasanian cities. Al-Kunduri, the predecessor of Nizam al-Mulk as Seljuq vizier, had persecuted the Shafi'is in the middle of the eleventh century and prominent scholars such as al-Juwayni were forced to flee from Nishapur.[5] Bulliet's approach makes it clear that this anti-Shafi'i policy was more about power politics within Nishapur than about legal or theological minutiae. After the murder of al-Kunduri in 455/1063, Nizam al-Mulk established in many cities of the Seljuq state his famous network of Shafi'i *madrasas*, known in his honour as the Nizamiyyas.

There is virtually no surviving material evidence of the Nizamiyyas. It is possible that a ruined building, situated in the remote village of Khargird to the south-east of Nishapur, may have been a *madrasa*, but that is not certain. Its beautiful but undated and fragmentary inscription, now in the Tehran Museum, nevertheless bears the name of al-Hasan b. 'Ali b. Ishaq, which clearly indicates that it was founded by Nizam al-Mulk himself.[6]

The lack of material evidence for the *madrasas* is in striking contrast to the wealth of information written about them in the medieval Arabic and Persian sources. Ibn al-Athir (died 630/1233) writes fulsomely, 'the The Nizamiyya *madrasas* are famous the world over; no city was without one, not even Jazirat ibn 'Umar, a town lost in a corner of the earth to which nobody pays any attention. Nizam al-Mulk built a beautiful big *madrasa* there, which is now known as the Radi al-Din *madrasa*.'[7] This is a grand way of saying that these Nizamiyyas were spread right across the Seljuq state. Other sources mention more precisely that they were found in Nishapur, Isfahan, Baghdad, Mosul, Herat, Balkh, Basra, Marv, Amul, and Tus.[8]

The first Nizamiyya was established in Nishapur in 450/1058. Its first director was al-Juwayni.[9] A Nizamiyya was then founded in Isfahan in 455/1063, and the most famous of all the Nizamiyyas, the one in Baghdad, was completed by 459/1067. And as van Renterghem has suggested,[10] there were many *madrasas* erected in Baghdad in the twelfth century, especially by 'Abbasid and Seljuq officials and even by private citizens of all four Sunni *madhhabs*.

How did the establishment of the Nizamiyyas occur? It seems likely that Nizam al-Mulk did not set out with a pre-conceived master plan to establish the network of Shafi'i *madrasas* that proclaimed his name across the whole Seljuq Empire. He was accustomed to the existence of *madrasas* that had long operated in Khurasan (some thirty-eight *madrasas* are known to have existed in Nishapur alone)[11] and he established his first Nizamiyya in that very city early on in his relationship with the Seljuq family.

Thereafter it would appear probable that while he served as vizier to Alp Arslan, he perforce accompanied this most peripatetic sultan who crossed the length and breadth of the Seljuq territories in time-honoured nomadic Turkish fashion. In the course of their travels, the vizier would endow *madrasas* as occasion offered in the cities that they visited, but the exact order in which they were built is not clear from the sources.

Nizam al-Mulk's Personal Oversight of His *Madrasas*

It seems that, once he was in full control of the Seljuq state, Nizam al-Mulk opted to stay for considerable periods in Isfahan, the city he pre-ferred, especially in the second half of his life.[12] Not surprisingly, he had chosen to build a Nizamiyya there, as already mentioned. Nizam al-Mulk made sure that control of individual Nizamiyyas remained in the trusted hands of his sons or other family members.[13]

The appointment of the academic staff to the Nizamiyyas, however, remained entirely the prerogative of Nizam al-Mulk himself. This was typical of his steely determination to keep a centralized grip on his *madrasas*. In modern parlance he was a 'control freak'. It was simply common sense for him not to become embroiled in local rivalries and conflicts and to appoint men whose credentials he could trust and who came from his own Khurasanian milieu. Thus, for the post of chief professor at the Nizamiyya in Nishapur, he chose the great Shafi'i/'Ashari scholar of that city, Imam al-Haramayn al-Juwayni. Al-Juwayni remained in the post until his death in 478/1085.[14] For the prestigious Nizamiyya in Baghdad, Nizam al-Mulk appointed another Persian, Abu Ishaq al-Shirazi, about whom more will be said later. Professors in charge of the Nizamiyyas did not always occupy the post for a long time. Sometimes they seem to have failed to get 'tenure', so to speak.[15] al-Ghazali, on the other hand, taught in two Nizamiyyas— in Baghdad and Nishapur.[16] He came to Baghdad in Jumada I, 484/ June–July 1091.[17] His brilliance is described in rapturous terms by 'Imad al-Din, as cited by al-Bundari, who writes, 'In knowledge he was an overflowing sea and a radiant full moon.'[18] Ibn al-Jawzi men-tions that Nizam al-Mulk gave al-Ghazali the honorific title of Zayn al-Din and says of the latter that 'his speech was honeyed and his mind was brilliant'.[19]

On some occasions, more than one professor was in post at the same time and they gave their classes on alternate days. Such was the case with Abu 'Abdallah al-Tabari and Abu Muhammad 'Abd al-Wahhab al-Shirazi, who both arrived within a few months of each other with diplomas appointing them to the Nizamiyya in Baghdad in 483/1090.[20]

The Nizamiyya in Baghdad

Let us now turn to the key monument under discussion in this chapter, the Nizamiyya in Baghdad, called by Hamdallah Mustawfi the 'mother of *madrasas*'.[21] Ibn al-Athir reports that in 457/1065, Nizam al-Mulk ordered Abu Sa'id al-Nishapuri to begin work on this Nizamiyya.[22] The choice of an architect hailing from Nishapur is surely significant. After all, Baghdad was the acknowledged capital of the Islamic world, culturally as well as politically, and it is next to impossible that the city which enjoyed the prestige of being the home of the 'Abbasid caliphate would lack competent architects. But it is natural to assume in the case of Nizam al-Mulk that he would choose someone from his own part of the world for this task because he was confident that such a man would understand his own vision for this building. After all, Nishapur already had its own Nizamiyya, built less than a decade earlier. It is clear, therefore, that Nizam al-Mulk, whose patronage dominated the building programmes in the Seljuq state during his lifetime, was inspired by architectural antecedents in Khurasan, and especially in the case of his *madrasas*. And it was these antecedents that he wanted replicated in Baghdad.

The splendid opening ceremony for this key building took place in 459/1067, presided over by the caliph himself, who was accompanied by his entourage. All the inhabitants of the city were assembled that day; their number filled the courtyard of the *madrasa* and the surrounding quarters of the city. The *waqfs* endowed to support the Nizamiyya included those for its library, as well *asbazaars*, caravanserais, and bathhouses.[23]

However, the appointment of Abu Ishaq al-Shirazi as the first professor of the Nizamiyya in Baghdad was not without its drama. There are signs that the building was completed in a hurry. According to Sibt ibn al-Jawzi, houses in Baghdad were pulled down in order to provide material for the building of the Nizamiyya.[24] On the opening day the people were assembled to welcome the arrival of al-Shirazi, but the great man did not show up.[25] Ibn al-Athir continues the story, relating that al-Shirazi had been visited by a youth who had reproached him for agreeing to teach within a building that was ill-gotten property. So al-Shirazi stayed away.[26] Another scholar was appointed temporarily at the Nizamiyya, but after twenty days al-Shirazi was persuaded to take up the post.[27] What made him change his mind is not recorded.

Even at a distance, Nizam al-Mulk dictated what happened in his *madrasas*. For example, when al-Shirazi died in 476/1084,[28] Mu'ayyad al-Mulk, the son of Nizam al-Mulk,[29] quickly appointed a new principal teacher at the Nizamiyya in Baghdad. Nizam al-Mulk was angered by this and ordered the *madrasa* to be closed for a whole year as a sign of mourning.[30] This demonstrates the control that Nizam al-Mulk exercised over the appointments to the Nizamiyyas and their curriculum. He hired and fired the staff and kept a close eye on their activities. The Nizamiyya in Baghdad was not just a teaching institution; it also served as a place to which the city's poor would come in order to receive alms. Ibn al-Athir mentions that when Malikshah visited Baghdad in 484/1091–2 the notables and amirs of his army dispensed alms on behalf of the sultan to countless indigent people.[31]

What did the Nizamiyyas Look Like?

The key fact is that they were large. According to Ibn Jubayr, 'The *madrasas* there number around thirty and they are all in the eastern part (of Baghdad). There is not one *madrasa* amongst them that falls short of the finest palace. The greatest and most famous of them is the Nizamiyya that was built by Nizam al-Mulk and was restored in 504/1110.'[32]

However, the vicissitudes of time, fire, flood, and invasion have ensured that no traces of any of the Nizamiyyas now remain.[33] This makes it difficult to imagine what they might have looked like. In the case of the Nizamiyya in Baghdad, however, there are perhaps a few clues to be found through looking at the still extant—though now much denatured—Mirjaniyya *madrasa* built by Amir Mirjan in Baghdad in 758/1357. According to the twentieth-century Iraqi scholar al-Alusi in his book *The Mosques and Monuments of Baghdad* (*Masajid Baghdad wa-atharuha*),[34] the Mirjaniyya mosque was built on the model of the Baghdad Nizamiyya. The Nizamiyya had three storeys; on the ground floor was situated the room facing the *qibla* where the students were taught; on the first floor were rooms for the accommodation of the boarders and a library. Al-Alusi goes on to say that the Nizamiyya was square in form and that in addition to the two storeys already mentioned, it contained basements with a kitchen and bathhouse. Unfortunately, al-Alusi does not state his source for this information about the Nizamiyya but he concludes that this short description accords almost exactly with the layout of the Mirjaniyya *madrasa*.[35]

The Curriculum

The medieval Arabic and Persian sources make it clear that the curriculum in the Nizamiyyas was not restricted to the teaching of Shafi'i *fiqh*. Indeed, it is likely that the whole range of the religious sciences was included in the programme followed by the students.[36] The Spanish traveller Ibn Jubayr attended a session in the Nizamiyya on Friday 12 Safar 580/25 May 1184; the speaker was Sadr al-Din al-Khujandi, the chief Shafi'i scholar from Khurasan (*sayyid al-'ulama' al-khurasaniyyawa-ra'is al-a'immat al-Shafi'iyya*), who discussed various branches of sciences (*afanin min 'ulum*) in his address to an audience delighted and honoured to see him.[37] Such a versatile scholar as al-Ghazali, for example, who taught in the Nizamiyya in Baghdad from 484–8/1091–5,[38] would have found it irksome just to limit his intellectual virtuosity to *fiqh*, which in one place in his magnum opus, the *Ihya' 'ulum al-din*, he describes as no more than a 'discourse on menstruation'.[39] The syllabus included the Qur'an, *hadith*, 'Ashari theology, Arabic grammar, literature, and arithmetic. [40]

Nizam al-Mulk seems to have practised a 'hands-on' approach regarding the teaching in his *madrasas*. He personally visited the Baghdad Nizamiyya in 479/1086, sat in the library and read and dictated sections of Prophetic tradition to the students.[41] According to 'Imad al-Din al-Isfahani, 'in the time of Nizam al-Mulk great attention was paid to instruction and education; parents busied themselves with the education of their children and would take them to the classes given by Nizam al-Mulk. He would question them and often take over the responsibility for directing the career of the most intelligent ones.'[42]

Why Were the Nizamiyyas Built

A number of sweeping statements have been made about why Nizam al-Mulk built his *madrasa*. It is important to point out first that Nizam al-Mulk himself did not come up with the idea of the *madrasa* as a separate building. Already in the sixth/thirteenth century Ibn Khallikan makes this mistake.[43] It is, moreover, unlikely that Nizam al-Mulk set out initially to establish a network of *madrasas* to combat the Isma'ili threat posed by the Fatimids in Cairo, as some have claimed.[44] This factor may have had some significance by the last decade of Nizam al-Mulk's life, but we should rather seek his motivation for embarking on the whole Nizamiyya enterprise inside rather than outside the Seljuq borders. Nor were his *madrasas* founded by the Seljuq state itself just because Nizam al-Mulk, a vizier, founded them. As Makdisi rightly pointed out long ago, 'any Muslim with full legal capacity could found a *madrasa*'.[45] However, I do not agree with another statement by Makdisi, namely that Nizam al-Mulk 'founded his network of *madrasas* to implement his *political* policies throughout the vast lands of the empire under his sway'.[46] Nor is Omid Safi's statement that the Nizamiyyas were for the propagation of state-defined 'Islamic thought' convincing.[47]

It would seem more generally that Nizam al-Mulk worked out religious policies at the micro-level early on in Nishapur while he was working alongside Alp Arslan, when the latter was still only governor of that city. Nizam al-Mulk then applied such policies more widely as his network of Nizamiyyas grew. Bulliet convincingly argues that Nizam al-Mulk aimed at creating a balance between rival religious factions within the Sunni fold. I do not believe that Nizam al-Mulk wanted every Muslim to be a Shafi'i Muslim, as he himself was. Bulliet goes on to argue that Nizam al-Mulk had planted the seed of 'state patriciate' by means of his *madrasas*.[48] But that little word 'state' begs the whole question: 'Who or what *is* the state at this time?' And if the state is to act, it needs actual people as its instruments. Step forward Nizam al-Mulk; his motto could very easily have been, foreshadowing Louis XIV, 'L'état c'est moï'. And if the next question is 'did this embodiment of the state use public funds or his own private purse for this purpose?' the answer must remain rather blurred. Most probably Nizam al-Mulk's motives for building the Nizamiyyas were complex and overlapping, perhaps pragmatic initially, and then more carefully thought out.

At all events, the evidence points clearly to a strongly accented local bias in the entire Nizamiyya enterprise. The various strands are easily enumerated: the development of the *madrasa* concept in Nishapur from at least the tenth century onwards; the fact that the earliest recorded Nizamiyya was built in that city; the choice of a Nishapuri architect to build the key Nizamiyya in Baghdad; the Khurasani provenance of one noted professor after another; and the fact that Nizam al-Mulk's career as a vizier began in that same city of Nishapur. He may well have been open-minded about which *madhhab* people belonged to, but one thing is clear: he was determined to propagate as widely as possible the intellectual culture of Nishapur, the capital of his home province of Khurasan, and his original power base.

* * *

The honorific title Nizam al-Mulk itself—'the ordering of the realm'—was taken by his admirers as a symbol of his power. To his biographer, al-Subki, Nizam al-Mulk *was* the government; 'His vizierate was no vizierate, but it rather stood above the sultanate.'[49] His role as vizier was even more significant than that of the Barmakid family of viziers under the 'Abbasids, because Nizam al-Mulk's so-called masters were Turkish warlords with no political experience. No wonder the Seljuq state at its height was punningly called *al-dawla al-nizamiyya*, the well-ordered state, or alternatively, the state of Nizam al-Mulk.

But history was to show that the centrifugal forces inherent in the Turkic concept of family rule worked against the centralized model of the Seljuq state that Nizam al-Mulk had tried to impose. Nizam al-Mulk was attempting to achieve balance and harmony between various conflicting forces:[50] the Turcomans and the sultans; the sultans and their relatives; the Seljuqs and their amirs; the cities and the nomads; the different *madhhabs* within Sunni Islam; and above all, he sought to establish stability in an empire that he had almost single-handedly built up and that eventually covered the landmass ruled by the ancient Sasanian Empire. This harmonizing and balancing he achieved through his various networks, one of which was the *madrasa* system. Whilst he was alive, the unity of the Seljuq state remained intact.[51] But once he was dead, nothing worked as well again.

However, there is an optimistic coda to this melancholic conclusion. In 625/1227, more than a century after the death of Nizam al-Mulk, in the very city where his most celebrated Nizamiyya stood, there rose the greatest medieval *madrasa* of them all, the Mustansiriyya,[52] whose global reach—for it catered to all four Sunni *madhhabs*—would surely have pleased him. In spirit, if not in name, it perpetuated his legacy—and indeed went further still, opening its doors to students all over the Muslim world.

Notes

1. For the life of Nizam al-Mulk, see Ibn al-'Adim, *Bughyat al-talab fi ta'rikh Halab*, partial ed. Ali Sevim, as *Biyografilerle Selcukular Tarihi Ibnu'l-Adim Büyyetul-taleb fi Tarihi Haleb* (Ankara: Türk Tarih Kurumu Basimevi, 1976), pp. 59–94; al-Subki, *Tabaqat al-shafi'iyya al-kubra*, ed. unidentified (Cairo: Al-matba'a al-Hasaniyya al-misriyya, 1964–76), vol. 3, pp. 135–45; Ibn al-Jawzi, *Muntazam fi ta'rikh al-umam wa'l-muluk*, ed. unidentified, (Hyderabad: Da'irat al-ma'arif al-'uthmaniyya, 1359/1940), vol. 9, pp. 64–8; al-Bundari, *Zubdat al-nusra wa-nukhbat al-'usra*, ed. Martinus Theodorus Houtsma, in *Recueil de textes relatifs à l'histoire des Seldjoucides* (Leiden: Brill, 1889), vol. 2, pp. 56–7; Ibn al-Athir, *Al-ta'rikh al-bahir fi'l-dawlat al-atabakiyya*, ed. Ahmad Tulaymat (Baghdad: Dar al-kutub al-haditha bi'l-Qahira wa-maktabat al-muthanna bi-Baghdad, 1382/1963), pp. 9–10; Ibn al-Athir, *Al-kamil fi'l-ta'rikh*, ed. Carolus Johannes Tornberg (Leiden: Brill, 1864), vol. 10, pp. 207–10; Ibn al-Athir, *Al-kamil fi'l-ta'rikh*, partial trans. Donald Sydney Richards as *The Annals of the Seljuq Turks* (London: Routledge, 2002), pp. 255–8; Ibn Funduq, *Tar'ikh-i Bayhaq*, ed. Ahmad Bahmanyar (Tehran: Islamiyya Press, 1938), pp.73–83; Ibn Khallikan, *Kitab wafayat al-a'yan*, trans. Baron MacGuckin de Slane as *Ibn Khallikan's Biographical Dictionary* (Beirut: Librairie du Liban, 1979), vol. 1, pp. 413–5; see also Harold Bowen and Edmund Bosworth, 'Nizam al-Mulk', *Encyclopaedia of Islam*, 2nd ed. (Leiden: E.J. Brill, 1954–); Neguin Yavari, 'Nizam al-Mulk', in *The Islamic World*, ed. Andrew Rippin (Abingdon: Routledge, 2008), pp. 351–8.

2. According to Ibn al-'Adim, Nizam al-Mulk died aged 76 years, 10 months, and 19 days. He was carried on a litter because of his old age, Ibn al-'Adim, *Bughyat*, p. 91. See also al-Athir, *Al-kamil fi'l-ta'rikh*, vol. 10, p. 204; Ibn al-Athir, *Al-kamil fi'l-ta'rikh*, trans. Richards, p. 253.

3. On the origins of the Nizamiyyas and discussions of the *madrasa* institution in general, see Heinz Halm, *Zeitschrift der Deutschen Morgenländischen Gesellschaft* (Wiesbaden), Suppl. III/1, XIX, Deutscher Orientalistentag (1977): pp. 438–48; Asad Talas, *L'enseignement Chez les Arabes: La Madrasa Nizamiyya et son Histoire* (Paris: Librairie Orientaliste Paul Geuthner, 1939), especially pp. 13, 26–31; Robert Hillenbrand, *Islamic Architecture: Form, Function and Meaning* (Edinburgh: Edinburgh University Press, 1994), pp. 173–250, and especially pp. 175–83; Richard Bulliet, *The Patricians of Nishapur* (Cambridge, Massachusetts: Harvard University Press, 1972), pp. 249–55; George Makdisi, 'The Madrasa as a Charitable Trust and the University as a Corporation in the Middle Ages', in *Actes du Ve Congrès International d'Arabisants et d'Islamisants* (Brussels: Publications du Centre pour L'Etude des Problèmes du Monde Musulman Contemporain, 1971), pp. 329–37; Abdul Latif Tibawi, 'Origin and Character of "al-madrasah"', *Bulletin of the School of Oriental*

and African Studies 25 (1962): pp.225–38; Ernst Herzfeld, 'Damascus: Studies in architecture—II', *Ars Islamica* 10 (1943): pp. 13–14.

4. Bulliet, *Patricians*, pp. 56–7, 72–5.

5. Richard Bulliet, 'Local Politics in Eastern Iran under the Ghaznavids and Seljuks', *Iranian Studies* 11 (1978): p. 50.

6. Ernst Herzfeld, 'Eine Bauschrift von Nizam al-Mulk', *Der Islam* 12 (1921): pp. 98–101; see also Sheila Blair, *The Monumental Inscriptions from Early Islamic Iran and Transoxiana* (Leiden: Brill, 1992), pp. 149–52 and plates 99–101; Hillenbrand, *Islamic Architecture*, p. 180.

7. Ibn al-Athir, *Al-ta'rikh al-bahir fi'l-dawlat al-atabakiyya*, ed. Ahmad Tulaymat (Baghdad: Dar al-kutub al-haditha bi'l-Qahira wa-maktabat al-muthanna bi-Baghdad, 1382/1963), p. 9; see also Richards, *Annals*, p. 257.

8. al-Subki, *Tabaqat*, vol. 3, p. 137.

9. Bulliet, *Patricians*, pp. 254–5, citing 'Abd al-Ghafir al-Farisi, *Siyaq li-ta'rikh Naysabur*, facsimile ed. Richard Frye (Cambridge, Massachusetts: Harvard University Press, 1965), ff. 48b, 72a, and 90a.

10. Vanessa van Renterghem, 'Controlling and Developing Baghdad: Caliphs, Sultans, and the Balance of Power in the Abbasid Capital (mid–5th/11th to late–6th/12th c.)', in *The Seljuqs: Politics, Society and Culture*, eds. Christian Lange and Songül Mecit (Edinburgh: Edinburgh University Press, 2011), p. 122.

11. Bulliet, *Patricians*, pp. 249–54; by the time Nizam al-Mulk was born, there were already four *madrasa*s in Nishapur; al-Subki, *Tabaqat*, vol. 3, p. 137.

12. David Durand-Guédy, *Iranian Elites and Turkish Rulers: A History of Isfahan in the Saljuq Period* (London: Routledge, 2010), p. 304.

13. Nizam al-Mulk had twelve sons to each of whom he gave a job (*shughl*) and governorship: see Nishapuri, *Saljuqnama*, ed. Alexander Hargreaves Morton (Chippenham: Gibb Memorial Trust, 2004), p. 31; Rawandi, *Rahat al-sudur*, ed. Muhammad Iqbal (London: Brill, 1921), p. 132.

14. The tradition of appointing local personages continued long after the death of Nizam al-Mulk. Ibn Khallikan mentions a Shafi'ite scholar named Qutb al-Din al-Nishapuri (d. 578/1183), who gave lessons in the Nizamiyya in Nishapur: Ibn Khallikan, *Kitab wafayat*, vol. 3, pp. 351–2.

15. Talas provides details of professors at the Nizamiyya in Baghdad; some stayed a long time whilst others were in the post only briefly; Talas, *L'enseignement*, pp. 52–64.

16. al-Ghazali was later persuaded to come out of retirement in Tus to take over as director of the Nizamiyya in Nishapur in 499/1105-6; Bulliet, *Patricians*, p. 255.

17. al-Bundari, *Zubdat*, vol. 2, pp. 36–44. Other Shafi'i scholars who taught at the Nizamiyya in Baghdad included Ahmad al-Ghazali (d. 520/1126), the poet and brother of Abu Hamid who gave lectures in the Nizamiyya in Baghdad, substituting for his brother; see Ibn Khallikan, *Kitab wafayat*, vol. 1, p. 79; a scholar named al-Mihani was appointed twice to

the Nizamiyya in Baghdad; see Ibn Khallikan, *Kitab wafayat*, vol. 1, pp. 189–90; and al-Usuli, who taught there for a month and then died; Ibn Khallikan, *Kitab wafayat*, vol. 1, p. 80.

18. al-Bundari, *Zubdat*, vol. 2, p. 80.
19. Ibn al-Jawzi, *Muntazam*, vol. 9, p. 55.
20. Ibn al-Athir, *Al-kamil fi 'l-ta'rikh*, trans. Richards, p. 247.
21. Hamdallah Mustawfi, *Nuzhat al-qulub*, ed. Guy Le Strange (Leiden: Brill, 1915), p. 35.
22. Ibn al-Athir, *Al-kamil fi 'l-ta'rikh*, vol. 10, p. 18.
23. Ibn al-'Adim mentions that Nizam al-Mulk endowed *madrasas* and plentiful *waqfs* and that he established libraries; *Bughyat*, p. 67.
24. Sibt ibn al-Jawzi, *Mir'at al-zaman fi tar'ikh al-a'yan*, partial edition, Ali Sevim (Ankara: Türk Tarih Kurumu Basimevi), 1968, p. 184.
25. Ibn Khallikan, *Kitab wafayat*, vol. 2, p. 164; Sibt ibn al-Jawzi, *Mir'at*, p. 185.
26. Ibn al-Athir, *Al-kamil fi 'l-ta'rikh*, vol. 10, p. 55; Ibn al-Athir, *Al-kamil fi 'l-ta'rikh*, trans. Richards, pp. 161–2.
27. Ibn al-Athir, *Al-kamil fi 'l-ta'rikh*, vol. 10, p. 55; Ibn al-Athir, *Al-kamil fi 'l-ta'rikh*, trans. Richards, p. 162.
28. Ibn al-Jawzi, *Muntazam*, vol. 10, p.7.
29. Ibn Khallikan, *Kitab wafayat*, vol. 1, pp. 5–6.
30. Ibn Khallikan, *Kitab wafayat*, vol. 1, p. 11.
31. Ibn al-Athir, *Al-kamil fi 'l-ta'rikh*, vol. 10, p. 55; Ibn al-Athir, *Al-kamil fi 'l-ta'rikh*, trans. Richards, p. 250.
32. Ibn Jubayr, *Rihla*, ed. Michael Jan de Goeje (Leiden: Brill, 1907), p. 229.
33. According to Hammer-Purgstall, the Nizamiyya was burned by a fire caused by an unprecedentedly large comet in 499AH/AD1105; see Joseph Hammer-Purgstall, *Geschichte der Ilchane* (Darmstadt: Verlag Leskr, 1842), p. 128. Unfortunately, Hammer-Purgstall does not mention his source. Sibt b. al-Jawzi mentions the comet but not the fire; *Mir'at al-zaman*, vol. 1, ed. unknown (Hyderabad: Matba'at majlis da'ira al-ma'ruf al-'uthmaniyya, 1370AH/AD1951), p. 16; Matthew of Edessa also refers to the comet which was both wonderful and terrifying. Matthew of Edessa, *Patmut'iwn*, trans. Edouard Dulaurier as *Chronique de Matthieu d'Edesse (962–1136) avec la Continuation de Grégoire le Prêtre jusqu'en 1162* (Paris: A. Durand, Libraire, 1858), pp. 262–3.
34. Al-Alusi, *The Mosques and Monuments of Baghdad (Masajid Baghdad wa-atharuha)* (Baghdad, 1346/1927), p. 101.
35. Quoted by Talas, *L'enseignement*, pp. 27–8. For a detailed account of the Mirjaniyya, see Tariq Jawad al-Janabi, *Studies in Mediaeval Iraqi Architecture* (Baghdad: Republic of Iraq, Ministry of Culture and Information, State Organization of Antiquities and Heritage, 1982), pp. 113–40.
36. Ibn al-'Adim, *Bughyat*, p. 67.
37. Ibn Jubayr, *Rihla*, p. 220.
38. Ibn Khallikan, *Kitab wafayat*, vol. 2, p. 622.

39. Tibawi, 'Origin and Character of "al-madrasah"', p. 228.
40. Talas, *L'enseignement*, pp. 37–8.
41. Ibn al-Jawzi, *Muntazam*, vol. 9, p. 36.
42. al-Bundari, *Zubdat*, vol. 2, p. 57.
43. Ibn Khallikan, *Kitab wafayat*, vol. 1, p. 414.
44. Tibawi, 'Origin and Character of "al-madrasah"', p. 234; Talas, *L'enseignement*, pp. xii and 18.
45. Makdisi, 'The Madrasa as a Charitable Trust', p. 332.
46. Makdisi, 'The Madrasa as a Charitable Trust' p. 334.
47. Omid Safi, *Politics of Knowledge in Pre-modern Islam: Negotiating Ideology and Religious Inquiry* (Chapel Hill: University of North Carolina Press, 2006), p. 7.
48. Bulliet, *Patricians*, p. 74.
49. al-Subki, *Tabaqat*, vol.3, p. 137.
50. Bulliet, 'Local Politics in Eastern Iran', p. 52.
51. 'This Hasan is a barrier against discords'; Ibn al-'Adim, *Bughyat*, p. 67.
52. Described by Hamdallah Mustawfi as the 'best building there': *Nuzhat*, p. 35.

Select Bibliography

Primary Sources

'Abd al-Ghafir al-Farisi. *Siyaq li-ta'rikh Naysabur*, facsimile ed. Richard Frye (Cambridge, Massachusetts: Harvard University Press, 1965).

al-Bundari. *Zubdat al-nusra wa-nukhbat al-'usra*, ed. Martinus Theodorus Houtsma, *Recueil de textes relatifs à l'histoire des Seldjoucides* (Leiden: Brill, 1889).

al-Subki. *Tabaqat al-shafi 'iyya al-kubra*, ed. unidentified (Cairo: Al-matba'a al-Hasaniyya al-misriyya, 1964–76).

Hamdallah Mustawfi. *Nuzhat al-qulub*, ed. Guy Le Strange (Leiden: Brill, 1915).

Ibn al-'Adim. *Bughyat al-talab fi ta'rikh Halab*, partial ed. Ali Sevim, as *Biyografilerle Selcukular Tarihi Ibnu'l-Adim Bügyetul-taleb fi Tarihi Haleb* (Ankara: Türk Tarih Kurumu Basimevi, 1976).

Ibn al-Athir. *Al-kamil fi'l-ta'rikh*, ed. Carolus Johannes Tornberg (Leiden: Brill, 1864), vol. 10, pp. 207–10; Ibn al-Athir, *Al-kamil fi'l-ta'rikh*, partial trans. Donald Sydney Richards as *The Annals of the Seljuq Turks* (London: Routledge, 2002).

——. *Al-ta'rikh al-bahir fi'l-dawlat al-atabakiyya*, ed. Ahmad Tulaymat (Baghdad: Dar al-kutub al-haditha bi'l-Qahira wa-maktabat al-muthanna bi-Baghdad, 1382/1963).

Ibn al-Jawzi. *Muntazam fi ta'rikh al-umam wa'l-muluk*, ed. unidentified, vol. 9 (Hyderabad: Da'irat al-ma'arif al-'uthmaniyya), 1359/1940).

Ibn Funduq. *Tar'ikh-i Bayhaq*, ed. Ahmad Bahmanyar (Tehran: Islamiyya Press, 1938).

Ibn Jubayr. *Rihla*, ed. Michael Jan de Goeje (Leiden: Brill, 1907).

Ibn Khallikan. *Kitab wafayat al-a'yan*, trans. Baron MacGuckin de Slane as *Ibn Khallikan's Biographical Dictionary* (Beirut: Librairie du Liban, 1979).

Matthew of Edessa. *Patmut'iwn*, trans. Edouard Dulaurier as *Chronique de Matthieu d'Edesse (962–1136) avec la Continuation de Grégoire le Prêtre jusqu'en 1162* (Paris: A. Durand, Libraire, 1858).

Nishapuri. *Saljuqnama*, ed. Alexander Hargreaves Morton (Chippenham: Gibb Memorial Trust, 2004).

Rawandi. *Rahat al-sudur*, ed. Muhammad Iqbal (London: Brill, 1921).

Sibt ibn al-Jawzi. *Mir'at al-zaman fi tar'ikh al-a'yan*, partial edition, Ali Sevim (Ankara: Türk Tarih Kurumu Basimevi, 1968); Sibt b. al-Jawzi, *Mir'at al-zaman*, vol. 1, ed. unknown (Hyderabad: Matba'at majlis da'ira al-ma'ruf al-'uthmaniyya, 1370/951).

Secondary Sources

Blair, Sheila. *The Monumental Inscriptions from Early Islamic Iran and Transoxiana* (Leiden: Brill, 1992).

———. 'Local Politics in Eastern Iran under the Ghaznavids and Seljuks'. *Iranian Studies* 11, 1/4 (1978): 35–56.

Bulliet, Richard. *The Patricians of Nishapur* (Cambridge, Massachusetts: Harvard University Press, 1972).

Durand-Guédy, David. *Iranian Elites and Turkish Rulers: A History of Isfahan in the Saljuq Period* (London: Routledge, 2010).

Halm, Heinz. 'Die Anfänge der Madrasa', *ZDMG*, Suppl. III/1, XIX, *Deutscher Orientalistentag vom 28.September bis 4 Oktober 1975 in Freiburg im Breisgau. Vortrage*, ed. Wolfgang Voigt (Wiesbaden: Franz Steiner Verlag,1977), pp. 438–48.

Hammer-Purgstall, Joseph. *Geschichte der Ilchane* (Darmstadt: Verlag Leskr,1842).

Herzfeld, Ernst. 'Damascus: Studies in Architecture', II. *Ars Islamica* X (1943): 13–70.

———. 'Eine Bauschrift von Nizam al-Mulk'. *Der Islam* XII (1921): 98–101.

Hillenbrand, Robert. *Islamic Architecture: Form, Function and Meaning* (Edinburgh: Edinburgh University Press, 1994).

Makdisi, George. 'The Madrasa as a Charitable Trust and the University as a Corporation in the Middle Ages', *Actes du Ve Congres International d'Arabisants et d'Islamisants* (Brussels: Publications du Centre pour L'Etude des Problèmes du Monde Musulman Contemporain, 1971), pp. 329–37.

Safi, Omid. *Politics of Knowledge in Pre-modern Islam: Negotiating Ideology and Religious Inquiry* (Chapel Hill: University of North Carolina Press, 2006).

Talas, Asad. *L'enseignement chez les Arabes: La Madrasa Nizamiyya et son Histoire* (Paris: Librairie Orientaliste Paul Geuthner, 1939).

Tibawi, Abdul Latif. 'Origin and Character of "al-madrasah"'. *BSOAS* 25 (1962): 225–38.

Van Renterghem, Vanessa. 'Controlling and Developing Baghdad: Caliphs, Sultans, and the Balance of Power in the Abbasid Capital (mid–5th/11th to late–6th/12th c.)', in *The Seljuqs: Politics, Society and Culture*, eds. Christian Lange and Songül Mecit (Edinburgh: Edinburgh University Press, 2011), pp. 117–38.

III

THE TURKS IN THE INDIAN SUBCONTINENT

6

TRANS-REGIONAL CONTACTS AND RELATIONSHIPS
Turks, Mongols, and the Delhi Sultanate in the Thirteenth and Fourteenth Centuries

Sunil Kumar

The establishment of the Delhi Sultanate in the early thirteenth century coincided with wide-ranging geopolitical shifts in the lands of eastern Iran. At the end of the twelfth century, under the leadership of the brothers Ghiyāth al-Dīn (558–99/1163–1203) and Mu'izz al-Dīn (569–99/1173–1206), the Shansabanid state of Ghur was poised to seize control over much of Khurasan and Khwarazm. Less than a decade later, with the reversal at the battle of Andkhud (598/1205) and murder of Mu'izz al-Dīn (599/1206), the Shansabanid state was in political disarray. With the loss of their political gains in Khurasan, their hold over north India also slipped away. The political flux of these years was aggravated by the ephemeral attempts of the Khwarazm Shah to dominate eastern Iran and the devastation that followed in the wake of the armies of Chinggis Khan and his generals.[1] The political landscape of the areas adjoining the subcontinent changed completely with the onset of the Chinggisid campaigns in the 1220s, a decade that also marked the expansion of the Delhi Sultanate into the distant regions of northern India. Although these two developments were virtually unrelated, the Mongol presence in the Afghanistan, Punjab, and Sindh regions had a huge impact on the making of the Delhi Sultanate. Even as Delhi sought to consolidate its recently annexed territories, it had to face the hostile Mongols and the residual members of the Shansabanid and Khwarazmian political dispensations across the Indus basin. The Mongols were redoubtable foes and through the thirteenth and fourteenth centuries they launched unremitting attacks on the Delhi Sultanate.

As I argue in my chapter, frontier conflicts tend to obscure the longer and more complex history of trans-regional relationships that existed between the Sultanate and the people of the Central Asian steppes. This was not entirely by accident or historiographical oversight. To Persian litterateurs, Chinggis Khan's devastation of Transoxiana, eastern Iran, and Afghanistan appeared as the holocaust that would presage the Day of Judgement. During this period of crisis, the Delhi Sultanate was the nearest sanctuary for Muslim migrants. And yet their sense of security in the Sultanate was hardly deep rooted and reports of each Mongol invasion replayed old fears.[2] These fears coloured the reportage of the Persian litterateurs, and memories of devastation and displacement caused by the Mongols left them as universally hated figures. This was somewhat awkward because many of the Sultanate elites were of the same social and cultural background as the Mongols and their retinues. Some of them had briefly served with Mongol contingents in the Afghanistan region. Thus it demanded a great deal of skill to condemn the Mongols without demonising their patrons. As I will point out in my chapter, the monochromatic description of the Mongols as hostile invaders made it difficult for Persian litterateurs to discourse freely about the character of their own patrons. A variety of narrative strategies were, therefore, deployed to underline the great distance between Sultanate heroes and Mongol infidels. As a result we remain rather poorly informed about the links between the Delhi Sultanate and the people of the steppe. This chapter analyses thirteenth-century Persian literature in an effort to unravel the complex and varied relationship that existed between different elements of Sultanate society, the Mongols, and their auxiliaries. It is divided into three sections that are more or less chronologically and thematically distinct. The first section focuses on the first half of the thirteenth century and develops two contrasting but interrelated themes—the special favour bestowed by the Delhi Sultans on Turkish military slaves, and the conflicted response of Persian chroniclers to the ethnicities and slave origins of their patrons. In the second section I focus on the middle of the thirteenth century and study how changes in the Mongol and Sultanate regimes complicated the way in which Sultanate military commanders and residents of Multan and

Lahore interacted with the Mongols. Although these Sultanate commanders were still Turks of slave origin, the years after Sultan Shams al-Dīn Iltutmish's death (633/1236) had altered their commitments to the Delhi Sultanate and they grasped the opportunities of political service on the frontier in ways quite different from the governors of a previous generation. I also study the ways in which these transitions affected the life and material circumstances of urban society in the Punjab and Sindh regions. The third section of the chapter studies the last quarter of the century and the recruitment of frontier commanders by the Delhi Sultans. This section of the chapter studies the early Khalajīs (689–720/1290–1320) and Tughluqs (720–817/1320–1414), whose founding dynasts had served in the Mongol auxiliary forces on the Sultanate frontier. Their background did not constrain their rapid rise to power and eventual seizure of the Sultanate itself. I focus upon the evidence for the transposition of Turkish and Mongol cultural traditions into Hindustan as these commanders transited from the frontier, seized power in the capital, and emerged as Sultans of Delhi. How did the Persian chroniclers, with their aversion to the Mongol hordes, respond to these developments? In the context of the antipathy of the Persian chroniclers towards the Mongols, how can modern historians study the presence of these steppe traditions in the Delhi Sultanate? The response of the Persian literati to the challenge of 'new Muslims' of indifferent social and cultural backgrounds emerging as leaders and protectors of the Muslim community was particularly interesting, given their portrayal of Delhi as the 'sanctuary of Islam.' Although I study this more closely in the last section, the question resonates throughout my chapter. Towards an effort at unravelling its different aspects, I commence my study at the beginning of the thirteenth century and the early deployment of Turkish military slaves by the Delhi Sultan Shams al-Dīn Iltutmish (607–633/1210–36) in the following section.

Migrations, Patronage, Turkish Ethnicities, and Thirteenth-Century Mamluk Legacies

The capture of urban settlements in north India by Mu'izz al-Dīn Ghūrī did not lead to a great deal of migration into the subcontinent from the regions of Afghanistan and Khurasan at the turn of the twelfth century. The people who did make their way into India with the Ghūrīd armies were a study in contrasts. On the one hand were social elites like Malik 'Izz al-Dīn Kharmīl who belonged to Ghur and came from a well-known aristocratic family that had distant affinal relations with the Shansabanids. He was appointed governor of Sialkot in 582/1186, participated in other campaigns in north India, but did not settle in the subcontinent.[3] For this aristocrat with important social and political connections in Ghazni, a life in the marches meant social and political oblivion. That is why he eventually left the frontier and returned 'home' to become by 602/1206 one of the powerful players in the politics of the capital.

By way of contrast, the social and political background of Muḥammad Bakhtiyār Khalajī, another soldier involved in Ghūrīd campaigns in north India, was hardly aristocratic. He was deemed unqualified for service (*mukhtaṣar*), too coarse to be recruited into the Ghaznavid or the Delhi armies. He made his career at the extremities of the eastern frontier, so successfully in fact that he accumulated a large army and became the governor of Lakhnauti. This humble soldier from Afghanistan, whose fortunes were transformed through his service in north India, found little to attract him 'home.' In one of his rare visits to Delhi, the valiant if simple hero of Bengal was needled and humiliated; in Lakhnauti he was the lord of the land and commander of armies. It was hardly surprising that he decided to make that his domicile.[4]

The examples of Kharmīl and Bakhtiyār Khalajī were not unique in the early thirteenth century. Until the Mongol invasions of the 1220s it was indicative of the kind of choices that people of different social backgrounds made as they contemplated service and/or migration to north India. These choices diminished once Chinggis Khan invaded Khwarazm and started his campaigns into Iran and Afghanistan. For the first time the Delhi Sultanate started receiving a large number of migrant social elites. A good example of such an individual is Quṭb al-Dīn Ḥasan 'Ali Ghūrī, the military commander of Tulak and Saifrud in Afghanistan. He had commandeered his soldiers and the residents of Tulak in a successful resistance against the Mongols. The residents of Tulak, however, feared the eventual wrath of the invaders at this show of defiance and eventually stopped helping the amīr. Faced with the ambivalence of the city's residents, Ḥasan 'Ali Ghūrī escaped from Tulak and fled even as the Mongols chased him across the Indus. The Delhi Sultan, Shams al-Dīn Iltutmish, received the émigré honourably but never offered him a public command. Ḥasan 'Ali Ghūrī's rise to political influence was dramatic, but only *after* Iltutmish's death when political competition allowed upward mobility for a greater diversity of personnel.[5]

The experience of Quṭb al-Dīn Ḥasan ʿAlī Ghūrī is a salutary reminder that the Delhi monarch was extremely astute and discriminating when it came to matters of bestowing patronage—émigrés of high status would receive respect at the Sultan's court, but not necessarily public office. A study of the monarch's patronage reveals that instead of aristocrats—people who might also have considerable political and military experience as military commanders—it was military slaves (*banda/bandagān*) who received privileged posts in the Sultanate. It would seem that rather than trusting people who had great titles and respectable genealogies, *laqab* and *nisba*, the Sultan favoured military slaves with high office—the one group of people whose deracination made them entirely dependent upon their master.[6]

Iltutmish secured a large number of slaves through his incessant campaigns in north India but only some of them were culled for military duties and service in the court. While we have little information about the general body of military slaves, we know more about the senior, elite ones called the *bandagān-i khāṣṣ*. It is actually hard to distinguish the singular qualities that might have separated the *khāṣṣ* from the rest of the slaves. But two important factors do stand out: first, the slaves who eventually became *khāṣṣ* were almost always purchased and seldom gained as war booty; second, they were almost always of Turkish origin. Most of Iltutmish's *khāṣṣ* slaves belonged to a variety of Turkish tribes, but Qipchaqs and their confederates predominated. The Chinggisid and Jochid campaigns in the *dasht-i Qipchaq* had flooded the markets with members of the Qipchaq confederacy and they were brought to the subcontinent by a variety of merchants. These merchants had provided some of the slaves an elementary education in the urbane traditions of Persianate life. This helped the slaves to acculturate to their new environs with greater facility, a quality that considerably improved their value in the market. Because they were valuable commodities Iltutmish expended considerable care in rearing these slaves. Most of them spent several years as pages in the court, some of them had close associations with members of the Sultan's family, and all of their conduct and training was carefully evaluated and scrutinized before they were gradually eased into public service as commanders and governors.[7]

The reaction of the Persian chroniclers to the large-scale deployment of slaves by Shams al-Dīn Iltutmish did not differ greatly. Writing in the mid–thirteenth century, Minhāj-i Sirāj Jūzjānī was unique in providing a considerable amount of information on the individual histories of some of these slaves. In the twenty-second section of his *Ṭabaqāt-i Nāṣirī*, Jūzjānī provided individual biographies of twenty-five slaves where he described their enslavement, how they were brought to the subcontinent, trained, and pursued glorious careers in the service of their masters.[8] With one notable exception, Jūzjānī's text communicated the extent to which the Sultan's slaves abided by the trust reposed in them.[9] If there was any discomfort in portraying slaves as heroes of Islam it appeared only parenthetically when the author mentioned the lineage of the two slave monarchs, Shams al-Dīn Iltutmish and Ghiyāth al-Dīn Balban. According to the author, the monarchs may have been slaves but they came from lineages of rulers—their fathers were great chieftains in the steppes and their abilities of leadership and governance were surely inherited. Jūzjānī went on to explain that God was responsible for Balban's enslavement and transportation to Hindustan. Balban's presence in India ensured the stability of Islam in the region; the Turk's enslavement, in other words, was God's boon to Muslims.[10]

Jūzjānī's was a sophisticated development of statements made by Fakhr-i Mudabbir far more bluntly earlier in the century. Fakhr-i Mudabbir's text was dedicated to Quṭb al-Dīn Ai-Beg, also a Turkish slave and ruler of Lahore and Delhi (602–7/1206–10). The author noted two associated qualities about Turks:

> [First] there is no group amongst the masses of unbelievers brought to Islam who do not hanker after their homes, their mother and father and relations ... except only the Turks who when they are brought to Islam place their heart so completely in it that they forget hearth and home and relations.... [Second] It is well known to the people of the world that all races and classes are loved and respected while they remain among their own people, their kindred and in their own town; but when they travel to some strange land they are friendless, miserable and disrespected. But the Turks are a case to the contrary. While they are amongst their own families and country they are merely one in a multitude and enjoy no wealth or power. But when they leave their own country and come to the land of the Muslims, the further they are taken from their hearth, their kin and their dwellings, the more valued, precious and expensive they become and they become amīrs and sipahsālārs.[11]

These records are particularly significant in their essentializing the qualities of Turks and depicting in this ethnic group the qualities that made them ideal servants of Islam. In these renditions, the capacity of the Turks to forget their original identities once they embraced Islam is applauded as a unique quality of this race of people. But notably, the trauma of enslavement that accompanied the experience of 'natal alienation and social death' was completely glossed.[12] According to these authors, it was not their deployment as military slaves that protected Muslim regimes; it was the quality inherent in their Turkish ethnicity—unique amongst all the people of the world—that came to the rescue of Islam.

The curious deployment of slaves of Turkish ethnicity may not be terribly surprising; the quality of the Turks as warriors in the cause of Islam has often been regarded as something of a literary trope, already evident in the ninth-century writings of al-Jāḥiẓ.[13] But there are some unusual aspects in the usage of these stereotypes by these two authors. Both Jūzjānī and Fakhr-i Mudabbir actually possessed fairly detailed information on Turkish tribes and the politics of the central Asian steppes. They were quite unique in this aspect, not just amongst Delhi Sultanate chroniclers, but amongst contemporary Persian authors writing in the eastern Islamic lands as well. They provided fairly precise names of tribes, their associations and locations, their languages, and scripts.[14] Despite their obvious access to all this information, the two authors homogenized the 'Turks' into analytically weak, ahistorical stereotypes. Other than accessing a relatively common and convenient literary trope, we need to ask whether the elisions present in the writings of the two authors were the product of larger structural factors that were in play in the construction of political authority and slave identities in the early Delhi Sultanate.

If we recall, Iltutmish empowered deracinated military slaves to build a reliable cadre of generals and governors in a bid to consolidate his authority. The reliance upon governors who were Turks and slaves created jural distinctions between civil (free) society and its governors who were slaves.[15] Providing an ethnic colouring to these groups reinforced these distinctions: a (nascent and threatened) Muslim society that was largely Persianate in its orientation was protected and governed by Turks. Noticeably, both Jūzjānī and Fakhr-i Mudabbir underplayed the slave–free juxtaposition; it was the racial binary that echoed in their texts.

On his part, Iltutmish hardly attempted to erase these binaries. He consolidated the chasm separating his senior military commanders from his subjects by underlining their proximity and dependence on him. Sometime during the training and fostering of his *bandagān-i khāṣṣ* Iltutmish gave them all new names. Without exception, all the slaves received Turkish names. At first sight this may not seem surprising: most of the *bandagān-i khāṣṣ* were of Turkish origin anyway.

But he could have given them Perso-Islamic names and titles as well. The import of the Delhi Sultan's actions becomes clearer when we consider that the period of the slave's training was the moment when the master consolidated his ties with his slaves and instilled in them the sense of belonging to a composite cadre. Apparently affixing a shared ethnicity was understood as an important part of the transitions in a slave's early life.[16] It must have been significant enough for the Sultan to give his non-Turkish slave a Turkish title. This happened in the case of Hindū *Khān*, a slave from the *qaṣaba* of Maihar in the Bundelkhand region in modern Madhya Pradesh. Iltutmish gave him the Turko-Mongol title of Khān and he became one of the monarch's trusted servants and the superintendent of all his slaves (*mihtar-i mubārak*).[17] Despite all of the tensions inherent in its making, the Delhi Sultan tried to provide the veneer of a composite Turkish ethnicity to his *bandagān-i khāṣṣ*.

Ironically, although the consolidation of the early Delhi Sultanate was carried out by Turks, they were depicted in such a way that very little of their steppe provenance or cultural identity filtered through. Instead, Turks carried a more general set of attributes related to valour and loyal conduct and, since it was an ethnic attribute, it served to measure this group off against others; one composite racial entity judged against another. In the hands of court chroniclers reporting on the Delhi Sultanate, the political system of the 'Turks' in north India was eulogized for creating a stable sanctuary for Islam, especially when eastern Iran, central Asia, and Afghanistan were suffering the Mongol apocalypse. At that fateful juncture in history, Sultan Iltutmish and his *bandagān-i khāṣṣ* stood united against the foes of Islam. The monolithic character given to the 'Turkish' military elite made it difficult for a thirteenth-century historian like Minhāj-i Sirāj Jūzjānī to explain the innumerable occasions of internal conflict amongst the *bandagān* later in the century. These were exceptional, unnatural moments and the author noted with some shock when

> the armies came close to each other—all brothers and friends of each other, two battalions of one dynasty *(daulat)*, two armies of the same capital *(haḍrat)*, [belonging to] the same mansion *(khāna)*, two parts of the same [saddle-?] lining—it was impossible for there to be a more amazing case. They were all of one purse, partakers of one dish between whom accursed Satan introduced much discord.[18]

In Jūzjānī's narration, the Shamsī *bandagān* would have never been in conflict with each other had Satan not intervened. Even as the great Sultan's political arrangements unravelled after his death, court chroniclers kept the memory of its ethnic homogeneity alive. It was for this reason that Baranī was surprised when the Khalajī dynasty removed the Turks from political power in 689/1286. As he put it, 'people ... wondered how the Khalajīs had replaced the Turks and seized the throne and how kingship had left the line *(aṣl)* of the Turks and gone to another'.[19] By the middle of the fourteenth century, when Ẓiyā' al-Dīn Baranī was composing his text, the years of slave dominance which had seen three slave families in power were scripted as a period of 'Turkish' dynastic rule. For this narration to possess credence, both 'slave' and 'Turk' were stripped of their historical contexts.

Mongol Invasions: Fluctuating Opportunities on the Sultanate Frontier

During Shams al-Dīn Iltutmish's reign Delhi protected itself from Mongol invasions through three strategic headquarters in the Punjab and Sindh regions. These were Lahore, Multan, and Uchch. Table 6.1 provides the information that we possess regarding their garrisoning under Shamsī commanders during Iltutmish's reign.

If we summarize this information we notice that the two oldest sons of Iltutmish controlled Lahore after it was annexed.[20] Their careers were separated by the brief tenure of a *bandagan-i khāṣṣ*, Naṣīr al-Dīn Ai-Tamar al-Bahā'ī. The governorship of Uchch was given to two senior slaves of Iltutmish, one after the death of the other. Two *bandagān-i khāṣṣ* were similarly appointed as governors of Multan. The first was removed because of some unreported misdemeanour. But this did not diminish Iltutmish's trust in his cadre of *bandagān*; another slave was appointed to Multan and he continued in office throughout the rest of Iltutmish's reign. It is significant that the governorships of strategic territories facing the Mongols were always given to people in whom the Sultan had the greatest amount of trust—his sons or his senior slaves. As the information in Table 6.1 brings out, the slaves were given these strategic governorships only after they had been trained and tested with a variety of administrative positions; these commands marked the apogee in their respective careers.

With Iltutmish's death in 1236 the sultanate plunged into political crisis. On the one hand Iltutmish's slave commanders and free amirs fought to maintain their autonomy and competed with each other on how to exert influence over their master's successor.[21] On the other hand, the Mongols intruded ever more energetically into the Punjab

Table 6.1   Shamsī Commanders and the Garrisoning of Lahore, Multan, and Uchch

Shamsi Military Commander	Area of Deployment
	LAHORE
Prince Nāṣir al-Dīn Maḥmūd, eldest son of Iltutmish, died 628/1230	614/1217 charge of **LAHORE**, (extended) to include Hansi; 623/1226> moved to Awadh > appointed Governor of Lakhnauti in 624/1227
Malik Naṣīr al-Dīn Ai-Tamar al-Bahā'ī, Shamsī slave	*sar-i Jāndār* > brief appointment in 623/1226 to *iqṭā'* of **LAHORE** > after 625/1227–8 *wilāyat* of Siwalik, Ajmer, Lawah (?), Kasli, Sanbharnamak and grant of elephant > killed during *ghazw* in Bundi region
Prince Rukn al-Dīn, second son of Iltutmish	625/1228 charge of Budaun > moved to Lahore in 631/1233 until end of Iltutmish's reign
	UCHCH
Malik Tāj al-Dīn Sanjar Kazlak Khān, Shamsī slave	Purchased by Iltutmish before his accession as Sultan > grew up with Prince Nāṣir al-Dīn > *chashnīgīr* > *amīr-i ākhūr* > 625/1228 *wilāyat* of Wanjrut in Multan > *iqṭā'* of Kuhram > *maḥrūsa*, garrison town, of Tabarhind, fort, town and suburbs of **UCHCH** > died 629/1231–2
Malik Saif al-Dīn Ai-Beg-i Uchch, Shamsī slave	Purchased by Iltutmish before his accession as Sultan > *sar-i Jāndār* > *iqṭā'* of Narnaul > Baran > Sunam > **UCHCH** after Tāj al-Dīn Kazlak Khān's death in 629/1231–2 >
	MULTAN
Kabīr Khān Ayāz al-Mu'izzī, Shamsī slave	Slave of Naṣīr al-Dīn Ḥusain Amīr-i Shikār > sold to Iltutmish by Naṣīr al-Dīn's heirs> 625/1227–8 town, fort, *qaṣabat*, market towns, and territory of **MULTAN** > removed c. 629/1231 and given Palwal for his maintenance
Malik Ikhtiyār al-Dīn Qarāqush Khān Ai-Tegin, Shamsī slave	An old slave of Iltutmish > *sāqī-yi khāṣṣ* > *iqṭā'* of Barihun (?) and Darnakwan (?) > *shaḥna* of *khālisa* of Tabarhind > after Malik Kabīr Khān's removal appointed to *iqṭā'* of **MULTAN** with title of Qarāqush >

Source: Minhāj-i Sirāj Jūzjānī, *Ṭubaqāt-i Nāṣirī*, ed. Abdul Hay Habibi (Kabul: Anjuman-i Tarikh-i Afghanistan, 1963–4).

and Sindh regions. The devastation of Lahore in 639/1241, the one-time capital of the Sultanate, merely marked the beginning of the Mongol incursions that would continue into the 1260s and lead to seizure of lands up to the Beas River in the Punjab and much of Sindh.[22] Jūzjānī reported on these invasions and the loss of territory in the most discreet fashion, but his anxieties were palpable. As Jackson put it, 'His prayer that the sovereignty of [the reigning sultan] Nāṣir al-Dīn Maḥmūd Shāh would endure until the Day of Resurrection (tā qiyām-i qiyāmat) is perhaps more than merely sycophantic hyperbole.'[23]

The geographical proximity of the Mongols to the core territories of the Sultanate was paralleled by increasing intervention in its political affairs. Rival contenders for power and disaffected military commanders sought sanctuary and military assistance from the Mongols. These included luminaries like Jalāl al-Dīn, the brother of the reigning Sultan, and important military commanders like Qutlugh Khān, Kushlu Khān, and even Shir Khān, the cousin of the future Sultan Ghiyāth al-Dīn Balban. The Mongols were always forthcoming in assisting disgruntled elites but seeking their assistance meant, in the protocol of the day, recognizing the suzerainty of the Great Khān and accepting the status of vassal. Thus, when Jalāl al-Dīn was installed as a rival Sultan in the recently despoiled city of Lahore, he had to accept a Mongol shaḥna, an intendant.[24]

There were diplomatic engagements between Hülegü (Il Khans), Batu (Golden Horde), Sultan Nāṣir al-Dīn, and his premier commander Ulugh Khān (the future Sultan Balban). The details of the negotiations are lost in the eulogistic dissimulation of the Delhi chroniclers who suggest that the Mongols were so impressed by the display of sultanate military might that they ordered their contingents to avoid campaigns in the territory of the Delhi sultan.[25] But in the fulsome record of Jūzjānī's narration of one such engagement is the inadvertent admission of Sultanate awareness of Mongol diplomatic etiquette. This is contained in a long anecdote where Jūzjānī described the presentation of letters from Ulugh Khān to Hülegü, the Il Khanid monarch. The letter to the Mongol monarch was in Persian and when it was translated into Mongolian the emissary replaced Khān in Balban's title with Malik. Jūzjānī clarified: 'The custom of Turkistan [qā'ida-i Turkistān] is this that there is but one Khān, no more, and all the others have the title of Malik.' In Jūzjānī's narration, Hülegü Khān knew of Balban's usage of the Khān title and honoured him sufficiently to protest its omission when his letter was read out with the honorific missing. He asked for the title of Khān to be restored.

Jūzjānī concluded his report: 'the titles of all of the Khāns from the lands of Hind and Sindh who went to the presence of the Khān were altered [*tabdīl kard*] in all of the documents proffered to the Mughal and they were referred to as *Malik*. But they confirmed the title of the great Ulugh Khān without change [as in] the original.'[26] The veracity of the incident is hardly of as much interest as Jūzjānī's knowledge of Mongol custom and hierarchic protocols and his sensitivity that the usage of the Delhi Sultan did not follow the prescribed custom. Since Hülegü chose to discount Mongol usage when dealing with Balban, the author suggested that a Great Khān could bestow the highest honour upon a non-Mongol.

We have already remarked on Fakhr-i Mudabbir and Jūzjānī's unique knowledge of the steppe people and their customs, but this fleeting insight into diplomatic relations helps to redirect our attention away from the litany of border conflicts that was only one part, albeit an important one, of trans-regional contacts at this time. The other aspect concerned migrants—displaced people and traders who had moved to the subcontinent and thus had left behind family, social networks, and markets in Afghanistan, eastern Iran, and Transoxiana.[27] Contacts between people separated by geographical distance required careful negotiation through arenas of conflict. The evidence for these contacts abounds in chronicles, travelogues, and in sufi *malfūzāt*. The casualness with which it is sometimes mentioned clearly demonstrates that different types of trans-regional contacts were hardly exceptional even during times of great hostilities.

An anecdote in the mystic saint Niẓām al-Dīn Awliyā's *malfūz* recalls how the imām of a mosque in Multan was pulled up by the sufi Ḥasan Afghān because rather than reading *namāz* with full intent, he was dreaming of bringing slaves from Delhi to Khurasan where they could be sold for a profit.[28] The fact that Khurasan was very much under the control of the Mongols caused the imām no nightmares. The anecdote is also noteworthy since it reported events from Multan. After the destruction of Lahore in 1241, Multan emerged as an important centre for trade into the 'upper lands', the euphemism for Khurasan and Transoxiana. Jūzjānī had occasion to test the services available in the city. He had a sister resident in Khurasan and in 648/1251 she sent messages to the author about being in dire straits. Jūzjānī appealed to his patrons and was given slaves and goods by Sultan Nāṣir al-Dīn and Ulugh Khān to send to her. When the author reached Multan that summer, it was in the midst of a tripartite struggle between two Shamsī slaves (Kushlū Khān and Shīr Khān) and the Qarlūq Saif al-Dīn Ḥasan, a Mongol ally. Multan eventually lapsed to the Qarlūqs, who had a Mongol *shaḥna* present in the city, but this conflict between different commanders and regimes over the city did not seem to complicate Jūzjānī's life. He successfully dispatched his goods to Khurasan and stayed on in Multan until the weather improved before making his way back to Delhi. Despite the military engagements between rival groups, the commercial life of the city remained undisturbed and, so far as our information allows us to gauge, Jūzjānī could travel undisturbed throughout the region.[29]

So how did these merchants traverse the trade routes into the 'upper lands'? We do not have information from Multan but Lahore provides a clue. When the Mongols besieged Lahore in 639/1241, the city was defended by Malik Ikhtiyār al-Dīn Qarāqush, his retinue and the residents of the town led by the *qāḍīs* and its notables, *ma'ārif*. The latter were hardly enthusiastic in resisting the Mongols and Jūzjānī explained that this was because the city possessed a large number of merchants involved in trade with Turkistan and the 'upper lands'. They visited these areas constantly and each had a *pā'iza* and a *mithāl-i amān* (literally, a tablet and an order of protection) from the Mongols.[30] The traders could use this *pā'iza* to travel undeterred in Mongol territories and they were aware that its receipt implied an acceptance of Mongol overlordship. While the *pā'iza* and *mithāl-i amān* gave merchants the opportunity to trade with the 'upper lands', where so many Sultanate residents still had families, it also left them—as the Lahore merchants discovered at their cost—as servants of two masters. This should not have been a problem if the Mongols and the Delhi Sultans had distinct political zones, but as we have already noticed, territorial control over the Punjab and Sindh areas in the middle of the thirteenth century was extremely fluid. Under the protection of the Sultanate commander, Qarāqush, the Lahore traders were the subjects of the Delhi Sultan. But as recipients of the Mongol *pā'iza* they were also subjects of the Mongols and, as a result, did not want to participate in a conflict where they had to choose between masters. Thus they only rendered the most lethargic support in the defence of the city. Without the support of the residents of the city, the Shamsī military commander, Malik Qarāqush, recognized the futility of defence and left the city to its fate. Unfortunately for the Lahore traders, the Mongols made little distinction between opposition, energetic or otherwise, and as was customary with subjects who had defied Mongol authority, the city of Lahore suffered devastating repercussions.

Great circumspection was necessary in negotiating the spaces between the warring Mongol and Delhi Sultanate regiments in the Punjab and Sindh regions. And yet prudence and entrepreneurship commingled adroitly amongst traders who saw in the vicissitudes of border confrontation, immigration, and displacement the opportunities to make their fortunes. It is doubtful if the Lahore traders were unique in carrying a *pā'iza* and a *mithāl-i amān*. As we noticed, the region of Multan profited from Lahore's misfortune, and trade from one port of call was transferred to another.

These developments should also make us question if our notions of 'frontier'—following, as they often do, the extremities of state control—obscure, rather than enable, a study of the complex trans-regional contacts during this period. Years ago, John Richards had argued that frontiers should be understood as 'zones' that were fluid and permeable, and which allowed for a variety of interactions. His own observations were restricted to an interaction between the Ghaznawid and Ghūrīd states and their Rajput counterparts in the subcontinent.[31] I am extending Richards's arguments somewhat to suggest that in the making of the Sultanate, the constant influx of immigrants and marauders through the thirteenth century never allowed for the development of a stable north-west frontier zone. The constant movement of people imbricated the Sultanate in larger trans-regional relations that had a profound impact on the character of the regime. In their portrayal of the Sultanate as a 'Sanctuary of Islam', an island of peace and stability for Muslims fleeing from the Mongol invasions, the Persian chroniclers sought to cohere the diverse body of immigrants into a composite Muslim community. But the making of this *idea* of the Muslim community meant that difference had to be policed and, failing that, glossed over. It would hardly help to dwell on Lahore traders who were subjects of the Mongol Khan; it was more useful to hold their fate as a warning to those who chose not to resist the Mongols.

Mongol Auxiliaries, Frontiersmen, and Late Thirteenth-Century Sultans of Delhi

The Mongols were one of the major threats to the stability of the Delhi Sultanate and it is not difficult to verify the grave military and political challenges they posed to the Delhi monarchs. Persian chronicles also describe in detail how the Chenggisid invasions deluged the subcontinent with immigrants during Iltutmish's reign in the first quarter of the thirteenth century. Less clear in their records—and therefore, in a later historiography as well—is the extent to which immigration from the 'upper lands' continued into the subcontinent, reaching another peak in the last quarter of the century. This was, in part, the consequence of developments that occurred within the Mongol and Sultanate dominions in the decades between the 1260s and 1290s.

To begin with, the concordance within the Mongol patrimony dissolved with the death of the Great Khān Möngke in 658/1260. Rival *uluses* emerged around the descendents of Chinggis Khān, and in the ensuing conflict the Chinggisid patrimony fragmented into rival states. Military contingents were sometimes stranded in areas distant from their parent body. The Delhi Sultanate felt the impact of these developments in the new body of Mongol personnel who appeared on their frontier. These were the Negüderids, known to Sultanate chroniclers as the Qara'unas. Unlike the past Mongol deployments in the Punjab and Sindh regions, the Great Khān did not direct the Negüderids to the area. They were the armed contingents of Negüder, a military commander affiliated with the Golden Horde, who escaped from Iran to avoid the persecution of the Il Khans. Unable to return to the trans-Caucasian steppes, the Negüderids made their way into the frontier marches of Hindustan where they were surrounded by hostile states: the Chaghadayids in Transoxiana, Il Khans in Iran, and the neighbouring Delhi Sultanate to the south-east. Quite inadvertently, their location made the Negüderids a buffer against any large-scale Mongol invasions into Sultanate territories.[32] Although Mongol incursions continued these were, for the moment, more localized engagements. They could nevertheless exact a heavy cost: in 684/1285 Balban's eldest son was slain during one such raid.

During the reign of Sultan Ghiyāth al-Dīn Balban (1266–87) the transitions in the Sultanate were equally dramatic. Its frontiers expanded once again into the Punjab and Sindh areas: Lahore was garrisoned and Multan secured under Sultanate commanders. The revitalization in Sultanate fortunes contrasted with the vicissitudes of many Mongol auxiliaries. The loss of patronage and reversals on the battlefield led some Mongol groups and their dependents to seek their fortunes with the Delhi court. Some Mongols made their residence in Delhi,[33] other groups like the Khalajīs—at one time dependents of the Qarlūqs, Mongol allies themselves—continued to reside on the frontier. Sometime in the early 1290s segments from the Negüderids—the Tughluqs—also sought service with the Delhi monarch.[34]

The Delhi Sultanate had already received and absorbed a large number of migrants of diverse backgrounds and, as in the past, these new migrants could also have disappeared in the subcontinent without a trace. But some of them could hardly be ignored: the immigrant families of the Khalajīs and the Tughluqs founded extremely influential, powerful Sultanate regimes. And yet the Persian chroniclers that recorded the histories of the Khalajīs and Tughluqs discussed the pasts of the dynastic founders in curious, elusive ways, systematically ignoring their prior service and associations with the Mongols. As a result we possess only incidental information concerning the social and cultural backgrounds or the early careers of Jalāl al-Dīn Khalajī and Ghiyāth al-Dīn Tughluq.

We know that Jalāl al-Dīn Khalajī's father's name was Yughrush only from a fifteenth-century chronicle.[35] For the early career of Jalāl al-Dīn we have to turn to Il Khānid chronicles to discover that the future monarch of Delhi was once the Mongol commander (*shāḥna*) of Binban, just west of the Indus.[36] Amīr Khusrau quotes him on his exploits against refractory Mongol and Afghan tribes in the Salt Range. He does not provide any context to these events which, if not hyperbole, might have occurred before he joined service with the Delhi Sultans.[37] An incidental reference in Jūzjānī informs us that the son of Yughrush (Jalāl al-Dīn?) visited Delhi with a Mongol embassy in 658/1260.[38] It is not clear when Jalāl al-Dīn started serving the Delhi Sultans but it must have been a few years later, sometime during Balban's reign. 'Iṣāmī mentions that he was in the service of Balban's younger son, Prince Bughra Khān.[39] The account is chronologically unclear but this must have occurred before 1280 while the prince was still located in Samana, a town that later became Jalāl al-Dīn's headquarters. Jalāl al-Dīn's political influence increased as commander of the north-west marches until Sultan Kaiqubād invited him to the capital as a counterweight to the old Balbanī elites and the parvenu commanders entrenched in Delhi. Although given the exalted title of Shaista Khān and the military assignment of Baran, Jalāl al-Dīn found it difficult to integrate himself in the politics of the court, especially with the murder of the young Sultan. Faced with political marginalization he acted against the clique who controlled the capital and seized the throne in 689/1290. Even after his accession, insurrection led by members of the old regime continued and it was not until 691/1292 that his reign approximated some degree of stability.[40]

As obscure as Jalāl al-Dīn's early history is the past of Ghiyāth al-Dīn Tughluq, the other military commander on the north-west frontier who went on to become Sultan. Although Amīr Khusrau provided a eulogy of Ghiyāth al-Dīn's campaign against the usurper Khusrau Khān Barwarī (720/1320), it is the Moroccan traveller Ibn Baṭṭūṭa, and not a chronicler of the Delhi court, who informs us that Ghiyāth al-Dīn was a Qara'una Turk.[41] Ghiyāth al-Dīn was not a great Negüderid amir when he migrated to India. According to Ibn Baṭṭūṭa he worked for a merchant as a humble keeper of the horses, perhaps a cattle-driver (*gulwaniya* > *guala*), and received patronage first from Ulugh Khān, the brother of Sultan 'Alā al-Dīn Khalajī.[42] Amīr Khusrau was less explicit. He recalled Ghiyāth al-Dīn's statement about his early years as a nomad (*āwāra mardī*) when the patronage received from Sultan Jalāl al-Dīn Khalajī (not Ulugh Khān in this version) raised him to a high status.[43] The discrepancies amongst his early patrons notwithstanding, there is no dispute about how Ghiyāth al-Dīn's military activities on the frontier improved his fortune until by the second decade of the fourteenth century he was commander of Dipalpur, with some respect as a successful general against the Mongols.[44] His frontier background and his successes did not endear him to the Khalajī military commanders in the capital, however, and Amīr Khusrau details their refusal to join him in his effort to remove the usurper Sultan Khusrau Khān Barwarī from power.[45]

Scant as this information might be, it underlines some common qualities shared by Jalāl al-Dīn Khalajī and Ghiyāth al-Dīn Tughluq: both had prior Mongol links, they served on the frontier under the Mongols until they migrated to the Sultanate and sought service with the Delhi Sultans. Both were deployed as frontier commanders and went on to eventually seize power in the capital. In this list of shared qualities we need to also add that both Jalāl al-Dīn Khalajī and Ghiyāth al-Dīn Tughluq were outside the charmed circle of military confreres in the capital and, as outsiders, not regarded worthy enough to be potential candidates to the throne of Delhi. Notably, neither of the powerful frontier commanders received support from Delhi courtiers when they shifted their base to the capital. In underlying these shared qualities, however, we need to keep in mind that no Sultanate chronicler ever underlined these similarities amongst the two Sultans of Delhi. Instead they sought to deflect their reader's attention from their close proximity and early service with the Mongols to a discussion of their qualities as Muslim monarchs. This should hardly surprise us. In the context of their unending diatribe against the Mongol hordes, it hardly helped for fourteenth-century Sultanate chroniclers like Ẓiyā' al-Dīn Baranī or 'Iṣāmī to recognize that the monarchs of

Delhi had made their early careers in the service of people described by Amīr Khusrau as individuals whose 'open mouth smelt like an arm-pit, [and] whiskers fell from his chin like pubic-hair'.[46]

If we recall thirteenth-century Persian chroniclers had been equally reticent in discussing the nature of their Turkish masters. They certainly did not dwell on their jural status as slaves, or attach any significance on their steppe, tribal antecedents. Instead they reworked these qualities to speak of a 'Turkish' racial quality that stood for a valorous, 'noble' soldier in the service of Islam. The 'Turk' was one individual who would gladly forsake his old social self and embrace a new identity as a Muslim. But the frontiersmen who entered the Sultanate in the last quarter of the thirteenth century were very different from these Turks. They had only recently transited from a pastoral milieu and service with the enemies of Islam. They were not deracinated, and they arrived in the Sultanate with their social networks, lineages, goods, and livestock intact. In other words, the social and cultural milieu of the frontier often followed in the footsteps of these migrants. Amīr Khusrau described the retinue of Ghiyāth al-Dīn Tughluq as they marched into Delhi saying, 'troopers [who] were mainly from the upper-lands (*iqlīm-i bālā*) and not Hindustanis or local chieftains. They included Ghūzz, Turks, and Mongols of Rūm and Rūs and some Khurasani Persians (*tāzīk*) of pure stock (*pāk aṣl*)'.[47] As Peter Jackson perceptively concluded: '[Ghiyāth al-Dīn] Tughluq's affinity ... was markedly regional; his lieutenants were commanders who had fought alongside him on the Mongol frontier, sometimes themselves Mongol renegades, or Hindu warlords who were his close neighbours in the western Punjab.'[48]

How did the migrations of these recent confederates of the Mongols affect the Delhi Sultanate? What aspects of their frontier milieu did they carry with them into their new homelands? Let us begin by focusing on administrative systems, a useful place to start because these are rarely invented *de novo*. Although these systems were strongly mediated by the Shansabanids, the early Delhi Sultans also borrowed, adapted, and inventively cobbled together forms of administration and governance from a diverse body of regimes. The lines of transmission are usually extremely unclear. Take for example the deployment of *shāhnas*, or intendants. As we have already noticed, the Mongols used *shāhnas* but so did Turkish Seljuqs much earlier. As Doerfer has pointed out, the office was of Chinese origin (*shao-chien*) and was introduced into the central Islamic lands by the Qārā Khitā.[49] It was already in common currency during Iltutmish's reign, and we cannot be certain how this office made its way into Sultanate usage.

Administrative borrowings can be traced somewhat more clearly at the end of the thirteenth century in the context of the *ulagh*. This was a mounted courier service organized by Chinggis Khān and sustained by the *qubchur* taxes collected from the Mongols. It is clear that the Delhi Sultans did not use the *ulagh* in the first half of the century; there are no references to it in Jūzjānī. On the other hand Baranī, writing in the middle of the fourteenth century, notes its usage under the Khalajīs and Tughluqs. But the way the office was manifest in Sultanate practice did not approximate early thirteenth-century Chinggisid usage. Baranī's description suggests that the Tughluq organization of the *ulagh* was closer in nature to its later thirteenth-century development in the Mongol *uluses* (post-Chinggisid patrimonies), where it was sustained by *qalan* or taxes that were imposed upon the local population and no longer on the Mongols. This would suggest that the Delhi Sultanate borrowed the system after its later evolution in the Il Khānid or Chaghadayid realms sometime during the 1260s and 1280s, decades that coincided with the migration of Mongol auxiliaries into Sultanate territory.

It is significant to note that no Persian chronicler discussed the provenance of the *ulagh* in their texts. This does not mean, however, that they were ignorant of its origins. They blithely glossed over the usage of Turkish titulature by the Delhi Sultans. Jūzjānī's remarks regarding Ulugh Khān's usage of the Khān title was a rare fleeting moment that revealed the awkwardness with which the author responded to the practice of Turkish and Mongol titulature by the Delhi Sultans. And yet, with the accession to power of the Khalajī monarchs, a chronicler such as Baranī could speak of the passing away of the age of the Turks even as he went on to record the plethora of Turkish titles used by the Khalajī ruling family—Yughrush, Garshasp, Ulugh, Qutlughtegin, Arkalī, Ikit. These were titles dispensed by Khalajī Sultans to relatives. These honours would possess little valence unless they possessed cultural significance to their recipients and a larger audience.

Despite their discretion, Persian chroniclers let slip enough information to clarify their knowledge of the complex, trans-regional constituency of Sultanate society and politics. And yet their narratives also clarify that they were not always familiar or able to comprehend some of the customs practised by their rulers. These would be customs and rituals associated with the recent immigrants, practices 'foreign' to the experience of the Persian chroniclers, and the two following examples will serve to illustrate my point.

The first example concerns Ẓiyā' al-Dīn Baranī's account of the circumstances that led to the brief enthronement of Qadr Khān in 695/1296, the younger son of Sultan Jalāl al-Dīn Khalajī. At the time of Jalāl al-Dīn's murder, of his two sons, Qadr Khān was too young to have received any prior political appointment. By contrast, Jalāl al-Dīn's older son, Arkalī Khān, had the old monarch's trust. He was given considerable authority over armies, territories, and in the punishment of rebels.[50] After Jalāl al-Dīn's murder Baranī expected that the competent Arkalī Khān would succeed his father and could not restrain his surprise when the queen mother, Malika-i Jahān, placed the younger sibling on the throne.[51]

Baranī's inability to comprehend these developments is apparent from his clichéd, gendered remarks about Malika-i Jahān. Baranī informs us that she was somewhat of a shrew, a stubborn, wilful person, who had dominated her husband while he was alive.[52] The impetuous act of placing the young Qadr Khān on the throne and assuming the regency herself was in keeping with her naïve, foolish character. She did not consult anyone and as her experiment led to disaster for the dynasty, Baranī had Malika-i Jahān confess to the folly of her actions. According to Baranī the queen admitted: 'I am a woman and women are deficient in judgement [*nāqiṣāt-i 'aql*]'.[53] Tenuous as the explanations provided by the author may be, they are rendered even more fragile at Baranī's recounting of the older son's reactions at the loss of the throne. The energetic, valiant Arkalī Khān, who had once had the sufi saint Sīdī Muwallih crushed by an elephant, accepted his exclusion from the throne as a *fait accompli*. Instead of disputing the succession, he retreated to his appanage in Multan. There he remained despite the apologies and entreaties of the queen to return to Delhi and oppose the rebel 'Alā' al-Dīn Khalajī.[54]

The Khalajīs ruled for three generations and every succession during their rule of thirty years (689–720/1290–1320) was disputed. Obviously the assumption of high office was never resolved to the satisfaction of rival claimants. Important to keep in mind is the fact that these claimants were *always* members of the ruling family and in attempting to curtail intra-lineage conflict, the fourth dynast, Mubārak Shāh Khalajī (716–20/1316–20), incarcerated many of his siblings, eventually blinding and executing them.[55] In this milieu, Malika-i Jahān's placing of young Qadr Khān on the throne—Baranī's horror notwithstanding—was one accession that remained unchallenged by his sibling. He seemed to accept—for the moment anyway—the right of his younger brother to the throne.

This was in contrast to 'Alā' al-Dīn Khalajī's own experience. After seizing the throne he was generous to many of his relatives and gave them high positions, but he also progressed toward an exclusive segregation of authority in his own person. Sometime around 700/1301 an attempt was made on 'Alā' al-Dīn's life. The perpetrator was Ikit Khān, 'Alā' al-Dīn Khalajī's youngest brother's son.[56] Baranī attributed base ambition as the motive for Ikit Khān's animosity but it should not escape our scrutiny that in seizing power, 'Alā' al-Dīn Khalajī had reversed the order of succession that had prevailed a generation earlier. If Malika-i Jahān had appointed the youngest son to the throne excluding the older sibling, 'Alā' al-Dīn was the oldest sibling and his right to the throne was challenged by the disaffected descendents of his youngest brother.

Baranī's reportage makes it extremely difficult to comprehend the workings of Khalajī customs of inheritance. Certainly one of their traditions seemed to privilege the rights of the youngest son. It is hard to say whether these traditions of ultimogeniture are reflective of the rights of the 'hearth-prince' [ot tegin/otčigin] recognized by some Turkish tribes and the Chinggisid family.[57] Tantalizing as the evidence might be, in its scantiness it remains hardly compelling. A careful prosopographical analysis of the Khalajī family may provide additional information on the subject but, for the moment anyway, more germane for our present discussion is to notice Baranī's complete inability to fathom what the regnant sultans of Delhi were about. While his diatribe against Malika-i Jahān reveals the author's own gendered location, it also underlines the Persian litterateur's inability to comprehend the cultural world of his protagonists—recent émigrés to the Sultanate but now its rulers.

Equally new to the cultural traditions of Delhi were the Tughluqs, whose dynastic founder, Ghiyāth al-Dīn, was hailed as the 'Saviour of Islam' even though his retinue consisted of Khokhars, Ghūzz, Turks, and Mongols from Rūm and Rūs, all of whom had challenged the authority of the Sultanate in the past. Now they were masters of Delhi. No Persian chronicler ever made anything of the disjunction between the past careers and present fortunes of the members of the early Tughluq political dispensation. And yet the travelogue of Ibn Baṭṭūṭa suggests that the Tughluqs placed a considerable premium that their notables acculturate rapidly to 'Muslim ways'. He noted that in Muḥammad Tughluq's reign (724–52/1324–51) 'all [courtiers] were required to show knowledge of the obligations of ablution, prayers and the binding articles of Islam. They used to be questioned on these matters; if anyone failed to give the correct answers he was punished and they made a habit of studying them with one another in the audience hall and the bazaars and setting them down in writing'.[58] This was an unusual requirement to demand of practising Muslims unless, of course, their ritual praxis was regarded as somewhat deficient.

While Persian chronicles gloss over some uncomfortable details about their lords and masters, the amateur ethnography of Ibn Baṭṭūṭa, the visitor from Morocco, carries interesting details about Tughluq court rituals and ceremonies. He provided the following description of Muḥammad Tughluq's royal procession on festivals:

> On the morning of the feast all the elephants are adorned with silk, gold and precious stones. There are sixteen of these elephants which no one rides, but they are reserved to be ridden by the Sultan himself, and over them are carried sixteen parasols of silk embroidered with jewels, each one with a shaft of pure gold.... The Sultan himself rides on one of these elephants and in front of him there is carried aloft the *ghāshiya*, that is his saddle-cover, which is adorned with the most precious jewels. In front of him walk his slaves and his mamlūks.[59]

Ibn Baṭṭūṭa added further details regarding the ritual at the time of the Sultan's entry into the capital:

> On some of the (sixteen) elephants there were mounted small military catapults and when the Sultan came near the city, parcels of gold and silver coins mixed together were thrown from these machines. The men on foot in front of the Sultan and the other persons present scrambled for the money, and they kept on scattering it until the procession reached the palace[60]

While *ghāshiya* has an Arabic etymology, meaning to cover, veil,[61] the origin of the ceremony lies in the accession and ceremonial rituals of the early Turks, where the 'Lord of the Horse' would be identified with the newly enthroned leader and the procession would celebrate the conquest of the four quarters by the Universal Emperor.[62] The tradition was followed in some of the major steppe-descended polities in the central Islamic lands—the Seljūqs, the Zangids, and the Baḥrī Mamlūks of Egypt (with a military elite of Qipchaq origin).[63] At least in Syria and Egypt, it was accepted as a ritual associated with royalty and performed by the Kurdish Ayyūbids, who learnt of it from their Turkish patrons, the Zangids. With the Ayyūbids it was integrated as a part of their accession ceremony together with the ritual pledge of allegiance, *bay'a*, and the investiture from the Caliph.[64]

Detailed descriptions of the *ghashiya* ritual exist from the Mamlūk Sultanate of Egypt, where Ibn Taghrībirdī clarified that it was a part of the accession ceremonies of the monarch and was repeated on major festivals. Its performance in Egypt mirrors Ibn Baṭṭūṭa's description of the ceremony from Muḥammad Tughluq's court and al-Qalqashandī provided the following description:

> [The *ghāshiya*] is a saddle cover of leather, decorated with gold so that the observer would take it to be made entirely of gold. It is borne before him (the Mamlūk Sultan) when riding in state processions for parades, festivals, etc. The rikābdāriyya (grooms, that is, ghulāms) carry it, the one who holds it up in his hands turning it right and left. It is one of the particular insignia of this kingdom.[65]

An important common feature between the Mamlūk state in Egypt and the Delhi Sultanate was their common reliance upon Turko–Mongol personnel from the trans-Caucasian steppes, the *dasht-i Qipchaq*. The Sultanate's link with the Eurasian steppe already present in Iltutmish's reign continued into the reign of Ghiyāth al-Dīn Tughluq who was of Negüderid background, and had a retinue of 'Turks and Mongols of Rūm and Rūs'.

Just as most of the Persian chronicles ignored the composition of Ghiyāth al-Dīn's retinue, they paid no attention to his royal procession ceremony. Since Ibn Baṭṭūṭa's observations remained largely 'unsubstantiated' in the accounts of the Persian literati they did not draw the attention of modern scholars. Yet, Baranī's description of 'Alā al-Dīn's triumphant march to Delhi after Jalāl al-Dīn's murder (695/1296) does possess some of the elements present in Ibn Baṭṭūṭa's description, although completely different motives are attributed by the author to the discharge of gold coins (*panj-man akhtar*, five mans of gold stars) amongst the crowds observing the Sultan's march.[66] Equally selective was Yaḥyā Sirhindī's early fifteenth-century account of Muḥammad Tughluq's celebratory procession after his accession. The narrative is close enough to Ibn Baṭṭūṭa's description of the *ghāshiya* ritual for us to follow its main features but the elisions are important as well. Sirhindī noted:

> The lanes were decorated with coloured and embroidered cloth. From the time that the Sultan set his foot in the city till he entered the imperial palace, gold and silver coins were rained from the back of the elephants among the populace, and gold was scattered in every street, lane, and house.[67]

In Baranī and Sirhindī's account the Sultan's triumphal processions receive due recognition but there is no reference to the *ghashiya*. Was the omission deliberate or was it an aspect of Turko–Mongol practice quite unfamiliar to Persian secretaries? Were they, in other words, just inadequate historians reifying the practice of their subjects either through ignorance or because of their own class and cultural prejudices?

Baranī was a contemporary of Ibn Baṭṭūṭa and both authors were in Delhi during Muḥammad Tughluq's reign. If the Moroccan visitor could notice and learn about the *ghashiya* during his visit, so, theoretically speaking, could Baranī. He noticed the *ulagh* and mentioned its presence in his *ta'rīkh*. But this detail did not complicate the larger point that the author wanted to make about Ghiyāth al-Dīn in his history. In Baranī's narrative Ghiyāth al-Dīn was a 'Saviour of Islam,' a morally righteous Muslim, renowned for his combat with the infidel Mongols and against the heathen menace that was suddenly threatening Delhi. The challenge to Islam appeared when the usurper Khusrau Khān Barwarī, a recent convert slave, killed his master and his heirs, despoiled his master's harem and apostatized. Just as Ghiyāth al-Dīn Tughluq had saved the Sultanate from the Mongols, this conflict with Khusrau Khān Barwarī was over the future well-being of the Muslim community. By incorporating details about the Turko–Mongol antecedents of Ghiyāth al-Dīn and the composition of his retinue, or noting the practise of [un-Islamic] steppe rituals by the frontier commander, Baranī would have complicated the simple binaries around which he had framed the qualities of his protagonist—the Muslim hero versus the non-Muslim—and his narration of the triumph of rectitude over evil. The author preferred not to tread these waters. Once the social and cultural backgrounds of Ghiyāth al-Dīn Tughluq and his frontier retinue were erased what was left was a relatively monochromatic picture of a Muslim Delhi Sultanate valiantly battling a sea of infidels, holding aloft the banner of Islam even as the Mongol deluge swept away the civilization of the *Dār al-Islām* elsewhere. In this narration the complex connections of the Tughluqs with regions and cultures outside the subcontinent were completely erased.

* * *

The social and cultural proximity of Sultanate elites and their political and administrative practices with the adjoining Turko–Mongol universe should be hardly surprising. Following the Mongol incursions

most of the central Islamic lands carried the imprint of steppe customs. Even areas relatively unscathed by Mongol campaigns, like
Mamlūk Egypt, were deeply tied into this new world through close
diplomatic and commercial links with the Golden Horde. By contrast, however, historians of the Delhi Sultanate have assumed that it
remained somewhat of an island, relatively untouched by these developments. It continued to honour the 'Abbāsid Caliphs and adhered
to a pre-Mongol matrix of political thought and conduct even as the
adjoining regions were altered irrevocably.

Conventional historiography on the Sultanate has argued that its
'Turkish' experience ended with the establishment of the Khalajī
dynasty in 689/1290. The Sultanate then proceeded to root itself in
its subcontinental milieu by the deployment of increasing numbers
of local converts to Islam. After the Ghaznavid and Ghūrid invasions, processes that were endogenous to the subcontinent touched
Sultanate history; the central Islamic lands impacted on it with the
occasional metaphysical idea: *waḥdat al-wujūd* (unity of being) in the
realm of mysticism or Mu'tazilite rationalism in theology and philosophy. The sense of history passing by the Sultanate is only emphasized by the great importance given to the Mughals whose rule saw
the introduction of new administrative, fiscal, and intellectual ideas.[68]

Many of these conclusions originate from the evidence available
to scholars. The Persian *tawārīkh* produced in the court of the Delhi
Sultans focused primarily on the military engagements between their
monarchs and the heathen invaders. The Mongols were looked at
with horror and dislike. Mongol migrants, when they were described
at all, were derisively called *naw musulamān* or new Muslims and
treated as despicable creatures. Their emissaries were awed by dis-
plays of Sultanate might and pomp. And yet, it is possible to develop
an alternate history of the Sultanate and its relationship with the
Mongol regimes and peoples adjoining the subcontinent. This is an
elusive, sometimes extremely disjointed history because the authors
of *tawārīkh* did not always find it politic to record its details. And yet,
the silence in our records, the fragmented evidence at hand, and its
many contradictions provide the questions that can be fruitfully inter-
rogated to enlarge not just on the nature of trans-regional relations
of the period but the complex and conflicted ways in which these
relationships textured the making of Sultanate politics and society.

Chinggis Khan's invasions triggered developments that directed the
history of the subcontinent in some unusual directions. The complex
constituency of the Muslim population in the subcontinent was one

of its products. Through the thirteenth and fourteenth centuries old and new immigrants from a variety of backgrounds jostled for power and eminence in the subcontinent. The threat of Mongol invasions provided more than just the context for the age; the lexicon of politics and governance was imbued by Turkish and Mongol traditions. The making of subcontinental Muslim society as much as the formation of the Delhi Sultanate was grounded in the manner in which these trans-regional connections were assimilated or rejected in the long duration. To ignore this dialectic and the Sultanate's extensive ties with regions beyond its boundaries would sublimate the politics of the age into a synchronic ahistorical homogeneity. Although we can appreciate the historical contexts and compulsions that led Persian litterateurs to create the picture of a monolithic social and political world under the Delhi Sultans, there is little reason for us to continue to peer into the past through the same lens.

Notes

1. For further details on the history of the period, see C.E. Bosworth, 'The Early Islamic History of Ghur', *CAJ* 6 (1961): pp. 116–33, reprinted in C.E. Bosworth, *The Medieval History of Iran, Afghanistan, and Central Asia* (London: Variorum Reprints, 1977); C.E. Bosworth, 'Notes on the Pre-Ghaznavid History of Eastern Afghanistan', *IQ* 9 (1965): pp. 12–24, reprinted in Bosworth, *Medieval History*; Finbarr Barry Flood, 'Ghurid Monuments and Muslim Identities: Epigraphy and Exegesis in Twelfth-century Afghanistan', *IESHR* 42 (2005): pp. 263–94; Sunil Kumar, *Emergence of the Delhi Sultanate* (Delhi: Permanent Black, 2007), pp. 46–63; and Peter Jackson, 'Jalāl al-Dīn, the Mongols and the Khwarazmian Conquest of the Panjāb and Sind', *Iran* 28 (1990): pp. 45–54; Peter Jackson, *The Delhi Sultanate: A Political and Military History* (Cambridge: University Press, 1999).

2. Note for example the sentiment of Minhāj-i Sirāj Jūzjānī, *Ṭabaqāt-i Nāṣirī*, ed. Abdul Hay Habibi (Kabul: Anjuman-i Tarikh-i Afghanistan, 1963–4), vol. 1, pp. 90–1.

3. Jūzjānī, *Ṭabaqāt-i Nāṣirī*, vol. 1, pp. 307, 324–7, 342, 397–8, 402, 412–13, 417.

4. Jūzjānī, *Ṭabaqāt-i Nāṣirī*, vol. 1, pp. 422–3, 424.

5. Jūzjānī, *Ṭabaqāt-i Nāṣirī*, vol. 1, pp. 450–2, 459–60, 468, 476; vol. 2, 134–5, 140–1.

6. For an extended discussion on migration and patronage see Kumar, *Emergence of the Delhi Sultanate*, pp. 65–78, 146–51.

7. Peter Jackson, 'Turkish Slaves on Islam's Indian Frontier', in *Slavery and South Asian History*, eds. Indrani Chatterjee and Richard M. Eaton

(Bloomington: Indiana University Press, 2006), pp. 63–82; P.B. Golden, 'The Ölberlī (Ölperlī): The Fortunes and Misfortunes of an Inner Asian Nomadic Clan', *AEMA* 6 (1986): pp. 5–29; Sunil Kumar, 'When Slaves Were Nobles: The Shamsī *Bandagān* in the Early Delhi Sultanate', *SIH* 10 (1994): pp. 23–52.

8. Jūzjānī, *Ṭabaqāt-i Nāṣirī*, vol. 2, pp. 1–89.

9. Note the example of Kabīr al-Dīn Ayāz; Jūzjānī, *Ṭabaqāt-i Nāṣirī*, vol. 2, pp. 5–7.

10. Jūzjānī, *Ṭabaqāt-i Nāṣirī*, vol. 1, p. 441; vol. 2, pp. 47–8, for Iltutmish and Balban respectively.

11. Fakhr-i Mudabbir, *Ta'rīkh-i Fakhr al-Dīn Mubārak Shāh*, ed. Ross, E. Denison (London: Royal Asiatic Society, 1927), pp. 35–6. This passage is a slightly amended translation of Ross, 'The Genealogies of Fakhr al-Din Mubarak Shah', in *'Ajab Namah: A Volume of Oriental Studies presented to E.G. Browne on His 60th Birthday*, eds. T.W. Arnold and R.A. Nicholson (Cambridge: University Press, 1922), pp. 402–3.

12. For the significance of 'natal alienation and social death', see Orlando Patterson, *Slavery and Social Death: A Comparative Study* (Cambridge, Massachusetts: Harvard University Press, 1982); and for a recent evaluation, see Sean Stilwell, *Paradoxes of Power: The Kano "Mamluks" and Male Royal Slavery in the Sokoto Caliphate, 1804–1903* (Portsmouth: Heinemann, 2004). I am grateful to Richard Eaton for making this book available to me.

13. C.T. Harvey Walker, trans., 'Jahiz of Basra to al-Fath ibn Khaqan on the "Exploits of the Turks and the Army of the Khalifate in General"', *JRAS* 23 (1915): pp. 631–97 and J.D. Latham, 'The Archers of the Middle East: The Turco–Iranian Background', *Iran* 8 (1970): pp. 97–102.

14. Fakhr-i Mudabbir, *Ta'rīkh-i Fakhr al-Dīn Mubārak Shāh*, p. 47 and Jūzjānī, *Ṭabaqāt-i Nāṣirī*, vol. 2, pp. 220–1, 175–6. See also Kumar, *Emergence of the Delhi Sultanate*, p. 162n76 for a more elaborate discussion.

15. See also Sunil Kumar, 'La Communauté Musulmane et les Relations Hindo-Musulmanes dans l'Inde du Nord au Début du XIIIᵉ siècl: Une Reevaluation Politique', *Annales* 60 (2005): pp. 239–64.

16. For some similarities with Mamluk Egypt, see David Ayalon, 'Names, Titles, and Nisbas of the Mamluks', *IOS* 5 (1975): pp. 189–232.

17. See Jūzjānī, *Ṭabaqāt-i Nāṣirī*, vol. 2, pp. 18–19.

18. Jūzjānī, *Ṭabaqāt-i Nāṣirī*, vol. 2, p. 73.

19. Żiyā' al-Dīn Baranī, *Ta'rīkh-i Fīrūz Shāhī*, ed. Sayyid Ahmad Khan (Calcutta: Bibliotheca Indica 1860–2), p. 175.

20. For the respective careers of Nāṣir al-Dīn Maḥmūd and Rukn al-Dīn, see Jūzjānī, *Ṭabaqāt-i Nāṣirī*, vol. 1, pp. 438, 447, 453–4.

21. For an account of these years see Kumar, *Emergence of the Delhi Sultanate*, pp. 238–98.

22. On Mongol invasions during this period see Jackson, *The Delhi Sultanate*, pp. 103–14.

23. Jackson, *The Delhi Sultanate*, p. 113.

24. Jackson, *The Delhi Sultanate*, pp. 73, 88–9, 111–14.

25. Jūzjānī, *Ṭabaqāt-i Nāṣirī*, vol. 2, pp. 83–8.

26. Jūzjānī, *Ṭabaqāt-i Nāṣirī*, vol. 2, p. 87.

27. For an early discussion of this subject, see John F. Richards, 'Outflows of Precious Metals from Early Islamic India", in *Precious Metals in the Later Medieval and Early Modern Worlds*, ed. John F. Richards (Durham: Carolina Academic Press, 1983), pp. 183–205.

28. Amīr Ḥasan Sijzī, *Fawā'id al-Fu'ād*, ed. Khwaja Hasan Thani Nizami Dihlawi (Delhi: Urdu Academy, 1990), p. 15.

29. Jūzjānī, *Ṭabaqāt-i Nāṣirī*, vol. 1, pp. 483–4; vol. 2, p. 61.

30. Jūzjānī, *Ṭabaqāt-i Nāṣirī*, vol. 2, pp. 123–4. On *pā'iza*, see also 'Alā' al-Dīn 'Aṭā Malik Juwainī, *Ta'rīkh-i Jahān-Gushā*, trans. John A. Boyle, *The History of the World–Conqueror* (Manchester: University Press, 1958), vol. 1, pp. 158, 255, 257; vol. 2, pp. 487, 488, 489, 499, 500, 508–9, 519–20, 523, 551, 598, 606; Gerhard Doerfer, *Turkische und Mongolische Elemente im Neupersischen* (Weisbaden: Frans Steiner Verlag, 1963–75), vol. 1, pp. 239–41; D.O. Morgan, 'Mongols', *EI2* 7: p. 234.

31. John F. Richards, 'The Islamic Frontier in the East: Expansion into South Asia', *South Asia* 4 (1974): pp. 91–109.

32. On the Negüderids/Qara'unas, see Jean Aubin, 'L'ethnogénése des Qaraunas', *Turcica* 1 (1969): pp. 65–94. See also Beatrice Forbes Manz, *The Rise and Fall of Tamerlane* (Cambridge: Cambridge University Press, 1990, reprint), pp. 159–61; Jackson, *The Delhi Sultanate*, pp. 119–22, 217–27, 328.

33. Baranī, *Ta'rīh-i Fīrūz Shāhī*, pp. 133–4, 218–19.

34. See notes 37–46 later for references.

35. Yaḥyā b. Aḥmad b. 'Abd Allah Sirhindī, *Ta'rikh-i Mubārak Shāhī*, ed. S.M. Hidayat Hosain (Calcutta: Bibliotheca Indica, 1931), p. 61. The text has Bughrush, which must be a mistake for Yughrush, the form found in Jūzjānī, *Ṭabaqāt-i Nāṣirī*, vol. 2, p. 88.

36. Cited in Jackson, *The Delhi Sultanate*, p. 80.

37. Amīr Khusrau, *Miftāḥ al-Futuḥ*, ed. Shaykh Abdur Rashid (Aligarh: Publication of the Department of History, Aligarh Muslim University, 1954), p. 8. Jackson, *The Delhi Sultanate*, p. 118, suggests a later date for these campaigns. The evidence is ambiguous on this point.

38. Jūzjānī, *Ṭabaqāt-i Nāṣirī*, vol. 2, p. 88.

39. 'Abd al-Malik 'Iṣāmī, *Futūḥ al-Salāṭīn*, ed. A.S. Usha (Madras: University of Madras, 1940), p. 195.

40. For an account of these years, see Baranī, *Ta'rīkh-i Firūz Shāhī*, pp. 170–84 and Jackson, *The Delhi Sultanate*, pp. 81–5.

41. Ibn Baṭṭūṭa, *Rehla*, trans. Mahdi Husain (Baroda: Oriental Institute, 1976, reprint) (Gaekwad's Oriental Series, no. 122), p. 47. See also the alternative translation of H.A.R. Gibb, 2nd series, no. 141 (Cambridge: Hakluyt Society, Cambridge University Press, 1971), vol. 3, p. 649.

42. Ibn Baṭṭūṭa, *Rehla*, trans. Mahdi Husain, p. 47; trans. Gibb, vol. 3, p. 649.

43. Amīr Khusrau, *Tughluq Nāma*, ed. Sayyid Hashmi Faridabadi (Aurangabad: Urdu Publishing House, 1933), p. 136.

44. For a useful account of Ghiyāth al-Dīn Tughluq's early career on the frontier, see Ibn Baṭṭūṭa, *Rehla*, trans. Mahdi Husain, pp. 47–9; trans. Gibb, vol. 3, pp. 648–52.

45. Amīr Khusrau, *Tughluq Nāma*, p. 84.

46. This is Amīr Khusrau's description of his Qara'una captor. See Amīr Khusrau, *Wasaṭ al-Ḥayāt*, cited in 'Abd al-Qādir Badā'ūnī, *Muntakhab al-Tawārīkh*, ed. Maulavi Ahmad Shah (Calcutta: Asiatic Society of Bengal, 1868), vol. 1, p. 153.

47. Amīr Khusrau, *Tughluq Nāma*, p. 84. To this group 'Iṣāmī (*Futūḥ al-Salāṭīn*, pp. 382–3) added the Khokars, a body of frontier pastoralists, forever in conflict with Sultanate armies and at least one Afghan commander. Although Amīr Khusrau ignored the Khokars in this list, he gives them a prominent role in the battle with Khusrau Khān. See *Tughluq Nāma*, p. 128.

48. Jackson, *The Delhi Sultanate*, pp. 178–9.

49. See Doerfer, *Turkische und Mongolische Elemente*, vol. 3, pp. 320–1, s.v. 'sihna'.

50. Baranī, *Ta'rīkh-i Fīrūz Shāhī*, pp. 182–3, 212–13, 243.

51. Baranī, *Ta'rīkh-i Fīrūz Shāhī*, p. 238.

52. For Baranī's portrayal of Malika-i Jahān as wife and mother-in-law, see *Ta'rīkh-i Fīrūz Shāhī*, pp. 196–7, 221.

53. Baranī, *Ta'rīkh-i Fīrūz Shāhī*, p. 245. Baranī provides the incidental information that Qadr Khān was married to Sultan Nāṣir al-Dīn Maḥmūd's granddaughter (Baranī, *Ta'rīkh-i Fīrūz Shāhī*, p. 196). He does not suggest, however, that the affinal link with the old ruling family strengthened the young prince's claim to the throne.

54. Baranī, *Ta'rīkh-i Fīrūz Shāhī*, p. 212, 239, 245–6.

55. Baranī, *Ta'rīkh-i Fīrūz Shāhī*, p. 313.

56. Baranī, *Ta'rīkh-i Fīrūz Shāhī*, pp. 273–6.

57. See J.A. Boyle, *The Successors of Genghis Khan, translated from the Persian of Rashīd al-Dīn* (New York: Columbia University Press, 1971), p. 163; Doerfer, *Turkische und Mongolische Elemente*, vol. 1, pp. 155–9, s.v. 'ötčigīn'; C.E. Bosworth, 'A Turco–Mongol Practice amongst the Early Ghaznavids', *CAJ* 7 (1962): pp. 237–40; C.E. Bosworth, *The Later Ghaznavids: Splendour and Decay* (New York: Columbia University Press, 1977), p. 146; P.B. Golden, 'The Kara Khanids and Early Islam', in *The Cambridge History of Early Inner Asia*, ed. Denis Sinor (Cambridge: Cambridge University Press, 1990), p. 359; René Grousset, *The Empire of the Steppes*, trans. from French by Naomi Walford (New Jersey: Rutgers University Press, 1970), p. 255–6.

58. Ibn Baṭṭūṭa, *Rehla*, trans. Gibb, vol. 3, p. 693.

59. Ibn Baṭṭūṭa, *Rehla*, trans. Gibb, vol. 3, pp. 663–4; trans. Mahdi Husain, p. 60. The translation is Gibb's.

60. Ibn Baṭṭūṭā, *Rehla*, trans. Gibb, p. 668; trans. Mahdi Husain, p. 64. The translation is Gibb's.

61. See also the Qur'an, chapter 88, *al-ghāshiya*.

62. For a review of Turko–Mongol ideals of universal dominion, see Osman Turan, 'The Ideal of World Domination among the Medieval Turks', *SI* 4 (1955): pp. 77–90; and for a discussion of iconographic representations from the Seljuq period of the monarch, 'the equerry and the honorific spare horse with saddle-cover', see Emel Esin, 'Ay-Bitigi, the Court Attendants in Turkish Iconography', *CAJ* 14 (1970): pp. 108–9.

63. See 'Ghāshiya', *EI2* 2: p. 1020; and P.M. Holt, 'The Position and Power of the Mamluk Sultan', *BSOAS* 38 (1975): p. 245.

64. See aforementioned notes 62–3, and P.M. Holt, 'The Structure of Government in the Mamluk Sultanate', in *The Eastern Mediterranean Lands in the Period of the Crusades*, ed. P.M. Holt (Warminster: Aris and Phillips Ltd, 1977), p. 47.

65. Al-Qalqashandī, *Ṣubḥ al-A'shā* (Cairo), vol. 4, p. 7, cited in Holt, 'The Position and Power of the Mamluk Sultan', p. 243.

66. Baranī, *Ta'rīkh-i Firūz Shāhī*, p. 243. Thomas, Edward, *The Chronicles of the Pathan Kings of Delhi* (Delhi: Munshiram Manoharlal, 1967), pp. 157, 169–70, explains that the *panj-man akhtar* referred to the gold coinage, *fanam/panam*, that is, fractions of the *hun*, seized as plunder by 'Alā al-Dīn in his Deccan campaigns.

67. Sirhindī, *Ta'rīkh-i Mubārak Shāhī*, p. 97; Yaḥyā b. Aḥmad b. 'Abd Allah Sirhindī, *Ta'rīkh-i Mubārak Shāhī*, trans. K.K. Basu (Baroda: Oriental Institute, 1932), p. 99. I have followed Basu's translation.

68. In contrasting texts from the Sultanate and Mughal periods, Muzaffar Alam's valuable study draws attention to the great distance travelled by political theorists between the two periods. And yet while Mughal theorists are disaggregated and shown as historical agents responding to the dynamic conditions of the sixteenth through the seventeenth centuries, Alam's arguments suggest that a vast amount of the generalizations in the writings of authors like Fakhr-i Mudabbir and Ẓiyā al-Dīn Baranī are derived from 'Abbāsid litterateurs of the preceding centuries. The dichotomy, wherein the Sultanate was the victim of intellectual ennui while the Mughals tapped into the creative ferment unleashed by the Mongol invasions, is problematic. See Muzaffar Alam, *The Languages of Political Islam in India, c. 1200–1800* (Delhi: Permanent Black, 2004).

7

THE GREAT MUGHALS
Relationships, Emotions, and Monuments

FRANCIS ROBINSON

Among the great legacies the Turkic peoples have left us are the relationships and emotions of the Mughal royal family, which ruled India in its full pomp from 1526 to 1707. On occasion these relationships and their attendant emotions lead us to some of the remarkable monuments built by the family. We are able to savour these relationships because of the rich record which remains. There is an autobiography and memoirs, correspondence, the work of historians—official and non-official—the accounts of European visitors to the Mughal court, to which should be added other forms of evidence—the pictorial record that reaches from the reign of Akbar to that of Shah Jahan, and of course, the monuments.

All the usual natural human relationships are open to inspection: the love between father and daughter, as demonstrated by Shah Jahan and his wise and gifted Jahanara, or that of Awrangzib and his brilliant Zib al-Nisa, whose support of his rebellious son, Akbar, forced him to imprison her for the rest of her life; the powerful affection between mother and son, as in that between Hamida Begam and the

Emperor Akbar, exemplified by her rushing to his side when he suffered from what seems to have been an epileptic fit and by his utter misery at her death in 1604; the competition between brothers which, given Mughal succession practices, was invariably murderous, and which was illuminated in particular by Awrangzib's jealousy of his elder brother, Dara Shikoh; the strong relationship between brother and sister, especially when they shared the same mother, which led Jahanara to persuade Shah Jahan before his death in 1666 to formally forgive Awrangzib, and which led Princess Zib al-Nisa to side with her brother Akbar in his rebellion against their father. Then, there are those examples of men struck by a lightning bolt of love—the *coup de foudre*, as when the adolescent Babur became infatuated with a boy and experienced for the first time all the madness and embarrassment of love, or when Awrangzib at the age of thirty-five became so infatuated with the singing girl Hira Bai as he saw her pluck a mango from a tree, that he was willing to drink wine to please her.[1] Because of the nature of the record, these relationships tend to come to light at times of crisis and family dysfunction. But, as Ruby Lal has shown for the sixteenth century, the Mughal royal family was a remarkable functioning unit in which women played a major role.[2] There are many examples of the pleasure men and women of the family took in each other's company. For instance, in 1582, when eight ladies of the family, under the leadership of Akbar's aunt Gulbadan returned from their pilgrimage to Mecca, Akbar and Salim (Jahangir) went out from Fatehpur Sikri to meet their caravan. Abul Fadl describes the family gathering, the many enquires after health, the joy at being together again, and the gifts brought back from Mecca: 'there were hospitalities, and that night they remained awake in pleasing discourses.'[3]

I wish to focus on the two most powerful relationships in the Mughal family context, those of father and son, and husband and wife. Examples will be drawn from the nearly two centuries in which the Mughals flourished. Each case will attempt to identify the emotions which the relationship reveals and whenever possible, a connection will be made to a Mughal monument.

Fathers and Sons

The relationships of Mughal fathers and their sons were marked by complex feelings. There was usually the love of the father for his son, and in return, again usually, the respect and veneration shown by the son for the father. Alongside these fundamental emotions there was the father's care for the rigorous training of the prince as a future ruler, a soldier, and a cultivated man. On the other side there was the prince's concern to win the respect, even words of appreciation and congratulation, from his father, which was no easy thing to achieve in this family. Furthermore, there was the inevitable competition between father and son, as the latter grew from adolescence into manhood, a competition which may have had oedipal dimensions, and as was the case in at least one instance, may have been sexual. This mix of emotions was further fraught by: a father's concern that a son or sons might overthrow him; the sons' concerns that a brother was favoured by the father and might have the advantage in winning the throne, an outcome likely to lead to their death and that of their children; and the actions of factions in the court to ensure they were on the winning side whenever the struggle took place.

Babur and Humayun

Babur came to the 'throne', in the sense that he became a leader in search of a kingdom, aged eleven in 1494 when his father's, Umar Shaykh's, dovecote collapsed into a ravine and he fell with it. Babur leaves us a picture of his father that combines strands of affection, humanity, and sharp observation which run throughout the autobiography:

> He was short in stature, had a round beard and a fleshy face, and was fat. He wore his tunic so tight that to fasten the ties he had to hold in his stomach; if he let himself go, it often happened that the ties broke.... He was well read and literate.... His sense of justice was great ... He was liberal, and his moral character was equal to his liberality. He was a good-natured, talkative, eloquent, and well-spoken man. He was brave and valiant.... He packed quite a punch ... and no one was ever hit by him who did not bite the dust. On account of his urge to expand his territory, he turned many a truce into battle and many a friend into foe. He used to drink a lot. Later in life he held drinking parties once or twice a week. He was fun to be with in a gathering and good at reciting poetry.[4]

Babur's relationship with his son, Humayun, was equally affectionate, but less indulgent. He records with pride Humayun's first military success in the skirmishing before the battle of Panipat in 1526 and notes that on that same day 'Humayun first put the razor and scissors to his face'.[5] He records Humayun's leading role in the battle of Khanua (1527), his actions after it, and his being stationed in Kabul. But, he also records harsh letters written to his son, a feature of Mughal father–son relationships.[6] One letter, which Babur reproduces in full in the autobiography, sums up a loving but testy relationship. It includes words of affection, advice on kingship, and behaviour towards his brother, and some complaints, of which the most striking is about the young prince's prose:

> As I asked you, you have written your letters, but you did not read them over, for if you had a mind to read them, you would have found that you could not. After reading them you certainly would have changed them. Although your writing can be read with difficulty, it is excessively obscure. Who has ever heard of prose designed to be an enigma.... Probably your laziness in writing letters is due to the fact that you try to make it too fancy. From now on write with uncomplicated, clear, and plain words. This will cause less difficulty both for you and for your reader.[7]

In spite of this testiness, Babur's primary emotion regarding Humayun was love, borne out by his own words and the strange manner of his death, as told by his daughter, Gulbadan. In the autumn of 1530 Humayun fell ill. Babur was distraught. Humayun's mother said in words that suggest the oral tradition of the harem: 'Do not be troubled about my son. You are a king; what griefs have you? You have other sons. I sorrow because I have only this one.' Babur replied: 'Maham, although I have other sons, I love none as I love your Humayun ... I desire the kingdom for him....'[8] Babur walked round Humayun's bed praying and saying: 'O God! If a life may be exchanged for a life, I who am Babar [sic], I give my life and my being for Humayun.' From that day Humayun became better and Babur grew ill until he died.[9] We cannot know how this deathbed scene came to be elaborated in the telling as it passed down through the family, but the powerful central emotion of love is often expressed by the Mughals.

Humayun died when Akbar was just thirteen, so there was little opportunity for a difficult relationship, which may have been a good thing given the nature of Akbar's self-assertion against his guardian, Bayram Khan, and others during his adolescence. The strong paternal affection, typical of the family, is recorded by Abul Fadl when Humayun recovers the young boy Akbar held prisoner by his uncle, Kamran: 'With excessive joy he [Humayun] clasped that divine nursling to his bosom.'[10] We do not hear of the cultivated Humayun's likely frustration as the boy Akbar wore out four teachers, and rejected learning in favour of hunting and martial arts. Of Akbar's feelings for his father, there is nothing recorded save for a favourite saying of his: 'Alas! That the emperor Humayun died so early and that I had no opportunity of showing him faithful service.'[11]

Akbar and His Sons

In the case of Akbar's relationships with his sons, in particular that with his eldest son and successor, Salim (Jahangir), we witness the first seriously bruising engagement. It was not easy being a son of this remarkable man. According to Abul Fadl, he 'kept his children under his own care and did not appoint any guardians to them, and was continually educating them in the most excellent manner of which there are few examples in ancient times'.[12] Children, particularly in adolescence, rarely respond well to such close supervision—not least when, as the Jesuit Monserrate tells us, Akbar found it difficult to show his real affection to them, giving them orders 'rather roughly whenever he wanted anything done' and sometimes punishing them 'with blows as well as with harsh words'.[13] Therefore it is not surprising that Akbar's two younger sons died of drink. Another son, Salim, was also deep in drink and opium but seems to have been made of tougher stuff. It is on his relationship with his father that we shall focus.

Akbar's feelings for Salim seem to have included love, irritation, and perhaps rivalry. There is no doubt that his birth was longed for. It did not happen until the summer of 1569 when Akbar was twenty-seven. Salim's mother, Akbar's wife from the Rajput house of Amber, was despatched to the Khanqah of Shaykh Salim Chishti for the birth in the hope that the saint's blessings would favour the occasion. As a result, the young boy was nicknamed Shaykhi Baba by his father. He also became a favourite of his stepmother, Salima, and his grandmother, Hamida Begam. Salim appears to have been a talented young man who hunted, accompanied his father on campaigns, and was an able student. Then, as Eraly has noted, from 1582, when he was thirteen, to 1600, when aged thirty-one he rebelled, Salim figures little in the official record.[14] Marriages and births are mentioned. So is Salim's failure on one occasion to bring the harem into camp, leading to strong criticism from Akbar and a massive sulk on the part of Salim.[15] There was also competition between the two in artistic patronage. There may have been too, on the basis of the legend relating to Anarkali (pomegranate blossom), Akbar's concubine, a sexual rivalry.[16] As time went on, Akbar may also have feared the political rivalry of his son. For whatever reason, he does not seem to have been given the usual tasks on which to cut his princely teeth.

In the last five years of Akbar's reign, Salim sprang back into prominence by opposing his father's will in various ways. Somewhat disingenuously in his memoirs, Salim denied any intention of rebelling:

> Short-sighted men in Allahabad had urged me also to rebel against my
> father. Their words were extremely unacceptable and disapproved by
> me ... acting according to the dictates of reason and knowledge I waited on
> my father, my guide, my *qibla*, and my visible God, and as a result of this
> good purpose it went well with me. [17]

But it is hard not to interpret Salim's behaviour as ranging from petu-
lance through insolence to rebellion. Twice he refused his father's
command to campaign in Mewar. He set up an independent court
in Allahabad and, according to one Dutch source, issued coins in
his name.[18] On one occasion he led 30,000 men from Allahabad
on Akbar's court at Agra, only retreating at his father's command.
On another, he had his father's close friend Abul Fadl assassinated
as he was about to come to Allahabad to negotiate with him; Salim
knew this would hurt his father deeply. Eventually, in November 1604
Akbar persuaded Salim with the promise of a full pardon to return
to the court at Agra. In public he received his son with affection and
honour. He then had him arrested and taken to the women's apart-
ments, where he slapped his face several times.[19] Akbar, according
to Muhibb Ali, Abul Fadl's successor as court chronicler, 'reproached
him, and after enumerating his transgressions gave him many cen-
sures. The prince cast his eyes on the ground and answered with
streaming eyes'.[20] He was then imprisoned and forbidden wine until
the importuning of the harem women gained his release. Akbar's
actions reveal an extraordinarily affectionate indulgence towards
Salim, though doubtless that indulgence was in part prompted by the
knowledge that Salim was the only son remaining to succeed him.

In retrospect Salim was full of reverence for his father, as his
memoirs reveal. In several pages of praise, which are more matter-
of-fact rather than eulogy, he tells of how Akbar was able to associate with learned men on equal terms with no one realizing he
was illiterate, of how his physique was athletic, his speaking voice
peculiarly rich, and his courage extraordinary. He also speaks of how
his father's good qualities were beyond the 'bounds of praise', of
how he had time for men of all conditions—high and low—and of
how he was deeply humble, never forgetting God.[21] Salim tells of
how the royal family would visit Akbar's tomb at Sikandrabad and
how he saw his father in his dreams. The shadow of this great man
looms over the first half of Salim's memoirs. The painting of c. 1614
in the Musée Guimet, Paris, in which Salim is made to gaze upon
the image of his father, is deeply suggestive of this relationship of
reverence (see Figure 7.1).

Figure 7.1 Jahangir gazes on an image of his father in a manner suggestive of the reverence in which he held Akbar. The divine light symbolism of the dynastic ideology is present in the halos of the two men and the six-pointed stars on Jahangir's collar. Painted c. 1614

Source: Musée Guimet, Paris, no. 3676B; from Francis Robinson, *The Mughal Emperors* (London, 2007), p. 139.

Jahangir and His Sons

One of the benefits of examining Jahangir and his sons is that we have in his memoirs what seem to be candid statements of his feelings about them. We do not, however, have any sense of how they may have felt about him. Of his four sons who reached adulthood, it is in his relationship with those who rebelled against him that Jahangir reveals himself most.

Jahangir's strong feelings about his children and their actions shine through everything he writes about them. His eldest son, Khusraw, was the first to rebel. In 1604, even before his grandfather had died, he was persuaded to involve himself with a rebellious court faction. His mother tried to keep him faithful to her husband. When he rebelled, she committed suicide. 'No evil fortune is greater', declared Jahangir,

> than when a son through the impropriety of his conduct, and his unapproved methods of behaviour, causes the death of his mother and becomes contumacious and rebellious against his father, without cause or reason.[22]

In April 1606 Khusraw launched a formal rebellion. Within three weeks the erring prince was captured, held in chains, and forced to witness his co-conspirators being impaled. Before many months passed he was caught plotting against his father again. Jahangir confided to his memoirs 'that my fatherly affection did not permit me to take his life'.[23] Indeed, he records time after time his fatherly affection, which has Khusraw's fetters struck off, permits him to come and pay his respects, and finally has him released from prison.[24] This affection, however, did not prevent Jahangir from surrendering Khusraw to his younger brother, Khurram, and a likely death.

Jahangir's relationship with his third son, Khurram, seems to have been stronger. For much of his life Jahangir's feelings about him were wholly positive. When Khurram was young Jahangir refers to him by his family nickname of 'Baba'. He reminds us that Khurram was Akbar's favourite grandchild: 'He recognised him as his real child.'[25] Jahangir refers to him as 'my fortunate son'.[26] When in 1617 he returned from an unusually successful campaign in the Deccan, Jahangir awarded him the title Shah Jahan, an unprecedented favour, which indicated that he was Jahangir's chosen successor. 'I showed him much attention and favour', Jahangir confided to his memoirs, 'I am very pleased with him.'[27] Then, reporting that Shah Jahan had fever, he declared him to be 'close to my heart'.[28] And recording that he had given the first copy of his *Jahangirnama* to Shah Jahan, he wrote: 'whom I consider in all respect the first of my sons'.[29] Shah Jahan had his father's love and respect.

Around 1619 the relationship between Jahangir and Shah Jahan began to change. He is mentioned less and less in the memoirs, and when he appears he is no longer given his fine title but just his name, Khurram. The problem was that Shah Jahan was increasingly having to position himself for the inevitable struggle for power as his father declined. He had already noted that Jahangir's favourite queen, Nur Jahan, was likely to be his chief rival. This meant that he was no longer able to blindly follow his father's orders. Then, when in 1622 Jahangir ordered him to proceed to retake Qandahar, which the Safawids had captured, he said he would go but only if he was given the rich governorship of the Punjab, in addition to those of Gujarat and the Deccan, Mewar, Malwa, Ahmadnagar, and Khandesh, which he already held. Jahangir was furious. He stripped Shah Jahan of all his governorships, plus his private estates, and made his youngest son, Shahriyar, commander of the Qandahar expedition, ordering Shah Jahan to release his troops into Shahriyar's service. From now on Jahangir refers to Shah Jahan as *Bi-dawlat* (outcast), or 'that wretch *Bi-dawlat*'. He confides in his memoirs, which were now written by Mutamid Khan, his sorrow that his son, for whom he had done so much, should be so ungrateful. For several years Shah Jahan went on the run, constantly harried by imperial troops. In 1626 there was one last engagement with his father, with Shah Jahan making a humble overture but unable to accept in full the terms his father offered. When in 1627 the succession struggle reached its final stages, Shah Jahan was the fortunate beneficiary of the determination of his wife's father, Asaf Khan, that his sister, Nur Jahan, should not rule the empire. The record of Jahangir and his rebel sons shows how powerful paternal feelings might moderate the treatment of their rebelliousness, but the business of power always came first.

Shah Jahan and His Sons

'I never saw so settled a countenance', declared the English ambassador, Sir Thomas Roe, of the young Shah Jahan, 'nor any man keepe so constant a gravitie, never smiling, or in face shewing any respects of difference of men.'[30] But behind this still, immobile face there was a man blessed with the capacity for affection and strong emotion, which ran through his family. There is a delightful miniature of c. 1620 showing Shah Jahan, the 'modern' father, with probably his second son, a clinging baby Shah Shuja, in his arms, a rare representation of father and baby son in the premodern period (see Figure 7.2).[31] Moreover, Shah Jahan's unusually powerful relations with at least two women of his family are well known. This said, I shall focus in particular on his relationship with his third son, Awrangzib, which inevitably draws in some comparison with his relationship with his eldest son, Dara Shikoh, of whom Awrangzib was intensely jealous.

Shah Jahan's early relationship with Awrangzib was one of open affection. In June 1633, when Awrangzib was watching an elephant fight with his father and Shah Shuja, one beast moved away from the fight and attacked Awrangzib. The fourteen-year-old prince on horseback, first threw his spear at the enraged animal and then, after being unseated, stood his ground with a sword. After he was rescued, Awrangzib went to his father. 'After tenderly embracing Prince Aurangzeb', the official record declared, 'His Majesty distinguished him by the title of *Bahadur*.'[32] The following year he was given his *mansab* with the rank of commander of 10,000 horses and given the royal prerogative of using a red tent. In 1635 he was permitted to command his first expedition. Two years later, we are told, Shah Jahan wrote him 'a most loving invitation in verse' to his marriage to Dilras Banu Begam.[33] Awrangzib was sure of his father's favour.

In 1637 Awrangzib began his first governorship of the Deccan which lasted until 1644. While he was in the field, his elder brother, Dara Shikoh, remained at court with Shah Jahan. Awrangzib found that his recommendations were overridden, his activities micromanaged from court, and as a consequence his prestige was lowered and it became difficult for him to govern effectively. He became insanely jealous of Dara. Amongst other things, he behaved badly at a feast given by Dara for his father and three brothers, which led to him being banned from the court. The process of losing his father's favour had begun.[34]

Relations between Awrangzib and Shah Jahan deteriorated further in the years 1647–52. Over this period, Awrangzib was given three difficult assignments. The first was to press Mughal power northwest to Balkh and into Badakhshan, but with inadequate troops. The expedition was a failure, as most such expeditions in Afghanistan have been, and Awrangzib was forced to retreat with heavy losses. The second and third assignments were the sieges of Qandahar in 1649 and 1652, both of which failed to dislodge the Safawid occupiers, because the Mughals did not have large enough cannon or the expertise to use effectively the cannon they had. 'I greatly wonder

Figure 7.2 In this charming painting of c. 1620 Shah Jahan shows his affection for one of his sons, probably Shah Shuja

Source: Victoria and Albert Museum, I.S. 90-1965; from Ebba Koch, *The Complete Taj Mahal* (London, 2006), p. 18.

how you could not capture the fort in spite of such vast preparations', Shah Jahan exclaimed in a bruising exchange of letters.[35] Awrangzib begged to be allowed to stay in the region to retrieve his honour in the next assault on Qandahar to be conducted by Dara. Shah Jahan dismissed his request and ordered him to the Deccan, saying: 'If I had believed you to be capable of taking Qandahar, I should not have recalled your army.... Every man can perform some work. It is a wise saying that men of experience need no instruction.'[36] It requires little imagination to understand how hurt Awrangzib would have been by this exchange.

Awrangzib's second governorship of the Deccan saw hurt piled upon hurt. There was constant interference in his posting of officials; there was a false accusation that he had given himself the best *jagir* (a grant of income from specified lands), when the decision had in fact been Shah Jahan's; there was a constant complaint, echoed at court, that Awrangzib was not restoring the prosperity of the Deccan fast enough. His plans for the sieges of Golconda (1656) and Bijapur (1657) were countermanded. Awrangzib accused his father of failing to keep to the financial understanding on which the Golconda campaign had been conducted:

> At the outset of this expedition, His Majesty had written to me that out of Qutb-ul-Mulk's indemnity the jewels and elephants should belong to the government, and the cash to me.... But now the entire Golkonda indemnity has been taken by the Emperor.... How can I repay my debt for the war and the arrears of my army, about 20 Lakhs of Rupees?[37]

Awrangzib's fall from his father's 'grace' is demonstrated by the five years of his second Deccan viceroyalty, when he was not once invited to visit his father, nor was one present from Awrangzib sent on the anniversaries of the emperor's birth and coronation, mentioned in the official record.[38] How far his rival Dara had risen in favour was demonstrated by his new title Shah-i Buland-Iqbal (King of Lofty Fortune), by his unprecedented rank of Commander of 40,000 horses, by his new position in court on a gold chair just below the throne, and by the fact that he conducted much of the administration, at times in the emperor's presence, and at times not. Dara was Shah Jahan's designated successor.[39]

In April 1657 Shah Jahan fell ill. Dara nursed his father, controlling access to him, and in turn was formally nominated his successor. This set off the greatest of all the Mughal succession struggles as the four sons of Shah Jahan fought for the throne and their lives. By June

1658 Awrangzib was firmly in control and began to exercise imperial authority. Awrangzib had imprisoned his father, who by now had recovered from his illness, in Agra Fort, where he was comforted by his eldest daughter, Jahanara. His brothers were about to suffer the fate of losers in such struggles. When Dara was captured and condemned to death, Awrangzib wrote in Arabic on his brother's final petition for mercy: 'You first acted as a usurper, and you were a mischief-maker.'[40] For nearly two decades Dara had blighted Awrangzib's life; there was no mercy. Awrangzib was almost as ruthless when dealing with his father—Shah Jahan was forbidden to correspond with anyone outside Agra Fort; he was subjected to numerous small indignities, and when he claimed his jewels as his property, Awrangzib told him: 'The royal property and treasures exist for the good of the community.... The king is only God's chosen custodian, and the trustee of God's money for the benefit of the people.' [41] What sweet revenge for Shah Jahan's failure to honour the financial terms of the Golconda campaign! In one of the several letters that Awrangzib sent his father during the first year of his captivity, he said that he had always been loyal to his father:

> My march on Agra was not due to a rebellious spirit, but to a desire to put an end to Dara's usurpation, his lapse from Islam and his exaltation of idolatry throughout the empire.... I was compelled, out of regard for the next world, to undertake the heavy load of this task and engage in looking after the interests of the populace and the peasantry.

Then, in a statement of compelling psychological revelation he declared:

> I ... remained loyal to you... till I knew for certain that you did not love me but were trying to place some other son in power.[42]

Awrangzib and His Sons

In their correspondence to and from Agra Fort, Shah Jahan warned Awrangzib that he would be treated by his sons as he had treated him. Not surprisingly, Awrangzib feared his sons. 'Never trust your sons', he wrote in his last will and testament, 'nor treat them during your lifetime in an intimate manner, because if the Emperor Shah Jahan had not treated Dara Shukoh in this manner, his affairs would not have come to such a sorry pass.'[43] Throughout his life Awrangzib was almost as good as his word. He could not prevent the odd sign of his affection from being revealed, news writers and spies reported to him regularly on the activities of his male children. Being a Mughal prince under Awrangzib was a particularly hard task.

Awrangzib was a man of strong feelings, as the way in which he was blown off his feet by his love affair with the singing girl Hira Bai suggests, and as the suppressed tension in many of his letters reveals. He was not used to displaying passion openly, Manucci tells us. Indeed, 'manliness does not consist in audacity and recklessness', he told Prince Azam, 'the perfection of manliness and humanity lies in self-control.'[44] So the self-controlled Awrangzib was cool, courageous, intellectual, abstemious, god-fearing in domestic relations, and always able to bring a Quranic or Persian verse forward to match a situation. 'He had a passion for work and a hatred of ease and leisure.'[45] He was a stickler for discipline and deeply concerned to achieve the best possible governance. 'He is the truly great king', he told his father, 'who makes it the chief business of his life to govern his subjects with equity.'[46]

This last quality meant that, while capable of strong affection, he was immensely hard on his five sons, as his correspondence with them reveals. He wrote to Prince Muazzam:

> Exalted son, through the representations of the spies I have come to know that the royal road between Bahadurpur and Khujasteh-buniad is not free from danger. Highwaymen rob the merchants and travellers of their goods.... How long will you allow this shameful mismanagement to go on?[47]

In another letter to Prince Azam he said:

> I have come to know about the occupation and action of the manager of the district of your 'jaghir' from the letter sent by the reporter. Why are you careless about the day of judgment?[48]

As he was dying in 1707 Awrangzib wrote to Prince Kam Baksh:

> My charming son, though in (this) world of free will ... I advised you about the divine will, and more than this about the divine power, it was destined that you would not listen to and accept this advice. Now I go away (to the next world) as a stranger from all; and I pity you for your want of intelligence and ability.[49]

Such a wounding style of correspondence, in addition to his constant monitoring of their activities, explains why Awrangzib 'crushed the latent ability of his sons so that at his death they were not better than children though turned of fifty years of age'.[50]

In this context we will focus on the relationship between Awrangzib and his fourth son, Akbar. Akbar was the son of Dilras Banu, who died four weeks after his birth. His elder full sister, the scholarly Zib al-Nisa, played a major role in his upbringing; he also became his father's favourite son. In 1681 Akbar was made commander-in-chief of the Mughal army in its campaign against the Rajputs in Marwar and Mewar. After a success in Marwar he met failure in Mewar, which led to sharp censure from Awrangzib. Akbar replied: 'I am merely learning the alphabet in the school of practical wisdom. Language can describe but part of the pain and shame I feel at the cursed infidel's astonishing exploit.'[51] He promised to do better next time, but failed only two days later. Awrangzib relieved him of his command in Mewar and sent him off to Marwar, where he failed again. The Rajputs, perhaps aware of how the young prince was smarting at his demotion, seduced him into rebelling against his father. Awrangzib, out of affection for his son, refused to believe that this was the case. It was only after Awrangzib confronted Akbar with the rumour that he discovered the truth. 'The whole realm', Akbar told his father, 'was tired at seeing his tyrannical acts, more especially the abrogation of the rights and privileges that his far-off ancestors had conceded to different persons in Hindustan.'[52] Akbar then issued an edict, validated by four ulama, deposing Awrangzib, proclaimed himself emperor, and set out with the Rajputs to confront Awrangzib in battle. He was outfoxed by his father and fled to seek shelter with the Marathas in the Deccan. Letters from Zib al-Nisa supporting Akbar's cause were found, Awrangzib imprisoned her. To the fugitive Akbar he gave the nickname *abtar*, meaning 'one who has severed the bonds of relationship'.[53]

Akbar's flight to the Marathas drew Awrangzib's armies into the Deccan; he could not risk another drive from the south to place his son on the throne. There he waged war for a further twenty-six years, devastating the region, greatly weakening the empire, and realizing at the end that he had failed.[54] Thus, his failed relationship with his son, Akbar, contributed to the decline of the Mughal Empire.

Fathers, Sons, and Monuments

What connections can we find between these father and son relationships and Mughal monuments? For our purposes we will focus on three: Humayun's tomb in Delhi, built by Akbar for his father, during 1562–72; Akbar's tomb at Sikandra, built by Jahangir for his father and completed between 1612 and 1614; and the tomb complex in Allahabad's Khusrawbagh, built between 1606 and the 1630s by Khusraw's sister, Nithar Begum, in response to the tragedy which befell her immediate family as a result of her brother's rebellion.

No documents exist relating to the construction of Humayun's tomb (see Figure 7.3) but, as Glenn Lowry has convincingly established, the driving force behind the building was Akbar. Construction began as the young prince began to assert himself in the governance of his realm. The building itself has the qualities of massive vision, boldness, and directness that accompanied his other projects, whether it was the great *Hamzanama* series of paintings completed between 1562 and 1577 or his imperial project as a whole.[55]

At one level the tomb was a magnificent act of filial piety, of that 'faithful service' he often declared he wished he had been able to do in his father's lifetime. At another level Akbar, through his father, was making a great dynastic statement in this first major Mughal building in India. Light symbolism is used throughout the building. One of the ways in which it is present is in the use of six-pointed stars at key sites [See Figures 7.4 and 7.5]. These, of course, have astrological significance, representing the conjunction of two opposing forces, but arguably they also suggest the divine light, which entered the mythical Mongol queen, Alanqoa, and passed down through the Timurids, and then through Humayun to Akbar. The time when divine light brought about the pregnancy of Alanqoa, declares Abul Fadl, 'was the beginning of the manifestation of his Majesty, the king of kings, who after passing through diverse stages was revealed to the world from the holy womb of Majesty Miryam-makani [Hamida Begam]'.[56] These stars were the concrete expression of Akbar's divine origins.[57]

The divine significance of the message conveyed by his father's tomb was supported by the way in which Akbar subsequently approached it. The tomb came to be treated in language and in ceremony like that of saint, a visit being *ziyarat*, involving circumambulation and the donation of alms. Akbar's historians came to call it the 'holiest of tombs'. Akbar visited it nine times from his various centres of power and came to give it preference, as time went on, over the Chishti shrine of Nizam al-Din Awliya.[58]

Jahangir's greatest monument was the tomb at Sikandra, which he built for his father (see Figure 7.6). That he was determined, like Akbar, to create something splendid for his father is made clear in the note in his memoirs of how on a visit to the construction site in 1608 he had told the builders to start again:

Figure 7.3 Humayun's tomb in Delhi, built by Akbar for his father, and the conveyor of the divine light symbolism of the imperial ideology

Source: Ebba Koch, *The Complete Taj Mahal* (London, 2006), p. 86.

Figure 7.4 Divine light and astrological symbolism. Six-pointed stars on both the main body of Humayun's tomb and on the drum of the dome

Source: © Amit Parischa

Figure 7.5 Akbar's tomb at Sikandrabad, built by Jahangir

Source: Picture by Ebba Koch; from Ebba Koch, *The Complete Taj Mahal* (London, 2006), p. 87.

> It did not come up to my idea of what it ought to be, for that would be approved which the wayfarers of the world would point to as one the like of which was not in this inhabited world.[59]

Jahangir's five-storeyed garden tomb with *chattris* (the small domed pavilions, indicating a royal presence, seen on Mughal and Rajput buildings) and a marble cenotaph at the top, open to the air and constructed in the style of contemporary palaces, certainly achieved the eye-catching innovation he sought, although it has not been regarded by all as a success.

Despite Jahangir's drastically different architectural vision for his father's tomb from that of Akbar's Timurid-influenced Humayun's tomb, it still conveys the light symbolism so prominent in Humayun's tomb. It has been suggested that, even though the uncovered cenotaph meets orthodox religious requirements, it should also be seen in the context of Mughal 'divine light' symbolism in its placement under the sun and the stars. Support for this view is found in the golden sun

Figure 7.6   Prince Khusraw's tomb, built by his sister Nithar Begum, at Allahabad

Source: Picture by Rajesh Vora; Neelam Sara Gaur, ed., *Allahabad: Where Rivers Meet: Marg* 61, no. 1 (September 2009), p. 51.

that features on the ceiling of the entrance gate and in the final verse of the inscription it bears: 'May his [Akbar's] soul shine like the rays of the sun and the moon in the light of God.'[60] At roughly the same time as the mausoleum was completed, the Musée Guimet picture of Jahangir and Akbar was painted, full of light symbolism, including six-pointed stars on Jahangir's collar [see Figure 7.1].[61]

In 1609 Jahangir and his womenfolk made a pilgrimage to Akbar's mausoleum. A *nazar* (gift of respect) was given, the shrine was circumambulated, there was recitation of the Quran, and singing and dancing (*wajd* and *sama*). Like Humayun's tomb, it was now treated as a Sufi shrine might be. 'The buildings of this blessed mausoleum have been made very lofty', Jahangir declared in his memoirs, 'at this time the money expended satisfied me.' Thus Jahangir felt he had done his duty both to his father and to his dynastic predecessor.[62]

The final connection between a father and son relationship and the building of monuments was the tragedy which accompanied the breakdown of relations between Jahangir and his eldest son, Khusraw. Khusraw's mother was Jahangir's first wife—the wife as he said of his adolescence—and the daughter of the Raja of Amber. Jahangir wrote fondly of her intelligence and her devotion to him. As the young prince began to turn against him, Jahangir notes, 'She constantly wrote to Khusraw and urged him to be sincere and affectionate to me. When she saw that it was of no use ... she from the indignation and high spirit which are inherent in the Rajput character determined upon death.' In 1604 she committed suicide by taking opium.[63] She was buried in the Charbagh garden in Allahabad which Jahangir had laid out while he held court there. Her tomb, known as the tomb of the Shah Begam, was constructed by Jahangir's chief artist at Allahabad, Aqa Rida, and its terraced design presages that of Akbar's in Sikandra. After Shah Jahan had Khusraw strangled in February 1622 to remove any threat that he might pose to his path to the throne, Khusraw's full sister, Sultan Nithar Begum, had him buried in a magnificent tomb close to that of their mother. In consequence the garden came to be known as the Khusrawbagh (see Figure 7.6). Nithar Begum built a third mausoleum there for herself, though when she died in 1646 she was placed in Akbar's tomb. This assemblage of the mausoleums of a mother, son, and daughter, remains witness to the tragedy which accompanied the breakdown of Jahangir's relations with Khusraw.[64]

Husbands and Wives

The Mughals offer some remarkable examples of relationships with passionate love, deep affection, genuine companionship, and respect between husbands and wives. The standard was set from the beginning in Babur's relationship with Maham, the mother of Humayun. Gulbadan Begam tells of how when she came from Kabul to Agra with her stepmother Maham, after the victory of Panipat, Babur, on hearing that they were close, did not wait to saddle a horse, but rushed out on foot to meet them, full of excitement. Gulbadan was told to stay back as husband and wife went on together to Agra.[65] There was also a trip made by the three to Dholpur and Sikri, and the remarkable exchange we have noted between Babur and Maham at what they feared was Humayun's deathbed.[66] Similar, and at times greater levels of feeling, which also came to be expressed in monuments built by the remaining partner after the death of the husband or wife, are to be found in the three relationships on which we will now focus: those of Nur Jahan and Jahangir, of Mumtaz Mahal and Shah Jahan, and of Dilras Banu and Awrangzib.

Nur Jahan and Jahangir

Nur Jahan (1577–1643) was a woman of high intelligence and many talents, ranging from the arts and food to shooting and politics. She was the daughter of a Persian noble who had joined Akbar's service at Fatehpur Sikri and had risen to become the superintendent of the royal household. Able, learned and polished, he rose to become *wazir* under Jahangir, with the title *Itimad Dawla* (Pillar of the Realm). After the death of her first husband, Nur Jahan, then known as Mihr al-Nisa, joined the retinue of Ruqayya Begam, one of Akbar's wives. It was in this capacity in 1611 that she caught Jahangir's eye at the Nawruz celebrations. By this time Jahangir had several wives and many concubines. Aged thirty-three (he was forty-two), Mihr al-Nisa became his last wife, soon being given the title, Nur Mahal (Light of the Palace) and then Nur Jahan (Light of the World).

Nur Jahan was gifted in the arts of pleasing a man. Jahangir revels in her care and affection, whether it was when he was ill—'I did not think anyone was fonder of me', or helping him cut down on his consumption of drink—'I relied on her kindness. She, by degrees, lessened my wine.'[67] He is constantly impressed by the feasts and entertainments she puts on (see Figure 7.7).[68] He feels for her when her mother dies, and even more so when her father, his friend, does

Figure 7.7   Jahangir embraces Nur Jahan, the love of his life. By Govardhan
c. 1620

Source: Govardhan, Los Angeles Country Museum of Art; Nasli and Alice
Heeramaneck Collection, Photograph Museum Associates, LACMA M.83.1.6; from
Francis Robinson, *The Mughal Emperors* (London, 2007), p. 145.

so soon after: 'I could not bear the agitation of Nur Jahan.'[69] He loves the fact that she shares his pleasure in hunting and is an outstanding shot (see Figure 7.8).[70] They had a companionate relationship as demonstrated by the English ambassador's charming picture of the two returning to camp at dusk having been out for a ride by themselves in an ox cart with Jahangir at the reins.[71]

Jahangir's admiration and affection for Nur Jahan enabled her to dominate him and then to take a leading role in the governance of the realm. 'In all actions of consequence in Court', declared the English Ambassador, 'a woman [meaning Nur Jahan] is not onely [sic] always an ingredient, but commonly a principall [sic] drug of most virtue.'[72] Her relatives began to rise in the Mughal administration, in particular her gifted brother, Asaf Khan. Nur Jahan had administrative gifts herself, which Jahangir recognized when he gave her her father's powers as *wazir* after his death in 1622. But her rise did not stop there; she came to exercise the royal powers in full. As Muhammad Hadi wrote:

> For some time she sat at the *jharoka*, and the nobles came to make their salutations and receive her commands. Coins were struck in her name, and the royal seal on *farmans* bore her signature. In short by degrees she became, except in name, undisputed Sovereign of the Empire, and the king himself became a tool in her hands. He used to say that Nur Jahan Begam ... is wise enough to conduct the matters of state and that he wanted only a bottle of wine and a piece of meat to keep himself merry.[73]

When one of Jahangir's leading nobles complained that 'the whole world is surprised that such a wise and sensible emperor as Jahangir should permit a woman to have so great an influence over him', he was ignored.[74]

The uncharitable might suggest that Nur Jahan's relationship with Jahangir was based solely on her interest in power. It is certainly true that in the years before 1622 she, her brother Asaf Khan, and Shah Jahan, operated as a troika in the affairs of the empire. It is also true that from 1622 she was positioning herself, through the marriage of her daughter by her first husband, Ladli Begam, to Jahangir's son Shahriyar, to become the key political player after her husband's death, a stratagem that was defeated by her brother, Asaf Khan. On the other hand Jahangir, a perceptive man, speaks so confidently of her devotion to him, her thoughtfulness, and her companionship, that it is hard not to imagine that there was genuine warmth of feeling between them. This warmth was underlined by Jahangir's burial in a garden she had prepared by the River Ravi in Lahore and by the

Figure 7.8 Jahangir was proud of Nur Jahan's many gifts, including that of shooting. On one occasion he records her killing four tigers with six shots from inside a howdah on top of an elephant

Source: Picture by Thalia Kennedy, Abu'l Hasan, Jahangir Album, Rampur Raza Library, India; from Francis Robinson, *The Mughal Emperors* (London, 2007), p. 145.

time she spent after her fall from power in devotion to her husband's memory.

Mumtaz Mahal and Shah Jahan

The relationship between Shah Jahan and Mumtaz Mahal is legendary not least because it came to be symbolized by the lady's tomb, the Taj Mahal, one of the wonders of the world. In 1607, Arjumand Begum, the daughter of Nur Jahan's brother, Asaf Khan, was betrothed to Prince Khurram. The full marriage did not take place until 1612, after Nur Jahan's marriage to Jahangir in 1611. Khurram was so delighted by her beauty and character that he gave her the title Mumtaz Mahal Begam (Chosen One of the Palace). Clearly blessed by the unusual gifts that ran through her family, she quickly became a partner in Khurram's princely enterprise, never leaving his side as he campaigned across India and bearing him fourteen children, seven of whom lived to adulthood, in nineteen years. Once Shah Jahan became emperor she herself began to play a role in government—business was deferred to her, she held the royal seal as her aunt had done, and she struck coins and issued edicts in her name.

Contemporaries were aware of the closeness of the relationship. 'His whole delight was centred in this illustrious lady', declared the court librarian Inayat Khan 'to such an extent that he did not feel towards the others one-thousandth part of the affection that he did for Her Late Majesty; and he never allowed that light of the imperial chamber to be separated from him whether at home or abroad.'[75] Muhammad Amin Qazwini, who in 1636 was ordered by Shah Jahan to write the history of the first years of his reign, had no doubt about the extraordinary nature of the relationship between this husband and wife:

> Always that Lady of the Age was the companion, close confidante, associate and intimate friend of that successful ruler, in hardship and comfort, joy and grief, when travelling or in residence... The mutual affection and harmony between the two had reached a degree never seen between husband and wife among the classes of rulers [*sultans*], or among the other people. And this was not merely out of sexual passion [*hawa-yi nafs*]; the excellent qualities, pleasing habits, outward and inward virtues, and physical and spiritual compatibility on both sides caused great love and affection, and extreme affinity and familiarity.[76]

What a testament to a marriage! And how extraordinary too in a seventeenth-century context, let alone a Muslim context, as Ebba

Koch notes, that an official chronicler, or any chronicler at all, should comment on erotic attraction.[77]

Against this background it was to be expected that Mumtaz Mahal's death in childbirth at Burhanpur on 17 June 1631 would be followed by a flood of grief. Shah Jahan wept without restraint. The whole court was made to wear clothes of white, a 'colour of mourning, especially in India'. 'For a whole week', Inayat Khan tells us, 'His Majesty from excess of grief did not appear in public nor transact any affairs of state.'[78] Shah Jahan's eyes came to be affected by his constant weeping and he had to wear spectacles. His beard and moustache, which had only a few grey hairs, became in a few days one-third white. He stopped listening to music, singing, and wearing fine linen.[79] He postponed for two years the weddings of Dara Shikoh and Shah Shuja, which he had been planning with Mumtaz Mahal. In future all entertainments were forbidden on Wednesdays, the day of Mumtaz Mahal's death, and the court was required to treat Dhi'l-Qa'da, the month of her death, as one of mourning.[80]

Dilras Banu and Awrangzib

The relationship between Awrangzib and Dilras Banu, his first wife, never reached such heights of emotion, but he did seem to hold deep respect for her; indeed, Jadunath Sarkar suggests that he was in awe of her.[81] Awrangzib married Dilras Banu, who was distantly connected to the Safawid rulers of Iran, in 1637. She died in 1657 as a consequence of giving birth to the ill-fated Prince Akbar. Awrangzib revealed his respect for her when he came to offer marriage counselling to his favourite grandson, Bidar Bakht. Awrangzib had heard from the Prince's minister that he had fallen out with his wife, calling her the daughter of a rascal (*paji*), and she replied: 'If you like, you may slay me, but I shall not speak to you again.'[82] Awrangzib wrote:

> Be it clear to this light of my eye [i.e. grandson] that in the season of youth which in the vile phraseology of his boon companions is styled 'mad youth', I, too, had this relation with a person [wife] who possessed extreme imperiousness, but to the end of her life I continued to love her, and never once did hurt her feelings.[83]

He went on to say that, if he did not hear that Bidar had made it up with his wife, he would be punished.[84]

Husbands, Wives, and Monuments

The connections between these relationships and monuments are expressed in the mausoleums which the surviving partners built to house the remains of their loved one but also in honour of their memory. We shall look at that of Jahangir in Lahore (completed 1637), which the evidence suggests was the work of Nur Jahan, that of Mumtaz Mahal at Agra (completed 1643), which was built by Shah Jahan, and that of Dilras Banu at Awrangabad (completed 1661), which was built by Awrangzib.

We do not know for certain that Nur Jahan built Jahangir's mausoleum and can only assert so on the balance of the evidence (see Figure 7.9). Some argue that Shah Jahan was the prime mover—for instance, the late nineteenth-century local historian, Latif, whose position has been accepted by Nur Jahan's biographer, Ellison Findly, and the architectural historian Ebba Koch.[85] Moreover, Shah Jahan was the greatest builder amongst the Mughals and it is difficult to see him readily surrendering control over such an important dynastic building. On the other hand, local tradition and several historians have long held that the design and construction of the mausoleum was Nur Jahan's work. The basis for this judgement is that the mausoleum was in Nur Jahan's garden; Nur Jahan had retired to Lahore; she had a track record of major architectural patronage; and she may well have had the resources to support the construction—in addition to the Rs 2,00,000 she received per annum from Shah Jahan, she had amassed a vast treasure in her years as queen, but we do not know how much of it she was allowed to keep. The following facts offer further support for this judgement: compared to the lengthy descriptions in the official record of Shah Jahan's major projects, his father's mausoleum has only the briefest mention; the building itself has features in common with the mausoleum Nur Jahan built for her father at Agra, and that which she built for herself close by that of Jahangir.[86] It is arguable that Nur Jahan had a hand in Jahangir's mausoleum, and perhaps a very big hand. Given the powerful relationship between the two of them, and Nur Jahan's positive nature, it seems likely that given half a chance she would have wished to lay her impress upon her husband's memorial.

There is little doubt that the Taj Mahal was the overall conception of Shah Jahan (see Figure 7.10). His historians tell us so. They also tell us that he had a team of architects working under his supervision and that during the daily meetings he would ask good questions, and from time to time required alterations.[87] One purpose in creating the Taj, recalling

Figure 7.9 Jahangir's tomb at Shahdera in Lahore in the construction of which Nur Jahan may have had a substantial role

Source: Picture by John Warburton, Lee Photography; from Francis Robinson, *The Mughal Emperors* (London, 2007), p. 147.

Figure 7.10   The Taj Mahal, Shah Jahan's tribute of love to Mumtaz Mahal

Source: Corbis; from Francis Robinson, *The Mughal Emperors* (London, 2007), p. 153.

the connections in Mughal thinking between fine and lofty buildings and the good name of kings, was to produce in the words of Qazwini, 'a masterpiece for ages to come'.[88] But the prime purpose was, in the words of Ebba Koch, to create 'a magnificent burial place for Mumtaz Mahal, an image here on earth of the heavenly mansion prepared for her in Paradise'.[89] This was such a successful act of love, in conception and in execution, that it has remained a symbol of conjugal love with an ongoing existence in popular culture down to the present.

Shah Jahan's concern to honour his dead wife is emphasized further by the treatment of her body during the construction of the Taj and his subsequent ceremonial practices. The coffin was brought from Burhanpur by her second son, Shah Shuja, her chief lady-in-waiting, and an entourage of attendants and Quran reciters. Food, drink, and coin were distributed to the poor along the way. At Agra the body was given a temporary burial on the construction site and covered by a domed building to protect it from males who were *na-mahram* (marriageable under Islamic law). A year later the cenotaph was surrounded by a golden rail, which cost Rs 6,00,000, or nearly 12 per cent of the total cost of the mausoleum. The tomb became the focus of celebrations of Urs on the anniversary of Mumtaz Mahal's death. It would be circumambulated and Shah Jahan would present gifts to learned men from all over the empire and charity to the poor.[90] The love story was completed by Shah Jahan spending his last years gazing out over the Taj from his imprisonment in Agra Fort, and then in death being taken to the Taj to lie beside his wife.

The mausoleum which Awrangzib built for Dilras Banu at Awrangabad, known as the Bibi ka Maqbara or the Taj Mahal of the Deccan, raises interesting questions (see Figure 7.11). The first relates to the extent of Awrangzib's involvement in the project. Understandings vary from asserting that Awrangzib built it,[91] to stating that Awrangzib asked Dilras Banu's eldest son, Azam, to build it,[92] to stating that Awrangzib just asked Azam to repair the finished building.[93] This said, we should note that as Awrangzib micro-managed every aspect of administration, it is unlikely that the concept for a project as important as this was not his. Nor was it surprising that the mausoleum was a smaller-scale copy of the Taj Mahal, although one which emphasized vertical lines as opposed to the symmetry of the original. Awrangzib seemed to care greatly about his mother's tomb. In 1652, after visiting it, he wrote to his father about the need for repairs and in 1691 he ordered the governors of every Mughal province to make a practice of sending Rs 2,000 to the caretaker of the Taj for maintenance.[94] So why would a man who cherished his mother's tomb ask for what has been described as a 'free copy' to be made for his wife? There could have been an element of backhanded compliment to his father in the decision, but arguably a building reflecting his father's act of love had already become the most powerful statement of affection and respect he could offer Dilras Banu.

* * *

The documentary, pictorial and built, record left by the great Mughals enables us to engage with the world of relationships and emotions in this extraordinary family. We have focused on the often fraught and dysfunctional relationships of fathers and sons, and the relationships between husbands and wives which, at their best, would seem to be models for men and women for all time. All kinds of emotions have been expressed. Within the former context there were those of fatherly love, fatherly anger, filial respect, filial resentment, and fraternal envy; while within the latter, the fondness of companionate marriage, the reality of erotic attraction, the desperation of

Figure 7.11 The Bibi ka Maqbara at Awrangabad, arguably Awrangzib's tribute of love to his proud queen, Dilras Banu

Source: Picture by Catherine Asher; from Catherine Asher, *Architecture of Mughal India*, New Cambridge History of India (Cambridge, 1992). p. 164.

passionate love, and the *coup de foudre*—the sudden intense feeling of love. At times these relationships and their attendant emotions led to the construction of some of the great monuments of Indo–Muslim civilization. The value of these monuments is widely understood. This said, it is the eternal quest of many historians to engage with what it was to be human in another place at another time. The Mughals, and the historians of their times, speak to us directly, lay out their feelings before us, and do so sometimes with a shocking directness. They enable us to engage with their humanity. Arguably, this legacy is as valuable to the modern world as the great monuments they handed down to us.

Notes

1. Wheeler M. Thackston, trans., ed., and annot., *The Baburnama: Memoirs of Babur, Prince and Emperor* (New York: The Modern Library, 2002), pp. 112–13; Jadunath Sarkar, *History of Aurangzib Based on Original Sources*, 2nd ed. (Calcutta: M.C. Sarkar & Sons, 1925), vol. 1, pp. 56–7.
2. Ruby Lal, *Domesticity and Power in the Early Mughal World* (Cambridge: Cambridge University Press, 2005).
3. Henry Beveridge, trans., *The Akbar Nama of Abu-l-Fazl*, reprint (Delhi, Low Price Publications, 1993), vol. 3, p. 569.
4. Thackston, *Baburnama*, pp. 40–2.
5. Thackston, *Baburnama*, p. 322.
6. Thackston, *Baburnama*, pp. 311, 391.
7. Thackston, *Baburnama*, pp. 413–14.
8. Gul-Badan Begam, *History of Humayun*, trans. Annette S. Beveridge, reprint (Delhi: Munshiram Manoharlal, 1983), pp. 104–5.
9. Begam, *History of Humayun*, p. 105; a slightly different version of this is told in Beveridge, *Akbar Nama*, vol. 1, pp. 275–77.
10. Beveridge, vol. 1, p. 571.
11. Abu l-Fazl Allami, *The A'in-i Akbari*, trans. Col. H.S. Jarrett, 2nd rev. ed. by Sir Jadunath Sarkar (New Delhi: Oriental Books Reprint Corporation, 1978), p. 428.
12. Beveridge, *Akbar Nama*, vol. 3, p. 105.
13. S.J. Monserrate, *The Commentary of Father Monserrate S.J. on His Journey to the Court of Akbar*, trans. J.S. Hoyland (London: Humphrey Milford at Oxford University Press, 1922), p. 53.
14. Abraham Eraly, *The Mughal Throne: The Saga of India's Great Emperor* (London: Weidenfeld and Nicolson, 2003), p. 236.
15. Beveridge, *Akbar Nama*, vol. 3, pp. 824–5.

16. Eraly, *The Mughal Throne* p. 237.

17. Jahangir, *The Tuzuk-i-Jahangiri or Memoirs of Jahangir*, trans. Alexander Rogers, ed. Henry Beveridge, reprint (Delhi: Munshiram Manoharlal, 1978), vol. 1, p. 65.

18. Joannes de Laet, *The Empire of the Great Mogol*, trans. J.S. Hoyland (Bombay: D.B Taporevala Sons & Co., 1928), pp. 166–7.

19. de Laet, *The Empire of the Great Mogol*, p. 169.

20. Beveridge, *Akbar Nama*, vol. 3, p. 1248.

21. Jahangir, *Tuzuk-i-Jahangiri*, vol. 1, pp. 33–8.

22. Jahangir, *Tuzuk-i-Jahangiri*, vol. 1, pp. 56–7.

23. Jahangir, *Tuzuk-i-Jahangiri*, vol. 1, p. 122.

24. Jahangir, *Tuzuk-i-Jahangiri*, vol. 1, pp, 111, 252; vol. 2, p. 107.

25. Jahangir, *Tuzuk-i-Jahangiri*, vol. 1, p. 19.

26. Jahangir, *Tuzuk-i-Jahangiri*, vol. 1, p. 256.

27. Jahangir, *Tuzuk-i-Jahangiri*, vol. 1, p. 401.

28. Jahangir, *Tuzuk-i-Jahangiri*, vol. 2, p. 14.

29. Jahangir, *Tuzuk-i-Jahangiri*, vol. 2, p. 27.

30. Observations from Sir Thomas Roe (English Ambassador to the court of Jahangir), 'Journal', in Samuel Purchas, *Hakluytus Posthumus or Purchas His Pilgrimes* (Glasgow: J. Maclehose and Sons, 1905), vol. 4, p. 379.

31. Robert Dankoff has informed the author of two others, a picture of Solomon with a young boy on his knee painted in Isfahan in 1664, in the David Museum, and a second of a young boy being led by the wrist from the Terceme-i Shahname, in the New York Public library.

32. Inayat Khan, W.E. Begley, and Z.A. Desai, eds., *The Shah Jahan Nama of Inayat Khan* (Delhi: Oxford University Press, 1990), p. 96.

33. Sarkar, *History of Auranzgib*, vol. 1, p. 51.

34. Jadunath Sarkar, *Anecdotes of Aurangzib: English Translation of Ahkam-i-Alamgiri Ascribed to Hamid-ud-din Khan Bahadur* (Hyderabad: Orient Longman, 1988), pp. 24–5.

35. Sarkar, *History of Aurangzib*, vol. 1, p. 145.

36. Sarkar, *History of Aurangzib*, vol. 1, p. 146.

37. Sarkar, *History of Aurangzib*, vol. 1, p. 215.

38. Sarkar, *History of Aurangzib*, vol. 1, p. 178.

39. Sarkar, *History of Aurangzib*, vol. 1, pp. 269–70.

40. Sarkar, *History of Aurangzib*, vol. 1, p. 545.

41. Sarkar, *History of Aurangzib*, vol. 3,, pp. 127–8n2.

42. Sarkar, *History of Aurangzib*, vol. 3, pp. 132–3.

43. Sarkar, *Anecdotes*, p. 37.

44. Eraly, *The Mughal Throne*, p. 384. In her subtle and perceptive article on Awrangzib's banning of music, Katherine Brown has indicated that

because Awrangzib really enjoyed music he also knew how it might move his emotions and lead him to lose the self-control he prized so highly. He was a highly emotional but deeply controlled man. K. Butler Brown, 'Did Aurangzeb Ban Music? Questions for the Historiography of his Reign', *MAS* 41 (2007): pp. 77–120.

45. Sarkar, *Anecdotes*, p. 18.

46. Eraly, *The Mughal Throne*, p. 387.

47. *Awrangzib to Prince Muhammad Azam*, nd, trans. Jamshid H. Bilimoria, *Ruka'at-i-Alamgiri* (Delhi: Idarah-i Adabiyat-i Delli, 1972), pp. 26–7

48. *Awrangzib to Prince Muhammad Azam*, p. 38.

49. *Awrangzib to Prince Muhammad Azam*, p. 73.

50. Sarkar, *Anecdotes*, p. 19.

51. Sarkar, *History of Auranzgib*, vol. 3, pp. 353–4.

52. Eraly, *The Mughal Throne*, p. 425.

53. This is the meaning in Arabic. The word *abtar* in this sense is used in the Qur'an 108:3. The context of that *sūra* is that when the Prophet lost his son/s, opponents who hated the Prophet taunted him with being 'cut off' without posterity. In Persian it is also used as in the Arabic meaning: 'whose tail is cut off, without offspring'.

54. He admits failure in his tragic last letter to Prince Azam; *Awrangzib to Prince Muhammad Azam*, pp. 70–2.

55. Glenn D. Lowry, 'Humayun's Tomb: Form, Function and Meaning in Early Mughal Architecture', *Muqarnas* 4 (1987): pp. 133–48.

56. Beveridge, *Akbar Nama*, vol. 1, p. 180.

57. Lowry, 'Humayun's Tomb', pp. 142–5.

58. Ebba Koch, *Mughal Art and Imperial Ideology: Collected Essays* (Delhi: Oxford University Press, 2001), p. 176.

59. Jahangir, *Tuzuk*, vol. 1, p. 152.

60. Catherine B. Asher, *Architecture of Mughal India: New Cambridge History of India* (Cambridge: Cambridge University Press, 1992), vol. 1, part 4, pp. 108–9.

61. Lowry, 'Humayun's Tomb'.

62. Jahangir, *Tuzuk-i-Jahangiri*, vol. 2, pp. 101–2.

63. Jahangir, *Tuzuk-i-Jahangiri*, vol. 2, pp. 101–2. It should be noted that while Jahangir's memoir says she died in May 1605, her tomb gives the date as 1604.

64. Asher, *Mughal India*, pp. 146–9; N.R. Farooqi, 'Akbar's Ilahabad', eds. Gour, Neelum, Saran, *Allahabad: Where the Rivers Meet* (Bombay: Marg Publications, 2009), pp. 44–55.

65. Begam, *History of Humayun*, pp. 101–2.

66. Begam, *History of Humayun*, pp. 102–5.

67. Jahangir, *Tuzuk-i-Jahangiri*, vol. 1, p.266, vol. 2, p. 214.

68. Jahangir, *Tuzuk-i-Jahangiri*, vol. 1, pp. 385–6, 397, vol. 2, pp. 192, 199–200, 214.

69. Jahangir, *Tuzuk-i-Jahangiri*, vol. 2, p. 222.

70. Jahangir, *Tuzuk-i-Jahangiri*, vol. 1, 375, vol. 2, p. 103.

71. Roe, 'Journal', p. 426.

72. Roe, 'Journal', p. 326. The *jharoka* was an overhanging enclosed balcony, placed on an external wall, in which the Mughal emperor would sit to be seen by the people.

73. M. Hadi, '*Tatimma-i Waki at-i Jahangiri*', in Sir H.M. Elliot and Prof. John Dowson, *The History of India as Told by Its Own Historians*, reprint (Delhi: Low Price Publications, 1990), vol. 6, p. 399.

74. Anonymous, '*Intikhab-i Jahangiri-Shahi*', in Elliot and Dowson, *The History of India*, vol. 6, p. 451.

75. Khan, *The Shah Jahan Nama*, p. 71.

76. A passage from Qazwini's, *Padshahnama*, trans. Ebba Koch, in Ebba Koch, *The Complete Taj Mahal and the Riverfront Gardens of Agra* (London: Thames & Hudson, 2006), p. 18.

77. Ebba Koch, *The Complete Taj Mahal*, p. 18.

78. Khan, *The Shah Jahan Nama*, p. 71.

79. Khan, *The Shah Jahan Nama*, p. 70

80. Koch, *The Complete Taj Mahal*, p. 20.

81. Sarkar, *History of Aurangzib*, vol. 1, p. 53.

82. Sarkar, *Anecdotes*, p. 56.

83. Sarkar, *Anecdotes*, p. 57.

84. Sarkar, *Anecdotes*, p. 57.

85. Ellison Banks Findly, *Nur Jahan: Empress of Mughal India* (New York: Oxford University Press, 1993), p. 285; Ebba Koch, *Mughal Architecture: An Outline of Its History and Development (1526–1858)* (Delhi: Oxford University Press, 2002), p. 97.

86. Findly, *Nur Jahan*, p. 285 and Asher, *Architecture of Mughal India*, pp. 172–4.

87. Koch, *The Complete Taj Mahal*, p. 89.

88. Koch, *The Complete Taj Mahal*, p. 6 and Koch, *Mughal Architecture*, p. 13.

89. Koch, *The Complete Taj Mahal*, p. 6.

90. Koch, *The Complete Taj Mahal*, pp. 97–9.

91. Koch, *Mughal Architecture*, p. 127

92. Asher, *Mughal Architecture*, p. 262.

93. Sarkar, History of *Aurangzib*, vol. 1, p. 53.

94. Koch, *The Complete Taj Mahal*, p. 250.

8

TURKISH LANGUAGE AND LITERATURE IN MEDIEVAL AND EARLY MODERN INDIA

Benedek Péri

'Notwithstanding that I grew up in Hindūstān, I am not ignorant of Turkī speech and writing'.[1]

Bu Hind yeri ḥāsılıdın köp köngül aldım
Ne sūd ki bu yer meni dil-gīr qılıptur[2]

The two Turkish[3] hemistiches chosen here as a motto are from a ghazal by Bābur. It serves here as an illustration of the general attitude of many Turkish military entrepreneurs who went to India of their own free will, planned to stay for only a short time after trying their luck, but eventually wished to return to their homeland with their gains. Nevertheless, the riches of the land and the career opportunities that Indian courts offered made them change their minds and so they stayed. The number of those who came and settled in Hindūstān is not known, but their constant stream started as early as the eleventh century during the age of the Ghaznavid rule in Northern India and went on for centuries. There is considerable knowledge of them. Historical sources have recorded many facets of their presence. These sources give a detailed account of the history of the dynasties they established, their political and cultural achievements, battles they took part in, and the buildings they erected. However, one aspect that is rarely mentioned in contemporary sources is the presence of Turkish language on the subcontinent.[4]

The first piece of evidence concerning the use of Turkish in India emerges during the fourteenth century. Our last record of it is during the middle of the nineteenth century. This last piece of information comes from a rather unexpected source, an English novel by an 'old India hand', whose knowledge of nineteenth-century India can hardly be surpassed.

Rudyard Kipling, in his novel *Kim*, set in the surroundings of the Anglo-Russian war of intelligence—the Great Game—describes the adventures of an orphaned Anglo-Indian boy called Kim. Kim, whose late father served in an Irish regiment becomes a trained secret agent. But before he is sent on his first mission, his training officer, Lurgan Sahib and Colonel Creighton, the head of the British network, meet in Simla to discuss what the most suitable test mission would be for the young secret agent.

> 'There is little business where he would be most useful—in the South,' said Lurgan, with peculiar suavity, dropping his heavy blued eyelids. 'E. 23 has that in hand,' said Creighton quickly. 'He must not go down there. Besides, he knows no Turki.'[5]

The reader learns the meaning of the phrase 'in the South' from the next chapter where Kim encounters his colleague on a train. The agent, who turns out to be a Maratha, relates to him his adventures—how he was recognized in Āgrā and how he had to flee the city without accomplishing his mission.[6]

This episode from the novel identifies two important conclusions. First, knowledge of Turkish in Āgrā, the former capital of the Mughal Empire, was still an essential skill in the nineteenth century. Secondly, it was still possible for anyone interested, even for a non-Muslim Maratha, to learn the language. This episode thus seems to reconfirm Annemaria Schimmel's suggestions published in a short article in 1982.[7] Schimmel's research clearly demonstrates that Turkish did not disappear from the palette of Indian languages in the late six-teenth century as most scholars of Turkish Studies tend to think.[8] Furthermore, it was not just a 'private patois of the Mughul family or the first generation immigrants from Central Asia'.[9]

Now let us revert to the first record of the use of Turkish in the Indian environment.

Amīr Khusrau (1253–1325), in his *Mathnawī Nuh Siphir*, which relates the events of the reign of the Delhi sultan Qutb ud-Dīn Mubārak-Shāh

(1316–1320), devotes a separate chapter to the languages of India.[10] In this chapter he mentions the existence of Turkish, whose popularity he attributes to the fact that most of the rulers in the area at that time were of Turkish origin. He states that the knowledge of Turkish is essential if someone wishes for a career in the army or in government circles. He emphasizes the practical use of Turkish and points out the fact that no one had ever learnt this language for academic purposes. He also claims that the universal demand in language-learning aids induced educated people well versed in this tongue to compile grammar books and dictionaries of Turkish.

Amīr Khusrau's report of the practical use of Turkish in India is confirmed by Abū' l-Qāsim Firishta who mentions that two of the Bahmanid sultans of the Deccan, 'Alā ud-Dīn Mujāhid (1375–78) and Tāj ud-Dīn Fīrūz (1397–1422), could speak Turkish.[11] The power and influence of Turkish courtiers and concubines at the Bahmanid royal court simply forced the kings to learn the language of their subjects.

Duarte Barbosa, the Portuguese traveller who visited India in the early sixteenth century, gives a detailed description of the inhabitants of Cambay—one of the major towns of the kingdom of Gujarat. He found a multi-ethnic society there, with a large non-Indian community he calls the 'Moors', who spoke four languages: Arabic, Persian, Gujarati, and Turkish.[12]

An important question must be raised here. Have any Turkish linguistic records survived from pre-Mughal India? The answer is in the affirmative—The *Farhang-i Zufān-gūyā wa Jihān-pūyā*, a Persian dictionary compiled by the Indian lexicographer Badr ud-Dīn Ibrāhīm, which includes a list of 509 Turkish words. The words are solely nouns, and some of them could be Turkish loanwords from contemporary classical Persian vocabulary. However, some scholars consider the Turkish words collected by the author of the aforecited dictionary to be from speakers of Turkish in India.[13] Unfortunately this is the extent of what one can say about the presence of the Turkish language and the role it played during the Sultanate period. The scarcity of data on the use of Turkish is not unprecedented in the cultural area of the Turko–Persian world, which stretched from the Balkans to Eastern India.

Large numbers of Turks became Muslims from the tenth century onwards. However, except for a few works that fortunately survived the vicissitudes of history and several pieces of information scattered in contemporary Persian and Arabic sources, we do not possess much information on the use of Turkish language during the Ghaznavid, Qarakhanid, or Seljuq rule. We can presume that Turkish was spoken in various fields of everyday life, but for a long time it did not threaten the position of Persian as the language of royal courts and the sole language of high literature. Persian was perceived as an ideal medium for composing sophisticated and elegant pieces of poetry while Turkish was considered the language of an uncultured and wary people—the *türk-i bî-idrâk*, the thick-brained Turks.[14] From the eleventh century onwards literary works started to be written in Turkish though their numbers were limited for several hundred years. This state of affairs is partly due to the reluctance of the Turkish literati, who chose not to use their mother tongue as a literary medium, but Persian instead. The possible reason behind their reluctance to write in Turkish is that they might not have considered this language suitable enough for literary purposes. Their opinion had a lasting effect and it is echoed even by Fuḍūlī (1480?–1556), a master of Turkish-language ghazals, who composed his poems during the golden age of classical Turkish poetry and whose Turkish *dīwān* was also read in India. He writes:[15]

> Poems in Persian are numerous because,
> It is difficult to compose elegant verses in Turkish.
> Order and arrangement does not suit the Turkish language,
> Its words are unpolished and unfitting for verse.[16]

While Fuḍūlī could rely on a rich tradition of classical Turkish poetry with established ways of solving basic problems of metre and rhyme and expressing elaborate thoughts in an elegant and delicate way, earlier poets who tried to compose in Turkish were in a far worse position. No one knew better the hardships of being a Turkish poet than Mīr 'Alī-Shīr Newā'ī (1441–1501). A genius of his age, Newā'ī devoted his whole life to creating a classical Turkish poetic tradition. In his pamphlet titled *Muḥākamat ul-Lughatayn*, which was dedicated to the purpose of persuading his fellow poets to use their mother tongue, Newā'ī describes the difficulties Turkish poets had to face as follows:

> Now it is clear from what has been said so far that there are many odd words and expressions in this language [Turkish]. It is very difficult to arrange them in a delicate and pleasant way. Fledgling poets get easily fed up with these hardships and choose an easier way. When it happens several times, it becomes a habit for them ...
>
> Budding young poets having composed their first verses that usually tender to their heart wish to show off with them in front of those who mastered this art. Since these experts are Persians and do not speak Turkish they [the young poets] give it up [composing poems in Turkish] and become attracted to them. When they become attracted to them they

establish contacts with them and eventually they become one of their folk.[17]

So it seems that Newā'ī and Fuḍūlī had to face the same problems: the incompatibilities of the Turkish language and the classical Persian quantitative metrical system. These difficulties did not pose insurmountable obstacles as was the case for many Ottoman, Azeri, or eastern Turkish poets, but in order to accomplish the task, that is to make Turkish suitable for composing classical poetry, poets needed a strong motivation to express themselves in that language. The reward of fame and material goods was worth the trouble. Nizāmī 'Arūḍī describes the relationship of poets and patrons as a tight bond in his treatise on the profession of poets. Poets depend on their patrons for a living and in exchange for their support, they guarantee that the name of their benefactor will survive for eternity.[18] But for a long time it was rare for a ruler or any other potential Maecenas to support someone who wrote poems or prose in Turkish.

The turning point in the western Turkish lands was a decree issued by the Qaramanid sovereign Mehmed in 1277 declaring Turkish as the official language of his kingdom. The Ottomans also made Turkish their official language and under their rule a well-established Ottoman Turkish literary tradition evolved. This development was facilitated by some of the Ottoman sultans who took an interest in poetry and composed poems in Turkish.[19]

Further eastwards, a similar development occurred. In the areas of eastern Anatolia, northern Iraq, and western Iran, with the support and personal involvement of Turkish rulers like Qāḍī Burhān ud-Dīn (1340–1398), who ruled in Sivas, the Qaraqoyunlu sovereign Jihān-Shāh (1405?–1467), who used the pen-name 'Ḥaqīqī,[20] or the first Safavid shah, Shāh Isma'īl 'Khaṭā'ī (1487–1524), a distinct literary idiom and literary tradition evolved. *Türkī-i 'ajamī* as a literary language and a literary tradition was very close to the language and tradition of the Ottomans.

Approximately at the same time a very similar process began in Transoxania and Khurasan. For a contemporary expert's account on the subject one should turn again to Newā'ī who says that:

> Arab kings supported Arab poets and Persian rulers nurtured poetry in Persian. Even when power was transferred from Arab and Sart sultans to Turkish khans, not a single poet appeared, from the time of Hülegü Khān to the reign of Sulṭān-i Ṣāhib-qirān Temür Küregen, whose works would have been worth reciting or recording in writing and not one sultan is mentioned who had composed poetry. However from the time of Sulṭān-i

Ṣāḥib-qirān Temür Küregen to the end of the reign of Shāh-rukh Sulṭān, his son and successor, poets started to compose in Turkish and also some of his Majesty's descendants proved to be a gifted poet.[21]

It is evident from his account that Newā'ī did not acknowledge the poetic efforts of earlier poets who lived before the advent of the Timurids. It is not clear whether he did not have any knowledge of them or he simply chose to ignore them, but it is quite obvious that he associates the real beginnings of classical Turkish poetry in Transoxania and Khurasan with Temür and his descendants. He is right in a sense because the hundred-year rule of the Timurids not only brought about the upheaval of interest in Turkish poetry but it also witnessed the establishment of an eastern Turkish literary tradition that came to be known by the name of its creator. In the western Turkish world it was called the style of Newā'ī.[22]

Regardless of how deliberate and hard working Newā'ī was, he could not have succeeded without circumstances that favoured his undertakings. The atmosphere he worked in was a period of 'cultural florescence that took place ... in the late fifteenth century as the climatic period of Timurid culture'.[23] The social and economic developments that made this boom of art patronage possible has been studied in depth,[24] but the support Timurids gave to classical Turkish literature cannot be adequately explained by these developments or by claiming that Timurid princes and Turkish nobles nourished their mother tongue by insisting on its use.

Research has shown that Timurids were always eager to demonstrate that they were equally comfortable with two simultaneously existing cultural environments: the Turco–Mongol and the Perso–Islamic world.[25] The adoption of two legal systems, the Mongol *yasa* and the Muslim *sharīʿa*, the existence of two tax systems, and the revival of the Uighur script,[26] which was the writing system of the Mongol Empire for official and artistic purposes, was all meant to demonstrate that both worlds were equally important to the Timurid rulers. They wanted to be accepted by all their subjects and show themselves, as Bābur the first in the line of Indian Timurids did, as men 'skilled in the accomplishments that mattered most to the Persianized, Islamized Turco–Mongol aristocrat of the late Timurid period: war, poetry and religion'.[27]

In fifteenth-century Muslim society, the legitimacy of a ruler depended on two key elements: a continous effort to comply with the rules of Islam set for a righteous ruler and a pious Muslim, and the ability to demonstrate divine support.[28] While the first of these requirements connected Timurid rulers to the Perso–Islamic world, the second attached them through their mythical progenitor Ālan Qū'ā, 'a Mongol woman who conceived her children by a ray of light or golden man whom Heaven had emanated', to their Turco–Mongol heritage.[29] This dual attachment can be observed through the activities of Timurid rulers and princes as patrons and writers of literary works. They supported Persian authors like many previous Turkish rulers of the Perso–Islamic world. Their support, however, also extended to those literati who were willing to use Turkish as a literary medium. This was a novelty for those of the eastern part of the Turco–Persian world. Timurid princes encouraged the usage of Turkish in poetry through financial support by being consumers of these literary products and also by actively taking part in promoting the case of Turkish. Quite a few of Temür's descendants tried their hands at composing Turkish poetry.[30] The keen interest Timurid princes took in classical literature written in Turkish became a part of the family's cultural legacy, a kind of family 'trademark'. Ẓahīr ad-Dīn Muḥammad Bābur (1483–1530), the founder of the polity that came to be known as the Mughal Empire, remained true to the family 'tradition' of using Turkish for artistic purposes. His oeuvre in Turkish prose is considerable and his lyrical poems amount to a full *dīwān*. The most exquisite among his poetical pieces are his ghazals and *rubā'īs*. In order to demonstrate that he was not only a poet well versed in the practical aspects of Turkish poetry, he also became an expert of the theory of this art form in which he compiled a treatise on Turkish prosody.[31] Nevertheless the work that earned him fame was neither his poetry nor his work on classical poetry but his magnum opus—his autobiography. His memoirs, often referred to as the *Bābur-nāma* (the Book of Bābur), is a unique encyclopaedia of early sixteenth-century Transoxania, Khurāsān, and Hindūstān. He wrote this book not in Persian, the customary language for chronicles, but in his mother tongue, because he wanted to demonstrate his 'stature as a Tīmūrid ruler, a leader of the Turco–Mongol aristocracy of Mawarannahr'.[32] Bābur's aim as a poet and theoretician was highly ambitious. He used every means available to surpass Newā'ī or at least to show that he was his equal.[33] Regardless of how ambitious he was as a man of the pen, he was only able to partially attain his objectives. Though sometimes his exeptional wit manages to shine through his lines, most of his poetry lacks the ingenious brilliance that is so characteristic of Newā'ī's verse. As for his prose it would not be accurate to compare the *Bābur-nāma* to any of Newā'ī's sophisticated prose compositions since the readership Bābur targeted was his companions—seasoned men of the sword who were not highly educated connoisseurs of literary delicacies.

In spite of all this criticism it can not be denied that Bābūr was a gifted intellectual and a first-rate poet in Turkish. Two of his four sons, his successor Humāyūn (1508–56) and the second-born Kāmrān (1509–57), were the ones who became renowned for their poetry. However, contemporary critics assert that the younger ones, both 'Askarī and Hindāl, were also quite skilful in the art of poetic composition.[34]

As for the Timurids' traditional love for Turkish classical poetry, we know from the account of Seydī 'Alī Re'īs, an Ottoman admiral and amateur poet who reached the imperial court of Humāyūn after many calamities, that the king appreciated Turkish poetry very much. 'Alī Re'īs was adept at composing poems both in his native Ottoman Turkish and in the style of Newā'ī. He claimed with great pride that Humāyūn loved his verses so much that he called 'Alī Re'īs a second Mīr 'Alī Shīr and gave him permission to return to his homeland only after 'Alī Re'īs presented his petition to Humāyūn in the form of two Turkish ghazals.[35] The Ottoman captain mentions several poets at the royal court who were gifted and skilful enough to enter a poetical contest in Turkish. It appears that Humāyūn, similiar to many Timurid princes before him, was well disposed towards Turkish poetry. Perhaps that is why Bābur presented him with a unique gift in 1529, the collection of his Turkish ghazals written in Hindūstān.[36]

Sources do not indicate whether Humāyūn was able to actively take part in the aforementioned poetical competitions. His poetical talent can only be assessed by his Persian dīwān and the scattered Persian verses preserved in various contemporary sources.[37] The sole existing copy of Humāyūn's dīwān does not contain a single verse in Turkish. But two contemporary anthologies preserved several of his Turkish lines, a single bayt (pairverse), and a short qiṭ'a,[38] suggesting that Humāyūn was also able to compose poetry in Turkish.[39]

Whether he chose to write almost exclusively in Persian for reasons outlined by Newā'ī or if his Turkish poems have been simply lost, it is difficult to conclude. But it is known that when the occasion arose he did not hesitate to use Turkish as a means of everyday communication.

A collection of various texts compiled during the reign of Akbar preserved a letter written in Turkish by Humāyūn in 1524.[40] Contemporary historians have also recorded several instances when Humāyūn spoke Turkish. While on a visit to Tabrīz during the years of his exile, he went to the marketplace whereupon he saw two Turks who saluted him, and he said in Turkish, 'give my compliments to your sovereign'; they replied in the same language: 'most certainly we will'.[41]

Bāyazīd Bayat,[42] Jawhar Āftābji (the historian who hailed from an Oghuz Turkish tribe), and also Abū'l-Faḍl in his *Akbar-nāma* recorded that Humāyūn sometimes spoke Turkish also at the court. During the skirmishes between the armies of Humāyūn and Kāmrān in the early summer of 1548, Ismaʿīl Beg Dulday, one of the group of rebellious officers who went over to Kāmrān, was captured by the royalists. He was brought before Humāyūn, who rebuked him in Turkish for his unfaithful behaviour.[43] Some time later, perhaps in August, after the siege of Tāliqān, when his rebel-turned-former prime minister, Qarača Khān was taken prisoner, Humāyūn, seeing him in a pitiful state, said to him a few soothing words in Turkish. He did the same to another captive, his former servant, Qurbān Qarawul. [44]

A few days later Mirzā Kāmrān also came to pay homage. The sovereign received his brother courteously and invited him to come closer using a Turkish word.[45] Five years later, in December 1553 Humāyūn defeated and captured Mirzā Kāmrān. He sought to find a final solution to the problem his brother represented and decided on blinding him. Humāyūn looked for a reliable person to do the job and discussed the matter with one of his followers, the would-be executioner ʿAlī-dūst. According to Jawhar the discussion was conducted in Turkish. [46]

Another incident was when the royal entourage was marching through the deserts of Rajasthan and they came across a place with water. At this site a quarrel broke out between the members of Humāyūn's retinue and the Turkish noble Turdı Beg Khān,[47] who would not let them water their camels and horses at the well assigned to his household. The king asked Turdı Beg in Turkish to let the royal attendants give water to their animals.[48]

The mere fact that the chroniclers thought it was important to mention that these conversations took place in Turkish clearly indicates that the official language of the Indian Timurid court was no longer Turkish but had become Persian by the time of Humāyūn's reign. But as the above stories demonstrate, Turkish was still in use among members of the Turkish élite, who seem to have switched to their mother tongue when they really wanted their message to have an impact or in situations where strong emotions were involved— brotherly love, sympathy for old acquaintences, anger, or as the story of Kāmrān's escape from Kābul suggests, despair.

According to Niẓām ud-Dīn Aḥmad as the siege of Kābul dragged on in 1547, Mirzā Kāmrān, seeing his situation as hopeless, made a hole in the wall and escaped one night. When a detachment of soldiers sent by Humāyūn caught up with him, he addressed their leader, Ḥājī Muḥammad Khān, in Turkish and desperately tried to convince him that he could not be held responsible for the death of the Khān's father. His words seemed to have had the the desired effect on his pursuer, since Ḥājī Muḥammad Khān let him go.[49]

Returning to poetry, we have seen that Humāyūn, who was able to compose classical poems in Turkish, hardly ever used this language for literary purposes. Nonetheless, his brother Mirzā Kāmrān followed his father's example and wrote various classical pieces of poetry in Turkish. Though he produced poems in Persian his Turkish ones are more numerous.[50] The bulk of his Turkish *dīwān* consists of ghazals and *rubāʿīs* (quatrains), which he mainly modelled on the lyrical compositions of famous masters of Persian classical poetry whom he named in a short *mathnawī*. He tried to imitate the style of Niẓāmī, Amīr Khusraw, and the poet laureate of the Timurids, Jāmī.[51] Mirzā Kāmrān used very skilfully the traditional arsenal of classical poetry and always aimed at reproducing the beauty present in Amīr Khusraw's and Newāʾīs works.[52] Still he humbly believed that his poetry was not good enough to reach those heights and his efforts were fruitless and in vain. For his failure, like Fuḍūlī in the western Turkish world, he blamed the Turkish language itself.

> When I start singing in the Turkish tongue
> It sounds as if I was beating an empty drum.[53]

Mirzā Kāmrān passed away in 1557 and the silence of our sources and the lack of other evidence suggests that for the next two-and-a-half centuries none of the Indian Timurid sovereigns or princes of the royal house was tempted or had the desire to compose verses in Turkish.

As mentioned before, ʿAskarī and Hindāl, the two younger sons of Bābur, had some sort of poetic talent. But unlike Kāmrān, they seem to have composed verses only in Persian. Several lines of their ghazals are quoted in contemporary anthologies.[54] Hindāl presumably was interested in Turkish classical poetry because his father sent him his poems and also his *qiṭʿas* written in the Bāburī script, but no sources indicate that he also produced poetry in Turkish.[55]

The successor of Humāyūn, Jalāl ud-Dīn Muḥammad Akbar (1542–1605), also had a talent for poetry though he was unable to learn the alphabet and remained illiterate throughout his life.[56] According to Abū'l-Faḍl, 'The inspired nature of his Majesty is strongly drawn to the composing of Hindī and Persian poetry and is critical and hair-splitting in the niceties of poetic diction.'[57] Abū'l-Faḍl's account suggests that Akbar did not compose verses in Turkish, only in the two languages mentioned before.

Interestingly enough, we do not possess any information on his knowledge of Turkish. Though contemporary sources remain silent on the subject, Muḥammad Ḥusayn Āzād asserts in his encyclopaedic work on the reign of Akbar that 'Akbar himself knew Turkish very well.'[58] And the *Dabistān-i Madhāhib*, a mid-seventeenth-century Indian work on the religions of the world,[59] even claims that 'His Majesty, Akbar as he was ordered by God, used to read prayers, containing the praise of the sun, in the Persian, Hindi, Turkish, and Arabic languages.'[60]

In any case, it is not without reason to suggest that Akbar learnt the language of his forefathers. But who did he learn Turkish from? There were many opportunities for him to pick it up. In his childhood he was surrounded by family members, courtiers, poets, and soldiers from whom he could have learnt the language since Humāyūn's 'court was not unlike that of his contemporary Suleimān the Magnificent, where Persian and Turkish flourished side by side as cultivated languages'.[61] For some time as a child Akbar was in the care of his uncle 'Askarī, and later in the custody of Kāmrān and his aunt Khānzāda Begum. His other aunt, Gul-badan Begum, is thought to have written her memoirs on Humāyūn in Turkish,[62] and his childhood tutor and trusted minister was a Baharlu Türkmen noble whose family once belonged to the most influential, leading clans of the Türkmen Qara Qoyunlu Empire.[63]

Bayrām Khān (1509–61) was not only a battle-hardened warrior and clever statesman, he was also a poet and such an outstanding poet in Turkish[64] that his poems deeply affected people. The force of his poetry is well illustrated by the story of how he comforted Shāh-qulı Maḥram Baharlu, a celebrated hero of his age. Shāh-qulı, who was a distant relative of Bayrām Khān, became famous for capturing the enemy commander Hemu in the second battle of Pānipāt (1556). Regardless of how battle-hardened a soldier he was, he had a weakness for young boys. He fell in love with a handsome dancer called Qabūl Khān. But Akbar did not approve of this kind of relationship and ordered the boy to be taken away. The love-stricken Shāh-qulı was deeply hurt and subsequently resigned from imperial service. He left behind his wealth and renounced worldly pleasures to become a yogi in the woods. In order to pacify and console him, Bayrām Khān composed a ghazal in Turkish and followed him into the jungle. According to Abū'l-Faḍl, his poem moved Shāh-qulı so deeply that Shāh-qulı became himself again and immediately returned to imperial service.[65]

There were other soldiers in the Mughal ranks who occasionally turned to poetry and composed in Turkish. Shāh-berdi Bayat, the brother of the historian Bāyazīd Bayat, wrote Persian and Turkish poems under the pen name, Saqqā Čaghatā'ī. According to his brother his Persian poems amounted to a full *dīwān* and they were well received by his contemporaries. In his Persian poetry he imitated the ghazals of Qāsim-i Anwār (1356–1433) and modelled his Turkish verses on the compositions of Seyyid Nesīmī (d. 1417).[66]

Mīr Muḥammad, the son of a simple farmer in Ghaznī, the brother of Shams ud-Dīn Muḥammad who became *wakīl-i muṭlaq* in 1562,[67] was also a famous military man. According to Badāuni his official duties kept him so busy that he could not devote much time to his favourite pastime, composing poetry.[68] But we know that he managed to find some time for his hobby and when the opportunity was given he wrote poetry, both in Persian and Turkish.[69]

The aforementioned Turkish nobles were not the only ones to enter imperial service. There were many others coming from various parts of the sixteenth-century Turkish world, from Central Asia, Iran, and the Ottoman Empire. The Turānī or Central Asian faction of nobility who caused considerable problems during the first decades of Akbar's reign mainly consisted of Uzbek and Central Asian Turkish nobles.[70] There were also many high-ranking officials of Türkmen origin who were counted among the members of the Iranian party.[71] Together with these nobles came their retainers, who were mostly recruited from their own clan. The number of Turks at the court or in the army cannot be verified but it can be said without much doubt that their presence and political influence made the knowledge of Turkish a very useful skill. Perhaps this consideration also played a role in Akbar's decision to appoint his former tutor Bayrām Khān's son, 'Abd ur-Raḥīm (1556–1627), to teach Turkish to the heir apparent, Prince Salīm, who later became the fourth Mughal emperor, Jahāngīr (1606–26). 'Abd ur-Raḥīm was trusted with another but almost equally important task—the translation of the *Bābur-nāma*. Akbar held his grandfather's memoirs in great esteem. He considered it an 'encyclopaedia of knowledge' and wanted to make it accessible for those who were unable to read the Turkish original. 'Abd ur-Raḥīm was a perfect choice for the job because as his biographer 'Abd ul-Bāqī Nihāwandī puts it: 'He has an excellent command of Turkī since it is the language of his forefathers.'[72]

The few sentences Nihāwandī devotes to praising his patron's knowledge of Turkish are worth quoting here because they express his admiration for 'Abd ur-Raḥīm's language skills. Nihāwandī provides readers with a glimpse of the state of the Turkish language in early seventeenth-century India. He writes:

> Turkī is not commonly used in Hindūstān. There are other people who are Turks and sons of Turks, for example the sons of Čaghatay amīrs, Qizilbash nobles and Uzbek grandees, but because they were born in Hindūstān and brought up among the people of India they do not have any share of this language. Not like this knower of languages ... who speaks in an elegant way the Turkī language of these peoples. The Turkī that used to be Uzbakī [Özbek] and Qizilbashī [Türkmen or Azeri] and Rūmī [Ottoman Turkish]. He also understands poems written in these three languages. He can explain their difficult words, he composes poems, writes various kinds of letters and other prose compositions in all three. Thus it would not be an exaggeration to say that he surpasses all those who are considered eloquent in these languages. On the order of the ruler of the Earth and Time, Jalāl ud-Dīn Muḥammad Akbar pādshāh he has translated into Persian the *Wāqiᶜāt-i Bāburī* written by Bābur Mirzā, the most exalted ruler who resides in Heaven. It is full of difficult Čaghatay Turkish words that even the Türkmens are unable to read and understand.[73]

Nihāwandī's account suggests that by the early 1600s the use of Turkish had become limited to a narrow circle of 'traditionalists' because even those who were of Turkish origin stopped speaking it. Nevertheless Turkī was still present in the subcontinent in the form of four distinct languages: Central Asian Turkish, Özbek, Türkmen, and Ottoman Turkish. The Turkish language Nihāwandī calls the language of 'Abd ur-Raḥīm's forefathers might have been Türkmen or Azerī, at least this is what Nihāwandī's remark on the Türkmens' difficulty in understanding certain Central Asian Turkish words might hint at.

The other Turkish languages 'Abd ur-Raḥīm learnt later, but he learnt them well, as is attested by the British ambassador to the Mughal court, William Hawkins, who was appointed to lead the British mission because he had learnt Turkish quite well during his stay in the Levant.[74] He was received by 'Abd ur-Raḥīm who bore the title 'Khan of the Khāns' at the time of their meeting and was one the most influential grandees in the Mughal Empire. The British gentleman's account of this official meeting largely confirms the eulogies of Nihāwandī regarding the Khān-i Khānān's knowledge of Turkish—Ottoman Turkish.[75]

'Abd ur-Raḥīm, as Nihāwandī's description of him shows, composed classical poetry in Turkish like his father had done. The quality of his Turkish verses can not be assessed because none of his Turkish lines have yet been found.[76] As for his prose compositions, only one letter, an epistle addressed to a certain Khwāja Dīwāna, has survived.[77] The letter, written in ornate prose, is embellished with quotations from the ghazals of Newā'ī, demonstrating that its author was in posession of a copy of Newā'īs *dīwān* and knew his poetry well enough to select the appropriate quotations.[78]

Besides being a man of letters 'Abd ur-Rahīm was also a patron of holy men, scholars, and poets. The third volume of Nihāwandī's work is a *tadhkira*, an anthology devoted to those scholars and poets who were supported by 'Abd ur-Raḥīm. Some of them were of Turkish origin[79] and three of them composed poems in Turkish as well. Kalb-i 'Alī Beg, who belonged to the Baharlu tribe of the Türkmens like the Khān-i Khānān himself,[80] came from Tabrīz, Siyānī from Hamadān,[81] and Dārwīsh Mithlī from Aleppo.[82] All three of them used western Turkish literary language in their poems. It is possible that Nihāwandī partly referred to their compositions when he asserted that 'Abd ur-Raḥīm was able to understand poetry in Qizilbashī and Rūmī.

As we have seen earlier, the Khān-i Khānān was appointed to teach Turkish to Akbar's son, Prince Salīm. The prince learnt his lessons well and prided himself in his language skills even when he became king. During the summer of 1607, he visited Kabul and took a copy of Bābur's memoirs with him in order to use it as a travel guide. This copy was special since it contained several long passages in Turkish that Jahāngīr added to the original text.[83] The title of the present article, a quotation chosen from his memoirs, clearly demonstrates that Turkish, the language of his forefathers, had great symbolic significance for Jahāngīr. Morley suggested in his catalogue that the first version of his *Tūzuk-i Jahāngīrī* was modelled on the work of his great-grandfather Bābur, and like the *Bābur-nāma* it was originally written in Turkish.[84] After reading Nihāwandī's remarks on the restricted use of Turkish, Morley's idea might not sound very convincing at first, but taking into account the importance Jahāngīr attributed to Bābur's memoirs and to his own knowledge of Turkish, it should not be dismissed out of hand. In any case, only a thorough comparative textual analysis of the *Bābur-nāma* and the *Tūzuk-i Jahāngīrī* could confirm Morley's theory.

Many things, like paintings made on his order or his insistence on the strict observance of court etiquette indicate that Jahāngīr was a man who attributed great importance to symbolic gestures. Since he was obsessed with his lineage,[85] knowing Turkish had great significance for him. It was an asset that linked him to his ancestors. In such circumstances an elementary level of knowledge of Turkish would never have satisfied him. With his skills in Turkish composition he intended to show that he was a true Timurid and like so many of his forefathers he was able and talented enough to produce at least a few passages of prose in Turkish that was of literary value. He did not write something of his own but chose to add passages to the *Bābur-nāma*, the highly revered book of his great-grandfather. Through this symbolic act he tried to put himself on an equal footing with Bābur, the first emperor, as far as literary achievement in Turkish is concerned. The passages he added to the *Bābur-nāma* conveyed the same symbolic message as the title he picked for his memoirs, the *Tūzuk-i Jahāngīrī*, since the Turkish word *tūzuk* connected him with his ancestor Temür, the author of the renowned *Tūzük-i Temürî* (the Ordinances of Temür).

The accounts of foreign travellers confirm Jahāngīr's attachment to the Turkish language. William Hawkins recorded in his account that during his official reception at the court, the emperor learnt that he could speak Turkish. This piece of news pleased him so much that he commanded the British envoy 'to follow him unto his Chamber of Presence.'[86]

The knowledge of Turkish at that time must have been so common at court that Thomas Kerridge of the East India Company in Ajmer warned his superiors in London in 1614, 'It is requisite that a lieger be sent to be continual resident in this court and if possible that he have either the Persian or the Turkish tongue so facile to have audience at his pleasure, which otherwise is more difficult and less effectual.'[87]

The ability to speak Turkish in early seventeenth-century Mughal India could easily smooth the way for all those who wished to do business in the great trade centres of the empire, like the port of Surat. The use of Turkish in Surat is attested by John Sandcroft, an East India Company official, who recorded in one of his letters that the 'Turkish tongue will pass as well here as Aleppo'.[88] Some twenty years later, in 1638, the German traveller Albert de Mandelslo also visited Surat, from where he went on to Ahmedabad, the capital of Gujarat.

He paid a visit to the governor of the province, a native of Shirwān, in Ādharbayjān; the governor evidently knew Turkish and had a long conversation with him.[89] Mandelslo's account of this meeting suggests that the British gentleman who accompanied him on this first visit acted as an interpereter. During their conversation it turned out that Mandelslo spoke some Turkish and when they were leaving, the governor said farewell to him in this language with the following words: '*Seni dahı görim*' (I shall see you again).[90]

Their next meeting took place two days later. The text suggests that Mandelslo was not helped by an interpreter this time and the conversation was conducted in Turkish.

Following the Mughal family tradition, Jahāngīr saw to it that Prince Khurram (1592–1666), his would-be successor, was also taught the ancestral language of the dynasty. He appointed Tatar Beg to teach the prince, and elevated him to the rank of *hasht ṣadī*.[91] Khurram was a hopeless and slothful student and though Tatar Beg was aided in his mission by Ruqayyā Sulṭān Begim,[92] the daughter of Mirzā Hindāl, their joint efforts proved futile.[93] But it is still likely that Khurram picked up at least some basic Turkish. If not from his tutors than from the 'many strong-limbed Tartara [Tatar], Calmac [Qalmaq], and Osbeca [Uzbak] women in his guard, all skilled in the use of arms'.[94] Shāh-jahān had a special and confident relationship with his Amazon guards. He trusted them so much that he assigned them to the most delicate missions where the highest degree of secrecy and circumspection was essential. One of these missions was the attempted capture of his son Aurangzeb, the future 'Ālamgīr I (1658–1707).[95]

Unlike his father who was largely indifferent to Turkish, Aurangzeb, as Sarkar puts it, 'has acquired a mastery over Chaghatay Turki, as he had served in Balkh and Qandahār, and the Mughal army contained a large body of men recruited from Central Asia'.[96] Some think that Turkish was his mother tongue[97] but since his mother, Mumtāz Maḥal, came from a family of immigrant Persians, this is highly improbable.[98] To Aurangzeb Turkish was not of the symbolic importance as it was for his grandfather, Jahāngīr. Besides being part of the family tradition as an educated prince of the royal family, there were practical reasons for knowledge of the language. The fields where knowledge of Turkish was particularly useful were military life and diplomatic correspondence. The Mughal army had large bodies of Central Asian Turkish mercenaries whom the emperor praised for their bravery and military skills.[99] A commander who was able to talk to his troops in their mother tongue could handle them more easily. In foreign relations, in addition to Persian, Turkish was also used as an intermediary language for Mughal–Ottoman[100] and Mughal–Russian relations.[101]

Aurangzeb made certain that his sons were educated in Turkish. Their education started at the age of five.[102] A contemporary historian, Sāqī Musta'id Khān, recorded that three of them had learnt the language. Muḥammad Mu'aẓẓam Shāh 'Ālam Bahadur (1643–1712), who later became king, had 'perfect knowledge of Turkish,'[103] Muhammad Kām-bakhsh (1667–1709) 'studied the standard books more than all his brothers and acquired a great knowledge of the Turkī language'.[104] Even Muḥammad Sulṭān (1639–78), who as a young man, used every possible excuse to get rid of his Turkish teacher and skip class, resulting in being severely scolded by his royal father for his unacceptable behaviour.[105] But eventually he learnt at least some Turkish. We do not know how fluent he was in it but his knowledge was enough to earn Sāqī Khān's approval.[106]

The knowledge of Turkish, however, was not restricted to the royal family or the families of Turkish immigrants in the second half of the seventeenth century. The author of the *Mirzā-nāma*, a guidebook intended for the perfect gentleman of the age, advised its readers to be educated in four languages: Arabic, Persian, Hindūstānī, and Turkish.[107] Many people might have taken this piece of advice seriously, as is suggested by the number of Turkish grammar books and vocabularies that started to appear during the latter part of Aurangzeb's reign.[108] The increasing need for language-learning aids does not necessarily mean an increase in the number of potential language learners. Perhaps it simply indicates that the native speakers from whom it was possible to learn the language were no longer as readily available. However, due to the lack of adequate information, it is impossible to give an estimation of the number of Turkish 'guest workers' employed in the empire from its establishment to the end of Aurangzeb's reign. But, by the end of the seventeenth century, the constant stream of Turkish immigrants seemed to have started to dry up. The decrease in their numbers might be attributed to several causes. The main cause was perhaps the general economic decline of the Mughal Empire. The once attractive opportunities for career and wealth that had been offered by a central government became less appealing.[109] Although princely states could have represented an alternative, especially for soldiers, the great changes that took place in military technology and warfare accelerated this process. As firearms, especially light guns and small arms, improved and became more easily available, infantry units greatly expanded.[110] The new weapons combined with new tactics led to more efficient infantry units that were of more use on the battlefields than traditional cavalry. New military skills required an expertise that Turks equipped with bows and arrows and trained in traditional warfare did not possess.[111] The importance of mounted archers started to fade away. Moreover, the manpower for infantry units was readily available on the Indian military labour market.[112]

Coming back to the role the Turkish language played during the reign of Aurangzeb, some scholars state that Turkish was the official language of the Mughal Empire in the late seventeenth century.[113] Though it can not be considered anything but a scholarly overstatement, it might be said that knowledge of Turkish had somehow become part of the ethos of the highly cultured Mughal gentleman, a trait that was not uncommon particularly among educated intellectuals. The case of the Rajput Prince Jai Singh[114] and the Muslim scholar 'Abd ul-Jalīl Bilgrāmī, the author of the *Kashkūl*, an Arabic–Persian–Turkish dictionary,[115] illustrates this point fairly well. Both of them were natives of India but both of them learnt Turkish quite well.

The relative popularity of learning Turkish continued after the death of Aurangzeb. Knowledge of Turkish proved to be very useful for the young Muḥammad Shāh (1719–48). He used it as a secret code of communication with his supporters with whom he conspired against his powerful *wazīr*, the Indian Shi'ite Ḥusayn 'Alī Khān.

According to the author of the *Siyar-i Muta'akhkhirīn*, the emperor and his allies were able to discuss how to do away with the *wazīr* even in the presence of their would-be victim because Ḥusayn 'Alī Khān did not know Turkish.[116] But Turkish was not only a secret means of communications at the court. Muḥammad Shāh liked to have small talks in Turkish with his Turkish nobles. On a hunting trip he 'took Aghyr[117] Qhan, the Turk with him, to whom he spoke Turkish during the whole hunt'.[118] Perhaps it was the fate of the *wazīr* and his brother that motivated the Persian Shi'ite noble, Najm ud-Dawla, to have his son Mirzā 'Alī Nāqī instructed in Turkish.[119] The use of Turkish in court circles must have been a common practice as it is indicated by a footnote attached to the text of the *Siyar* by its first translator, a half-French gentleman who spent most of his life in India. Raymond, writing in 1785, calls it a 'Bizarery' that the language of government in India is not Turkish but Persian.[120]

Muḥammad Shāh was not the only eighteenth-century Mughal ruler who learnt the ancestral language of the Indian Timurids. Shāh

'Ālam II (1760–1806) also knew Turkish well.[121] He spoke several native languages of India and was educated in Persian and Arabic. Like so many Timurids before him he also composed poems. He wrote his verses under the pen name 'Āftābī. We do not know if he composed poems in Turkish but he might not have been indifferent to poetry written in this tongue.

Mirzā 'Alī-bakht Gurgānī (1759–1818),[122] a Mughal prince who indulged in writing verses in Persian, Urdu, and Turkish, relates in his memoirs that once Shāh 'Ālam visited him in his home. Knowing that the king liked his poetry, the Mirzā presented him with a copy of his Urdu and Turkish poems.[123] Mirzā 'Alī-bakht wrote his poems under the pen name Aẓfarī, 'Long Nailed'. This nom de plume was not his original choice. He was persuaded to change his *takhalluṣ* from Gham-khwur, 'One Who Suffers in Patience' to Aẓfarī by the *wazīr* of 'Ālamgīr II, 'Imād ul-Mulk Ghāzī ud-Dīn Fīrūz-jang, one of the most powerful Turkish nobles of the age.[124] 'Imād al-Mulk was a learned man who knew the Qurān by heart and composed poems in Persian and Turkish.[125]

Aẓfarī, in addition to writing poetry, was also an amateur scholar of Turkish linguistics. He spent the first thirty years of his life in confinement in Delhi in the *Salāṭīn*,[126] where he acquired good knowledge of Arabic, Persian, and Turkish. Later he taught Turkish to his uncle, Mirzā Ḥusayn,[127] and gave Turkish lessons to two of the young Mughal princes, Mirzā Moghul and Mirzā Toghul, with whom he remained on friendly terms even after his escapade from Delhi. Aẓfarī was proud of his students' Turkish skills and in a letter written in Turkish, Aẓfarī asked the young princes to send their replies in the very same language. Mirzā Moghul and Mirzā Toghul complied with his request and wrote him a letter in the language they had learnt from him.[128] During his wanderings through India Aẓfarī spent a long time in Lucknow, where he got acquainted with the ruler of Avadh, Āṣaf ud-Dawla (1775–97). Aẓfarī also befriended one of the Nawāb's highest-ranking officials, Madār ud-Dawla Bahadur Samsām-jang, who asked him to write a book for him on Turkish because he wished to learn the language.[129] Samsām-jang was a distant relative of Aẓfarī, so his Timurid lineage would explain his interest in the language of his ancestors. But in Lucknow Aẓfarī had a student with a very different background. He was neither a Timurid nor a *turkzā*, a person of Turkish origin. He was an Indian *sayyid* who had already learnt the rudiments of Turkish and wanted to enhance his skills.[130]

Late eighteenth-century Lucknow seems to have been a place where there were people who were interested in learning Turkish. The predecessor of Āṣaf ud-Dawla, Shujā' ud-Dawla (1754–75) had a good command of the language[131] and Aẓfarī met a certain Mirzā Kāzim, who was of Turkish origin and not only spoke Turkish well but could also recite Newā'ī's *dīwān* by heart.[132]

Aẓfarī eventually left Lucknow and after enduring many hardships travelled south to the Karnatik where he hoped to find refuge in the realm of Umdat ul-Umarā Ghulām Ḥusayn Khān Bahadur (1795–1801). Before arriving in Madras he sent his collected Arabic, Persian, and Turkish verses to the *nawāb* as a sign of his respect.[133]

As mentioned earlier besides being a poet, Aẓfarī was also an amateur linguist and lexicographer. He compiled several works on Turkish grammar and vocabulary. During his stay in Lucknow he compiled a dictionary titled *Lughat-i Turkī-yi Chaghatā'ī* and sword list in verse, the *Niṣāb-i Turkī*.[134] Unfortunately we do not know the title of a longer word list also in verse, which he wrote for his Hindu friend Lāl Tīkā Rām.[135] The most comprehensive of his lexicographical works is a dictionary titled *Ma'rūf ul-Lughat* or *Lughat-i Aẓfarī*. The dictionary consists of three parts: a Persian–Turkish section, a Turkish–Persian section, and a foreword on Turkish grammar.[136] The foreword survived as an independent hundred-odd page work, under the title *Mīzān ut-Turkī*. It is considered a summary of all the knowledge Aẓfarī managed to gather on Turkish from various sources—books, language teachers, and most importantly, his own research.[137] Aẓfarī was also a translator of Turkish works. He prepaired a rhymed Persian abridgement of Bābur's treatise on prosody[138] and rendered Newā'ī's *Maḥbūb ul-Qulūb* into Persian.[139]

Aẓfarī was not the only poet who wrote verses in Turkish in early nineteenth-century south India. In his new home in Madras he continued to teach Turkish. His student Khān-i 'Ālim Khān Bahadur (1792–1854) could speak Persian, Arabic, English, and Turkish and composed verses in three of these languages, in English, in Arabic, and in Turkish under the pen name Fārūq.[140]

The oeuvre of Aẓfarī suggests that Turkish grammar and vocabulary still had a readership in the early nineteenth century. The Mughal prince was not the only one to compile such a work. Qatīl (d. 1817), a Hindu convert to Islam, whose works on Persian grammar became much debated later, added a chapter on Turkish grammar to his treatise on the science of literature titled *Chār Sharbat*.[141] Besides being a linguist he was also the author of several shorter texts in Turkish, two tales,[142] and a brief eulogy on the Prophet Muḥammad.[143] From his Persian letters it is clear that he knew the works of Newā'ī and had a correspondence in Turkish.[144]

In a multi-ethnic society like eighteenth-century India, it was not considered an extraordinary feat if someone learnt several languages, but even in such an environment the achievements of Inshā-allāh Khān 'Inshā' (1758–1817), the first native author to compile the grammar of Urdu, earned him fame. Born to a family of Turkish immigrants from Najaf, he not only spoke Arabic, Persian, Urdu, Kashmiri, Purbi, Pashtu, and Turkish but was also able to compose poetry in these languages.[145] His oeuvre in Turkish consists of several shorter pieces in his *dīwān*, a few scattered verses in his *Shikār-nāma*,[146] and a short prose diary titled *Turkī Rūz-nāmcha*.[147]

A fellow poet and one of Inshā's most intimate friends was Sa'ādat-yār Khān 'Rangīn' (1767–1835). Rangīn's father Tahmāsp Beg Khān I'tiqād-jang was a Turk from Anatolia who arrived in India with the army of Nādir Shāh as a seven-year-old boy. Rangīn spent most of his life in Lucknow in the service of a Mughal prince, Mirzā Sulaymān-shukūh.[148] His works in Turkish include a Turkish–Urdu word list titled *Nisāb-i turkī*[149] and a few Turkish verses in his *Majmū'a-yi Rangīn*.[150]

The last representative of the nineteenth-century Indian literati whom we know to have written anything in Turkish or on Turkish is Mirzā 'Abd ul-Bāqī ul-Sharīf ul-Riḍawī 'Wafā' (1789–1856). Like the families of Inshā and Rangīn he also came from the western Turkish world. He was born in Baghdad and though it might not have been his mother tongue, he knew Turkish well. He arrived in Madras in the early 1830s and at the request of Nawāb Ghulām Ghawṣ Khān set to translating the *Majālis un-Nafā'is*, the famous poetical anthology of Newā'ī, into Persian.[151] He found the task a most difficult one because he discovered that the western Turkish he knew differed greatly from the language of Newā'ī. To sum up the differences he discovered, he attached a short, ten-page long sketch of Turkish grammar to his work and where he thought it neccessary, he added notes in the margin to the text of his translation.[152]

In the 1830s the Great Game, the Anglo-Russian war of intelligence that serves as a background to Kipling's novel, had already been going on for quite some time. It is not known when exactly the story of *Kim* takes place but it might well be around this time. Is it possible to confirm Kipling's piece of information suggesting that Turkish was still spoken in Āgrā or in any of the great cities that once belonged to the Mughal Empire? The scarcity of data on the subject makes a definitive answer very difficult but it seems probable that in some families with Turkish ancestry Turkish was still taught. Mirzā Asadullāh Ghālib, the famous poet of the nineteenth century, was born to a family with Turkish origin. Even though it is not known whether he had ever learnt Turkish, his closest friend and a relative of his wife, Mirzā 'Alā'ī, who also came from a Turkish family of immigrants from Transoxania, knew Turkish well.[153] So it is not without reason to believe that in the great cities of the Mughal Empire, especially in those where families with Turkish origin lived, Turkish was still spoken as the language of the community.

As a summary, it can be said that Turkological research has only recently discovered Mughal India as a promising field for Turkish Studies. Fieldwork has just begun, more data is being collected, and a catalogue of Turkish language manuscripts is in preparation.[154] But even with the posession of the meagre results presented here, it can be stated with all certanity that the land of India was witness to a rich Turkish tradition that was kept alive from the fourteenth till the mid-nineteenth centuries. Turkish became a means of communication at the courts of various sovereigns and in their armies during the Sultanate period. The first Indian Timurids took their tradition of cultivating classical literature in their mother tongue to Hindūstān, so Turkish started to serve also as a literary medium in the middle of the sixteenth century. But as a language of literature Turkish could never compete with Persian and it was soon restricted to the royal family and the households of Turkish nobles. During the late seventeenth century the knowledge of Turkish became an inseparable part of the Mughal court culture and thus the circle of those who became interested in Turkish grew wider. Contemporary sources show that in the eighteenth and early nineteenth century many educated people learnt Turkish even if they were not of Turkish lineage.

Notes

1. Alexander Rogers, trans., *Tūzuk-i Jahāngīrī or Memoirs of Jahāngīr* (New Delhi: Low Price Publications, 1994), vol. 1, pp. 109–10. For the original text see Syud Ahmud, ed., *Toozuk-i-Jehangeeree* (Aligarh [Ally Gurh]: Private Press by Syud Ahmud, 1864), p. 52.
2. 'I have conquered a lot of hearts with things I got in India, but it was all in vain because this place has made me sad.' Bâbur 124/IV, in Bilal Yücel, *Bâbür Dîvânı* (Ankara: Atatürk Kültür Merkezi, 1995), p. 190.

3. The word Turkish is applied in this article as an equivalent of the native term Turkī used in contemporary sources for all Turkic languages.

4. For a summary of the research done on the field, see Benedek Péri, *Az Indiai Timuridák és a Török Nyelv: A Török írás- és Szóbeliség a Mogulkori Indiában* (The Indian Timurids and Turkish Language: The Use of Turkish in Mughal India) (Piliscsaba: The Avicenna Institute of Middle Eastern Studies, 2005), pp. 12–18.

5. Rudyard Kipling, *Kim* (New York: Oxford University Press, 1997), p. 173.

6. Kipling, *Kim*, pp. 200–01.

7. Annemarie Schimmel, 'Türkisches in Indien', in *Scholia. Beiträge zur Turkologie und Zentralasienkunde. Annemarie von Gabain zum 80. Geburtstag am 4. Juli 1981 dargrebracht von Kollegen, Freunden und Schüler* (Wiesbaden: Otto Harrassowitz, 1982), pp. 156–62.

8. Mehmet Fuat Köprülü, 'Çağatay Edebiyatı', *Islam Ansiklopedisi* 3 (1993): p. 314.

9. Stephen Frederic Dale, 'The Legacy of the Timuirds', *JRAS*, Third Series 8, no. 1 (1998): p. 51.

10. M. Wahid Mirza, ed., *The Nuh Sipihr of Amir Khusraw: Persian Text with Introduction, Notes, Index, etc.* (Calcutta and Madras: Oxford University Press, 1950), pp. 172–81.

11. John Briggs, trans., *History of the Rise of Mahomedan Power in India: Translated from the Original Persian of Mahomed Kasim Ferishta*, vol. 2 (New Delhi: Low Price Publications, 1990), pp. 203, 228. See also H. Kh. Sherwani, *The Bahmanis of the Deccan* (New Delhi: Munshiram Manoharlal, 1985), pp. 82, 100.

12. Henry Edward John Stanley, trans., *A Description of the Coasts of East Africa and Malabar in the Beginning of the Sixteenth Century by Duarte Barbosa a Portuguese* (London The Hakluyt Society, 1864), p. 56. Agusto Reis Machado, ed., *Livro em que dá Relação do que viu e Ouviu no Oriente Duarte Barbosa* (Lisboa: Divisão de Publicações e Biblioteca Agencia Geral das Colónias, 1946), p. 69. Duarte Barbose mentions two groups among the 'Moors' living in Cambay that were of Turkish origin: Turks and Türkmens.

13. Emir Nadžipovič Nadžip, 'Tyurkskiy Yazyk Deliyskogo Sultanata XIV Veka', *ST* 2 (1982): pp. 70–85; *ST* 3 (1982): pp. 72–85; Robert Dankoff, *The Turkic Vocabulary of the Farhang-i Zafān-Gūyā* (Bloomington, Indiana: Indiana University Research Institute for Inner Asian Studies, 1987); András Bodrogligeti, 'Review Article of Dankoff, Robert: *The Turkic vocabulary of the Farhang-i Zafān-Gūyā*' (Bloomington: Indiana University Research Institute for Inner Asian Studies. 1987), in *Ural–Altaic Yearbook* 64 (1992): pp. 188–97.

14. The commonplace-like scornful opinion of the intellectual capabilities of Turks was so persistent that it was still present in sixteenth-century Ottoman literature. Güvāhī (d. 1520) in his *mathnawī* titled *Pend-nāme*

relates two short stories illustrating the blockheaded foolishness of this people. He ends his stories with the following couplets:

'Ajā'ib ṭā'īfedür qavm-i Etrāk
Eyü yatlu nedür itmezler idrâk.

(Strange are the people of the Turkish race
What is good or what is bad they cannot comprehend.)

Güvāhī, *Pend-nāme*, ed. Mehmet Hengirmen, (Ankara: Kültür Bakanlığı, 1983), pp. 166–8.

15. Out of the twenty-six manuscripts of Turkish dīvāns preserved in Indian libraries, seven are collections of Fuḍūlī's poems. Ali Fuat Bilkan, 'Hindistan Kütüphanelerindeki Türkçe El Yazmaları ve Hindistan'da Türkçe', in *Tarihte Türk Hint İlişkileri: Sempozyum Bildirileri 31 Ekim–1 Kasım 2002* (Ankara: Türk Tarih Kurumu 2006), p. 265.

16. *Ol sebebden Fārsī lafẓıla čokdur naẓm kim,*
    Naẓm-i nāzik türk lafẓıla iken düshvār olur.
    Lehče-i türkī qabūl-i naẓm-ı terkīb etmeyip,
    Ektheren elfāẓı nā-merbūṭ ü nā-hemvār olur.

Hamid Araslı, ed., *Məhəmmed Füzuli Əsərləri* (Bakı: Şarq-Gərb, 2005), vol. 1, p. 362.

17. Sema Barutçu Özönder, ed., *'Alî Şîr Nevâyî: Muhâkemetü'l-Lugateyn: İki Dilin Muhakemesi* (Ankara: Türk Dil Kurumu, 1996), p. 179.

18. Edward Granville Browne, *The Chahár Maqála ("Four Discourses") of Nidhámí-I-'Arúdí-I-Samarqandí*, reprinted from *JRAS* (July and October, 1899): pp. 45–7. For the various aspects of the patron–poet relationship in an Ottoman environment, see Halil İnalcık, *Şâir ve Patron: Patrimonyal Devlet ve Sanat Üzerine Sosyolojik Bir İnceleme* (Ankara: Doğubatı, 2005).

19. For a complete list of sultans who composed poems see Mustafa İsenand Ali Fuat Bilkan, *Sultan Şairler* (Ankara: Akçağ, 1997).

20. His Turkish poems were edited by Muhsin Macit, in *Karakoyunlu Hükümdârı Cihânşâh ve Türkçe Şiirleri* (Ankara: Grafiker Yayınları, 2002).

21. Özönder, *'Alî Şîr Nevâyî: Muhâkemet*, p. 188.

22. Speaking of Jemīlī, a poet of Central Asian origin who composed his poems in eastern Turkish, the sixteenth-century Ottoman biographer Latīfī characterizes him with the following words: 'He is one of the poets who are from Türkistān. He composed most of his poems in the style of Newā'ī.' Mustafa İsen, *Latîfî tezkiresi* (Ankara: Kültür Bakanlığı, 1990), p. 147. The poems of Newā'ī became so popular in the Ottoman Empire that Ottoman poets started composing verses in eastern Turkish. For a detailed account of the subject see Yusuf Çetindağ, *Ali Şîr Nevâî'nin Osmanlı Şiirine Etkisi* (Ankara: Kültür ve Turizm Bakanlığı Yayınları, 2006).

23. Dale, *The Legacy of the Timuirds*, p. 43.
24. M. E. Subtelny, 'Socioeconomic Bases of Cultural Patronage under the Late Timurids', *IJMES* 20 (1988): pp. 479–505.
25. F.B. Manz, 'Temür and the Problem of a Conqueror's Legacy', *JRAS*, Third Series 8, no. 1 (1998): pp. 21–41.
26. István Vásáry, 'Az Ujgur Irásbeliség az Arany Hordában és a Timuridáknál', *Keletkutatás*, (1986/tavasz), pp. 39–47. For additional information on the usage of the Uighur script during the reign of the Timurids, see Osman Fikri Sertkaya, 'Some New Documents Written in the Uigur Script in Anatolia', *CAJ* 18 (1974): pp. 180–92; Osman Fikri Sertkaya, *Uygur Harfleriyle Yazılmış Bazı Manzum Parçalar* (İstanbul: İstanbul Öniversitesi Edebiyat Fakültesi, 1975).
27. Stephen Frederic Dale, *The Garden of Eight Paradises: Bâbur and the Culture of Empire in Central Asia, Afghanistan and India (1483–1530)* (Leiden: Brill, 2004), p. 466.
28. Douglas E. Streusand, *Formation of the Mughal Empire* (New Delhi: Oxford University Press, 1997), p. 26.
29. Streusand, *Formation of the Mughal Empire*, pp. 29–30. The same dual attachment can be observed in the case of Bābur's archrival, the Özbeg khan, Muḥammed Shibānī. In some of his ghazals that were composed in Turkish, he boasts about his Čingisid descent, and quite often depicts himself as a deputy of Allah whose duty is to wage war against the infidels and the heretics.

> *Bu Tîmür oghlanları taghyīr kıldı medhhebin*
> *Kim kızıl börk dīnige kirdise ber-bâd eyledük*
> (These Timurids had changed their religion,
> All those who took the redcaps' ways we have scattered in the wind.)
> *Ḥaq ta^c ālānıng yolıda ol qadar kim berdi dast*
> *Čapıban Islām t tīghini ilni irshād eyledük.*
> (Taking the road of God, as far as I was able to,
> I wielded the sword of Islam in order to herd the people onto the right path.)

Shibānī, Gazel no. 139, couplets no. II, IV, in Yakub Karasoy, ed., *Şiban Han Dîvânı: (İnceleme-Metin-Dizin-Tıpkıbasım)* (Ankara: Türk Dil Kurumu, 1998), p. 165.

> *Diyür men Ḥaq sözin ilge ishitsün kh^{v}āh ishitmesün*
> *Bular barčası bughday u yalghuz men semendür men*
> (I convey the words of God to the people whether they listen or not,
> They are grains of wheat, I am a jasmin flower.)
> *Shibān yalghan demes kim Ḥaq anı şāhib-qirān qıldı*
> *Ḥasebde Tengrige qul men, nesebde Čingizīdür men.*
> (Shibān is not lying when he asserts that God made him a chosen one
> I am slave to God and a Čingisid by birth.)

Shibānī Gazel no. 240, verses IV, VII, in Karasoy, *Şiban Han Dîvânı*, pp. 234, 235.

30. According to Newā'ī, who was also the first author to compile a *tadhkira* in Turkish, the following Timurids composed Turkish pieces of poetry: Abū Bakr Mīrzā (1387–1408), Sulṭān Iskandar Mīrzā (d. 1415), Khalīl Sulṭān (1384–1411), Abū' l-Qāsim Bābur Mīrzā (d. 1457), Sayyid Aḥmad Mīrzā (1391–1429), Sulṭān Aḥmad Mīrzā (d. 1494), Badīᶜ uz-Zamān Mīrzā (d. 1515), Shāh Gharīb Mīrzā (d. 1496), Sulṭān Masᶜūd Mīrzā (before 1477–1507); Farīdūn Ḥusayn Mīrzā (d. 1509), Sulṭān 'Alī Mīrzā (d. 1500), Abū' l-Ghāzī Sulṭān Ḥusayn Mīrzā Bayqara (1438–1506). Kemal Eraslan, ed., *Alî-Şîr Nevayî Mecâlisü'n-Nefâyis. I. (Giriş ve Metin)* (Ankara: Türk Dil Kurumu, 2001), pp. 192–202.

31. Zahiriddin Muhammad Bobir, *Muxtasar*, ed. Hasan Saidbek, (Tashkent [Toshkent]: Fan, 1971).

32. Dale, *Garden of Eight Paradises*, p. 149.

33. Bābur, for example, criticizes Newā'ī in *Bābur-nāma* for alleged mistakes he made in his work on prosody. Bābur, *Bābur-nāma*, ed. Eiji Mano (Kyoto: Shōkadō, 1995), p. 265 (fol. 171a).

34. M. Ishaque, ed., *Haft Iqlīm: The Geographical and Biographical Encyclopaedia of Amîn Ahmad Râzî*, vol. 2 (Calcutta: Royal Asiatic Society of Bengal, 1963), pp. 606–9.

35. Seydī 'Alī Re'īs, *Mir'āt ul-Memālik* (İstanbul: Ikdām Matbaᶜası, 1313/1895–96), pp. 54–5.

36. Bābur, *Bābur-nāma*, p. 571 (fol. 357b).

37. For an evaluation of Humāyūn's poetry and the verses included in his *dīwān* see Hadi Hasan, 'The Unique Diwan of Humayun Badshah', *IC* 25 (1951): pp. 212–76.

38. Lit. Fragment, which is usually of a philosophical, ethical or meditative character. The rhyme pattern is *ba, ca, da*, and so on. It was popular for use in improvizations; often a touchstone for new poets. It allowed the introduction of unaccustomed arbitrary themes.

39. *Men ki bülbül-dek gülidin küymishem āhang ile*
    Ot saḥıptur jānıma ruhsāra-i gülreng ile.
    (I am burning with passion for her rose like a sweet voiced nightingale
    Her rosy cheeks have thrown flames into my heart.)

    Hasanhoja Nisoriy, *Muzakkiri ahbob (Do'stlar yodnomasi)*, trans. Ismoil Bekjon (Toshkent: Abdullo Qodiriy Nomidagi Halk Merosi Nashriyati, 1993), p. 57. The Delhi edition of the original Persian texts contains the couplet in a corrupted form. See: Nithārī Bukhārī, *Mudhakkir-i aḥbāb*, ed. Syed Muhammad Fazlullah (Delhi: Published with financial assistance from the Ministry of Education, Government of India, 1969), p. 102.

    Gharīblık ghamıdan mihnet ü melālım bar
    Bu ghamdan ölmege yetdim gharīb hālım bar
    Wiṣāḥ devletidin ayrılup men-i maḥzūn
    Tirik men ü bu tiriklikden infiᶜālım bar.

> (The sorrow of loneliness causes me misery and pain,
> I am almost dying because of this sorrow, I have a strange feeling,
> Having left her blessed company, I feel miserable,
> I am alive and I am ashamed of this.)

Sādiqī Kitābdār, *Majma' ul-khawāṣ*, ed. A. Khayyāmpūr (Tabrīz: Chāpkhānah-i Akhtar-i Shumāl, 1327), p. 14.

40. Z.V. Togan, 'Tahran Kütüphanelerinde Hindistan'dan Gelen Eserlerde Çağatay Dil ve Temürlü Sanat Abideleri', *Belleten* 24 (1960): pp. 441–5.

41. Charles Stewart, trans., *The Tezkereh al Vakiât or the Private Memoirs of the Moghul Emperor Humâyûn Written in the Persian Language by Jouher* (London: Oriental Translation Fund of Great Britain and Ireland, 1832), p. 75.

42. For the Oghuz Turkish tribal name Bayat, see Soltanşa Atanıyazov, *Şecere: Ansiklopedik Türkmen Etnik Adları Sözlüğü* (Konya: Tablet, 2005), pp. 102–4.

43. Hidayat Mohammad Hosain, ed., *Tadhkira-i-Humāyūn wa Akbar of Bāyazīd Biyāt: A History of the Emperor Humāyūn from A.H. 949 (A.D. 1542) and of his Successor the Emperor Akbar up to A.H. 999 (A.D. 1590)* (Calcutta: The Asiatic Society of Bengal, 1941), pp. 90–1.

44. Abū'l-Faḍl 'Allāmī, *Akbar-nāma*, ed. Maulawī 'Abd-ur-Raḥīm (New Delhi: Kitab Publishing House, 1977), vol. 1, p. 280; Hosain, *Tadhkira-i-Humāyūn*, pp. 94–5. Neither Abū'l-Faḍl nor Bāyazīd has recorded the original Turkish words.

45. *Keling!* (Come!). Hosain, *Tadhkira-i-Humāyūn*, p. 98.

46. Stewart, *The Tezkereh*, p. 106. Alī Dūst expressed his unwillingness to execute Humāyūn's orders with the following words: *Bu ishgä heč kishi qılmaydur* ('Nobody is willing to do this job'). Humāyūn reproached him by answering: *Iti qaltaq! Sangha ne boluptur? Sen qılıng!* ('Oh, you worthless one! What has happened to you? You should do it!') The two Turkish sentences are in such a corrupted state, both in the manuscript I consulted and in Ghani's book, that at certain points they hardly help reconstructing the original text. Jawhar Āftābčī, *Tadhkirat al-Wāqiᶜāt* (Jamia Millia Islamia, Dr Zakir Husain Library), C-86, 80b, available at http://www.new1.dli.ernet.in/scripts/FullindexDefault.htm?path1=/data2/upload/0041/019&first=1&last=186&barcode=99999990186713, last accessed 20 November 2015; Muhammad Abdul Ghani, *A History of Persian Language and Literature at the Mughal Court, Part I: Humâyûn* (Allahabad: Indian Press 1930), p. 7. After submitting the first version of this paper I managed to consult Thackston's new edition of Jawhar's text and it confirmed my reconstruction. Wheeler M. Thackston, *Three Memoirs of Homayun* (Costa Mesa: Mazda Publishers), p. 158.

47. Authors writing on Mughal history tend to erroneously spell his name Tardi Beg. Turdı means 'stopped' in Turkish. His name belongs to a traditional category of Turkish names given in order to protect the new-born from evil spirits. For the name Turdı see L.Rásonyi, I. Baski,

Onomasticon Turcicum: Turkic Personal Names (Bloomington: Indiana University Press, 2007), pp. 796–7.

48. Stewart, *The Tezkereh*, p. 42; Ghani, *A History*, p. 8.; Jawhar Āftābčī, *Tadhkirat*, p. 36b. This time Jawhar has not recorded the Turkish words. Jawhar relates yet another instance when Turkish was used at court. After an encounter with enemy forces, a Mughal deserter was taken captive. When he was brought before Humāyūn he started abusing the king. One of the royal attendants, switching to Turkish, suggested that he should be killed but the king pardoned him and set him free. Jawhar does not say whether Humāyūn answered in the same language. Stewart, *The Tezkereh*, p. 45; Ghani, *A History*, p. 9. Jawhar Āftābčī, *Tadhkirat*, p. 39a.

49. Niẓām ud-Dīn Aḥmad, *Tabaqāt-i Akbarī*, ed. Brajendranath De, (Calcutta: Asiatic Society of Bengal, 1931), vol. 2, p. 69. The Turkish sentence as it appears in the printed edition is exactly the opposite of its Persian translation: *Bābā Qashqanı men öldürüp* ('I have killed Bābā Qashqa.') All the contemporary historians have their own version of the story. Abū'l-Faḍl, *Akbar-nāma*, vol. 1, p. 269; Hosain, *Tadhkira-i-Humāyūn*, p. 83; Stewart, *The Tezkereh*, p. 84; 'Abd ul-Qādir Badā'ūnī, *Muntakhab ut-Tawārīkh*, ed. Mawlawī Aḥmad 'Alī (Calcutta: Asiatic Society of Bengal, 1868), vol. 1, p. 450.

50. For his poems in eastern Turkish, see Hasan Saidbek, *Komron Mirzo: Devon* (Toshkent: Fan, 1993).

51. Saidbek, *Komron Mirzo*, pp. 15, 32. As an anecdote preserved in the *Tārīkh-i Dā'ūdī* shows, Kāmrān was famous for his knowledge of the Persian language classics. Fleeing from his brother, he sought refuge at the court of Humāyūn's main rival, the Afghan Salīm Shāh, who was also famed for his familiarity with classical poetry. Salīm Shāh, trying to put to test his guest's expertise, quoted three bayts and asked Kāmrān to explain them. To the audience's utter astonishment Kāmrān recognized the verses and could name their authors. Henry Miers Elliot and John Dowson, *The History of India as Told by Its Own Historians* (New Delhi: Low Price Publications, 1996), vol. 4, p. 498.

52. Saidbek, *Komron Mirzo*, pp. 15, 16 (gazel no. 24, couplet no. VII; gazel no. 29, couplet no. V)

53. *Mendin agar türkīde bolsa nawā*
    Ṭabl-i tihīdin čiqarsa ṣadā.
    Saidbek, *Komron Mirzo*, p. 32.

54. See endnote 34.

55. Bābur writes in his memoirs that he had sent his poems to four people in 1529: three of his sons Humāyūn, Kāmrān, and Hindāl and also to Khwāja Kalān. Bābur, *Bābur-nāma*, p. 571 (fol. 357b).

56. One of his latest biographers, Andre Wink suggests that Akbar might have been dyslexic. Andre Wink, *Akbar* (Oxford: Oxford University Press, 2009), p. 11.

57. Abū'l-Faḍl, *Akbar-nāma*, vol. 1, pp. 270–1.

58. Muḥammad Ḥusayn Āzād, *Darbār-i Akbarī* (Lucknow: Maktaba Kalyan, 1910), p. 648.

59. M. Athar Ali, 'Pursuing an Elusive Seeker of Universal Truth—The Identity and Environment of the Author of the Dabistān-i Mazāhib', *JRAS*, Third Series 9, no. 3 (1999): p. 365.

60. David Shea, trans., *The Dabistan or School of Manners, Translated from the Persian Original with Notes and Illustrations* (London: Oriental Translation Fund, 1843), vol. 3, p. 94. For the Persian text see *Dabistān-i Madhāhib* (Lucknow: Munshī Nawal Kishūr, 1877), p. 325.

61. Aziz Ahmad, *Studies in Islamic Culture in the Indian Environment* (Delhi: Oxford University Press, 1999), p. 226.

62. Anette S. Beveridge, *The History of Humāyūn: Humāyūn-nāma by Gulbadan Begam* (New Delhi: Low Price Publications, 1996), p. 79. On the Turkish words in the text of the *Humāyūn-nāma*, see A. Hafizova, '"Kelurname" Muhammeda Yakuba Čingi', *ST* 3 (1973): p. 95.

63. On Bayrām Khān see Sukumar Ray, *Bairam Khan* (Karachi: Institute of Central and West Asian Studies, 1992).

64. For the latest edition of his Turkish poetry see Münevver Tekcan, *Bayram Han'ın Türkçe Divanı* (İstanbul: Bulut, 2005).

65. Abū'l-Faḍl, *Akbar-nāma*, ed. Mawlawī 'Abd ur-Raḥīm (Calcutta: Asiatic Society of Bengal, 1879), vol. 2, p. 79.

66. Hosain, *Tadhkira-i-Humāyūn*, p. 50. Shāh-berdi Bayat left the imperial service in 1545. He became a dervish and headed for Turkistān where during his stay in Samarqand, Qāsim-i Anwār appeared to him in a dream and instigated him to start composing poetry. After his return to Delhi, he moved into the *čilla-khāna* of Niẓām ud-Dīn Awliyā. Hosain, *Tadhkira-i-Humāyūn*, pp. 234–5. He chose the pen name Saqqā because he earned his living as a water carrier. According to Badā'ūnī, he composed his poems in a religious trance. His verses amounted to several *dīwāns* but when he 'was overcome by religious ecstasy he would wash the ink from the pages of the *dīwāns*, one by one, but the remains of his poems form a large *dīwān*.' He passed away on his way to Ceylon. George S.A. Ranking, Sir Wolseley Haig, and W. H. Lowe, *The Muntakhabu-t-Tawârîkh by 'Abdu-'l-Qādir Ibn-i-Mulūk Shāh known as Al-Badāoni* (Calcutta: Royal Asiatic Society of Bengal, 1925), vol. 3, pp. 338–40.

67. Badā'ūnī, *Muntakhab ut-Tawārīkh*, ed. N. Lees and Ahmad Ali (Calcutta: Asiatic Society of Bengal, 1865), vol. 2, p. 52.

68. Ranking, *The Muntakhabu-t-Tawârîkh*, p. 396.

69. Ishaque, *Haft iqlīm*, p. 437.

70. For one of the most influential of the Central Asian noble families, see B. Péri, 'A Turkic Clan in Mughal India: The Qaqshals in Akbar's Service', *AOH* 60 (2007): pp. 363–98.

71. B. Péri, 'The Ethnic Composition of the "Iranian" Nobility at Akbar's Court (1574–1605)', in *Irano-Turkic Cultural Contacts in the 11th–17th*

Centuries, ed. E. Jeremiás (Pilicsaba: Avicenna Közel-Kelet Kutatások Intézete, 2003), pp. 177–201.

72. ʿAbd ul-Bāqī Nihāwandī, *Maʾāthir-i Raḥīmī*, ed. Hidâyat Husayn (Calcutta: Asiatic Society of Bengal, 1925), vol. 2, p. 591.

73. Nihāwandī, *Maʾāthir-i Raḥīmī*, vol. 2, p. 591.

74. Ram Chandra Prasad, *Early English Travellers in India* (New Delhi: Motilal Banarsidass, 1995), p. 83.

75. 'I went to the Court to visit Chanchanna, being then Lord Generall and Vice-Roy of Decan giuing [sic] him a Present; who kindly tooke [sic] it; and after three houres conference with him, he made me a great Feast.... The Language that we spoke was Turkish, which he spake very well.' C.R. Markham, *The Hawkins' Voyages During the Reigns of Henry VIII, Queen Elizabeth and James I* (London: The Hakluyt Society, 1878), p. 399; W. Foster, *Early Travels in India* (Oxford: Oxford University Press, 1921), p. 80.

76. A very meagre part of his poetic composition has been hitherto discovered. His Persian lines were collected and published by Ḥusayn Jaᶜfar Ḥalīm. H.J. Ḥalīm, *Sharḥ-i aḥvāl wa āthār-i ʿAbd ur-Raḥīm Khān-i Khānān va khadhamāt-i ū barā-yi pīshraft-i adabiyāt-i fārsī* (Islāmābād: Markaz-i taḥqīqāt-i fārsī-i Īrān u Pākistān, 1992), pp. 257–73.

77. For the text see Nihāwandī, *Maʾāthir*, vol. 2, pp. 554–5.

78. He inserted a few *bayt*s from three different ghazals to make his composition more elegant. It is not clear which *dīwān* of Newāʾī he used because all three poems are included in both Newāʾī's first collection, *Badāyiᶜ ul-Bidāya* and in the first of the *Čār Dīwān*, the *Gharāʾib uṣ-Ṣighar*. Navoiy, *Badoyiʿ ul-Bidoya*, ed. Sharofiddin Sharipoʾv (Toshkent: Fan, 1987), pp. 329, 330 (gazel no. 413, couplet no. I–II; gazel no. 414, couplet no. I; gazel no. 415, couplet no. I–II); Nevāyī, *ʿAlī Şīr, Ġarāʾibüʾṣ-Ṣiġar*, ed. Günay Kut (Ankara: TDK, 2003), pp. 294, 296 (gazel no. 385, couplet no. I–II; gazel no. 386, couplet no. I; gazel no. 387, couplet no. I–II). The *maṭlaʿ* of ghazal no. 414 quoted in the text of the letter slightly differs from the versions of the critical editions.

79. Yol-qulı Beg Anīsī was from the Shamlu [Nihāwandī, *Maʾāthir-i Raḥīmī*, vol. 3, ed. Hidāyat Ḥusayn (Calcutta: Asiatic Society of Bengal, 1931), pp. 517–604], Shāh-naẓar Beg was from the Afshar [Nihāwandī, *Maʾāthir-i Raḥīmī*, vol. 3, pp. 1471–4], Mullā Shaydāʾī was from the Tekkelü [Nihāwandī, *Maʾāthir-i Raḥīmī*, vol. 3, pp. 1487–97] tribe of the Türkmens. Qaplan Beg's family came from Transoxania [Nihāwandī, *Maʾāthir-i Raḥīmī*, vol. 3, pp. 1089–95]. None of them seems to have composed poems in Turkish or their Turkish pieces have not survived.

80. Nihāwandī, *Maʾāthir-i Raḥīmī*, vol. 2, p. 663.

81. Nihāwandī, *Maʾāthir-i Raḥīmī*, vol. 3, pp. 1391–2.

82. Nihāwandī, *Maʾāthir-i Raḥīmī*, vol. 3, pp. 1363–7.

83. Ahmud Syud, *Toozuk*, p. 52. It is highly possible that these passages are the so called 'Rescue passages(s?)' starting on p. 144 of the Ilminski

edition [Nikolay Ivanovitch Ilminski, ed., *Baber-nameh Diagataice ad Fidem Codicis Petropolitani* (Kazan, 1857)] and the passages at the end of the same edition [Ilminski, *Baber-nameh*, 494/8–504/12]). Anette Beveridge,. trans., *Bābur-Nāma (Memoirs of Bābur)* (New Delhi: Munshiram Manoharlal, 1990), p. 52. For the English translation of the rescue passage, see Beveridge, *Bābur-Nāma*, Appendix D, pp. xi–xiii. For a detailed analysis of the passages at the end of the text see F. Teufel, 'Bâbur and Abû'l-Fazl', *ZDMG* 37 (1883), pp. 141–87. Teufel, who did not consult the *Tūzuk*, did not know that the possible author of the passages was Jahāngīr.

84. William H. Morley, *A Descriptive Catalogue of the Historical Manuscripts in the Arabic and Persian Languages Preserved in the Library of the Royal Asiatic Society of Great Britain and Ireland* (London: J.W. Parker, 1854), p. 116.

85. Lisa Ann Balabanlilar, 'Lords of Auspicious Conjunction: Turco–Mongolian Imperial Identity on the Subcontinent', *JWH* 18, no. 1 (2007): p. 39.

86. Markham, *The Hawkins' Voyages*, p. 400; Foster, *Early Travels*, p. 81.

87. W. Foster, ed. *Letters Received by the East India Company from its Servants in the East*, vol. 2 (London: S. Low, Marston & Co., 1896), p. 108.

88. The letter is dated 19 December, 1614. W. Foster, ed., *Letters Received by the East India Company from its Servant in the East*, vol. 3 (London, 1899), p. 305.

89. Mānekshāh Sorābshāh Commisariat, *Mandelslo's Travels in Western India (1638–39)* (New Delhi and Madras: Asian Educational Services, 1995), p. 35.

90. James Talboys Wheeler, *Early Records of British India: A History of the English Settlements in India* (Calcutta, W. Newman & Co., 1878), p. 25. The governor was called Aᶜzam Khān and not 'Arab Khān as Mandelslo states. The mistake is clear from Mandelslo's remark that the Khan's daughter 'had been married to the Mogul's second son.' It is clear from A'zam Khān's farewell words that the Turkish he spoke was Azeri. Shāh Nawāz Khān asserts that Aᶜzam Khān was a *sayyid* from Sāwah. Henry Beveridge, *The Maâthir-ul-Umarâ being the Biographies of the Muhammadan and Hindu Officers of the Timurid Sovereigns of India from 1500 to about 1780 A.D. by Nawwâb Samsâm-ud-Daula Shâh Nawâz Khân and His Son 'Abdul Hayy* (New Delhi: Low Price Publications, 1999), vol. 1, p. 315.

91. S.M. Azizuddin Husain, trans., *Tazkiratul-umara of Keval Ram: The History of Nobles from Akbar to Aurangzeb's Reign, 1556–1707 A.D* (New Delhi: Munshiram Manoharlal, 1985), p. 37; 'Abd ur-Raḥmān Sabāḥ ud-Dīn, *Bazm-i Tīmūriya* ('Azamgarh: Dār ul-Maṣannifīn Shiblī Ākīdimī, 1991), vol. 3, p. 1.

92. 'Abd ul-Ḥamīd Lāhūrī, *Pādshāh-nāma*, vol. 1, ed. Kabīr ud-Dīn Aḥmad, 'Abd ur-Raḥīm and W. N. Lees, (Calcutta: Asiatic Society of Bengal, 1866), p. 67.

93. Ali Khan Mubarak, _The Court of the Great Mughuls_ (Bochum: Ruhr-Universität, 1976), p. 118.
94. William Irvine, trans., _Mogul India 1653–1708 or Storia do Mogor by Niccolao Manucci_ (New Delhi: Low Price Publications 1996), vol. 1, p. 278.
95. F. Bernier, _Travels in the Mogul Empire, A.D. 1656–1668_ (Oxford: Oxford University Press, 1916), p. 61. Because of their warlike nature and their skill in using various weapons, it was a common practice to employ Central Asian Turkish women in harems. According to Manucci, an Italian adventurer who spent most of his life in India, their job was mainly to carry palanquins or to stand guard at night. The embassy from Balkh in the early 1660s brought several such women for sale and one of them called Yakhshı (Good) was purchased and presented to the king by a courtier. She bore a son to Aurangzeb whom the emperor adopted and brought up in a princely manner. Irvine, _Mogul India_, vol. 2, p. 38.
96. J.N. Sarkar, _History of Aurangzeb_ (Calcutta: M.C. Sarkar & Sons, 1912), vol. 1, p. 5.
97. S.M. Jaffar, _Education in Muslim India_ (Peshawar: S. Muhammad Sadiq Khan, 1936), p. 99.
98. The father of Mumtāz Maḥal was Abū'l-Ḥasan, Āṣaf Khān, the brother of Nūr Jahān. For the details of the family's ancestry see Ellison Banks Findly, _Nur Jahan: Empress of Mughal India_ (Oxford: Oxford University Press, 1993), pp. 8–9.
99. Aurangzeb in his alleged will highly praised the Turānī people who 'have ever been soldiers' and advised his sons to confer 'favours on this race, because on many occasions these men can do the neccessary service, when no other race can.' Jadunath Sarkar, _A Short History of Aurangzeb_ (Calcutta: Orient Longman, 1979), pp. 325–6.
100. The only Ottoman Turkish letter published so far was sent by Suleymān II to Aurangzeb in 1688. Hikmet Bayur, 'Osmanlı Pâdişahı II. Süleyman'ın Gürkanlı Pâdişâhı I: Âlemgîr (Evrengzîb)'e Mektubu', _Belleten_ 14 (1950): pp. 269–85.
101. Two official documents in Turkish have hitherto been published. One is a letter written to Aurangzeb by the tsar Aleksey Mihaylovič in 1675, and the other one is a letter of safe conduct that was issued by Aurengzeb to a Russian tradesman called Malenkiy. _Russko-indiyskie Otnosheniya v XVII. v. Sbornik Dokumentov_ (Moscow [Moskva]: Izd-vo vostochnoy lit-ry, 1958), pp. 205–9, 369–70.
102. Irvine, _Mogul India_, vol. 2, p. 323.
103. Jadunath Sarkar, trans., _Maāsir-i-'Ālamgīrī: A History of the Emperor Aurangzeb-'Ālamgīr (Reign 1658–1707 AD) of Sāqi Musta'ad Khan_ (New Delhi: Oriental Books Reprint Corporation, 1986), p. 319. For the Persian text see Musta'id Khān, _Ma'āthir-i 'Ālamgīrī_, ed. Āghā Muḥammad 'Alī (Calcutta: Asiatic Society of Bengal, 1870), p. 535.

104. Sarkar, *Maāsir-i-'Ālamgīrī*, p. 322; Musta'id Khān, *Ma'āthir-i 'Ālamgīrī*, p. 538.

105. For Aurangzeb's letter written to his son in October 1654, see Sabāḥ ud-Dīn, *Bazm-i Tīmūriya*, vol. 3, pp. 220–1. For an English summary, see Jadunath Sarkar, *Studies in Aurangzib's Reign* (Calcutta: Orient Longman, 1989), p. 29.

106. Sarkar, *Maāsir-i-'Ālamgīrī*, p. 319; Musta'id Khān, *Ma'āthir-i 'Ālamgīrī*, p. 533.

107. M.M. Hidayat Hosain, 'The Mirzā Nāmah (The Book of the Perfect Gentelman) of Mîrzâ Kâmrân, with an English Translation'. *JRAS*, new series 9 (1913): pp 1–13. For a detailed analysis of the work, see R. O'Hanlon, 'Manliness and Imperial Service in Mughal North India', *JESHO* 42, no. 1 (1999): pp. 47–93.

108. The only hitherto published specimen of this genre is the *Kelür-nâme* by Muḥammad Ya'qūb Čingī (Muḥammad Ya'qūb Čingī: *Kelür-nāma*, ed. A. Ibragimo'v (Tashkent: Fan, 1982). Many such works are to be found scattered in libraries mainly in India and the United Kingdom. For a preliminary list, see Ali Fuat Bilkan, 'Hindistan Kütüphanelerindeki Türkçe El Yazmaları ve Hindistan'da Türkçe', in *Tarihte Türk-Hint İlişkileri Sempozyumu. Bildiriler* (Ankara: Türk Tarih Kurumu, 2006), pp. 355–65; C. Rieu, *Catalogue of the Turkish Manuscripts in the British Library* (London: British Museum, 1888), pp. 264, 266–9. Though these works could immensely improve our knowledge of the presence and role of Turkish languages on the Indian subcontinent from the seventeenth through the nineteenth centuries, scholars of Turkish studies have just started to work on the subject. For early eighteenth-century grammar see, Benedek Péri, *A Török Irás- és Szóbeliség Nyomai a Mogul-kori Indiában: Mīrzā 'Alī-bakht Gurgānī Azfarī Mīzān ut-Turkī címū Grammatikai Értekezése és ami Körülötte van* (The Traces of Turkish in Mughal India: Mīrzā 'Alī-bakht Gurgānī Azfarī and His Treatise on Turkish Grammar Titled Mīzān ut-Turkī) (PhD diss., University of Budapest, 2000). The text of Azfarī's treatise is included in the Appendix.

109. The shrinkage in employment opportunities was mainly caused by the crisis of the *jāgīrdārī* system that caused a 'stoppage of patronage to the stream of immigrants from abroad'. Satish Chandra, *Parties and Politics at the Mughal Court, 1707–1740* (New Delhi: Oxford University Press, 2002), p. xviii.

110. Andrea Hintze, *The Mughal Empire and Its Decline: An Interpretation of the Sources of Social Power* (Aldershot, England: Ashgate, 1997), pp. 269–70.

111. Niẓām ul-Mulk, the founder of the Ḥaydarābād state employed Ottoman Turkish marksmen as well. Yusuf Husain, *The First Nizām: The Life and Times if Nizāmu'l-Mulk Āsaf Jāh* (Bombay: Asia Publishing House, 1963), p. 109. Their numbers are not known and soon enough, they were gradually replaced with European soldiers.

112. Jos Gommans, *Mughal Warfare* (London: Routledge, 2002), p. 205.
113. Hafizova, *Kelurname*, p. 96.
114. Sarkar, *History of Aurangzeb*, vol. 1, p. 5
115. Sabāḥ ud-Dīn, *Bazm-i Tīmūriya*, vol. 3, p. 98; Hadi Nabi, *Dictionary of Indo-Persian Literature* (New Delhi: Abhinav Publications, 1995), p. 10; Henry F. Hofman, *Turkish Literature: A Bio-Bibliographical Survey* (Utrecht: Royal Asiatic Society of Great Britain and Ireland, 1969), vol. 5, p. 241.
116. John Briggs, *The Siyar-ul-Muta'akhkhirîn: A History of the Mahomedan Power in India during the Last Century by Mir Gholam Hussein Khan* (London: Oriental Translation Fund, 1832), pp. 206, 239, 242. See also William Irvine, *Later Moghuls* (New Delhi: Munshiram Manoharlal, 1996), vol. 2, p. 57; Muhammad Umar, *Muslim Society in Northern India during the Eighteenth Century* (New Delhi: Munshiram Manoharlal, 1998), p. 270.
117. The name should be read as Aghar. The title Aghar Khān refers to an Oghuz tribe, the Aghar, where the first bearer of this title, the father of the Aghar Khān mentioned here, hailed from. For the Aghar tribe, see, Atanıyazov, *Şecere*, pp. 61–3. Either the father or the son wrote poems in Turkish under the pen name Aghar. This poet's collection of Turkish poems is preserved in the Raza Library, Rampur. Bilkan, *Hindistan*, p. 357.
118. Mustafa Raymond, trans., *A Translation of the Seir Mutaqherin or View of Modern Times being an History of India from the Year 1118 to the Year 1194 of the Hedjrah* (Calcutta: Printed by T.D. Chatterjee, 1902), p. 226.
119. Muhammad Umar, *Islam in Northern India during the Eighteenth Century* (New Delhi: Munshiram Manoharlal, 1993), p. 279. For the family of Najm ud-Dawla see, Saiyid Athar Abbas Rizvi, *Shâh Walî-Allâh and His Times* (Canberra: Ma'rifat Publishing House, 1980), p. 147.
120. Raymond, *A Translation*, p. 152n133.
121. Jean De Lauriston Law, *Mémoire sur Quelqes Affaires de l'empire Mogol, 1756–1761* (Paris: E. Champion, 1913), p. 329.
122. For a detailed account of his life see, Benedek Péri, 'Egy 'amatőr turkológus' a 19. Századi Indiából: Mirzâ 'Ali-bakht Gurgânî 'Azfarî' élete és Munkássága', in *Keletkutatás* (2002. ősz – 2006. ősz.), pp. 131–52; Iqtidā Hasan, 'Wāqi'āt-i Azfarī: Adventures of a Moghul Prince', in *Un ricordo che non si spegne: Scritti di docenti e collaboratori dell'Istituto Universitario Orientale di Napoli in memoria di Alessandro Bausani* (Napoli: Istituto Universitario Orientale), 1995, pp. 147–61.
123. Mīrzā 'Alī-bakht Gurgānī Aẓfarī, *Wāqi'āt-i Azfarī*, ed. T. Chandrashekharan (Madras: Madras Government Oriental Manuscripts Library, 1957), p. 17.
124. Aẓfarī, *Wāqi'āt*, p. 74.
125. For his career see, Beveridge, *The Maâthir-ul-Umarâ*, vol. 1, pp. 674–8. A Turkish quatrain composed by him has been preserved in Aẓfarī's memoirs. Aẓfarī, *Wāqi'āt*, p. 74.

126. On the *Salāṭīn* see, Percival Spear, 'The Mogul Family and the Court in the 19th Century Delhi'', *JIH* 20 (1941): pp. 38–60; Percival Spear, *A History of Delhi under the Late Moghuls* (New Delhi: Low Price Publications, 1995), pp. 62–3.

127. Azfarī, Wāqi'āt, p. 99.

128. Azfarī, Wāqi'āt, pp. 189, 193. The Turkish in the printed edition is in a garbled state. For the reconstructed and transcribed version see Péri, *Az Indiai Timuridák*, pp. 97–8.

129. Azfarī, Wāqi'āt, p. 99.

130. Azfarī, Wāqi'āt, p. 115.

131. Umar, *Muslim Society*, p. 421.

132. Azfarī, Wāqi'āt, p. 114. Azfarī does not tell which *dīwān* it was.

133. Azfarī, Wāqi'āt, p. 147. The poems have not been located yet. As I was informed at the court of H.H. Nawab Mohammed Abdul Ali, the Prince of Arcot, the library was burnt down sometime in the mid-1800s.

134. Azfarī, Wāqi'āt, p. 226.

135. Azfarī, Wāqi'āt, p. 226.

136. For the two complete copies see Edward Rehatsek, *Catalogue Raisonné of the Arabic, Hindostani, Persian and Turkish MSS of the Mulla Firuz Library* (Bombay: Mulla Firuz Library, 1873), p. 54; A. Ḥusaynī, *Fihrist nuṣkha-hā-yi khaṭṭī-yi Kitābkhāna-yi 'Umūmī-yi Ḥaḍrat Āyatullāh ul-'Azmī Najafī Mar'ashī* , vol. 14 (Qum: Chāpkhāna-i Mihr Ustuwār, 1367/1988), p. 170.

137. Azfarī, *Mīzān ut-Turkī*, Madras Government Oriental Manuscripts Library, Persian D. no. 459, fol. 2a. I have consulted the manuscript itself which is an autograph. For the edition of the text see Péri, *A Török írás- és Szóbeliség Nyomai*, pp. i–lxvi.

138. Azfarī, 'Arūḍ-zāda, Madras Government Oriental Manuscripts Library, Persian D. o. 698.

139. M.S. Muzhir, 'Azfarī', *DMBI* 19: 336.

140. Ghawṣ Khān, *Tadhkira-yi gulzār-i a'zam* (Kabul: Maṭba'-i Sarkārī, 1272/1855–6), pp. 274–5; M.Y. Kokan, *Arabic and Persian in Carnatic 1710-1960* (Madras: Copies may be had from Hafiza House, 1974), p. 381.

141. Mirzā Qatīl, *Chār Sharbat* (Lucknow: Muḥammadī, 1261/1845), pp. 77–85.

142. Hofman, *Turkish Literature*, vol. 5, pp. 60–1.

143. Qatīl, *Ruqa'āt-i Mirzā Qatīl* (Kānpūr: Nawal Kishūr Press, 1873), pp. 4–5.

144. Qatīl, *Ruqa'āt*, pp. 7, 11.

145. 'Abid Pīshāvārī, *Inshā-allāh Khān 'Inshā'* (Lucknow: Uttar Pradesh Urdū Akādmī, 1985), pp. 99–100.

146. Inshā, *Kulliyāt-i Inshā*, Ms. Salar Jung Museum, Hyderabad, India, Urdu Ms. 145, fols. 226b, 230b, 231a, 245b.

147. The original Turkish text has not been published yet. A copy of this work is preserved in the Raza Library, Rampur. See A.S. Bazmee Ansari, 'Inshā', *EI2* 3: p. 1244. For the Urdu edition see, Sayyid Na'īm ud-Dīn,

trans., *Inshā kā Turkī rūznāmcha* (New Delhi: Taraqqī Urdū Biyūro, 1980).

148. M. Sadiq, *A History of Urdu Literature* (Delhi: Oxford University Press, 1995), p. 197.

149. J.F. Blumhardt, *Catalogue of Hindustani Manuscripts in the Library of the India Office* (Oxford: Oxford University Press, 1926), p. 106.

150. Hofman, *Turkish Literature*, vol. 5, p. 108.

151. Kokan, *Arabic and Persian*, pp. 372–3.

152. The only copy of the work is preserved in the Government Oriental Manuscripts Library, Chennai. Persian D no. 445. Hopefully I will be able to edit and publish the text of this autograph copy in the near future. Subrahmanya P.P. Sastri, *A Descriptive Catalogue of the Islamic Manuscripts in the Government Oriental Manuscripts Library Madras* (Madras, printed by the superintendent, government press, 1939), vol. 1, pp. 490–1.

153. R. Russel, and Khurshidul Islam, *Ghalib: Life and Letters* (New Delhi: Oxford University Press, 1994), p. 371.

154. A. F. Bilkan, 'Hindistan Kütüphanelerinde Bulunan Türkçe El Yazmaları', in *Türk Dili* (1996: Nisan, 1096–1105).

IV

TURKISH ACHIEVEMENTS IN CARTOGRAPHY AND GEOGRAPHY

9

PIRI REIS AS A RENAISSANCE
OTTOMAN TURK

Svat Soucek*

The theme of this chapter is the place of the Ottoman Empire, and of Ottoman civilization itself, in the initial period and context of the rise of the contemporaneous West, as seen through the cartographic and geographical literature produced by Turks. The focus of my theme

* The first time I met Edmund Bosworth was almost four decades ago, but his name and scholarly calibre had been known to me since 1964 when I read *The Ghaznavids*. He writes in the Preface that the genesis of the book was a doctoral thesis, and this detail together with the scope and quality of the work reminded me of another classic that had roots in a doctoral thesis, W. Barthold's *Turkestan Down to the Mongol Invasion*. My friendship and cooperation with Professor Bosworth since that encounter has been lasting, and became a source of profound satisfaction for me, especially when another book brought to my mind the qualities that these great Russian and British scholars shared: Barthold's *Istoriko-geograficheskiy Obzor Irana*, which Princeton University Press decided to publish in English, and asked me to carry out its translation. The Russian original came out of St Petersburg in 1903; obviously, by 1982 the notes needed massive updating. Up to a point, this had already been done by the Oriental Institute of the Soviet Academy of Sciences, which published Barthold's *Sochineniya* in nine large volumes (1963–76), the *Obzor* being in vol. 7. The editorial committee, presided by Yuriy Bregel, had done splendid work, but there was only so much they could do on their side of the Iron Curtain, and an English version called for additional effort. I could have undertaken that task, but Princeton University

is the life and work of Piri Reis and related matters in the critical sixteenth century.[1]

If Islam was the defining feature of the Ottoman Empire and an essential element of the glue that held it together, the Turkish language was the other indispensable component. Arabic and Persian may have been part of the cultural heritage that the Ottoman sultans and the educated class received during their upbringing, but the dominance of Turkish—with the possible exception of strictly theological writings where Arabic long remained supreme—was beyond dispute. The Ottoman administrative system—from the sultans' edicts to the mass of detailed administrative records maintained by bureaucrats—was conducted in Turkish; prominent Ottoman poets and historians wrote in Turkish; and it was under the aegis of their Turkish identity that the Ottomans ranked among the foremost cultural achievers of the Islamic world. The Ottoman Turkish civilization could be called 'une culture-monde', to paraphrase Fernand Braudel.

Press wanted the very best scholar in the field, and that person was without a question Edmund Bosworth. The result, published in 1984 as W. Barthold, *An Historical Geography of Iran*, is thus even better than the excellent Soviet edition. Moreover, the Russians 'cheated' slightly when they prepared their volume: they used the author's personal copy, which he had profusely annotated in the margins over the years, and they began by using his annotation. This was of course perfectly legitimate, in fact mandatory. However, Barthold included in his notes often longish excerpts from Turkish, Persian, and Arabic sources in the original, and the editors reproduced these excerpts without translating them into Russian. The passages were often difficult to interpret, which put me in a quandary: the task specified in my contract was to translate the Russian text, so what about the classical Islamic trio, Arabic, Persian, and Turkish? The answer given by Margaret Case, the Princeton University Press editor, was unequivocal: the only language in which we allow quotations to be left in the original is French. It was an arduous chore, but in retrospect I am grateful to Margaret—it made the book that much more useful. The story does not stop here, however. Barthold's work has long been admired in Iran and published in Persian translations, and this included the Obzor. That translation had been made, however, from the 1903 edition. Not surprisingly, the Persians have not only noticed our English version but have translated and published it as Vasili Vladimiruvich Bartuld, *Jughrafiya-ye Tarikhi-e Iran; Tarjamah az Rusi bih Inglisi Tavassut-e* Svat Suchik, *ba Virastari va Muqaddamah-e* (Tihran: K.E. Buzvurs; Tarjamah-e Humayun San'atizadah, 1999). In other words, the fruits of Edmund Bosworth's labours are being savoured by his Iranian colleagues in this respect as well.

At the same time, however, geopolitical and historical circumstances placed this empire on the front line of the Muslim world's confrontation with its historic adversary, Christian Europe. The Ottoman sultans resumed the war to advance the frontiers of Islam into the European continent, the jihad that the Arabs had waged against Byzantium but then allowed to lapse with the decline of the 'Abbasid caliphate in the tenth century. That drive was resumed by the Seljuq Turks towards the end of the eleventh century, and was taken to new heights by the Ottoman Turks in the fifteenth and sixteenth centuries. Territorial acquisitiveness, sometimes revealing a desire to control trade routes and obtain productive territories, the expansiveness characteristic of great powers, and even ideas of messianic grandeur in the time of Suleyman the Magnificent (1520–66),[2] no doubt formed part of the motivation. Nevertheless, devotion to Islam as the only true religion and one that mandated *gaza*—the term more popular among the Turks—against the infidels for the sake of expanding *Dar al-Islam* (the land of Islam) formed an inseparable component and legitimizing factor in the sultans' wars on the empire's European frontier during the halcyon days of their rule, and they pursued it with a zeal and assiduity that attained its apogee in the reign of Suleyman.[3] The Ottoman Turkish Empire was viewed as the strongest military power of the day, and indeed, a virtually unceasing string of victories on land as well as at sea solidified this sultan's and his subjects' conviction not only of the righteousness of their religious cause, but also of the superiority and self-sufficiency of their civilization. All the same, although *gaza* acquired an almost ritual cadence in the sultans' efforts to expand *Dar al-Islam* westwards, war was not the only form of relations between the Porte and Christian Europe. During long periods of peace, visitors of all kinds streamed into the Ottoman Empire: diplomats, pilgrims, merchants, travellers, and so on in search of curiosities or just plain knowledge about the Muslim world, as well as those in quest of employment and ready to become renegades if that was required to succeed. A hospitable Ottoman government was eager to cultivate relations of this kind as well. Even these peaceful and friendly relations, however, contained elements of the contest that animated *gaza*: in terms of direct, active engagement, there was little reciprocity. The conviction of superiority and self-sufficiency within the orbit of *Dar al-Islam* was compounded here by the reprehensibility of visiting *Dar al-Harb* (the Land of War) for its own sake.[4]

On land, the grandiose campaigns usually led by the sultans themselves, *gazis* par excellence, became the dominant form and symbol of this historic process. If we attempt to highlight this contest by date, we can start with the year 1354, when Orhan occupied Gallipoli; we can say that it reached its first spectacular success with the conquest of Constantinople by Mehmet II in 1453; and that this success was followed up with Suleyman the Magnificent's conquest of Belgrade in 1521; it peaked with the same sultan's siege of Vienna in 1529; and ended with his death in 1566 as he was laying siege to the Hungarian fortress of Szigetvar.

While Gallipoli was one of the earliest points of departure for campaigns in the European continent, it also became the Ottoman Empire's first naval base from where the sultan's fleets sailed to support maritime or amphibious cruises. However, if on land the dominant form was the large-scale campaign of an army led by the sultan or the grand vizier, at sea their counterparts were Turkish corsairs who likewise considered themselves *gazis*. These mariners acted to a considerable degree independently of the sultan, but when summoned to serve in campaigns of the imperial fleet they readily obeyed, and eventually became an essential, often decisive, component of Ottoman naval strength. The ports and islands of Aegean Turkey were their original home. They had illustrious predecessors, the *gazi* beys of the pre-Ottoman beylicate period, the most renowned among these being Gazi Umur Bey of Aydin, who in the fourteenth century gained great fame among his Muslim peers and Byzantine contemporaries with his daring forays into the Aegean Sea.[5] The Ottoman seafaring *gazis*, however, expanded the maritime horizon of their campaigns, eventually reaching the farthest shores of the western Mediterranean. This happened in the last two decades of the fifteenth and the first decade of the sixteenth centuries, thus during the reign of Sultan Bayezid II (1481–1512). Given the energy and zeal of Turkish seafaring *gazis*, their eventual spread over the entire Mediterranean was no doubt pre-ordained, but because of their unofficial status, the earliest ones have remained unknown to this point. The first to emerge from anonymity was Kemal Reis, a Turk from Anatolia, who came to Gallipoli as a young man. He participated in Mehmet II's conquest of Euboia in 1470, and then took up the maritime *gaza* that he pursued for the next forty years, until his death in 1510. He became the first Turkish corsair famous all over the Mediterranean, renowned among Muslims as *gazi* or *mujahid*, notorious among Christians as a pirate.[6]

Meanwhile momentous events occurring in Spain may have accelerated the activities of Turkish corsairs in the western Mediterranean. The Christian offensive against Granada gained momentum after the unification of Castile and Aragon in 1479, and the Arabs along the

North African coast also felt threatened by the increasingly aggressive infidels. Many of these Muslims, from the last Nasrid king Muhammad XII in Granada to ascetic holy men and the boisterous populace on the African coast, were looking to the Turks as the coreligionists capable of protecting them.[7] The Ottoman sultan, preoccupied elsewhere, could do little to save the last Muslim kingdom on the Iberian peninsula from the final onslaught of the Reconquista in 1492, but at least the freelance Turkish *gazis* were seen by the Arabs as champions of Islam who successfully combatted the infidels. The latter aspect is vividly illustrated by a passage found in the *Kitabi Bahriye*, a portolan compiled by Kemal Reis's nephew and companion Piri Reis. It describes the reception that the Turkish seafaring *gazis* were given in the Algerian port of Bijayah (Bougie) at an undisclosed date, which must have been in the late 1480s or early 1490s:

Once Kemal and I came to Bijayah whose sultan, Mawlay Abd al-Rahman, was a relation of the sultan of Tunis. As we approached Bijayah, boats manned by the inhabitants of the city came ten miles out toward us. They asked who we were and came right up to us and climbed onto our ship. The late Kemal Reis asked them, 'Why were you not wary of us? After all, no Turk has come here as yet!' They answered: 'Three days ago Sidi Muhammad Tuwati informed us that a gazi was coming from Turkey and told us to go and meet him. When we saw you today, we went and told the shaykh. He asked how many ships there were, and we answered: "Three, one a square-rigger." No sooner had we said this than the shaykh exclaimed, "Go forth, it is the gazi!" So we have come to you.' They stayed a short while and then returned to the city. One of our ships was a barça. The weather was suitable for putting into port. We slowly approached the harbor. No words can describe how much they celebrated and fired the cannon. After we had cast anchor, first of all we went with several of our companions to the zaviye of Sidi Muhammad Tuwati. The shaykh inside— a holy man said to be 122 years old—was told about our coming. They helped him come to the door, and he greeted us. Each of us kissed his hand after our fashion. He placed his right hand on Kemal Reis's head, recited the Surat al-Ikhlas three times, and said: 'God willing, the Ottoman sovereign will bestow his favor upon you.' He gave both Kemal Reis and me a rod of aspen wood, saying, 'In the next three days, you will meet enemy ships. Brandish these rods at them!' We did indeed meet enemy ships, and did as the shaykh had told us: the wind turned in our favor, and we sailed forth unharmed.... Out of love for this saint, we spent two winters at Bijayah, sailing out each summer on our raids.[8]

Kemal Reis's renown spread far and wide, and reached the ear of Sultan Bayezid II who was planning the conquest of Venetian possessions along the coasts of Greece. In 1495 he summoned Kemal Reis to Istanbul, and from then on the *gazi*-corsair intermittently sailed in government service and on his private *gaza* expeditions. Both he and his nephew prominently participated in the 1499–1502 war with Venice. By an ironic coincidence, those were the years of great alarm in Venice also for another reason: in 1499 Vasco da Gama returned with two ships to Lisbon from an expedition that had left two years earlier and arrived on the south-western coast of India in 1498; Pedro Alvarez Cabral then sailed with a larger fleet of thirteen ships and returned in 1501 laden with spices, the result being that the lucrative spice trade began to be re-routed from the partly overland route through the Middle East to the all-maritime route around the Cape of Good Hope, reaching European markets via Lisbon instead of Venice. This should have made Venice and the Ottoman Empire natural allies, for the latter, although not a merchant state the way the republic was, also benefited from the spice trade both as a consumer and as a transit area, and Venetian diplomats had indeed endeavoured to draw the Porte's attention to the new danger. How soon and how much the sultan and his viziers awoke to this alarm is uncertain, but the first Muslim state to react to it was for obvious reasons the Mamluk sultanate: Egypt was the principal transit area in the Middle East through which the spice trade passed, and thus it had the most to lose from its deflection to the Cape route. The Mamluks tried to respond with a counter-offensive by sending a war fleet to the Indian Ocean, but to do this they first had to build one. Egypt was not a naval power, and its rulers appealed to the Ottoman sultan for help. Bayezid II, a pious Muslim, responded generously, and during the final years of his reign, convoys with supplies in men and matériel sailed from Istanbul to Alexandria. The most prominent captain escorting these convoys was Kemal Reis, as we can read in the chronicle of the Egyptian historian Ibn Iyas:

> On 19 Jumada I 913 [27 September 1507], an individual named Kemal, one of the special retainers of the Ottoman Sultan, arrived at the noble residence. This Kemal has a great reputation as a man who tirelessly wages the Holy War (jihad) on the Franks, to the point where the latter have despaired of ever getting rid of him. In short, he is chief of the dedicated warriors of Islam (mujahidin). When he arrived, the [Mamluk] sultan gave him a lavish reception and placed a robe of honor on him. [Kemal] stayed a short time in Cairo and then returned to his country.[9]

From then on Kemal Reis convoyed other shipments sent by Bayezid to the Mamluks, until his death in 1510, when his ship, caught in a storm, sank in the Aegean. We know this from another passage in Ibn Iyas' chronicle:

On 16 Dhu l-Qa'dah 916 [14 February 1511] there came an ambassador from Ibn 'Uthman, king of Rum. He brought a message, which the sultan kissed and placed on his eyes before passing it on to the chancellor. The latter read it aloud in the sultan's presence and that of his officers. Its style was forceful, with daring metaphors, and it contained glorious titles honoring the sultan. The dispatch announced that ships bringing military equipment had been sent to the sultan, and that he would be glad to find out if they had reached their destination. The letter brought news of the death of the mujahid Kemal Reis, drowned at sea, of whom there had been no news. The ambassador stayed in Egypt a few days; a response was written to the letter which he had brought, and he was then allowed to depart for his country.[10]

The Ottoman naval help to the Mamluks had mixed results. Their fleet failed to oust the Portuguese from the Indian Ocean and recover the flow of the spice trade through the Middle East, but Turks in Mamluk service succeeded in repelling the infidel's incursions into the Red Sea, which had a special significance because of the danger they represented to Islam's holy cities.

Among the contemporaries of Kemal Reis and his nephew who took up the seafaring profession, first as merchants and then as corsairs, were two brothers from the island of Lesbos, Oruç and Hızır. In 1512 they were caught up in the succession struggle between Bayezid's sons Selim and Korkut, during which the victorious but still apprehensive Selim forbade all maritime activities along Turkish coasts lest Korkut should escape abroad. Oruç,[11] who as a seafaring *gazi* had benefited from Korkut's support, felt threatened but managed to leave Ottoman waters and, after spending the winter of 1512–13 in Egypt, headed west. The island of Djerba, which he may have known from previous forays as a *gazi*-corsair, first served him as a base from where he resumed these activities. He was soon joined by his brother Hızır, and both men then asked the sultan of Tunis to allow them to use its port as a base for their corsair forays in return for the canonical fifth, which they gave him from their booty. They, especially the younger brother Hızır, had success that outshone even the exploits of Kemal Reis, and similarly gained fame among Muslims and notoriety among Christians. To Muslims, Hızır became known as Hayreddin, 'Virtue of the Religion', to Christians as Barbarossa, apparently because of his red beard.[12] This development intensified after the two brothers had moved to Algiers, where Hayreddin eventually seized power, the corsair thus turning into a political chieftain. In 1519 he sent several galleys with gifts to Selim I, proclaiming his loyalty. In 1520 the sultan in turn sent a ship with presents and an investiture document naming Hayreddin *beylerbey* of Algiers. Official Ottoman presence in the central and western Mediterranean dates from that year.

Meanwhile Selim I's conquest of Egypt in 1517 took the Ottoman Empire's maritime frontier to the threshold of the Indian Ocean. The sultan was thus offered the possibility of conceiving a plan to penetrate that maritime space and substitute Ottoman for Portuguese dominance of the spice trade. While in Cairo, Selim might have wanted to appoint a task force charged with preparing such a project. A lucky coincidence brought into his presence two men whom he could have used as the nucleus of such a force. They were Piri Reis and Selman Reis. Piri Reis, who came with the Ottoman fleet to Alexandria, was among those who sailed up the Nile to the Egyptian capital. Presumably introduced to the sultan, he presented him with a world map that he had made at Gallipoli in 1513. As for Selman Reis, he was an Ottoman Turk previously in Mamluk service who came to Cairo after repulsing a Portuguese attack on Jedda.[13]

Piri Reis in the Mediterranean

After the death of his uncle Kemal in 1510, Piri Reis continued to sail on the Mediterranean as before, sometimes—perhaps even often—as one of the companions of Hayreddin Barbarossa. However, he must also have spent an increasing amount of time at Gallipoli, for that was where he had made the map mentioned earlier, as he states in a colophon on it. During the many years of criss-crossing the Mediterranean by the side of his uncle, Piri Reis did far more than just chase infidel ships and raid the Christian coasts. He also engaged in a wide range of information-gathering in the field of navigation, cartography, hydrography, geography, and discovery literature. Among other things, he gathered a number of maps made by Christians that encompassed larger segments of the oceans or were even of the comprehensive *mappamundi* kind. The most advanced type of these world maps, which soon attained a remarkable degree of accuracy, was a direct result of the ongoing voyages of discovery. Piri Reis used several of these maps—specimens that figured among the booty found on captured ships or during descents on Spanish and Italian coasts—to make his own map; he also benefited, however, from an advantage that none of the Europeans had—the ability to understand and use Muslim, primarily Arab, cartography of the Indian Ocean, so that his *mappamundi* was in certain respects the most original and valuable cartographic work of its time. Here is his story of how this map came into being.

> This is a unique map such as no one else has ever produced, and I am its author. I have used twenty [regional] maps and world maps—the latter derive from a prototype that goes back to Zulkarneyn's time and that comprises the entire inhabited world—Arabs call such maps 'ja'feriye'—I have used eight such 'ja'feriyes'; then I have used an Arab map of [the] India[n ocean], as well as maps made by four Portuguese who applied mathematical methods to represent India and China; finally, I have also used a map of the Western regions drawn by Columbus. I have brought all these sources to a single scale and this is the result: In other words, just as the sailors of the Mediterranean have reliable and well-tested charts at their disposal, this [new] map of the world oceans [lit. 'Seven Seas'] too is reliable and worthy of recognition.[14]

Only one third of Piri Reis's *mappamundi* has survived, for someone— possibly the sultan himself—tore it into two parts; the extant piece covers the Atlantic with its eastern and western fringes, the latter thus showing the newly discovered part of the New World. Fortunately, this segment also includes the colophon recording the name of the author, the year (1513), and place of its creation, the story of how it was produced, and the mention of Columbus's map. As far as is known, Selim I, other than receiving the map and possibly himself mutilating it, paid little attention to it and to its author.[15]

As for Selman Reis, he was one of the Turkish mariners Bayezid had sent to help the Mamluks to build up their navy. He stayed in their service as commander of the arsenal of Suez and of the Mamluk navy during Selim I's reign until this sultan's conquest of Egypt. Here is what Ibn Iyas writes:

> On Saturday 18 Muharram [mid-February 1514] ... the sultan traveled to Suez in order to inspect the ships which he had built there.... Upon his arrival, the day when he entered Suez was a festive one.... The captain Salman the Ottoman and a company of Ottoman mariners—some two thousand Ottomans—were there, and the sultan expressed his great appreciation of this company.... When the sultan arrived he inspected those vessels which he had had built at Suez, some twenty grabs. Those whose construction had been finished were launched in the sultan's presence; it was a great day.... Captain Salman the Ottoman was the one who had supervised the construction of these vessels.... When the sultan arrived captain Salman gave him an enthusiastic welcome, and the sultan dressed him in a red robe lined with sable and gave him a gift of one thousand dinars; he also gave robes of honor to each member of the company of carpenters, ironsmiths and caulkers.[16]

Selman Reis's final duty in that role was the defense of Jedda from a Portuguese attack that coincided with Selim's conquest of Egypt. Once that had been accomplished, he hurried to Cairo to join the sultan. He had much to offer. Several years in Mamluk service included cruises in the Indian Ocean, which gave him an opportunity to closely observe the new situation. If Piri Reis was a unique version of a Muslim Renaissance man, Selman Reis was the exact type of an Ottoman Turk whom the sultan needed if he wished to challenge Christian Europe in the Indian Ocean. Here again, Selim I did not respond; worse, after the sultan's departure from the Egyptian capital, Selman Reis was arrested and imprisoned in the Cairo citadel, where he spent the winter; the next spring the governor of Egypt Hayr Beg sent him, in chains, via Damascus to Istanbul. The reasons for this treatment were not disclosed, but Selim's irritation that Selman had not joined him forthwith at the outset of the campaign is the most plausible explanation.[17] The mariner was ultimately exonerated and even sent back as commander of the now Turkish naval base at Suez, but the opportunity to start a planned, methodical Ottoman penetration of the Indian Ocean was lost, although the concept itself would have meant nothing to the sultan: Selim I's conceptual framework was essentially territorial; at the maritime level, it remained confined to the Mediterranean orbit, with the Red Sea as an important but still lateral issue. This would, in fact, be the case with all his successors as well.[18]

The empire that Suleyman the Magnificent inherited from his father in 1520 had expanded almost beyond recognition when compared with the one that Selim himself had received from Bayezid eight years before. With Syria, Egypt, and Algiers now Ottoman possessions, the empire spread over three continents, and its Mediterranean waterfront surpassed in length that of any other power. The sultan and his subjects could legitimately feel invited to engage this sea in a variety of ways. By another historical coincidence, a dynastic event in Europe created a link between the land and sea *gaza* pursued by Suleyman or his proxies: from 1526 on, both on land and at sea the sultan's principal adversaries were Habsburg monarchs, those of Austria on land, those of Spain at sea.

On the very eve of Suleyman's enthronement, the empire's maritime reach had been extended all the way to the western Mediterranean through the merit of Hayreddin Barbarossa. Among the benefits this represented was the special nature of sea space and coasts around it into which the Turks were introduced. By being inherently international, this different milieu enabled the sultan's subjects to meet people from the Christian side more frequently and with a greater variety of contacts than was possible on land. In particular, penetrating the central and western Mediterranean offered the Ottoman Turks an unprecedented opportunity to observe Europe and to deal with it in ways that harboured great promise. One of the Turks who did so was Piri Reis.

Seaborne trade had existed in the Mediterranean since antiquity, but it rose dramatically with the expansion of Italian and Catalan commerce in the eleventh century. The captains needed sea charts and texts describing routes, coasts, and ports, and by the time Turkish *gazis* had spread all over the Mediterranean, there existed a large body of these tools and manuals, as a rule made by members of those two communities in their respective languages, or rather in a lingua franca whose romance base was peppered with accretions from other Mediterranean idioms such as Greek and Arabic. The charts they used were called portolans, a genre that with the introduction of the compass in the thirteenth century attained a remarkable degree of accuracy. They depict the totality of the Mediterranean or its specific segments.[19] Besides charts, there were also textual descriptions of the Mediterranean for the purpose of navigation, which were likewise called portolans. A few Arab ones are known to have existed, but no Turkish ones did prior to the time under discussion. Piri Reis filled this gap, and what an achievement his was! The *Kitabi Bahriye*, his book describing the Mediterranean, is a portolan, but it is unlike any portolan produced by Christian cartographers and hydrographers. It is the only known case that covers the entire Mediterranean while combining both charts and texts. Piri Reis drew on the existing literature produced by his Christian counterparts, but also on his own experience and notes, to create this masterpiece of the portolan genre. In the preface he explains his motives. One was to join all those who wished to offer a gift to Suleyman on the occasion of his accession to the throne, and he expressed the hope that the sovereign would deem it worthy of recognition and reward; the other was to make available to his fellow seamen a manual that would make their trade easier and safer. He certainly succeeded in the second respect; this is shown by the number of manuscript copies that have survived, some considerably modified, compiled by scribes in the arsenal or other seamen who quite often identified themselves as well as recorded the place and date of production in the colophon. Piri Reis failed, however, in the first respect. We know this because he writes about it in the preface to a second, expanded version he produced by 1526. It was a lucky chance that led to the creation of this new version. In 1524, the grand vizier Ibrahim Pasha was sent to Egypt to reorganize the *vilayet*'s administration after the suppression of the rebellion of the governor Hain Ahmet Pasha, and the pilot of the ship on which he sailed was Piri Reis. As the ship proceeded through the Aegean, the mariner kept consulting the *Kitabi Bahriye*, and the minister showed interest in the manual. When told about the author's disappointment, Ibrahim Pasha suggested that a new, physically more accomplished copy be produced, which he would then present to the sultan. The result was a new version with not only an expanded number of places and charts but also a long introduction. This is a versified description of the art of navigation and navigation tools from charts to the compass, of the world's oceans, and of the recent voyages of discovery. For the first time an Ottoman Turk could read about the Spanish discovery of America and the New World itself, as well as the Portuguese penetration into the Indian Ocean and the challenge that meant for Islam, especially the Ottoman Empire. Piri Reis laments the danger and harm the infidels' penetration of the Indian Ocean represented, exemplified by the Portuguese seizure of Hormuz (in 1515), where they were reaping the benefits of lucrative trade. We thus find in the *Kitabi Bahriye* the following passage:

Now that you have heard about the situation of Bahrayn, come and listen to what it is like at Hormuz. Know that it is an island. Many merchants visit it.... But now, O friend, the Portuguese have come there and built a stronghold on its cape. They control the place and collect the customs— see into what condition that province has sunk! The Portuguese have prevailed over the natives, and their own merchants crowd the warehouses there. Whatever the season, trading cannot now happen without the Portuguese.[20]

Another passage mentions the Portuguese attack on Jedda (in 1517) which, although repulsed, represented an unforgettable affront to Muslims, threatening as it did the holiest sites of Islam, namely Mecca and Medina.

While Ibrahim Pasha was in Egypt, he was given a *Layiha*, a memorandum, dated 10 Sha'ban 931/2 June 1525. It is anonymous, and no known record mentions who was its author. Internal as well as circumstantial evidence argues, however, in favour of Selman Reis.[21] By the time Suleyman the Magnificent succeeded his father on the throne in 1520, the mariner had been exonerated in Istanbul and then—the exact date is unknown—returned to Suez in the role of commander of the Ottoman base and fleet now stationed there.[22] The *Layiha* describes the naval situation in the Red Sea and the Indian Ocean, and presents a plan for confronting the infidels and substituting Ottoman for Portuguese dominance along the coasts and the waters of that ocean. Like Piri Reis, Selman Reis too laments the current situation and implicitly exhorts the Ottoman sovereign to recover the spice trade for Muslims:

> Description of how the infidel Portuguese seized [a number of] places in [the ?] India[n Ocean?]. First the island of Hormuz, which pertains to the country of Persia: they built there a small fortress and garrisoned it with two hundred infidels. Fifty to sixty large ships call there every year, and [the infidels] levy a tithe of 100,000 florins and send it to Portugal.... All the spices come from these islands [of Indonesia, but] at present they are sent to Portugal. Previously, before the Portuguese took these countries, the spice trade brought great revenue to Egypt.[23]

It is not known whether the report, presumably written by Selman, reached Suleyman, nor is it known whether the new version of the *Kitabi Bahriye* did so. Since Ibrahim Pasha was the sultan's favourite vizier, however, we can assume that they probably did. Several beautifully executed manuscript copies of the *Kitabi Bahriye* included specimens that may have been produced in the imperial workshop, destined for important or wealthy customers rather than for mariners practicing their rough trade. On the other hand, there is no evidence that Piri Reis received any special reward, recognition, or support for expanded activity in the field of cartography and geography. For a few years he produced more maps, as witnessed by the fragment of a world map made in 1528, his last known work, but after this date, he slips into obscurity until he emerges in 1547 as the captain of the Suez fleet, as we shall see subsequently.

The significance of the *Kitabi Bahriye*, both its first and second version, can hardly be overstated. First of all, its more modest earlier version must have been a godsend as a practical manual for his fellow sailors, from local shippers to captains of the imperial fleet. Furthermore, the fact that it describes the entire Mediterranean, thus also its Christian side, represents a new feature in a Muslim approach to the infidel world; traditionally, the Christian side was either ignored or viewed as something hostile—an attitude that skewed and limited its intelligibility. The *Kitabi Bahriye* is the first Ottoman, in fact Muslim, discussion of the other side for its own sake. An Ottoman Turkish reader could thus now read about such things as the foundation and growth of Venice and the history of Corfu. This new attitude was facilitated by the difference between land and sea. On land, a line is drawn: the boundary's purpose is chiefly separation. At sea, the space, inherently international, has no boundary, enabling those who venture into it to meet and engage with any other humans inclined to do likewise. The other coast has a variety of tempting features: it is studded with ports inviting trade, functioning as centers of exchange, as gates of entry to a world with things to offer. In Piri Reis' and Suleyman the Magnificent's time, the Christian side had a lot to offer. Some of it was not new. Seaborne trade carried chiefly by Italians and Catalans that crossed the religious divide had begun to flourish before the rise of the Ottoman Empire, and the Turks may have felt tempted to do what the Arabs had rejected, picking up the challenge and doing likewise. They now had an even better portolan, which in turn they may have wished to continue to update and improve. But there was more. In the first place, news of the conquest of the oceans and the capture of overseas trade by the infidels might have inspired Suleyman the Magnificent to respond in kind, and not just in concrete terms by sending a war fleet to confront the Portuguese; to succeed, he needed a carefully elaborated project that would have included a team of expert cartographers and mariners with experience in the Indian Ocean—men such as Piri Reis and Selman Reis. He could have had his curiosity awakened while reading, in the *Kitabi Bahriye*, about the Mediterranean coast of Europe and the world at large, including the discovery of America. Had he done so, he might also have grasped that something altogether new was happening in Europe at the hands of the Europeans. The Renaissance had burst into full bloom, and Piri Reis had approached it from the Turkish side. The Renaissance, of course, is a complex and broad concept whose Christian component could hardly have suited Muslim candidates for membership. However, it also comprised a scientific, cultural, and a commercial revolution, and the spread of printing, each of which deserved interest and participation, not least because they eventually made Europe militarily stronger.

There is no evidence that either the *Kitabi Bahriye* or the *Layiha* succeeded in stirring Suleyman the Magnificent's interest. True, in 1526 the monarch was too busy to pay attention to his two mariners and the Indian Ocean, for that was the year of a triumphal campaign in which victory at Mohács enabled him to conquer an important part of Hungary. Once back from the war in 1527, however, the sultan might have thought the time was right for summoning the two mariners and doing what his father had neglected to do ten years earlier:

assemble a team of experts and prepare, under their leadership, a plan to challenge the Portuguese. Had he done so, he would have emulated his Habsburg and Portuguese peers, Charles V and John III, each of whom had assembled teams of seafaring and cartographic experts to support their overseas projects and legal rights. Some of these men, appreciated and well-paid by their sovereigns, worked at the Casa de Contratacion in Seville and the Casa da India in Lisbon, government agencies established for the purpose of administering and supporting overseas exploration and trade. Maps and charts made by the experts were invaluable for the voyages of exploration and commerce undertaken by Spanish and Portuguese fleets. The decade of the 1520s witnessed some of the greatest events and achievements of this kind. It began with the circumnavigation of the earth: Sebastian Elcano returned to Spain in 1522 as captain of the only surviving ship of a five-ship flotilla that under the command of Fernando Magellan had set out from Seville in 1519. One of the purposes of this expedition sponsored by Charles V had been to ascertain which part of the Spice Islands belonged to Spain or Portugal. Negotiations to settle this matter, begun at Badajoz in 1524, ended in 1529 with the Treaty of Zaragoza.[24]

By contrast, the Ottoman sultan paid little attention to Piri Reis, Selman Reis, the Indian Ocean, and the spice trade, or to sending out expeditions for the exploration and mapping of the world. Piri Reis remained at Gallipoli, where he continued his cartographic work, producing a second world map in 1528, of which again only a fragment is extant. Selman Reis, stationed in Suez and without adequate means, accomplished little. In 1525, during a desultory cruise outside the Bab al-Mandab, he made an attempt to seize Aden, but given a report that a Portuguese fleet was approaching, he raised the siege and sailed back. The mariner was then charged with a decidedly non-naval mission—to suppress the rebellion of Mustafa Beg, governor of Yemen; he did so, and assumed the administration of the province himself. Shortly afterwards, Hayreddin Beg, an aide who had assisted him in the assignment, gained the support of the local *levends*, rebelled and ultimately assassinated Selman Reis in 1528.[25]

While he paid little attention to the two mariners, the Portuguese infidels, or the spice trade, Suleyman invested energy and resources of the state in the *gaza* against the Habsburgs. This effort went through several stages, the most dramatic being a three-year phase from 1529 to 1532 and a two-year phase in 1537–8. The earlier phase was bracketed by campaigns to conquer Vienna; the later phase opened with the landing of troops in the Habsburg part of Italy, an operation implicitly aimed at Rome, and culminated in the battle of Preveza in September 1538. It was a contest with Charles V for world domination: that is, at least, how the Ottoman monarch saw it, a stance directed outwards from his milieu towards a Europe that was Christian, and more—a world whose past was remembered as a glorious Roman Empire. He saw himself as a monarch whose conquests and power justified his ambition to emulate or surpass that almost mythical conqueror, Alexander, and as a sovereign destined to complete the mission bequeathed by his ancestor Mehmet II by also conquering the other Rome.[26] This multi-tiered ambition created a contradictory psychological climate: confrontation with the infidel as well as fascination with some aspects of Europe's own past and present, engendering a desire to partake of it and imitate it. The symbolism of this apotheosis of the Ottoman sultan's greatness is truly remarkable, for we witness here this monarch's desire to step beyond the original meaning of the *gaza* and assume the title of a universal ruler, one who adds to his credentials the status of being heir to Roman grandeur and the substitution of a Muslim Ottoman for a Roman Catholic universalism. According to a recent book, 'whereas, in the 14th and 15th centuries, the Ottomans had borrowed some of the structures of the European state, under Suleyman they seem to have challenged the Catholic version of European history itself—to re-imagine it as a vision that harkened back to the pre-Christian past and to fashion the Ottoman Empire rather than the papacy or the Holy Roman Empire as the rightful successor to the Greek and Roman civilizations'.[27] It was part of a stupendous display of power, wealth, and magnificence designed by Suleyman to impress Europe's Christendom in general and his Habsburg opponents in particular.

As for Suleyman the Magnificent's Habsburg adversary, Charles V, he for his part claimed a divine mandate to unify Christendom and become the supreme sovereign of a *monarquia universal*—an idea which arose with his election as Holy Roman Emperor in 1519 and was sanctified when in 1530 he was crowned and anointed at Bologna as Holy Roman Emperor by Pope Clement VII, who placed on his head a triple crown symbolizing universal sovereignty. A woodcut portrait of the emperor thus crowned was made and then widely distributed. Wishing to surpass the emperor, the sultan ordered a far more elaborate and costly headgear made by a jeweller-craftsmen in Venice.[28] Its base was a golden helmet surmounted by four crowns with enormous twelve-carat pearls, a head band with pointed diamonds, a neck-guard with straps, and topped with a plumed aigrette with a crescent-shaped mount. The Venetian diarist Marino Sanuto saw the headgear on 13 March 1532 in the jewellers' district of the Rialto, after which it was put on public display at the Ducal Palace before being sent to the Ottoman court; the invoice, according to Sanuto (listing fifty diamonds, forty-seven rubies, twenty-seven emeralds, forty-nine pearls, and a large turquoise), was for 1,44,000 ducats.[29] During the march of Ottoman troops through the Balkans towards Vienna in the summer of 1532, Suleyman the Magnificent wore it on select occasions when receiving foreign dignitaries in the imperial tent.

Meanwhile Charles V and the rest of Christian Europe were far less concerned with Suleyman the Magnificent and Islamdom than with their own problems, conflicts, and ambitions. The Habsburg emperor's claim that he had a divine mandate to become the supreme sovereign of a *monarquia universal* was directed primarily at Christendom, but by this time it had become virtually bankrupt because of its medieval and backward-looking content at a time when one part of Europe was evolving into a continent of modern nation states with different agendas, while another part was disintegrating into a mosaic of small independent or semi-independent, mostly Protestant principalities. As a historian states in a recent book,

> It is clear that the myth of the three crowns was ineluctably destined to fade away, inasmuch as it was a mark of a distant and elapsed epoch.... Only the coronation in Bologna, this extraordinary hiatus between dream and reality, could temporarily revive it.[30]

The main effect of the emperor's claim was resentment and fear among other Christian rulers on the continent, and utter rejection by the ever more numerous and assertive Protestants.

Suleyman the Magnificent did not concern himself with such matters when on his march towards Vienna he donned his extraordinary headgear to impress Europe's ambassadors, or with the fact that Charles V's ambition, confined within the boundaries of Christendom despite the rhetoric of world domination, liberation of Jerusalem, and the Holy Land, or a crusade against the Turk remained primarily focused on Europe. While the sultan's ambition on the battlefield was resolutely turned towards Europe, the emperor's never turned toward the Ottoman Empire.[31] Moreover, Charles's inward orientation mirrored that of the rest of Europe's Christendom. Despite the popular fear of the Turk and the elevated rhetoric of uniting for a crusade against him, Europe's real preoccupation was with its own goals and antagonisms within its own boundaries. Among them the struggle between the Holy Roman Emperor and the Most Christian King, and that between the rising tide of the Reformation and the gathering momentum of the Counter-Reformation stood out as the most prominent.[32] There was thus a striking asymmetry between East and West: while the wars waged by the continent's Christian leaders were totally wasteful, their peoples' engagement in both kinds of exploration—the Renaissance at home and discoveries overseas—brought them great dividends, leaving the Ottomans by the wayside.

This fact mattered little to Suleyman the Magnificent, if he ever grasped its existence. His empire had the structure of an efficient military bureaucracy, governed from a centee in which the sultan's authority was absolute. He had unfettered access to financial resources, and possessed a standing army of *janissaries* and a readily mobilized *sipahi* cavalry—luxuries the like of which no Christian monarch had at his disposal.[33] The empire's vastness and unity enhanced its economic strength, reaching new heights thanks to the recent conquest of the Mamluk sultanate, which added an enormous and steady source of revenue. With Anatolia, the greater part of the Balkans, Syria, Egypt, Iraq, and the Algerian part of the Maghreb forming its components, the Ottoman Empire surpassed any other European state in the old world with the possible—and for the time being irrelevant—exception of Russia. By contrast, Charles V was an adversary hamstrung by the peculiar structure of the Habsburg Empire—a disparate, partly scattered mosaic, in some of whose components the emperor's authority was limited, while revenues in the form of taxes had first to be approved by the representatives of a conglomerate of local constituencies. Both monarchs had to combat dangerous heresies, but only Charles waged the other dynastic-territorial kind of war, financially exhausting and morally degrading. What is more, it turned his principal adversary, the king of France, into an ally of the Ottoman sultan. Under these circumstances, the idea of a crusade against the Ottoman Empire rarely passed from the realm of pious talk to that of military action. Only once in his long reign did the emperor undertake a campaign to confront the sultan directly: this was in 1532 on the occasion of a siege that Suleyman laid to Güns (Köszeg, a town in Hungary near the border with Austria 100 kilometres south of Vienna), presumably with the Austrian capital as the ultimate target. But Charles never got so far as to glimpse a single Turkish soldier: he came to Vienna only on 23 September, after the sultan with his main body of troops had begun their retreat,[34] and he then turned back to attend to more pressing matters in Germany. The year 1532 was thus an exception; in 1529 and in all campaigns after 1532, the Austrian Habsburgs, beginning with Charles V's brother Ferdinand I, were left virtually alone to bear the brunt of the Turkish assault or to mount an attack to recover Hungary. This was one of the several asymmetries despite what standard historiography considers a great contest for world domination between two empires and religions. Defence of Christendom against the infidels and a crusade to recover Constantinople or Jerusalem may have been an oft-mentioned ideal professed by Charles V, but while during his long reign the emperor never set out to combat the sultan except for the above-mentioned aborted campaign of 1532, he waged six wars with France (four with his brother-in-law Francis I, two with Henry II), besides also taking on the Pope himself (a quarrel whose side effect was the sacking of Rome in 1527). By contrast, Suleyman undertook five campaigns against his Habsburg enemy, or seven if we include the proto-Habsburg Belgrade and Mohács campaigns.[35] A crusade to recover Constantinople or Jerusalem or both these sacred cities for Christendom may indeed have been Charles's obsessive daydream, but even to make a start he would at least have had to make peace with Francis I; in order to do that, however, the emperor and the king would have had to reach a compromise, especially with respect to the possession of Milan; and neither was willing to do that. This and other quarrels stood in the way of a campaign on land, but the expansiveness of sea space might have rendered conceivable naval actions confronting the infidel or even bringing the crusaders to his doorstep.

For a seaborne campaign, however, the participation of Venice was indispensable, and even then the Holy League against the Ottomans would not have been signed on 8 February 1538 without forceful prompting by Pope Paul III. The formation of the Holy League—as latter-day crusades, especially the seaborne ones, came to be called—preceded the signing of a ten-year truce between Charles and Francis on 18 June, but it too took place only through the prodding of the Pope. Moreover, Venice would hardly have joined the League if she had not been attacked the year before by Turkey. Furthermore, while war dominated relations between the empire and France, there was no love lost between the republic and the emperor either. The last thing Charles V wished to see was an emboldened and strengthened Venice, which might have complicated his designs in Italy. Hence the strange behaviour of Andrea Doria and the imperial component of the allied fleet in September 1538 at the battle of Preveza, where the emperor's admiral visibly eschewed a full confrontation with Hayreddin Barbarossa and the Turkish fleet. Needless to say, the Most Christian King stayed out of this Holy League, and the ten-year truce signed in 1538 collapsed by 1543.[36]

Be that as it may, war with the Habsburgs also became the centrepiece of the sultan's warfare at sea. While the offensive on land reached its farthest limit with the first siege of Vienna, in the same year of 1529, Hayreddin Barbarossa completed the conquest of Algiers by storming the Peñón, a fortress built by the Spaniards on the islet facing the entrance to the city's harbour. Algiers, strategically well-placed for naval operations in the western Mediterranean, functioned as the principal base from which Turkish squadrons sailed to pursue Christian shipping and raid the coasts that belonged to the Habsburg Empire, chiefly those of Spain and southern Italy as well as the Balearics, Sardinia, and Sicily. This port city was the centre of the westernmost Ottoman province, and the Turkish presence retained its initial character as established by the seafaring *gazis*, Oruç and Hayreddin. Maritime *gaza* was its dominant characteristic, and continued to be so virtually until the end of Ottoman rule in the nineteenth century.

In Suleyman's time, Hayreddin's opponents were Christian squadrons now under the command of Andrea Doria, a Genoese admiral who had been in Charles V's service since 1528. One of the few times Doria ventured into the Ottoman home waters of the eastern Mediterranean was in 1532, when he seized Koron, possibly as a rather lame diversion during the second Viennese campaign. A garrison that Doria placed there before leaving proved inconsequential and within two years had to be withdrawn, revealing the imbalance of the contest for the Mediterranean between the two sides. The Turks had a pronounced geostrategic advantage at sea: while the coasts of the two western thirds of the Mediterranean were equally divided between the Christian north and the Muslim south, in this sea's eastern third both sides belonged to the Ottoman Empire; moreover, the *gazi* spirit as well as maritime *gaza*'s ever-present corollary, economic motivation, that animated Hayreddin Barbarossa and his ilk far surpassed the initiative displayed by Andrea Doria and such Christian corsairs as the Knights of St John.

In 1533 Suleyman the Magnificent, summoning Hayreddin Barbarossa to Istanbul, appointed him commander of the Ottoman navy, a post which the mariner then held until his death in 1546. The new commander threw his prodigious energy into the preparation of an important campaign: the conquest of Tunis, whose Hafsid ruler, Hasan, had murdered all his brothers except Rashid, who fled to Istanbul, hoping to be brought back and reinstalled by the Ottomans. Hayreddin arrived with the imperial fleet in June 1534 and easily occupied Tunis, but instead of reinstalling Rashid remained there himself, presumably planning not only to turn it into another Ottoman *beylerbeylik* on a par with that of Algiers, but also to use it as a naval base ideally suited to promote Ottoman dominance of the strategically crucial central Mediterranean. A permanent year-round Ottoman naval base in the splendid anchorages of the Bay of Tunis had the potential of radically raising the effectiveness of Ottoman penetration into the western Mediterranean, perhaps even enabling a recovery of southeastern Spain for Islam. This must have been Hayreddin's thinking, to judge from a memorandum he reportedly sent to his sovereign before he left Istanbul on this campaign:

> That frontier [the maritime frontier of central and western Mediterranean] is far away from the Gate [of Felicity, that is, the Ottoman capital]. The army of Islam [that is, the Ottoman fleet and troops] heading there inevitably suffers hardship and fatigue. If the domain of Tunis were [sic] devolved on Reşid and the harbor of Goletta were [sic] taken and protected by the [Ottoman] sovereign, the imperial fleet could be stationed in it most of the time. In that case, with the help of God the Sublime, it would be feasible to conquer and subdue Spain from there.[37]

Hayreddin thus occupied Tunis in the summer of 1534, but a year later Charles V, benefiting from a lull in his French and Italian wars, undertook a colossal amphibious expedition that took Tunis and forced the Turkish commander to flee to Bone and then to Algiers. Back at his original base, Hayreddin reconstituted his fleet and before returning to his post at the Ottoman capital, undertook several successful forays of the standard corsair type.

Despite the great fame that Charles V's expedition to conquer Tunis acquired in historical annals,[38] neither this site, nor even the Mediterranean, occupied a prominent place in his policy as far as confrontation with the Ottoman Empire itself was concerned. The campaign could pass for a crusade to recover Constantinople or Jerusalem for Christendom only at the propaganda level, as part of Charles V's lifetime contest with the king of France. This is already suggested by the fact that the emperor did not follow up the conquest with a permanent occupation of the city and country, nor did he found there a naval base from which to challenge the Turks in their home waters, to say nothing of organizing a crusade to recover the holy sites. He placed a Spanish garrison in Goletta, the fortress by the shore guarding the entrance to the lake of Tunis, turned the city and country over to Hasan, henceforth a Spanish vassal, and left for Italy where before an assembly presided over by the Pope and attended by the college of cardinals and the diplomatic corps, he delivered a fiery speech against his Catholic coreligionist, brother-in-law, and primary opponent, the *roi très chrétien* Francis I.[39]

On land, as we have seen, the armies of the sultan and the emperor thus never clashed directly, by reason of geopolitical circumstances in the case of the former, by force of other priorities in that of the latter. In the Mediterranean, on the other hand, there was greater opportunity for direct confrontation. Here too, however, there was asymmetry, although of a different kind. After the Tunis campaign, Charles V undertook an expedition to Algiers in 1541, but this time the main purpose was not so much to score a publicity advantage over Francis I as to eliminate a bothersome pirate base, in order to protect the coastal population from enemy raids and make the empire's home waters safer for communications and trade.[40]

Christian attempts to seize strategic or commercial points on the North African coast went back several centuries. Crusading against infidels may sometimes have been part of the motivation, especially during the two decades after the fall of Granada when Melilla, Mers el-Kebir, Oran, Algiers, Bougie, and Tripoli were occupied, but they never generated any serious undertaking with Constantinople or Jerusalem as the ultimate goal. Gaining viable presence in the critical sea space and facilitating trade and traffic remained an essential part of the Christians' motivation. As for the Muslim side, the case was different again. Significantly, Muslims, whether Arabs or Turks, hardly ever reciprocated by trying to seize and hold strategic sites on the Christian side, once the conquests achieved in Umayyad and early 'Abbasid times had run their course. This was true even at the height of their naval power in the time of Suleyman the Magnificent, because except for the eastern third of the Mediterranean, sea space and the infidel's coasts meant different things to the two sides. To Suleyman and his subjects, sea space was a *dar al-harb* (or, more correct lexically, *bahr al-harb*), an area of unceasing confrontation offering a wide range of opportunities, ranging from grandiose campaigns by the imperial fleet with the purpose of seconding the land *gaza* against the Habsburgs to lucrative *gaza* forays by smaller squadrons; whereas to Charles and his subjects, it was an expanse whose commercial and passenger shipping, communications, and coasts had to be protected.

The Turks challenged the enemy with impressive demonstration cruises through Spanish home waters, and in 1543–4 Hayreddin came with the imperial fleet to assist the French in their struggle against the Habsburgs, visiting Marseilles and wintering in Toulon. This was a spectacular tour de force, enabling the Ottoman sovereign to assume the stature of a supreme arbiter in Europe's power politics and also reinforcing the Ottoman Empire's reputation of being the foremost naval power.[41] Here indeed, he took a bold step of yet another kind beyond his canonical *gaza* against the Austrian Habsburgs, taking a place of prominence in the vortex of European inter-state politics. In the strategic and economic sense, however, this policy was sterile. It did not convert the western Mediterranean into an area where Muslim commercial shipping would have been competitive with Christian shipping, nor did it aim at re-conquering for Islam the Arab part of Spain or other strategically important sites, especially those along the southern coast of Sicily (or the entire island, for that matter).[42] Instead of laying siege to the fortress of Nice for the benefit of the Most Christian King, Suleyman would have been wiser to expel the Spaniards from Goletta and found an Ottoman naval base at Tunis, as Hayreddin had advised him, or to besiege and seize Malaga or Almeria on the Spanish coast. Paradoxically, it was the corsair-turned-fleet commander whose thinking was strategically statesmanlike, whereas the sultan himself ordered him to carry out missions that did not go beyond the routine pursuits of corsairs: rather than undertaking a re-conquest of Muslim Spain or conquering and holding a base in Sicily, Suleyman preferred to have Hayreddin raid the Habsburg coasts of Italy, returning to Istanbul laden with booty and captives.[43]

After this last and most famous campaign, Hayreddin Barbarossa spent the last two years of his life in Istanbul, respected by most and especially by the sultan. An often reproduced miniature painting shows the two men, Suleyman and Hayreddin, the admiral honoured by what may have been a frequent audience.[44] On one such occasion the sultan, who no doubt enjoyed listening to the seaman's narration of his long life filled with victorious adventures, may have suggested that it be recorded in written form. The result was the *Gazavat-i Hayreddin Paşa* or Hayreddin Pasha's Wars, composed in two forms, one in prose, the other in verse, the latter ghost-written by the poet Muradi.[45] It is a priceless historical document, besides being captivating reading. The account was written none too soon: Hayreddin died in 1546, a sexagenarian or septuagenarian, and was buried in a *turbe* built by the architect Sinan at Beşiktaş on the bank of an anchorage in the Bosporus, which then became a ritual gathering point for the Ottoman fleet as it was setting out on large-scale campaigns.

While Hayreddin basked in the limelight of fame and favours received from the sultan, Piri Reis languished in obscurity. No new edition of the *Kitabi Bahriye* made by him is known, nor is any world map made after 1528. Clearly, neither the sultan nor the rest of the ruling elite gave him any encouragement to compete with the infidels at the level of cartography and navigation science. The only man who made an effort in this direction was Ibrahim Pasha, mentioned earlier, but he too may have been discouraged by the lack of interest displayed by Suleyman when shown the 'new and more handsome edition' of the *Kitabi Bahriye*. Besides this the vizier himself was running into a dead end because of palace intrigue and was executed by the sultan in 1536.

Piri Reis in the Indian Ocean

In 1547 Piri Reis emerged from obscurity not as the head of a cartographic or geographic workshop established at Gallipoli or Kasımpaşa, but as commander of the Indian Ocean fleet based at Suez. He must have been in his seventies by then, and considering the fact that in contrast to his scientific work he had not done much as a naval commander, the appointment is somewhat puzzling. It may well have been that it was he himself who had kept on soliciting for this appointment, arguing for a bolder policy on the Indian Ocean. His tenure started auspiciously. In 1548 he led an expedition to recover Aden, which had been conquered during the course of Hadim Suleyman Pasha's expedition to Diu in 1538, but whose Arab leaders then rebelled and expelled the Ottoman governor. After a brief siege the troops landed there, seized the port city, and, having restored law and order, Piri Reis returned with his squadron to Suez. For the next few years no action undertaken by him is known, but he may have been proposing an expedition to Hormuz. At any rate, in April 1552 a fleet of some thirty ships under his command sailed from Suez with this island as the target. It took almost five months to reach the destination, and Piri Reis began the siege of the Portuguese fortress only at the end of September. The defenders put up a stiff resistance, the Turks saw their gunpowder supplies and other provisions dwindle, and there came reports of the approach of a Portuguese relief fleet from Goa. All that moved him to lift the siege and retreat to Basra. He left the fleet there and returned with two swift galleys to Suez, whence he

hurried to Cairo, where Semiz Ali Pasha, the *vali* of Egypt,[46] arrested
him and sent a report to Suleyman the Magnificent, who happened at
that moment to be in eastern Anatolia, waging his third war against
the Safavids. The sultan's response was swift and trenchant: death,
so that the great cartographer–geographer was executed in Cairo,
where thirty-six years earlier he had presented Suleyman's father
Selim with his masterpiece, the 1513 map of the world.[47] The verdict
has puzzled historians, Ottoman and modern. Two types of accusation raised against him have usually been mentioned as the possible
reason: failure to conquer Hormuz, made worse by the suspicion that
he took a bribe from the Portuguese commander; and abandonment
of the fleet under his command in Basra. There is no indication that
he would have received what we would call a 'fair hearing'.[48] If leaving
the fleet under his command in Basra was what they blamed him for,
this accusation only emphasizes his superiors' incomprehension of
the situation. Had he been given a chance to defend himself, he would
doubtless have argued that leaving the fleet in the safety of Basra was
the only sensible thing to do. Its crew was exhausted by November
from the campaign that had begun half a year earlier, its munitions
and victuals were depleted, and the Portuguese fleet, newly arrived
from Goa, could not only have prevented the Turks from returning to
Suez but would almost certainly have annihilated them. Even one year
later, when the flotilla tried to return to Suez under the command of
Seydi Ali Reis, local Portuguese squadrons off the Omani coast mauled
it and forced the remnant to seek safety on the coast of Gujarat.[49] By
contrast, while still intact, the fleet could have constituted a welcome
element of an expanding Ottoman naval base in Basra, whose logistical
and strategic advantages were superior to those of Suez with respect
to the Indian Ocean. There is also no record of what happened to Piri
Reis's collection of maps and other nautical equipment, or even where
he was buried. This silence speaks volumes about the standing of the
cartographer and geographer—of whom modern Turks are so proud—
in the eyes of the Ottoman sultan and the empire's elite; the tragedy,
and Piri Reis's entire trajectory, symbolizes this elite's incomprehension or indifference towards the ongoing exploration and discoveries,
to which Piri Reis had endeavoured to awaken his countrymen.

* * *

Piri Reis thus can serve as a gauge as well as a symbol of another facet
of the asymmetry dividing the Ottoman Empire and Western Europe

in the critical period of the sixteenth century. Scientific revolution, voyages of exploration and discovery, the spread of printing and propagation of discoveries in their myriad varieties, overseas trade, and incipient colonization were all hallmarks of the dawn of the modern era, and the great cartographer was among those subjects of the sultan who had focused on one or another aspect of these dynamic forces fuelling the rise of the West. In 1526, the year when he presented the second, expanded version of the *Kitabi Bahriye* to Suleyman the Magnificent, Piri Reis was in an ideal position to launch a most rewarding career; all he needed was the sultan's support for organizing an Ottoman counterpart to the Spanish Casa de Contratacion or the Portuguese Casa da India, where a team of gifted and eager adepts, using the remarkable collection of maps, charts, and texts the master had gathered during three decades of sailing and research, would give birth to a splendid Ottoman school of cartography and oceanography. Istanbul was a city like no other in the world, a centre where East and West met, where Turkish, Arabic, Persian, Greek, Italian, and Slavic idioms were understood, where Islam, Christianity, and Judaism could coexist, a place that could have turned into a convergence of civilizations. But Piri Reis's work disappeared or remained frozen in time. His and Selman Reis's advice went unheeded, and they left no human legacy because Suleyman the Magnificent resolutely turned his back on them and their ilk, as did the rest of the ruling class. This attitude was also reflected in the fate of the *rasathane*, an observatory built near the Ottoman capital in 1575. Taqi al-Din, who had previously held the posts of *kadi* and *müvekkit* at Cairo and Damascus, was placed in charge of it. There are indications that he was a brilliant man who had also constructed new types of mechanical clocks. He succeeded in gathering a team of colleagues and disciples eagerly availing themselves of the various instruments and tools of observation and study (including a remarkably modern-looking globe), and his workshop is portrayed in a famous Ottoman miniature.[50] In 1580, however, the *şehülislam* Ahmed Şemseddin Efendi persuaded Murad III that the observatory was harmful to nobler pursuits, upon which the sultan ordered its demolition.[51] The observatory's destruction is no less symbolic than Piri Reis's execution. It is also significant that in the same year, 1580, the King of Denmark Frederic II built an observatory for Tycho Brahe on the island of Hven; the accurate observations carried out by Brahe subsequently provided Kepler with data indispensable for his solution of the problem of planetary orbits, which in turn facilitated Newton's discovery of the laws of gravity and motion.[52]

What the sultan and his viziers did connect with was the wrong side of Europe—the second Rome to conquer, the Habsburg emperor to emulate or surpass by crowning the sultan with ever more stupendous headgear, the quarrels between its two greatest Catholic monarchs to meddle in and exploit—all that besides the still-legitimizing mission of the *gaza* along its prime frontier on land and in its special form at sea. These ambitions brought few dividends to the Ottomans, while in Christendom their counterparts, such as they were, belonged to an era that was on its way out.[53] Kanuni Suleyman could afford to pay little attention to the outside world because of the immensity and self-sufficiency of his empire and the strength of his armies—assets that in the long run would turn into a trap.

Postscript

It may be worthwhile to examine both Piri Reis and the civilization of which he was a citizen not just in terms of his time but also in terms of our own. He had passed into virtual oblivion soon after his death. No one knows where he was buried, and his possessions, confiscated, were dispersed; there may have been a valuable collection of nautical maps, texts, and tools in his home at Gallipoli or Kasımpaşa, but that too would have been scattered. His resurrection—or should we say rehabilitation?—four centuries later, however, has been dramatic. It began in 1929 when the director of the Topkapı Sarayı Halil Ethem Eldem and the German scholar Adolf Deissmann, examining maps in the collection of the library, came across the map made by Piri Reis in 1513. Its existence had not been unknown to the staff of the library, who apparently sometimes had used it as a tablecloth at lunchtime. The renowned Orientalist Paul Kahle also happened to be present, and quickly recognized the map's true identity. The realization that the map was partly based on an early but lost map made by Columbus caused an international sensation and a swell of pride in Turkey.[54] To Kemal Atatürk it represented the tremendous potential the Turks had possessed for entering the arena of participation and competition with the rising West, and the great Gazi ordered the Turkish Historical Society to publish a reproduction of the map together with a thorough description and analysis of it. The Society complied, and in 1935 there appeared a beautiful facsimile edition with a booklet that includes all the names and legends on the map, either transliterated or translated into modern Turkish as well as into English, French, German, and Italian.[55] The Turkish Historical Society also published a facsimile of one of the manuscripts of the 1526 version of the *Kitabi Bahriye*, with an excellent scholarly introduction and an exhaustive geographical index.[56] Piri Reis's star thus finally rose, and has been shining in the Turkish firmament ever since. More editions, reproductions, and studies have appeared, and in 2004, the Turkish Admiralty organized an international symposium on Piri Reis with participants coming from Europe, America, and Australia. A *Piri Reis Araştırma Merkezi* has been founded at the Istanbul Deniz Müzesi Komutanlığı, and there is a Piri Reis museum at Gallipoli. History has thus come full circle. To Atatürk Piri Reis more than Hayreddin Barbarossa emerged from the Ottoman past as the truly great Turk, and many agree. Remembering how proud Kemal Atatürk was when told about the map made by Piri Reis, we can imagine how jubilant he would have been if scholars delving in the treasures of the Topkapı Palace had discovered another, complete map of the world—or perhaps even a collection of maps—made by the cartographer in compliance with an order issued by Suleyman the Magnificent. Based on sources streaming in from East and West, such maps would have symbolized the role of Istanbul and the Ottoman Empire as the site not of a clash but rather of a convergence of civilizations, in fact the rise of a splendid new one. Alas, that did not happen, for Suleyman, instead of ordering ever more accurate world maps to be made by his loyal subjects for the empire's scientific and intelligence-gathering centre in Istanbul, ordered a stupendous crown to be made for himself by artisans in Venice.

Notes

1. For a perceptive discussion of the background to this subject, see Gottfried Hagen, 'Some Considerations on the Study of Ottoman Geographical Writings', *ArOt* 18 (2000): pp. 183–93.

2. From among several studies devoted to this subject, the best examples are Gülrü Necipoğlu, 'Suleyman the Magnificent and the Representation of Power in the Context of Ottoman–Hapsburg–Papal rivalry', *AB* 71, no. 3 (1989): pp. 401–27, reproduced in *Suleyman the Second and His Time*, eds. Halil Inalcik and Cemal Kafadar (Istanbul: ISIS Press, 1993), pp. 163–94; Cornell Fleischer, 'The Lawgiver as Messiah: The Making of the Imperial Image in the Reign of Suleyman', in *Soliman le Magnifique et son temps*, ed. Gilles Veinstein (Paris: Documentation Française, 1992), pp. 163–79; and Gábor Ágoston, 'Information, Ideology, and the Limits of Imperial Policy: Ottoman Grand Strategy in the Context of Ottoman–Habsburg Rivalry', in *The Early Modern Ottomans: Remapping the Empire*, eds. Aksan Virginia and Daniel Goffman (Cambridge: Cambridge University Press, 2007), pp. 75–102.

3. The thesis of *gaza* as a catalytic element in the Turks' drive into Byzantine and Balkan territory and in the foundation of the Ottoman state, popularized in the 1930s by Paul Wittek, has in recent decades come under attack, and some historians have virtually dismissed it from the roster of plausible motivations. While not denying the need to be wary of assigning *gaza* an exclusive or excessive role, I think that totally banning it from this roster would be like claiming that there would have been an Ottoman Empire even if Islam had not been its guiding religion. *Gaza* and *gazi* as Islamic concepts persisted throughout the greater part of Ottoman history, from the time of Osman *Gazi* (1258–1326) and the *gazavat* of the seafaring *gazi*-corsairs in Hayreddin Barbarossa's time to the title *Gazi* that Mustafa III (1757–74) tagged onto his name during the celebrations following the successful defense of Khotin in June 1769, and its inclusion in the name of Cezayirli *Gazi* Hasan Paşa in October 1770 after this captain's recovery of the island of Lemnos from the Russians during the same war. Even the great secularizer of the Turks, Mustafa Kemal, could not refuse this honorific title, which the National Assembly gave him in September 1921 after his victory on the Sakarya, dropping it only in 1935 when he, like all citizens of Turkey, had to adopt a family name, Atatürk in his case.

4. Thus, while there appeared from the fifteenth century onwards a growing number of European travel accounts as well as descriptions and reports dealing with the Ottoman Empire, there is very little in the reverse sense, that is, Turkish literature on Christian Europe, prior to the eighteenth century. Nicolas Vatin's introduction to his articles published as *Les Ottomans et l'Occident (XVe-XVIe siècles)* (Istanbul: Les Éditions ISIS, 2001), pp. 5–7, implies this, his articles bear it out, and the very last sentence of the book, on p. 193, states: 'Comme me le fait remarquer Gilles Veinstein, le fait même de résider hors du *daru-l-islam* était condemnable en soi.' (As Gilles Veinstein has pointed out to me, the fact alone of residing outside the daru-l-islam was reprehensible in itself.) This does not mean that the Porte ignored Europe altogether. It had keen interest in its political events, especially those that could have an impact on the Ottoman Empire, and assiduously gathered this type of information, but even here it was chiefly through a network of mostly Christian agents who were Ottoman subjects.

5. Elizabeth Zachariadou, 'Umur I Pasha, Baha' Din 'Umar (Aydınoghlu)', *EI2* 10: p. 867.

6. Kemal Reis is mentioned countless times in Marino Sanuto's *Diarii*, 58 vols (Venice: F. Visentini, 1879–1903), usually referred to as *corsaro*, but at least once as *archipirata famosissimo* (the most famous arch-pirate); see also Hans-Albrecht von Burski, *Kemal Re'is: Ein Beitrag zur Geschichte der türkischen Flotte* (Bonn: Bonner Universitätsdruckerei gebr. Scheur, 1928); Cevat Ülkekul, *Büyük Türk denizcisi Kemal Reis* (Istanbul: Piri Reis Araştırma Merkezi, 2007); and Necat Göyünç, 'Kemal Re'is', *EI2* 4: pp. 881–2.

7. According to Kâtip Çelebi, *Takvim ül-tevarih*, year 892/1487, 'Kemal Reis sailed with a squadron to devastate Spain, after the prince of the Beni Ahmar had besought help by means of a beautiful *qasida*.' The poem had presumably been sent to Bayezid, and Kemal Reis would have been sent by the sultan. There is some confusion about the date, however, for the corsair entered government service only in 1494. Şemseddin Sami in his *Kamus al-Alam*, vol. 5 (Istanbul: Mihran Matbaası, 1889), p. 3886, does not solve the problem either with a note that not Muhammad XII but his father Hasan had sent this *qasida* between 1483 and 1485.

8. *Kitabi Bahriye*, 1st version, Dresden, Staatsbibliothek, Ms. Eb 389, fols. 107b–108a; Bologna, University Library, Ms. Marsigli 3613, fol. 106a–b; Topkapı Sarayı Kütüphanesi, Ms. Bağdat 337, fol. 107a–b.

9. Ibn Iyas, *Bada'i' al-zuhur*, ed. M. Muṣṭafā, 2nd ed. (Cairo: al-Hay'a al-Misriyah al-'Ammah lil-Kitab, 1984), vol. 4, p. 119.

10. Iyas, *Bada'i' al-zuhur*, pp. 202–3.

11. Roger Le Tourneau, 'Arūdj', *EI2* 1: pp. 677–9.

12. Aldo Gallotta, "Khayr al-Din, (Khıdır) Pasha, Barbarossa', *EI2* 4: pp. 1155–8; Svat Soucek, 'The Rise of the Barbarossas in North Africa', *ArOt* 3 (1971): pp. 238–50, reprinted in Svat Soucek, *Studies in Ottoman Naval History and Maritime Geography* (Istanbul: ISIS Press, 2008), pp. 67–78.

13. Svat Soucek, 'Selman Re'is', *EI2*. 9: pp. 135–6.

14. As mentioned in the colophon on the map.

15. Svat Soucek, *Piri Reis and Turkish Mapmaking* (London: Nour Fondation, 1996), pp. 49–79.

16. Iyas, *Bada'i' al-zuhur*, pp. 362, 365–6.

17. Topkapı Sarayı Müzesi Arşivi no. E 8337; see Şehabettin Tekindağ, 'Süveyş'te Türkler ve Selman Reis'in arizası', in *Belgelerle Türk Tarih Dergisi* (Istanbul: Mentes Kitabevi, 9 1968), pp. 77–80, and Muhammad Yakub Mughul, 'Portekizlerle Kızıldeniz Mücadele ve Hicaz'da Osmanlı Hakimiyetinin Yerleşmesi Hakkında bir Vesika', in *Belgeler: Türk Tarih Belgeleri Dergisi*, 2 (3–4) (Ankara: Türk Tarih Kurumu Basımevi, 1967), pp. 37–48. A thorough study of the attack on Jedda and its defence in Jean-Louis Bacqué-Grammont and Anne Kroell, *Mamlouks, Ottomans et Portugais en Mer Rouge: l'Affaire de Djedda en 1517* (Cairo: Insitut Français d'Archéologie Orientale, 1988); Selman's letter is reproduced in transliteration and translation on pp. 30–6. This book also includes a second letter, a kind of postscript or corrective, written on the last day of Rabi' I 923/22 April 1517, thus five days later, both then being taken by the same envoy to the Ottoman sultan (Topkapı Sarayı Müzesi Arşivi no. 5902); a facsimile, transliteration, and translation are on pp. 36–40; see also notes 192–233 on pp. 95–8.

18. Cengiz Orhonlu, *Osmanlı İmparatorluğunun Güney Siyaseti: Habeş Eyaleti* (Istanbul: Edebiyat Fakültesi Matbaası, 1974), p. 6n34; Iyas, *Bada'i' al-zuhur*, vol. 5, pp. 307–8; Feridun Bey, *Münşeat es-Selatin* (Istanbul: Daru'-Tibaat el-Amire, 1848), vol. 1, pp. 491, 498. The 1538

campaign to seize Portuguese-held Diu and the 1552 campaign to seize Portuguese-held Hormuz, ended in failure, and no further attempts were made. The principal cause was the fact that the Ottomans had never invested the necessary amount of planning and effort needed for a successful penetration of the Indian Ocean. Instead, we hear of orders given by Suleyman the Magnificent that were as grandiose as they were patently unrealizable. In 1538, he ordered Hadım Suleyman Pasha: 'You who are Governor-General of Egypt, Suleiman Pasha, as soon as this imperial edict arrives, will immediately gather weapons, supplies, and provisions and prepare for holy war in Suez; having equipped and out-fitted a fleet and mustered a sufficient quantity of troops, you will cross over to India and capture and hold the ports of India; you will free that country from the harm caused by the Portuguese infidels, who have cut off the road and blocked the path to the sacred cities of Mecca and Medina (may God Almighty ennoble them!), and you will put an end to their depredations at sea', Hasan b. Tulun, *Tarikh-i Misir*, fol. 353b, British Museum, Ms. Add. 1846, quoted by Giancarlo G. Casale, in *The Ottoman Age of Exploration* (Oxford University Press, 2010), p. 82. In 1546 Ayas Pasha, governor of Baghdad, reported in a message to Ali ibn Ulayyan, the Arab chief of Jazayir, a similar order he had received from his sovereign: 'I have received an order from His Majesty the Sultan to go to Basra, conquer it, and from there to proceed to Hormuz and India, to combat the infidel Portuguese, to put an end to their rule and annihilate them', quoted by Salih Özbaran, *Yemen'den Basra'ya sinirdaki Osmanlı* (Istanbul: Kitap Yayınevi, 2004), pp. 149–50.

19. Tony Campbell, 'Portolan Charts from the Late Thirteenth Century to 1500', in *History of Cartography*, eds. J.B. Harley and David Woodward (Chicago: Chicago University Press, 1987), vol. 1, pp. 677–9; Svat Soucek, 'Islamic Charting in the Mediterranean', in *History of Cartography*, eds. J.B. Harley and David Woodward (Chicago: Chicago University Press, 1992), vol. 2, book 1, pp. 263–92; Svat Soucek, *Piri Reis and Turkish Mapmaking after Columbus* (London: Nour Foundation, 1996), pp. 20–33; Konrad Kretschmer, *Die Italienischen Portolane des Mittelalters: ein Beitrag zur Geschichte der Kartographie und Nautik* (Hildesheim: G. Ohms, 1962).

20. Piri Reis, *Kitabı Bahriye*, ed. F. Kurdoğlu and Haydar Alpagot (Istanbul: Türk Tarihi Araştırma Kurumu, 1935), pp. 65–6.

21. Topkapı Sarayı Müzesi Arşivi, E. 6455. See Michel Lesure, 'Un Document Ottoman sur l'Inde Portugaise et les pays de la Mer Rouge', *MLI* 3 (1976): pp. 137–60.

22. Cengiz Orhonlu, 'XVI. Asrın ilk Yarısında Kızıldeniz Sahillerin'de Osmanlılar', in *Tarih Dergisi*, vol. 16 (Istanbul: Ibrahim Horoz Basımevi, 1961), pp. 9–13; Cengiz Orhonlu, *Osmanlı Imparatorluğunun Güney Siyaseti: Habeş Eyaleti* (Istanbul: Edebiyat Fakültesi Matbaası, 1974), pp. 6–18.

23. Lesure, 'Un Document Ottoman'.

24. The process, subsequent to Columbus' return from his first voyage, began in Rome on 4 May 1493 with a papal bull promulgated by Alexander VI; it granted sovereignty over all newly discovered territories situated 100 leagues (1 league = 4.8 kilometres) west of the meridian passing through the Cape Verde archipelago to Spain, and those east of that meridian to Portugal; this was then amended by moving the dividing line to 370 leagues west of the meridian, and finalized on 7 June 1494 in Tordesillas, Spain, with a treaty signed by representatives of the two kingdoms. It was further amended by the Treaty of Zaragoza concluded on 22 April 1529 between Emperor Charles V and King John III. More than a question of universal dominion, privileged access to the spices of the Orient was the issue on the Christian side. Because of the difficulty of determining longitude before the eighteenth century, locating a place by longitude was speculative and could serve special interests. The Treaty of Zaragoza incorrectly assigned the Philippines and Moluccas to Spain, but Charles V agreed to cede the latter archipelago to Portugal against payment of 360,000 gold ducats, money he needed for his war with the French king, Francis I.

25. Orhonlu, 'XVI. Asrın ilk Yarısında', p. 12.

26. Paolo Giovio, (1483–1552) writes in his *Commentario de le cose de' Turchi...a Carlo Quinto Imperadore Augusto* (Rome, 1531) [the edition used here is *Commentario de le Cose de' Turchi*, a cura di Lara Michelacci, (Lara, Bologna: CLUEB, 2005), p. 156]: 'Sultan Suleyman thinks of nothing else but to occupy your realms, avid as he is for glory and, having made himself daring and audacious through so many victories and the greatness of the Empire, he often says, as I have heard from trustworthy people, that the Empire of Rome and of the entire West rightfully belongs to him, by virtue of his being the legitimate successor of Emperor Constantine who transferred the Empire to Constantinople; and Your Majesty should know that he is determined and perfectly informed about Christian affairs.'

27. Goffman, *The Ottoman Empire*, p. 109.

28. Marino Sanuto, *Diarii* (Venice: F. Visentini, 1858–91), vol. 56, pp. 594, 634–5. The crown is known pictorially from three Venetian woodcuts as well as from an engraving by Agostino Veneziano, and textually from several sources. See Gulru Necipoğlu, Gülrü, 'Suleyman the Magnificent and the representation of power in the context of Ottoman-Hapsburg-Papal rivalry', *AB* 71, no. 3 (1989): pp. 401–27; reprinted in Halil Inalcik and Cemal Kafadar, *Suleyman the Second and His Time* (Istanbul, Beylerbey: ISIS Press, 1993), pp. 163–93.

29. Sanuto, *Diarii*, vol. 56, pp. 10–11.

30. Juan Carlos d'Amico, *Charles Quint maître du Monde: Entre Mythe et Réalité* (Caen: Maison de la Recherche en Sciences Humaines, 2004), pp. 161–2. The process stemming from the 'collapse of any prospect of European unity based on dominion by a "universal Empire" or a

"universal Church"', leading to the 'long, slow and often tortuous process by which a number of independent sovereign states succeeded in defining their territorial boundaries against their neighbours and in establishing a centralized authority' is discussed by John Elliott, in his *Spain, Europe and the Wider World, 1500–1800* (New Haven: Yale University Press, 2009), pp. 3ff.

31. On the battlefield, that is. In other respects, as I have already suggested, Europe's interest in the Ottoman Empire and the Islamic world was intense and increasing.

32. I am not suggesting that the people and rulers of Christian Europe had no fear of the Turks. The fear was real, but not to the point of generating an adequate commitment to unification for a crusade, despite the perennial, though not always consistent, efforts of the popes. The overall stance was one of defensive efforts to hold the land frontier if attacked by the sultan's armies, and at sea, to protect the coasts and shipping preyed upon by the *gazi*-corsairs.

33. A counterpart, however remote, nevertheless existed in the form of the Spanish *tercios*. They proved themselves to be the best infantry of contemporary Europe, but never had an opportunity to be tested against the *janissaries*.

34. Suleyman the Magnificent, after a brief period of raiding enemy territory, decided to call off the campaign. He may have done so because this time, more than laying siege to Vienna, his goal had been to confront Charles V directly, something his Habsburg opponent had avoided by simply staying back in Regensburg. As I have pointed out, it was only after the frustrated sultan had begun his retreat that the emperor proceeded to Vienna, entering the city on 23 September 1532. 'On 27 September he could inform Maria [Mary of Hungary, his sister and regent of the Habsburg Netherlands] about the withdrawal of the Turk ... Charles has been blamed for not taking advantage of the opportunity to pursue the Turks in their retreat and bringing the Hungarian campaign to a successful completion. For reasons of prestige, however, the emperor deemed that he should not undertake in such action. He helped his brother, ceding to him troops recruited in Italy; this aid had little effect, inasmuch as a majority of those Italians refused to serve under Ferdinand's orders, and deserted.' Manuel Fernández Álvarez, *La España del Emperador Carlos V* (Madrid: 1999), p. 473, vol. 20 of *Historia de España*, ed. Menéndez Pidal (Madrid: Espasa-Calpe, 1935–2007). Also Manuel Fernández Álvarez, *Corpus documental de Carlos V* (Salamanca: Universidad, 1973–81), vol. 2, p. 263, letter from Martin Salinas to Ferdinand, Mantua, 28 March 1530, stating that 'the soldiers doubtless preferred to join the campaign of Florence, hoping to sack this city instead of having to confront a tough enemy such as the Turks, whom they would have had to fight in the plains of Hungary.'

35. Yet we read in Goffman's *Ottoman Empire*, p. 110: 'Charles over and over again attacked Suleyman's realm in both the Mediterranean Sea and the Balkans.'

36. See James D. Tracy, *Emperor Charles V, Impresario of War: Campaign Strategy, International Finance, and Domestic Politics* (Cambridge: Cambridge University Press, 2002), especially pp. 164–6.

37. Ibrahim Peçevi, *Tarih* (Istanbul: 1283/1866), reprint, Ibrahim Peçevi, *Tarih* (Istanbul: Enderun Kitabevi, 1980), vol. 1, p. 493 (no explicit publisher for the original; I have used the reprint).

38. The excellent annotation in Tracy, *Emperor Charles V*, section 'The Tunis Campaign', pp. 145–57, gives a good idea of the European primary sources.

39. Heinz Durchhardt, on p. 517 of *Carlos V, 1500–2000: Simposio Internacional: Viena 7–11 de Marzo de 2000* (Madrid: Sociedad Estatal para la Conmemoración de los Centenarios de Felipe II y Carlos V, 2001), writes in his article 'Túnez, Argel, Jerusalén: La Política Mediterránea de Carlos V', pp. 515–20, 'However, this symbolic act was not followed by a second step which would have been necessary to put an end, with [the conquest of] Algiers, to the nightmare of the Barbarossas in northern Africa and the western Mediterranean. Instead of that, Charles resolved to undertake a journey for his glorification and to make an eloquent speech against Francis I in Spanish in the presence of the Pope, the college of cardinals and the diplomatic corps.'

40. Fernand Braudel writes on p. 363 of his seminal article 'Les Espagnols et l'Afrique du Nord', *RAfr* 69 (1928): pp. 184–233, 351–428: 'La Sardaigne, la Sicile, Naples se trouvaient exposées aux incursions repétées des corsaires barbaresques. Les galères algéroises rendaient difficiles les relations par voie de mer entre l'Espagne et l'Italie. La liberté des routes maritimes qui conduisaient vers les pays italiens était indispensable à l'impérialisme espagnol depuis que le Roi Catolique avait des possessions en Italie ... La rupture du lien maritime entre la péninsule et l'Italie était aussi l'un des buts de la politique française qui trouva, dans les corsaires d'Alger, de précieux auxiliaires. C'eût été chose accomplie sans le revirement politique d'André Doria qui mit à temps, au service de l'Espagne, la flotte de la république génoise. La piraterie algéroise ne mettait pas seulement en périle les intérêts politiques de l'Espagne, elle constituait un danger permanent pour ses intérêts commerciaux.' (Sardinia, Sicily, and Naples were exposed to repeated incursions of Barbary corsairs. Algerian galleys impeded maritime communications between Spain and Italy. Freedom of maritime routes that led to Italian domains was indispensable for Spanish imperialism ever since the Catholic king had possessions in Italy.... The rupture of the maritime link between the peninsula and Italy was also one of the goals of French policy, which found in the corsairs of Algiers valuable auxiliaries. What prevented a successful achievement of this policy was the sudden

reversal of Andrea Doria, which placed the fleet of the Genoese republic in the service of Spain. Algerian piracy not only imperiled Spain's political interests, it presented a permanent threat to its commercial interests.) Charles V's descent on Algiers in 1541 is sometimes explained as a blow to parry the Turkish offensive to seize Buda from Ferdinand I earlier that year. If such a desire formed part of the motivation, the emperor could have done so only on the level of propaganda waged against his perennial opponent, Francis I, not because he would have expected that a Spanish seizure of Algiers might force Suleyman to withdraw his troops from Hungary.

41. At the formal level, this reputation arose with the battle of Preveza in 1538, was reflected in the cruises of the *donanma-yi humayun* under Hayreddin Barbarossa and his successors, and received a final consecration with the battle of Djerba in 1560. Even more effective, however, were the unceasing raids of the *gazi*-corsairs, which began with Kemal Reis and peaked with Barbarossa.

42. As in the case of Spain, there should have been religious justification— not to speak of duty—for a conquest of Sicily, anticipating thereby the conquest of Cyprus. Selim II wished to conquer this island, but it was a Venetian possession, and the Porte had a peace treaty with the republic. This obstacle was circumvented by the *şeyhülislam* Ebussud Yahya Efendi's *fetva* stating that Cyprus had once been ruled by Muslims, and that it was the duty of Muslims to recover such territory at the earliest convenience regardless of other considerations. See Svatopluk Soucek, 'The Naval Aspects of the Ottoman Conquest of Rhodes, Cyprus and Crete', *SI* 98/99 (Paris: 2004): pp. 219–61, reprinted in Soucek, *Studies in Ottoman Naval History*, pp. 113–46.

43. An illustration of this attitude was Suleyman's reaction to the conquest of Tripoli from the Knights of St John of Jerusalem in 1551, an operation led by Sinan Paşa, commander of the fleet, and Turgut Reis, Hayreddin's most famous successor as a *gazi*-corsair. The conquest apparently provoked the sultan's irritation because it had been carried out at the expense of the instructions he had issued to devastate the coasts of Sicily, Calabria, and Puglia, possessions of the emperor. See Gilles Veinstein, 'Les Campagnes Navales Franco-Ottomanes en Méditerranée au XVIe Siècle', in *La France et la Méditerranée: Vingt-sept siècles d'interdépendance*, ed. Irad Malkin (Leiden: Brill, 1990), p. 321n32, and Stéphane Yerasimos, 'Les Relations Franco-Ottomanes et la Prise de Tripoli en 1551', in *Soliman le Magnifique et son Temps* (Paris: La Documentation Française, 1992), pp. 529–47. His neglect of Tunis and reaction to the conquest of Tripoli were not the only indications of Suleyman's inability to grasp strategic aspects of the Mediterranean scene. His order to virtually scuttle the conquest of Corfu in September 1537 was another glaring example; he overruled Hayreddin who was insisting that the fall of the fortress was imminent. See Soucek, 'Naval

Aspects of the Ottoman Conquest of Rhodes', p. 230. This incomprehension may be partly due to the fact that genuine thalassocratic strategy was not this sultan's—or any other Ottoman sultan's—'cup of tea', hence the lack of attempts to permanently occupy vital points on the other side's coasts—Christian in the case of the Mediterranean, mostly Muslim in the case of the Indian Ocean.

44. Farsça Yazmaları 1404, University Library, Istanbul. Reproductions of this miniature have become extremely popular with authors and publishers of books on the Islamic civilization.

45. Aldo Gallotta published what he considered its most authentic version as *Il "Gazavat-i Hayreddin Paşa" di Seyyid Murad* (Napoli: Centro di Studi Magrebini, 1983), in facsimile with variants at the bottom of the page and an exhaustive introduction; the same scholar also discusses the *Gazavat* on p. 1158 of Gallotta, "Khayr al-Din, (Khıdır) Pasha, Barbarossa'.

46. There has been some confusion as to the identity of the *vali* of Egypt at that time, Davud Pasha often being mentioned as the incumbent.

47. Cengiz Orhonlu, 'Hint kaptanlığı ve Piri Reis', *Belleten* 34 (1970): pp. 246–8. Piri Reis's tragic fate was followed by another killing a few months later, which was likewise an Ottoman tragedy: the 'execution' of Suleyman the Magnificent's eldest and ablest son, *şehzade* Mustafa. The prince came to pay homage to his father during the Iranian campaign, but as he entered the imperial tent, he was faced by seven mutes charged with killing him. While the sultan stayed behind a curtain, they pounced on Mustafa, and after a brief struggle strangled him. The use of *dilsizler*, mutes, was characteristic of crimes for which testimony against those responsible had to be prevented. As for Mustafa's crime, it was the accident of being the son of an ageing mother who could not compete with Hurrem Sultan, the enticing younger wife for whom Suleyman the Magnifcent had shown preference, and who strove, with masterly assistance from the grand vizier Rustem Pasha, to clear the path towards the throne for her own sons. See Celalzade Mustafa, 'Koca Nişancı', in *Tabakât ül-memālik*, ed. Petra Kappert (Petra, Wiesbaden: Steiner, 1981), fol. 436b; Ogier Ghiselin de Busbecq, *The Turkish Letters of Ogier Ghiselin de Busbecq, Imperial Ambassador at Constantinople, 1554–1562*, trans. from Latin by E.S. Forster (Oxford: Clarendon Press, 1927), pp. 31–3.

48. I address this question in my *Studies in Ottoman Naval History and Maritime Cartography*, pp. 61–5.

49. Svat Soucek, 'The Portuguese and the Turks in the Persian Gulf', *Revisiting Hormuz: Portuguese Interactions in the Persian Gulf Region in the Early Modern Period*, eds. Dejanirah Couto and Rui Manuel Loureiro (Wiesbaden: Harrassowitz Verlag, 2008), pp. 36–7, reprinted in Soucek, *Studies in Ottoman Naval History*, pp. 89–90.

50. Farsça Yazmaları 1404, University Library, Istanbul.

51. Adnan Adıvar, *Osmanlı Türklerinde İlim* (Istanbul: Remzi Kitabevi, 1982), pp. 99–109; Aydın Sayılı, *The Observatory in Islam* (Ankara: Türk Tarih Kurumu Basımevi, 1988), pp. 289–305.

52. Svat Soucek, 'Piri Reis and the Ottoman Discovery of the Great Discoveries', *SI* 79 (1994): pp. 121–42, reprinted in Soucek, *Studies in Ottoman Naval History*, pp. 57–65.

53. The collapse of Charles V's *monarquía universal* and the peace of Cateau-Cambrésis that in 1559 put an end to the Habsburg–Valois wars did not initiate an age of peace and political reason in Europe. A century of murderous wars of religion took the centre stage, a nightmare that was further exacerbated by the Holy Inquisition on the Catholic side and the burning of witches on the Protestant. The remarkable thing is that these destructive forces could not prevent the continuous rise of the West in its essential respects, although at times they did manage to hamper it.

54. Voluminous literature on the subject has appeared since then, but the authoritative introduction by Paul Kahle has retained its value; see his *Die Verschollene Columbus-Karte von 1498 in Einer Türkischen Weltkarte von 1513* (Berlin: Walter de Gruyter, 1933).

55. *Piri Reis Haritası*, introduction by Yusuf Akçura (Istanbul: Türk Tarihi Araştırma Kurumu, 1935).

56. Reis, *Kitabı Bahriye*,. This 1935 edition is a one-volume facsimile edition of the manuscript Suleymaniye Library, ms. Ayasofya 2612, enriched by an excellent introduction and analysis by the editors and provided with an index of place names. In 1988, the Historical Research Foundation, Istanbul Research Center published under the auspices of the Ministry of Culture and Tourism a four-volume facsimile edition of the same manuscript accompanied on facing pages by a transliteration of the Ottoman text, a version rendered into present-day Turkish, and an English translation (*Piri Reis, Kitab-ı Bahriye*).

10

EVLIYA ÇELEBI'S EXPEDITIONS ON THE NILE

ROBERT DANKOFF

Evliya Çelebi arrived in Cairo on 4 June 1672 (7 Safer 1083), having completed the Hajj pilgrimage. After decades of traveling throughout the Ottoman Empire, with forays into Iran and Western Europe, he might well have considered the nine large volumes that culminated in his account of the Hajj to be a lifetime accomplishment. But his travel career was not over. He spent the next ten years exploring Egypt and its African hinterland. These explorations resulted in two monumental achievements.

One is Volume 10 of the *Seyahatname*—arguably the richest, certainly the longest, of the ten volumes. Roughly half is devoted to Cairo, with excurses on the history and geography of Egypt, the Ottoman administration in Egypt, the fauna of the Nile, the Mevlud of Seyyid Ahmed el-Bedevi in Tanta, and many other topics. The other half is a description of his Nile expeditions. First he goes from Cairo to Alexandria and to Damietta along the two branches of the Nile in the Delta. Setting out once again from Cairo, he travels as far as Sudan and returns via Ethiopia and the Red Sea coast.[1] His accounts of these journeys contain some of the richest material in the *Seyahatname*.

The second monumental achievement of his explorations is a map of the Nile, preserved in the Vatican Library (Vat. Turc. 73). While it has been known to the scholarly world since 1949,[2] it is only now being edited and studied in detail. An edition of the map, prepared by

Nuran Tezcan and myself, has now been published as *Evliya Çelebi'nin Nil Haritası 'Dürr-i bî-misîl în ahbâr-ı Nîl'*.³ From our study, we have arrived at two basic conclusions:

1. Although Evliya's name does not appear on the map, it is clearly by him, in conception if not wholly in execution.
2. The map is largely an original creation.

Evliya Çelebi's Map of the Nile

The map consists of an introduction and 475 entries—distinct geographical areas demarcated by lines, characterized in a text, and often marked by a drawing. (Most of the drawings represent either a walled city or mountains.) For ease of reference, we have divided the map into zones as follows (see Table 10.1).

In some ways, Vat. Turc. 73 can be viewed as the culmination of Islamic mappings of the Nile, going back to the ninth-century Arab geographer al-Khwārazmī. In particular, Evliya depended on this Arab tradition for the southern-most parts of the Nile that he had no access to.

The real origin of the Nile always remained unknown to Muslim scholars and travellers. It is a curious fact, however, that the information on this subject which we find uniformly repeated in the Islamic sources from the treatise of al-Khʷārazmī (c. 215/830) onwards gives an idea of the origin of the Nile which does not correspond entirely to the data furnished by the classical sources. This conception makes the Nile emerge from the Mountains of the Moon (Djabal al-ḳamar) to the south of the equator; from this mountain come ten rivers, of which the first five and the second five reach respectively two lakes lying on the same latitude; from each lake one or more rivers flow to the north where they fall into a third lake and it is from this lake that the Nile of Egypt begins. This conception is largely schematised and corresponds only partly to Ptolemy's description of the Nile sources; Ptolemy knows only of two lakes, not lying on the same latitude and does not speak of a great number of rivers coming from the Mountains of the Moon. The third lake especially is an innovation.... The system described by al-Khʷārazmī of the origin of the Nile is represented on the map in the Strasbourg ms and is repeated many times after him (Ibn Khurradādhbih, Ibn al-Faḳīh, Ḳudāma, Suhrāb, al-Idrīsī and later authors).⁴

The top portion of Vat. Turc. 73 follows this schema. It is certainly based on a map in this tradition, although it contains additional material (the Magnetic Mountain, the eleven bridges) not found in any of

Table 10.1   The Zones in Evliya Çelebi's Map of the Nile

Zone	Entries	Description
A	4	Sources of the Nile: Magnetic Mountain and Mountain of the Moon; the eleven bridges
B	5	Rivers of the Nile
C	7	Valleys of the Nile; City of Wardân; Funj Kingdom
D	12	Sindi, Kandi, Hafîr-i Sağîr, Hafîr-i Kebîr
E	15	Cezîre-i Hammâm, Narinte, Sese, Mağrak, Sây, İbrim
F	29	İsne, Ermen, cataract, Etfu, Azrak Câzû, Vâdî 'Urbân, Vâdî Sübû', Kûştâmine; Bedouins (Kelâfîş, Mihriyye, Künûz)
G	10	Aswan, Kolombo, Cebel-i Silsile
Ha	11	Luxor, Ahmim, Kına, Füvve; Bedouins (Hüceyze, Havvâre, 'Abâbide)
Hb	19	Hû, Farşût, Semennût, Menşiyye, Ebû Tîc, Menfalût, Ümmü'l Kusûr
Hc	14	Oases, Behnisa, Feyyûm
İ	25	Feyyûm, Mellevî, İşmûnîn, Minye, Meymûne; Tunisian coast (Tunus, Sousse)
Ja	13	Tunisian and Libyan coast (Barca, Djerba, Tripoli), pyramids, Gize, Inbaba
Jb	21	Cairo, Bulaq, Şubre
Ka	33	Branching of the Nile: Menuf, Tarrâne
Kb	52	Western branch of the Nile, west bank: Demenhûr, Alexandria, Ebûkîr, Rosetta
Kc	28	Western branch of the Nile, east bank: Farasdak, shrine of Seyyid İbrâhim-i Dessûkî, Füvve, Burlos
La	45	Eastern branch of the Nile, west bank: Matariyye, Şubre, Minyet Şubre
Lb	31	Eastern branch of the Nile, east bank: Manzara, Fereskûr, Damietta
M	51	Red Sea and Gulf of Suez: Zeyla', Suakin, Mocha, Jedda, Yenbû','Akabe, Sinai Desert, Suez, Mt. Sinai
N	50	Bilbeys, 'Arîş; Palestine, Syria, Iraq, Eastern Anatolia and Western Iran

the maps cited in the note 4. We have not yet traced the particular source.[5]

Zones A and B of our edition are largely based on this traditional lore regarding the sources of the Nile. But as soon as we reach Zone C we find material that is mainly based on Evliya's journey in the Funj kingdom and Ethiopia.[6] And in Zone E we reach Qasr Ibrim and Ottoman territory.[7] We may assume that Evliya had access to Ottoman maps, and possibly European maps, that showed the Nile from here to the capital at Cairo and from Cairo to the Delta; but there is no specific evidence that he made use of any. Rather, nearly all the information given on the map seems to be based on his own travels. He says:

> Y392a I have recorded so many fortresses and lands, as in the Mappamundi, and rivers and mountains and lakes, in the manner that I have learned from my master Nakkâş Hükmîzîde Alî Beğ—may God vouchsafe that I may complete this journey of the Nile and the Funj kingdom and that I may record their forms.

We have not yet traced Nakkâş Hükmîzâde Alî Beğ. Presumably he was a scholar and a court painter (*nakkâş*) with whom Evliya studied during his youthful years in the Ottoman court in Istanbul.

We would expect Evliya to have been familiar with at least one previous Ottoman map of the Nile, that of Piri Reis. This Ottoman sea captain sailed up the Nile as far as Cairo shortly after the Ottoman conquest of Egypt in 1517; and he included his mappings of the river and of the metropolis in his *Kitâb-ı Bahriyye*, which otherwise is confined to the Mediterranean coastal waters.[8]

If we compare Piri Reis's maps of the Nile with the corresponding section of Vat. Turc. 73, we see that there is little resemblance.[9] For example, between Rosetta and Farasdak, Piri Reis has the following (see Mantran, Figures 5–6), compared with Vat. Turc. 73 (see edition, Kc9–25, Kb12–19, 23–9) and the *Seyahatname* (Y337a–338b)—(see Table 10.2 later):[10]

While the dependence of Vat. Turc. 73 on the *Seyahatname* is clear, there is no obvious instance where Evliya depends on Piri Reis, either on the map or in the book.

Kâtib Çelebi—Evliya's contemporary, also known as Haci Halife—drew a map of the Nile as one of numerous maps that he made for his cosmography known as *Cihannüma*.[11] Another contemporary, Abu Bekr b. Behram ed-Dimaşki, has an even more elaborate map of the Nile in his *Nusretü'l-İslam ve'l-Surur fi Tahrir-i Atlas Mayor*, completed in 1685. There is no evidence that Evliya had contact with either of these scholars or knew of their work.

Another possibility is that Evliya knew of European maps of the Nile. He sometimes refers to a world map ('Papamunta' or Mappamundi, as in the above quotation) and to works known as *Geography* and *Atlas* and *Minor* (that is, the *Atlas Minor* of Mercator),[12] but always

Table 10.2 Comparisons between Piri Reis's maps of the Nile, Vat. Turc. 73, and the *Seyahatname*

Piri Reis	Vat. Turc. 73	Seyahatname
Reşîd	Reşîd	Reşîd
	Üzbe	İzbetü'l-Ma'dî
	Ciddiye	Hadiyye
	Mahalle-i Emîr	Mahalletü'l-emîr
Burinbal	*Birimbâl	Birimbâl
Minya		
Sidi Yut		
	*İdfine	İdfine
Mutbis	Mutûbis	Mutûbis
Sidi Musa		
Sidi Salim		
Sidi Abdallu		
Sidi Hasan		
Alf		
	*Cemşîre	Cemşîre
	Fezâre	Fezâre
Davut	Deyrût	Deyrût
	Sindiyyûn	Sindiyyûn
'Atıf	'Atıf	'Atıf
Füvve	Füvve	Füvve
Manta Şerife	Şürefe	Şürefâ
Surunbay	Şurum Beg	Şurum Beg
Salimiya	Sâlimiyye	Sâlimiyye
	Mâlik	Mâlik
	Şumrûhât	Şumuhzât
Mahallat Abd ar-Rahman	Rahmâniyye	Rahmâniyye
Didi İbrâhîm el-[De]sûkî	İbrâhîm-i Dessûkî	İbrâhîm-i Dessûkî
Cimcamun		
	Mahalle-i Ebû 'Alî	Mahalle-i Ebû 'Alî
	Merkâs	Merkâs
Diyai	Diyey	Diyey-i Kebîr
Şubra Hit	Şibir H(ad)îs	Şibir Hîs
Bihnac		
Şibriş	Şibir R[î]ş	Şibir Rîş
Sada		
al-Sath		Sâh
Sidi Ma'ruf		
	*Mihalicse	Mihalicse
	Kefr-i Cedîd	Kefr-i Cedîd
	Nakle	Nakle
Farastak	Farasdak	Farasdak

in non-specific terms, and it is unlikely that he had access to such a work while he was in Egypt. He also shows no sign of being aware of European maps of Cairo, such as those of Matteo Pagano (1549) or Ferrandeo Bertelli (1568), or contemporary maps of Egypt such as that of Jan Jansson (1659).[13]

Relation of the Map and the Book

We must imagine Evliya during his last years (roughly 1673–83), when not engaged in travelling, as residing with his servants in his apartment in the Cairo citadel and drawing up both his magnum opus and his map of the Nile. Regarding the *Seyahatname*, we possess the autograph manuscripts of volumes 1–8. A close study of this manuscript suggests that he employed a scribe or amanuensis to write up the fair copy, adding diacritics and marginal notes in his own hand.[14] Similarly, he must have employed an assistant to work on Vat. Turc. 73 or its prototype.

All the information on the map corresponds to material in the book, but rarely using the exact terms. Rather, there is much abbreviation and paraphrasing, often including erroneous readings or misunderstandings, plus some eccentric spellings and grammatical usages that are different from those in the autograph manuscript of the *Seyahatname*. The ductus (handwriting style) of the map is also different. From all this, we may conjecture that at some point Evliya lost control of the map, or at least never checked it for errors as he did the first five volumes of the autograph manuscript of the *Seyahatname*. The conception of the map, and possibly the specific outlines and drawings, are Evliya's. But the hundreds of texts were inscribed by someone else, an assistant or secretary, probably from Evliya's written notes.

The contents of these texts reflect some of Evliya's preoccupations in his travel account. These include the following:

- Climate
- Flora and fauna
- Sources of wealth and commerce
- Civilized amenities or their absence
- Details of government and administration, military structure, tribal organization, and religious persuasion
- 'Noteworthy sights' (*'ibretnümâlar*) and the lore surrounding places and monuments.
- Distances and geographical coordinates are given only occasionally

While Vat. Turc. 73 is primarily a map of the Nile, it extends beyond the Nile in three directions:

- To the east: Suez and Sinai, the Red Sea ports, and the stations of the Hajj route (Zone M).
- To the northeast: Bilbeys and the desert beyond, plus indication of important towns in Palestine, Syria, Iraq, Eastern Anatolia, and Western Iran (Zone N).
- To the northwest: the Mediterranean ports extending from Alexandria as far as the Maghreb (Zones İ1,11,14; Ja1–4; Ka1–2,9–11).

While these extensions may seem gratuitous in a map of the Nile, they certainly reflect Evliya's mental geography.

In sum, Vat. Turc. 73, while perhaps not drawn by his own hand, thoroughly reflects his mind and unquestionably deserves to be called 'Evliya Çelebi's Map of the Nile'. The following is not a complete survey of the map but a highlighting of some sections, proceeding from top (south) to bottom (north) and comparing entries in the map with information in the book. When comparing the two sources, I use 'book' when citing the *Seyahatname* and 'map' when citing Vat. Turc. 73. In order not to prejudge the issue, I refer to the author of the map as 'the mapmaker'. Citations from the book are preceded by the manuscript folio number. Citations from the map are preceded by zone and number assigned to each entry in our published edition.

Sources of the Nile and Sources of the Two Works

The mapmaker claims to have consulted seven or eight classical sources of Arab geography, which are named at the end of the introduction. Except for some of the details regarding the headwaters of the Nile, there is no evidence that any such work was directly used in drawing up the map. None of these is mentioned explicitly in the book. (Evliya's use of written sources for volume 10 of the *Seyahatname* requires further study.)

A possible exception is *Cografyâ-i Batlîmûs* (that is, the *Almagest* of Ptolemy). At the beginning of Chapter 46 of the *Seyahatname* on the Description of the Nile, he cites Batlîmûs Hakîm/Ptolemy the Philosopher on the rivers of the world. He goes on to say:

> Y156b According to Ptolemy the Philosopher, the source of the Nile is the Mountain of the Moon, a seven months journey south of Cairo. It rises from twelve great springs/streams (*'ayn*). South of (? – *cenûba halef*) the equator these twelve great streams flow into a large lake, which is like a sea.

The book goes on to describe the course of the Nile after it flows out of this lake, through the *vilayet*s of Kırmanka, Kakan, Fûncistân, Berberistân, Nûbe, and Sây; and then through Egypt to the sea. The information on the map seems to have a different source:

> A2 Brief account of the Mountain of the Moon: Because the moon's rays are intense and shine brightly over this mountain, it is named after the moon. This mountain is located south of the equator at 11 degrees latitude. It is very lofty and difficult to climb. At sunrise the eastern slope becomes very red, while at sunset the western slope reddens. God knows best.

Following this on the map comes the Magnetic Mountain (*Cebelü'l-mağnâtîs*) and the eleven bridges out of which issue the twelve sources, all of which flow into the large lake (see Figure 10.1).

Figure 10.1 Headwaters
Source: Vatican Library (Vat. Turc. 73).

The Western Arm of the Nile

A curious feature of the last-mentioned text is the western arm of the Nile:

Y156b The blessed Nile (that emerges from) the lake at the above-mentioned source of the Nile divides into nine branches and flows westward toward the countries of Sudan and Fez and Marrakesh.... After 1000 parasangs all nine branches flow into the Atlantic Ocean, as I learned in Funjistan from some individuals who had gone there.

What seems to be the counterpart of this on the map are the two sections just below the eleven bridges on the western (right hand) side:

B1 This river flows westward through the regions of Ethiopia, Zanzibar, and the countries of Jaslâq and Amlâq. Finally it reaches human habitation at the city of Jâbalsâ, which has one thousand gates. Alexander Dhu'l-Qarnayn reached this country, but it did not submit to him; as testified by the Koranic verse (18:86): [*He journeyed on a certain road*] *until he reached the West*....

B2 This river is formed from the valleys in the mountains of central Ethiopia. It goes to the city of.... Then, after passing through desolate regions, flows to the inhabited area of the Maghreb and reaches Ceuta (?), which is the 'confluence of two seas' of the Maghreb.

Evliya appears to have no knowledge of the Blue Nile. For him, whatever part of the Nile is in Ethiopia somehow has the same source as the White Nile and somehow ends up in the Maghreb!

The mapmaker alludes to the western arm twice more:

F15 The Nile used to flow from these places toward the Maghreb. Traces of monuments are still visible.

İ12 This place is the course (? – *cirm*) of the *Lâhûn River. It flows from the Nile, under the bridge (and) under ground, toward Tunus (and) the city of Hadra. The ancient rulers (or philosophers? – *hükemâ*) reportedly brought it (i.e., as a tributary from the Nile).

The Funj Kingdom

While Evliya claims to have travelled as far south on the Nile as (Old) Dongola, Arbaci, and Sennar, these well-known places are not found on the map. Instead, the first recognizable place to be encountered is Vardân (C2 = C6) followed by Sindî (D1 = D9), Navrî (D2 = D10), Kandî (D3 = D11), Hafir-i Sagîr (D4 = E9), Narnarinte (D6 = E10), and Hafîr-i Kebîr (D12). As Petti Suma has pointed out, 'the map does not contain toponyms south of the southern limit of the region governed by ... [the Funj viceroy] Kör Hüseyn'.[15]

Hafîr-i Kebîr

D12 This is a great fortress and large city known as Hafîr-i Kebîr. The inhabitants are black Negroes, all believers [that is, Muslims]. There are

Figure 10.2 Hafîr-i Kebîr
Source: Vatican Library (Vat. Turc. 73).

many[16] Friday mosques, small mosques, hans, public baths and charitable institutions in this city. It is under the rule of Kör Hüseyn Beg. The twill fabric and cotton cloth for shirts are very fine. Ivory, rhinoceros horn, lizard skin, ebony and teak lie spilled out on the roads and alleys. It is a very safe and secure country. In this fortress Kör Hüseyn Beg has 70,000 black-skinned Negro soldiers, ready to do battle.

Y396b This great fortress is a strong Shaddadian structure, triangular in shape, on the west bank of the Nile. It is the capital of Kör Hüseyn Beg.... It contains a total of 1060 houses. There are 20 prayer-niches. All the people are Sunnis of the Shafi'i rite and perform the ritual prayer.... There are perhaps 50 dervish lodges, 1 soup kitchen, 2 small *vekâles* (=han), 6 elementary schools, 20 water-dispensaries, 1 small public bath, perhaps 100 shops, 10 coffee houses and 20 boza houses. All the shops are open day and night, the merchandise lying there [unguarded], very safe and secure. The fortress has 700 soldiers and 50,000 Berberî and Zâgî [that is, Nubian and black-skinned] subjects. They practice agriculture and produce plentiful crops.... Praise be to God, in this city we saw wheat bread.... It is a city with plentiful supplies [or, cheap prices].... The qibla is toward the north ... because the city lies on the equator.

Y397b In this fortress of Sindî, in the bazaars and storehouses, ivory, rhinocerus horn, lizard skin and ebony lie piled up like mountains in the marketplace, trampled in the dust and without value.

In the book, Evliya mentions the triangular shape of the fortress, and this is clearly evident in the drawing on the map (see Figure 10.2).[17] The figure for the garrison given in the book is much more credible than the map; the discrepancy can be accounted for if we assume that the mapmaker added the 700 soldiers and 50,000 subjects in the book and somehow came up with 70,000 soldiers.[18] The list in the map of the precious commodities that lie unguarded in the marketplace clearly depends on the corresponding list in the book, which, however, is not found in the notice of Hafîr-i Kebîr but in nearby Sindî.

Ibrim

Figure 10.3   Ibrim
Source: Vatican Library (Vat. Turc. 73).

E3 This place west of the Nile is the end (?) of the fortress of İbrim Sağîr.

E4 This fortress is known as İbrim-i Garbî (Western Ibrim) of the Copts. It was built by King Mukavkıs.

E15 The name of this fortress is İbrim of the Copts. It was built by the last Coptic king, King Mukavkıs, and conquered by 'Amr ibnü'l-'Âs. Now it is ruled from Cairo. It has a castle warden and more than 7000 soldiers ... of the governor.

Y391a Description of the ancient castle, city of Ibrim: It was built by King Mukavkıs, one of the Coptic kings. In the year of the Hijra (---) it was conquered after a two-month siege by several thousand Companions of the Prophet, including Amr ibnü'l-Âs, Ka'bü'l-Ahbâr, Ubeyde ibn Cerrâh, Câbirü'l-Ensâr, Ebû Hüreyre, Sâriyetü'l-Cebel and Esved ibn Mikdâd. It is a solidly-constructed fortress, small but strong, atop a bare hill that rises toward the heaven on the eastern shore of the Nile. It is pentagonal in shape, with a circumference of 800 paces.... It has a castle warden, 200 garrison troops and a splendid military band. The castle warden is one of the Müteferrika troops of Cairo, according to the *kanun* of Selim (I). Every year 300 men belonging to the seven corps are sent from Cairo to protect the fortress, and another 300 guards from the seven corps for the governor. They collect the state taxes and grain supplies and have exclusive control over the bureaus.

The mapmaker apparently misunderstood *Kabâbıta* as modifying the name of the city rather than the earlier kings. The castle as depicted on the map (lower left of the inset) is generic, not pentagonal as specified in the book (see Figure 10.3). The smaller forts on the other side of the Nile also called Ibrim (E3, if interpreted correctly, and E4, on the right side of the inset) are not mentioned in the book. These fit a pattern in the map of carrying over the toponomy to the other side of the Nile (cf. examples in The Funj Kingdom earlier and Vâdî Sübû' later). It remains to be studied whether this is simply a pattern in the mind of the mapmaker or whether it has a counterpart on the ground.

Ermen

F9 This place west of the Nile is the great city of Ermen. There are traces of its monuments that confound the beholder. The Coptic historians mention that Moses son of Imran was born here, and from fear of Pharaoh they were in this tranquil place.

Y445a A town near the Nile with 100 houses and one Friday mosque. The people are Shafi'is who perform the ritual prayer religiously. It was such a great city in ancient times that we were unable to traverse its monuments and wondrous and noteworthy domes and halls and palaces in a single day. The urban space was extremely large. Indeed, some reliable historians have written that Moses son of Imran was born in this city and that, from fear of Pharoah, they bound him atop a board and let him go in the Nile. By God's wisdom, as baby Moses floated past Pharoah's palace, Pharoah's wife Asiye took him and fed him. When Pharoah saw Moses he was pleased at the baby's sprightly movements and said nothing. It is a long story found in the chronicles of Tabari and all the Koran interpretations; there is no need to record it here.

The notice on the map is clearly an abbreviated version of the notice in the book.

Vâdî Sübû' (Wadi al-Sabua)

Figure 10.4 Vâdî Sübûa
Source: Vatican Library (Vat. Turc. 73).

F3 The mountains here are called Vadî Sübû' (Valley of Lions). In olden days it was reportedly a great city. The porphyry statues of lions as big as elephants, petrified, are still extant, and traces of construction are visible. One side of it is inhabited. There are 500 houses of reed and matting. The inhabitants are black Arabs.

F23 This place is called Vadî Sübû' (Valley of Lions), and also Fir'avn Sahrâsı (Plain of Pharaoh), because here on both sides of the Nile there are porphyry statues of lions as big as elephants—by God's command, they were petrified and turned to stone.

Y390a Noteworthy lions: In order to view this site we dismounted and let our horses graze and spent an hour touring the site. By God's wondrous power, on both sides of the Nile are lions of porphyry and granite, as big as elephants, in various poses and attitudes, several thousand of them broken in pieces and lying trampled in the sand and dust. Viewing them, one is overcome with terror, since the lions standing there firmly seem to be alive. They are such well-wrought statues.... [Also seven-headed dragons.] Apparently Moses battled with Pharaoh in this place and these are the beasts that his diviners and magicians conjured up.... [Cites Koran 7:107.] Apparently the carved beasts that we viewed are those that escaped being swallowed up by Moses's staff that turned into a serpent. Later, by God's command, they turned to stone.

The site on the map apparently includes the mountainous regions on both sides of the Nile, that on the eastern side (F3) having a village, and that on the western side (F23) having the ancient monuments (see Figure 10.4). In the latter, the mapmaker, with limited space at his disposal, compressed everything between 'lions as big as elephants' and 'turned to stone,' inserting in place of the suppressed passage the word *meshût*. This word, properly *meshût* meaning 'metamorphosed,' is used in Egypt to mean 'petrified, turned to stone by the wrath of God.' It is not found in the *Seyahatname*.

Kûştâmine

F26 This place is a city known as Kûştâmine. It has 200 reed houses. Its people are obedient. They have a mosque and a dervish convent, also a coffee house and a boza shop. Here the Zînûr(?) Künûz ... Senyâl Arabs, a people numbering around 2000, pass as Muslims. But their women do not cover themselves, they go around naked, it is not considered disgraceful.

Y389b–Y390a Tribe of Senyal: A people encamped in tents in a vast plain, totalling 2000 Muslims. Since they are Bedouin Arabs, their women's faces are naked.... Town of Kûştâmine: 200 peasant reed houses. Its people are obedient. They have a mosque and a dervish convent, also a coffee house and a boza shop. Here too a tribe of Künûz Arabs live in their tents.

The mapmaker has conflated two notices in the book and regarding the women being uncovered has added 'it is not considered disgraceful' (*ayıb değildir*), one of Evliya Çelebi's hallmark expressions.[19]

Kelâfîş

F27 In this place east of the Nile dwells the Arab tribe of Kelâpiş (Kelâfîş). It is a place of black rocks and many caves. These people live in caves. There are no date palms here and no crops are sown, it is only a black valley. There is agriculture in some places, because this place is toward ... They eat crocodiles and have sex with crocodiles. They are a ... people.

Y389b Tribes of the rebellious Kelâfîş: Among the Bedouin they are known as *kelâfîş* meaning 'They are nothing.' They have no tents but dwell in the caves that are in these cliffs. Their shaikh Çâdillâ showed us a Cave of Orphans that we entered with our horses and escaped from the heat. They are very cold caves.

These are a rebellious tribe of 3000 blacks in this black stony region. They have many goats but no other animals. They eat millet and camel flesh and *teys* meaning goats. They also make crocodile kebabs and eat them.

What is more, they have sex with female crocodiles. When they talk about sex with crocodiles their mouths water. They are a tough and tyrannical people from eating crocodiles. They are in possession of crocodile musk and crocodile gallstones. They remove the gallstones from the crocodiles' galls. At night they grasp these gallstones and are able to have sex with their wives 40 or 50 times. They can keep having sex as long as they do not let them out of their hands. Reportedly, their wives too have an undiminished appetite for sex as long as they keep them in their hands.

The Nile tributaries do not reach these places, and so there are no date palms and no berseem (Egyptian clover). The only produce is red millet. To make a living the people arm themselves and go into the Ethiopian mountains where they do battle with elephants. They take elephant tusks and rhinoceros horns to Ethiopia and sell them there and buy twilled cotton.

It is unclear why the mapmaker changes Kelâfîş to Kelâpiş.[20] Having very little space, he drastically reduces the sexual lore about crocodiles.[21]

Aswan

Figure 10.5   Aswan
Source: Vatican Library (Vat. Turc. 73).

G2 This place on the east bank of the Nile is the fortress of Aswan. It was built by 'Âd bin Şeddâd. It now has a castle warden and the garrison is appointed from Cairo. This place is the frontier of the Funj kingdom and the 'Urbân (or bedouin) Arabs. It is predominantly the frontier of the Bedouin Arabs.

G3 This fortress is called İsvân-ı sânî ('Second Aswan'). It was built by 'Âd bin Şeddâd. It now has a castle warden and the garrison is appointed from Cairo. It is the frontier of the Funj and the rebellious 'Urbân.

Y385a–b The fortress, on the summit of a lofty mountain on the shore of the Nile, is octagonal in shape, truly a Shaddadian structure. Its circumference is 3600 paces. It has three gates to the land and to the river. Within the fortress are around 500 squalid houses, large and small, with no orchards or gardens. It has a castle warden and a garrison of 150 soldiers, also a military band, an armory and 20 şâhî cannon. It is now a great frontier, since it is surrounded by rebellious Bedouin Arabs.

The book has a great deal more about Aswan. The mapmaker used only this portion, dealing with the fortification (see Figure 10.5). Having split Aswan in two (I don't know the reason for this—they are on the same side of the Nile, so it does not fit the pattern noted above) he repeated what he knew about the garrison and the frontier. Neither of the drawings bears any resemblance to the octagonal shape of the fortress mentioned in the book.

Luxor

Ha4 This place is called the town of Aksureyn (Luxor). It is a *kâşiflik* (provincial governorship) and in the (territory of the) 'Urbân (or bedouin) and the subdistrict (*nâhiye*) of Kûs, but it is not very built up (or prosperous). The one known as Ebu'l-Hac is buried there.

Y382b–383a Because of these two castles it was given this name, which means city of two castles. If I were to record the description of this great city as I observed it, I would run out of writing space, so it is better to abbreviate. It is an independent governorship in the province of Girga. With its garrison of 200 soldiers it obtains a grain-tax of 40 purses. There are no other guards or officials, also no mufti, superintendent of descendants of the Prophet, or notables.

It was a grandly built ancient city of 1200 houses on the shore of the Nile. Thousands of lofty buildings are still visible, with their skyscraping Vaults of Chosroes and countless domes and thousands of precious columns now trampled in the dust. The lofty columns used by past sultans to build their hans and grand mosques in Cairo all originated from here. And the four noteworthy lofty pillars inside the Süleymaniyye in Istanbul were brought from this city to Alexandria on the Nile by rafts.... Sultan Süleyman himself went to see these pillars as they were raised according to the science of mechanics from ships at Unkapanı and accompanied them to Vefa Square, giving some instructions. I heard this from my late father, whose life goes back to the time of Süleyman. In short, such rosy columns have gone from the city of Luxor to Cairo and to Istanbul. And still countless porphyry columns lie there toppled and trampled.

The present city, however, is not very built up. There are 20 prayer-niches, three of which have the Friday sermon. The one with a large congregation is the Mosque of Ebülhaccâc in the marketplace. There is a han and public bath, a number of busy dervish lodges, a primary school, water dispensary and coffee houses. The climate is very fine and the people are very poor.

In the book Evliya goes on to describe his visit to the shrine of Ebülhaccâc, apparently the only touristic activity in Luxor in those days. The mapmaker mentions this shrine but omits information on the ancient city.

Mountain of Birds

Hb15 This is a mountainous region, with large mountains and caves. And in those caves are millions of storks, buried and preserved. Once a year all the storks in the world come to this place and visit this mountain, because the talismans of the storks are here.

Y369b–370b Description of the Mountain of the Birds [It is also called Mt Taylimun]: It is a wondrous spectacle. The tongue falls short at describing this great mountain. Every year in the spring several hundred thousand birds of various—but mainly storks and goldfinches—come from the direction of Turkey and settle on this mountain. The mountain plains swarm with them, so that one can hardly find a place to set one's foot, and their cries are loud enough to make one's gall bladder burst. The people of the region are aware of the spectacle and come to view it from a distance; but no one can seize any of the birds or throw stones at them. On top of the mountain, on a sandy plain, is a cemetery. Each sarcophagus contains thousands of birds of various sorts—but mainly storks—buried in their shrouds (that is, mummified). The (living) birds all come to visit this cemetery, circling above it and squawking and lamenting. Then they land in the mountain plains. Most of the buried birds are visible outside the graveyard. Their bodies and feathers are fresh and have not decayed inside their shrouds, which are made of date-palm fibers. No one knows the reason why these birds are buried here in their shrouds. Nor have I seen it mentioned in any of the histories. This humble one actually brought two of these mummified birds to Kethüda Ibrahim Pasha so he could see them.

Evliya goes on at great length about the birds' behaviour at this place and about bird migration. The notice on the map is a drastically reduced version of the account given in the book.[22]

Deyr Kıbtî

Figure 10.6   Deyr Kıbtî
Source: Vatican Library (Vat. Turc. 73).

İ20 In this place is a Coptic monastery, founded during the time of Moses. It is a very noteworthy ancient Pharaonic structure.

Y363b–364a Opposite Semennut on the other side of the Nile is a church known as Deyr Kıbtî, like the fortress of Kahkaha at the summit of a lofty cliff. Believing it to be a Pharaonic construction, the Copts make an annual 'pilgrimage' to it—saving the comparison!—and its monks obtain an Egyptian Treasure's worth of money. The western side of its sheer cliff stretches over the Nile like an elephant's trunk, with the blessed Nile flowing underneath. The monks atop this cliff draw water from the Nile with firm ropes 100 fathoms long and fill the cisterns. If anyone climbs up for the view, they treat him as an honored guest and bring him a breakfast consisting of the staff of life (*can otu*, lit. grass of life), which is bread, and bird's milk, which is eggs, and honey. They bring the guests bedclothes of silk and brocade and their Magian boys (that is, servants) provide all sorts of services.

The mapmaker as usual omitted all the personal adventure and stylistic flourishes characteristic of the book. But he also added something that is not in the book (see Figure 10.6). From the information on the Pharaonic structure, he deduced that it was founded in the time of Moses. Were the structure depicted not on the Nile but closer to the Red Sea coast, it might be identified with the Monastery of St Anthony.

Mediterranean Coast

A curious feature of this part of the map is the depiction of the Mediterranean coast paralleling the Nile on the western (right hand) side, just as the Red Sea parallels it on the eastern (left hand) side. Thus, opposite Fayyum, we find Hadra 'in the Maghreb,' Kairouan 'under the rule of Tunis' and Sousse; then, opposite the pyramids and Cairo, Barca 'where coral is brought up from the sea, under the rule of Tunis' and the island of Djerba; and opposite Gize, Tripoli. The area around Cairo is stretched out, while the thousand-mile distance between Cairo and Tunisia across the Sahara Desert is compressed to almost nothing and the Mediterranean coast is twisted southeastward to run parallel to the Nile.

It is tempting to treat the phenomenon on the Nile map as indicative of the mapmaker's limited mental geography. And we may recall that Evliya thought there was a western branch of the Nile that went to the Maghreb. On the other hand, it is perhaps more fruitful to examine the phenomenon as one (perhaps extreme) example of the stretching and compressing of spatial topography observable in this map.

Pyramids

Figure 10.7 Pyramids and Barca
Source: Vatican Library (Vat. Turc. 73).

Ja5 This place is the pyramids. They were built before the Flood, on the hope that they would be saved from the Flood, but they were not saved. From here the road to Feyyûm is through the mountains, traversed by caravans.

Y232a A marvel, the mountain of the Pyramids: One hour from the town of Gize on the west bank of the Nile are the three 'mountains' known as the pyramids. They are the tallest and most ancient buildings on the face of the earth. They are huge man-made mountains, each one a veritable Mt Qaf.... Some chroniclers say they were built before the Flood by 'Ad ibn Shaddad. Others maintain that before the Flood, King Surid, at the urging of his soothsayers, built them as a tomb for himself. When they were finished he filled the three pyramids with treasure, put in weapons, and also placed therein the books of all the sciences written by the prophet Idris. He set up talismans and guardians (?) and covered the pyramids with brocade, making them a hidden treasure. He also built a great city on the shore of the Nile where the guards of the pyramids resided. Every year, in spring, all the people of the world came and circumambulated the pyramids, as they do the Ka'ba ...

Again, the book has much more on the pyramids, including a large dose of personal adventure.[23] Instead, the mapmaker substituted a different version of the relation of the pyramids to the flood, and added a topographical note not in the book (see Figure 10.7).

Footstep of the Prophet and Dam of Cânpûlâdzâde Hüseyn Pasha

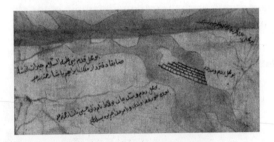

Figure 10.8   Footstep of the Prophet, Dam and Barrier
Source: Vatican Library (Vat. Turc. 73).

Jb1 This place is the Footstep of the Prophet, a charitable foundation built by the former Defterdâr Melek İbrâhîm Paşa, may God have mercy upon him.

Y115b–116b Description of the dervish lodge of the Footstep of the Prophet: In the year 1074 (1663–4) Defterdâr İbrâhîm Paşa, for love of the messenger of God, Muhammad Mustafa, set aside 50 Egyptian purses of his own money and constructed a lofty dome above the Footstep of the Prophet, and attached thereto a large Friday mosque at the description of which the tongue falls short.

Ja7 This place is a dam and barrier.

Jb2 This place is the dam and barrier of Canbulatzade Hüseyn Paşa. Afterward it became a tributary and, by God's command, nourished an island (?).

Q351a–P345a Afterwards our lord Hüseyn Paşa governed for two full years, administering justice, so that the province of Egypt enjoyed great Ottoman security and plenty. He had a great trench dug from the Nilometer to Kademü'n-Nebî, a distance of 80,000 royal cubits, employing 70,000–80,000 men and 10,000 buffaloes, allowing the Nile to flow in front of Eski Mısır (Fustat) as far as Bulaq, so grain ships could fearlessly approach the Anbâr-ı Yûsuf. He also constructed two dams on the Nile in the territory of Giza, in front of Kademü'n-Nebî and Beled-i Besâtîn. Each one entered the Nile a distance of 100 cubits and was 80 cubits high and 50 cubits broad. This humble one commemorated them in the following chronogram:

When Evliyâ saw its foundation
He uttered its date: 'A great construction' (*binâ-yı azîm*) Year (---)

In short, they are noteworthy dams and tributary trenches, beyond human capacity.

The book has much more about the mosque at the Footstep of the Prophet. The report about the dam in the book comes just after Evliya's account of the removal from office of Kethüda Ibrahim Pasha and the arrival of the new governor, Cânpûlâdzâde Hüseyn Pasha, in 1673 (see Figure 10.8).

Cairo

The map depicts an urban area stretching from the Nilometer on the island of Roda, through the aqueduct of Sultan Gavri, Old Cairo or Fustat, the city walls of Cairo, and the Karâfe cemeteries, ending at Kubbe-i 'Azebân. Only the notice on Fustat has something more than the bare essentials:

Jb3 This place is Old Cairo, formerly known as the city of Fustat. When first ruled by the Umayyads it reportedly had 7000 public baths. A man would get up in the morning and go to the bath to wash up, but he would find no room because of the crowd, so he would go around from bath to

Figure 10.9   Cairo
Source: Vatican Library (Vat. Turc. 73).

bath, finally finding a place at the 120th bath. Judge from that how magnificent a city Old Cairo, i.e. Fustat, was in olden days, and how populous it was with Muslims; may God have mercy on them.

This peroration on the baths of Fustat is not found in the book, which otherwise has quite a bit about Cairo baths (Y117a–118b). The book, of course, has a huge amount of material on Cairo, the Karafe cemeteries, the Nilometer, and so on; but barely mentions the aqueduct of Gavri and the Kubbe-i 'Azebân.

> *Y128b* (Ch. 37, on fountains): The upper citadel has a total of 21 fountains, all of them fed by the aqueduct of 360 arches extending from the blessed Nile, a charitable work of Sultan Gavri.... Another fountain is the water-of-life fountain with a lofty dome and six steps leading down, in the middle of the Azeb barracks. It has two waterspouts side by side, each as thick as one's arm. This too is [an endowment of] Gavri.

The one monument within the Cairo city walls that is labelled on the map is Bi'r-i Yûsuf (Joseph's Well) (see Figure 10.9). This construction by Saladin (Salâhaddin Yûsuf) is clearly something that impressed Evliya, who has a detailed description of it in the book (Y84b-85a), ending:

Y85a In sum, the world traveler who has not seen this Joseph's Well has no idea of what craftsmanship there is in the world and what a noble creature man is and what miraculous things he is capable of.

The Delta

A curious feature of this part of the map is that some very important places are missing. Amidst the several hundred villages and towns that are listed, one looks in vain for Tanta, Mahalletü'l-kebîr, Âbyâr, and Mansûra, all of which Evliya visited and devoted long sections to in the book.

Tanta especially was important to Evliya for its annual festival of saint Seyyid Ahmed el-Bedevi, to which he devotes a particularly long and rich description (Y177b–295a). Of Mahalletü'l-kebîr (al-Mahalla al-Kubrâ), Evliya asserts that it is the second-largest city in Egypt, after Cairo and before Rosetta and Damietta (Y355b). The closest place to Mahalle that is shown on the map is La40 Semennût[24]—a mere two hours away (Y358b).

The reason seems to be that in this part of the map Evliya only lists the towns and villages that are directly located on the major Nile tributaries.

For the same reason, Demenhur is not on the map, although it is mentioned in the following (see Figure 10.10):

Figure 10.10 Tur'at Seyfüddin
Source: Vatican Library (Vat. Turc. 73).

Kb5 This place is the tributary known as Seyfü'd-dîn. It waters the clime of Buhayre and connects to Demenhur. The entrepot known as Demenhur is in this place.

Needless to say, in the book Evliya has a lot to say about Demenhur (Y304b–310a).

Rahmâniye/Shrine of İbrâhim-i Dessûkî

Kc11 This place named Rahmâniyye is the shrine of Seyyid İbrâhim-i Dessûkî.
Y301a–304a Description of the town of İbrâhîm-i Dessûkî.
Y304b Town of Rahmâniye.

The book has a lengthy description of the shrine and the associated *mevlud*. The mapmaker omits that and also compresses into one entry what is in two entries in the book. Properly, Rahmâniye is across the river from Dessûk, between Merkas [Murquṣ] and Şumrûhat [Sumukhraṭ].

Ciddiye to Şumrûhât

Figure 10.11   Ciddiye to Şumrûhât
Source: Vatican Library (Vat. Turc. 73).

Kb18–19, 23–29 Şumrûhat, Şurum Beg; 'Atıf, Deyrût, İtfibe (*İdfine), Diyey, Mahalle-i Emîr, Hemmân(?), Ciddiye
   Kc12–20 Mahalle-i Mâlik, Sâlimiyye, Şürefe, Füvve, Sindiyûn, Fezâre, Mutûbis, İmşîre (*Cemşîre), Mîrî Bal (*Birimbal)
   Y337a–338a Beled-i Hadiyye (*Ciddiye) ... Kasaba-i Mahalletü'l-emîr ... opposite this in the territory of Garbiyye, the delightful city of Birimbâl ... opposite this one mile up in the territory of Buhayre, the town of Mahalle-i

Diyey ... one mile up again in the territory of Buhayre on the bank of the Nile, the town of İdfîne ... opposite this in the territory of Garbiyye, the town of Mahalle-i Mutûbis ... one mile up from this city in the territory of Garbiyye, Mahalle-i Cemşîre ... opposite this in the territory of Buhayre, Mahalle-i Fezâre ... in this place the blessed Nile turns sharply to the east. Two miles above that again in the territory of Buhayre, Mahalle-i Deyrût ... opposite this in the territory of Garbiyye opposite this in the territory of Mahalle-i Sindiyûn ... andan bir mîl yukaru Buhayre hâkinde Mahalle-i ma'mûr-ı Atıf ... one mile up in the territory of Garbiyye, the town of Füvve ... opposite this is an island, encompassed by the Nile, known as Cezîretü'z-zeheb ... one mile above this island again in the territory of Garbiyye, Mahalle-i Şürefâ ... opposite this in the territory of Buhayre, Mahalle-i Şurum Beg ... opposite this in the territory of Garbiyye, Mahalle-i Sâlimiyye ... one mile up again in the territory of Garbiyye, Mahalle-i Mâlik ... opposite this city in the territory of Buhayre, Mahalle-i Şumuhzât.

This sample of an area of the western branch of the Nile shows the intimate relation between the map and Evliya's itinerary in the book (see Figure 10.11). At the same time, there are several examples of misreadings or misunderstandings of place names, as well as other discrepancies.

We can follow the itinerary starting from Ciddiye (lower right on the inset). The itinerary seems to skip the next item on the map, Hemmân(?), going directly to Mahalletü'l-emîr. We then cross the river to Birimbal; (re)cross to Diyey; continue one mile up to İdfîne; cross the river to Mutûbis and continue one mile up to Cemşîre—but on the map these two are reversed (Shamshīra is actually south of Mūtūbīs). According to the itinerary, we then (re)cross to the Buhayre side and go to Fezâre—but the map mistakenly shows Fezâre on the Garbiyye side. Evliya says that at this point the Nile takes a sharp turn to the east, which is perhaps the source of the confusion. Next on the Buhayre side is Deyrût. We cross the river to Sindiyûn; (re)cross to 'Atıf. Back on the Garbiyye side the itinerary continues with Füvve. Evliya says that opposite Füvve is a small island called Cezîretü'z-zeheb (not shown on the map). We continue up to Şürefâ; cross over to Şurum Beg; (re)cross to Sâlimiyye; go one mile up to Mahalle-i Mâlik; and finally cross back over to Mahalle-i Şumuhzât.

This exercise leaves the strong impression that the drawing up of the map and the recording of the itinerary in the book were done at the same time.

The form in Y338a, Q290a Şûmûhzât is erroneous for Şûmûhrât. The form on the map is smudged but can be tentatively read as Şumrûhat. The form on modern maps is Sumuhrat. The form in

Y336b, Q289b Ḥadiyye is erroneous for Ciddiye. These are two cases where the form on the map is more accurate than the form in the book.

Bi'r Matariyye

La1 The place known as Matariyye.

La2 This place is Bi'r Matariyye, one of the miracles of Jesus. Mary came to this place with Jesus and asked the villagers for water, but they refused. She put Jesus down on the ground and went in search of water, but could not find any. When she came back she saw that water had emerged from Jesus's two hands and made a circle and become a well (?). Mary prayed that if the villagers drank this water it would be bitter, but if anyone else drank it, it would be sweet. And so it was, by God's command.

Y227a Picnic Grounds and Shrine of Bi'r Matariyye: Two hours north of Cairo amidst orchards and gardens, a place empowered by the vision of Jesus. There were great buildings here when Egypt was in the hands of the Greeks; now only a vault and a dervish lodge are left. There is also a basin where all those who are sick bathe and find a cure. It is recorded in all the Greek chronicles that Jesus and his mother Mary migrated from the city of Nablus and settled here. And the Christians claim that Jesus and his mother dug this well of Matariyye and bathed in it, and that this basin is their construction. And that is correct, because all the wells of Egypt are bitter, but this well of Matariyye is sweet since it is a miracle of the Messenger of God.

The accounts in the book and on the map are very different.

Damietta

Figure 10.12   Damietta
Source: Vatican Library (Vat. Turc. 73).

Lb26 This place is the city known as the entrepot of Dimyât (Damietta). It was founded by Zü'lyezen son of Mısrâyim son of Ham son of Noah.

Lb27 This place east of the Nile is the ancient fortress of Dimyât (Damietta).

Lb23 This is the fortress recently constructed at the western strait of the Nile, built by Sultan Ahmed son of Sultan Mehemmed.

Y344b–348b Description of the great city and entrepot of Ancient Dimyât: ... It was built after the flood by a great ruler named Dimyât, one of the sons of İşma'ûn b. Mısrâyim.

Y348b Three miles below that, again on the Dimyât side, where the blessed Nile flows into the Mediterranean. Description of Ancient Dimyât, bulwark of the Nile: It was built by the conqueror of Egypt himself, Sultan Selim I, in the year (---), at the hands of Hayra Bey, the first governor of the newly conquered province of Egypt. There is no trace of the earlier fortress conquered by Aswad b. Miqdâd at the time of Amr b. al-Âs. At present this fortress is a solid square-shaped building on a sandy place at the promontory where the Nile flows into the Mediterranean. It is 500 paces in diameter and has four towers at the four corners ...

Y349a Opposite this eastern castle, on the shore of the Nile: Description of the Western Castle opposite the Eastern Castle: It was built during the reign of Sultan Ahmed by Tavâşî Müteferrika Ca'fer Ağa using his own money, for the sake of God. However, it has become known as the Castle of Abdüssamed. It is a small round castle on the shore of the Nile. Later a large redoubt was added outside the wall and the castle became even stronger.

The two castles as depicted on the map are generic, not square and round as specified in the book (see Figure 10.12). Nor do their relative sizes and dimensions correspond. Zü'lyezen is clearly a misreading of İşma'ûn. In the book, Evliya says that when he inspected the Western Castle he discovered that seven garrison soldiers were missing and sent a report with their names to the Pasha.

Alexandria and Rosetta

Figure 10.13 Alexandria and Rosetta
Source: Vatican Library (Vat. Turc. 73).

Kb38 Fortress of Alexandria.
Kb36 Pillar of the Mast.
Kb44 This place is the fortress of Ebûkîr.
Kb46 This place is the entrepot of Reşîd (Rosetta). In the city and (?) its surroundings are date groves.
Kb45 This place is the village of Köm Efrâh and the shrine of Shaikh *Mansûr.
Y319b–324b (Alexandria), *329b–330b* (Ebûkîr), *332b–335b* (Reşîd, Köm Efrâh).

Pillar of the Mast (*'Amûd-i Sârî*—see Figure 10.13) is not mentioned in the book, which does, however, describe the obelisk (*dikilitaş*)—one of 'Cleopatra's needles'—500 paces east from Galleon Harbour (*kalyon limanı*) in a ruined area with many fallen columns:

Y321a These columns are called Cârûdü'l-Mü'tefikî. They are noteworthy monuments, constructed to serve as talismans during the period of the prophet Solomon. Some were built by Ya'mer b. Şeddâd.

According to Piri Reis (348b–350a; Mantran, 293–295 + Figure 3), the 'mast' (Ar. *sarî* or *sarâ*) was set up as a marker on the island west of the city known as Island of the Mast (Direk Adası in Turkish, Jazîrat al-Sarâ in Arabic). Both authors must be referring to what is known today as Pompey's Pillar (actually erected in 293 for Diocletian, not for Pompey).

* * *

These comparisons show that the map and the book, while intimately related, are conceived as separate works with different aims. The *Seyahatname* seeks to record all of Evliya Çelebi's travels and explorations in great detail, with full attention to historical, administrative, and ethnographic aspects of the places described; it is expansive in nature, a travel narrative with encyclopedic aspirations. The map is limited in scope and focused on the topographical. Still, the two are obviously the product of the same mind and reflect the same attitudes and preoccupations.

With regard to the map, at this stage of our research we have concentrated on textual and philological concerns, trying to get an accurate reading of all the entries and establishing their relationship with the corresponding texts in the book. At a later stage, now that a usable edition is in hand, we can turn to more interesting questions: What accounts for the discrepancies between the map and the book? How accurate is the map in its topographical information? What does the map teach us about this region of the world at that historical moment? And what can we extrapolate about the mentality of the map's author and about the Ottoman cultural universe? For now, my contention is that the Nile River runs through both of these monuments—volume 10 of the *Seyahatname* and Vat. Turc. 73—like a red thread. It is the organizing principle of both works, providing structure and pattern for a myriad of heterogeneous details. The two were conceived and executed together, as the twin culminations of a fifty-year career of travel, exploration and writing.

Notes

1. For reasons not yet understood, he dates the beginning of this second journey (Y360b) to the year 1082 of the Hijra, corresponding to 1671-2—the same year that he was travelling in Syria and the Hijaz in volume 9. He gives the date of his return to Cairo from Upper Egypt as 1 Muharrem 1084/18 April 1673 (Q350a). The dates in 1083/1672 that he mentions in connection with the Mevluds in Lower Egypt (Y277b, 307b) cannot be squared with the dates he gives for this second expedition.

   References to the *Seyahatname* are to the 'Yıldız' manuscript of vol. 10 (İstanbul Üniversitesi Kütüphanesi Türkçe Yazmalar 5973). Occasionally I cite passages not found in this manuscript, in which case the references are to manuscripts P and Q (Süleymaniye Kütüphanesi Pertev Paşa 462 and Süleymaniye Kütüphanesi Hacı Beşir Ağa 452). All of the references may be located in the critical edition of vol. 10: Seyit Ali Kahraman, Dağlı Yücel and Robert Dankoff, eds. *Evliya Çelebi Seyahatnamesi 10. Kitap* (Istanbul: Yapı Kredi Yayınları, 2007). References to vol. 9 (signaled by IX) are also to the 'Yıldız' manuscript (Topkapı Sarayı Kütüphanesi Bağdat 306) and can be located in the critical edition of vol. 9: Dağlı Yücel, Seyit Ali Kahraman, and Robert Dankoff, eds. *Evliya Çelebi Seyahatnamesi 9. Kitap* (Istanbul: Yapı Kredi Yayınları, 2005).

2. Ettore Rossi, 'A Turkish Map of the Nile River, about 1685', *Imago Mundi* 6 (1949), pp. 73-5. Rossi provided the following information:

   The map (Vat. Turc. 73) is 543 cm long, 45 cm wide in the southern and 88 cm wide in the northern half; it is drawn upon rough cloth and represents the Valley of the Nile from its sources at the fabulous Mountains of the Moon to the Mediterranean Sea between the Red Sea and the Libyan Desert. The map has suffered injuries from time and seems to have been eaten by mice: in some parts there are lacunas.

   Rossi went on to describe the contents of the map in rough outline and to speculate on its date and authorship. He pointed out that it must have been composed around 1685, the death date of Defterdâr Melek İbrâhîm Paşa who is mentioned on the map as having passed away. Rossi also noted the 'strict correspondence' between the contents of the map and volume 10 of the *Seyahatname*. He suggested that 'the map was drawn in connection with Evliyá Celebî's book by one of his readers, perhaps by a person of the author's suite.'

3. Robert Dankoff and Nuran Tezcan, *Evliya Celebi'nin Nil Haritası 'Durr-i bi-misil in ahbar-ı Nil'* (Istanbul: Yapı Kredi Yayınları, 2011).

4. J.H. Kramers, 'al-Nīl', *EI2* 8: p. 37. For an illustration of the Strasbourg ms of al-Khwārazmī's map and other Arab maps of the Nile, see J.B. Harley and David Woodward, eds, *Cartography in the Traditional Islamic and South Asian Societies, The History of Cartography* (Chicago: University of Chicago Press, 1987), vol. 2, book 1, plate 4 and figs 7.10–7.13, 7.17–7.18. See also Konrad Miller, *Mappae Arabicae* (Stuttgart, 1926); repr. (Wiesbaden: L. Reichert, 1986), pp. 59–62: 'Die arabische Darstellung der Nilquellen und des Nillaufes' (Tafelband: Tafeln), pp. 2–7.

5. For a stylized and abbreviated seventeenth-century map of the Nile in this tradition, see Nebes Norbert et al., *Orientalische Buchkunst in Gotha: Ausstellung zum 350 jährigen Jubiläum der Forschungs-und Landesbibliothek Gotha* (Gotha: Forschungs-und Landesbibliothek Gotha, 1997), pp. 168–9.

6. See A Bombaci, 'Il viaggio in Abissinia di Evliyā Čelebī (1673)', *AIUON*, NS 2 (1943): pp. 259–75; Maria Teresa Petti Suma, 'Il Viaggio in Sudan di Evliya Čelebi (1671–72)', *AIUON*, NS 14 (1964): pp. 432–52; Erich Prokosch, *Ins Land der geheimnisvollen Func: Des türkischen Weltenbummlers Evliyā Çelebi Reise durch Oberägypten und den Sudan nebst der osmanischen Provinz Habeş in den Jahren 1672/73* (Graz: Styria, 1994); John O. Udal, *The Nile in Darkness: Conquest and Exploration 1504–1862* (Wilby, Norwich: M. Russell, 1998), pp. 17–35; Intisar Elzein, Ottoman Archaeology of the Middle Nile Valley in the Sudan', in *The Frontiers of the Ottoman World*, ed. A.C.S. Peacock (Oxford: Oxford University Press, 2009), pp. 371–83.
    Petti Suma was the first scholar to have made use of Vat. Turc. 73 in studying the *Seyahatname*. Udal followed suit (with acknowledgment to Professor Ménage). Elzein, in her recent survey, states (p. 383): 'In terms of documentary research, a more detailed study of the text of Evliya Çelebi as well as the Vatican map than has been undertaken to date is needed.'

7. See John Alexander, 'The Turks on the Middle Nile', *ANM* 7 (1996): pp. 15–35; Martin Hinds and Hamdi Sakkout, *Arabic Documents from the Ottoman Period from Qaşr Ibrīm* (London: Egypt Exploration Society, 1986).

8. See especially Svat Soucek, *Piri Reis and Turkish Mapmaking after Columbus: The Khalili Portolan Atlas* (Oxford: Oxford University Press, 1996), pp. 149–58. The original 1521 and 1526 versions of these mappings are not extant. Some later copies have been published as follows:

- ? [late sixteenth century] (Topkapı Sarayı Müzesi Kütüphanesi ms H. 642, fol. 352): M. Rogers, 'Itineraries and Town Views in Ottoman Histories', in *Cartography in the Traditional Islamic and South Asian Societies, The History of Cartography*, eds. J.B. Harley and David Woodward (Chicago: University of Chicago Press, 1987), vol. 2, book 1, p. 232.
- 1574 (Ayasofya Kütüphanesi ms 2612, 347b–362a): Piri Reis, *Kitabı Bahriye*, eds. F. Kurdoğlu and H. Alpagot (Ankara, 1935); Piri Reis, *Kitab-i Bahriye*, ed. Ertuğrul Zekai Ökte, 4 vols (Istanbul: Historical Research Foundation, 1988), vol. 4.
- 1628–9 (Nuruosmaniye ms 2997, 166b) Mine Esiner Özen, *Piri Reis and his Charts* (Istanbul, 1998), p. 62.
- Circa 1670 (Khalili ms 718, 48b–49a): Soucek, *Piri Reis and Turkish Mapmaking*, pl. 16, 27.
- ? (İstanbul Üniversitesi Kütüphanesi Türkce Yazmalar 6605); *Evliya Çelebi Seyahatnamesi, onuncu cilt* (Istanbul: Devlet Basımevi, 1938), after pp. XXVIII, and 668; Özdemir Kemal, *Ottoman Nautical Charts and the Atlas of Ali Macar Reis* (Istanbul: Creative Yayıncılık ve Tanıtım, 1992), pl. 26.
- Circa 1730 (Walters Art Museum, ms W658): available at http://art. thewalters.org/viewwoa.aspx?id=19195.

9. For this section of Piri Reis's book, see Robert Mantran, 'La Description des Côtes de l'Égypte dans le *Kitâb-ı Bahriye* de Pîrî Reis', *AI* 17 (1981): pp. 287–310.

10. Entries marked with asterisk (*) in the second column are reconstructed from the forms in the text, miscopied (according to our hypothesis) from the original. For this section of Evliya's journey, see also Paola Cirillo, 'Evliyâ Çelebî in Egitto: Il viaggio da Rosetta al Cairo', *AIUON* 53, no. 1 (1993): pp. 1–34. And see the section later titled 'Ciddiye to Şumrûhât'.

11. See Gottfried Hagen,'Kâtib Çelebi and Sipahizade', in *Essays in Honour of Ekmeleddin İhsanoğlu*, ed. Mustafa Kaçar and Zeynep Durukal (Istanbul: Research Centre for Islamic History, Art, and Culture, 2006), pp. 525–42, fig. 3. This is Kâtib Çelebi's autograph, which Hagen discovered in the University of Michigan Library. For some later copies, see Dorothea Duda, *Islamische Handschriften II Teil 2: Die Handschriften in türkischer Sprache* (Wien: Verlag der Österreichischen Akademie der Wissenschaften, 2008), fig. 243, 246.

12. For example, Y157b: *Ammâ Nîl'in ma'mûr [u] âbâdân yerleri Sây kal'ası ve Der şehri ve İbrîm kal'ası ve Şellâl vilâyeti ve İsvân ve İsne ve şehr-i Kûs ve şehr-i Kınâ ve Füvve ve Circe'ye, andan bâlâda tahrîr olunan Mısır'a varınca şehirler ve Dimyât ve Reşîd'e varınca Nîl'in iki cânibi kat-ender-kat ma'mûr [u] âbâdândır. Tevârîh-i Hıtat'da ve Hey'et-i Papamunta ve Atlas ve Minor ve Coğrafiyye kitâblarında Mısır'ın berren ve bahren eşkâliyle âbâdân yerlerin*

tahrîr eylemişlerdir. Cf. Gottfried Hagen, 'Ottoman Understandings of the World in the Seventeenth Century', afterword in Robert Dankoff, *An Ottoman Mentality: The World of Evliya Çelebi* (Leiden: Brill, 2004), pp. 207–48, p. 228n43.

13. See B. Blanc et al., 'A Propos de la Carte du Caire de Matheo Pagano', *AI* 17 (1981): pp. 203–85. Ferrandeo Bertelli's map is reproduced in Soucek, *Piri Reis and Turkish Mapmaking*, pl. 16. For Jan Jansson's map titled *Ægypti recentior descriptio: Ægyptis & Turcis Elchibith, Arabibus Mesre & Misri, Hebræis Mitsraim,* see http://ids.lib.harvard.edu/ids/view/13501006?buttons=Y.

14. See Pierre A. MacKay, 'The Manuscripts of the *Seyahatname* of Evliya Çelebi, Part I: The Archetype', *Der Islam* 52 (1975): pp. 278–98; Robert Dankoff, 'Şu Rasadı Yıkalım mı? Evliya Çelebi ve Filoloji', in *Evliya Çelebi ve Seyahatname,* eds. Tezcan Nuran and Kadir Atlansoy (Gazimağusa: Doğu Akdeniz Üniversitesi, 2002), pp. 99–118; English original as 'Shall We Tear Down That Observatory: Evliya Çelebi and Philology', in *From Mahmud Kaşgari to Evliya Çelebi: Studies in Middle Turkic and Ottoman Literatures* by Robert Dankoff (Istanbul: Isis, 2008), pp. 329–51.

15. Petti Suma, 'Il Viaggio in Sudan', p. 434. And see Udal, *The Nile in Darkness,* p. 20. Udal's study is a heroic attempt to reconcile the information on the map with that provided in the *Seyahatname* and by later travellers such as Burckhardt. See further Elzein, 'Ottoman Archaeology', pp. 376–82.

16. Reading *çokdur,* not *yokdur* as Petti Suma, 'Il Viaggio in Sudan', p. 441 'non vi sono moschee ...'

17. With few exceptions, wherever there is a drawing of a walled city, there is mention of *kal'e* in the accompanying text. The inverse is true as well in most of the map, but there are quite a few *kal'es* in Zone M that lack an accompanying drawing.

18. The slapdash use of figures is actually a feature of Evliya's style; see Dankoff, *Ottoman Mentality,* pp. 154–8.

19. See Robert Dankoff, 'Ayıp değil! (No Disgrace!)', *JTL* 5 (2008): pp. 77–90; Turkish translation as: 'Ayıp Değil!' in *Çağının Sıradışı Yazarı Evliya Çelebi,* ed. Tezcan Nuran (Istanbul: Yapı Kredi Yayınları, 2009), pp. 109–22.

20. Petti Suma, 'Il Viaggio in Sudan', p. 44n43 identifies this with the tribe of Kabâbîsh.

21. For more on this topic see Dankoff, 'Ayıp değil!'; Robert Dankoff and Sooyong Kim, *An Ottoman Traveller: Selections from the Book of Travels of Evliya Çelebi* (London: Eland, 2010), pp. 390–2.

22. See Dankoff and Kim, *An Ottoman Traveller,* pp. 436–9. This Jabal al-Tayr/Taylimun is mentioned by several of the earlier Arab geographers and also by Evliya's Turkish predecessor Mehmed Aşık and his German contemporary Johann Michael Vansleb. See Jean-Louis Bacqué-Grammont and Catherine Mayeur-Jaouen, '*Evliyâ Çelebi Seyahatnâmesi*'nde

Çeşitli Kaynakların Kavşak Noktası: Mısır'daki Kuşlar Dağı', in *Evliyâ Çelebi'nin Sözlü Kaynakları*, ed. Öcal Oğuz (Ankara: UNESCO Türkiye Millî Komisyonu, 2012), pp. 1–8, available at https://www.scribd.com/doc/269229356/Evliya-CelebiSozlu-Kaynakları.

23. See Ulrich Haarmann, 'Evliyā Čelebīs Bericht über die Altertümer von Gize', *Turcica* 8, no. 1 (1976): pp. 157–230; Dankoff and Kim, *An Ottoman Traveller*, pp. 403–6.

24. This is a village in the Delta (modern Samannūd, ancient Sebennytos), not to be confused with two other Semennûts, both in Upper Egypt: Hb4 (Samhūd) and İ9 (Şamalūṭ).

V

TURKISH CONNECTION OF THE SAFAVIDS

11

REVISITING SAFAVID ORIGINS IN LIGHT OF SOME CONTEMPORARY DOCUMENTS

Ali Anooshahr

Throughout the 'middle' and 'early modern' periods of Islamic history (about 1000 to 1750 CE), Sufi orders played a major role in the society, culture, economics, and politics of western Asia. However, in one case, a Sufi order captured the very seat of power and converted itself into a veritable bureaucratic empire. The order was known as the Safavids, originating in the city of Ardabil (north-western Iran), and the empire named after it was roughly in present-day Iran and the Caucasus for over two centuries.

The larger-than-life apocalyptic charisma of the dynasty's founder Shah Isma'il has caused many modern scholars to evaluate early Safavid history as a teleology of revolutionary millenarian propaganda that reached its completion at the beginning of the sixteenth century. Few have seriously questioned the 'personality' and 'religious' explanations of the events provided in sixteenth- and seventeenth-century Persian chronicles. The objective of this chapter is to question and problematize the immediate background of the Safavids prior to Shah Isma'il's emergence through the utilization of a number of contemporary but neglected sources. Isma'il's father Haydar and his grandfather Junayd were very much products, and almost victims, of social and economic processes in the formation of which they played no role at all. Once pushed on to the historical stage by chance and with the unintended consequences of developments far beyond their control, they made the best of a bad situation with little success. The charges of heresy and sedition, interpreted today as religious ideology and revolution, were applied by their contemporaries only after their murders as justification. Finally, their Anatolian supporters did not simply consist of Turcoman tribes of religious devotees.

Modern Scholarship

Modern scholars of the early Safavids acknowledge that Shaykh Junayd, the grandfather of the future Shah Isma'il, began the political activity of the order, that this activity was subsequently presided over by his son Shaykh Haydar, and that it was finally brought to completion under his grandson Shah Isma'il. This broad thesis is, however, modified by minor disagreements that fall into two categories. There are those who believe that Junayd used the teachings of his Sufi order as a political ideology. The earliest proponent of this view was Franz Babinger who combined the history of two events at the beginning and end of the fifteenth century—the rebellion of Shaykh Badr al-Din and that of the Safavids—as interrelated ideological phenomena brought about by the pressures of war and civil strife.[1] Some years later, Walther Hinz asserted that Junayd had indeed transformed the Safavids from a Sufi order to a priestly state.[2] Junayd did this by making changes in the secret teachings of his illustrious ancestors, which since the time of his grandfather Khwajah 'Ali had been influenced by Shi'ism, and by gathering many devotees for the purpose of seizing political power: hence his early exile from Ardabil by the Qaraquyunlu ruler Jahanshah.[3] After Junayd's death during a holy war in the Caucasus, argued Hinz, his Anatolian disciples flocked to his son Haydar, who simply carried on his father's work by donning the mantle of *ghaza*.[4] More recently still, Roger Savory suggested that the Safavids had in fact been planning to capture power from the time of their formation around the turn of the fourteenth century, and Junayd had merely launched the first overt attempt after nearly two centuries of patient preparation.[5] The fact that the movement continued under Haydar and did not disappear with Junayd's death was the result of such ideological groundwork by the Safavid organization.[6] As for Haydar, Savory believed that he 'wielded both spiritual and temporal authority: 'inwardly, following the example of shaykhs and men of God, he walked the path of spiritual guidance and defense of the faith; outwardly, he was a leader sitting on a throne in the manner of princes'.[7] Along the same lines, John Woods believes that Junayd had begun a radical militant wing of the Safavids, which included followers among the extreme Shi'i Turcoman of Anatolia and Syria, and whose activities were maintained by Haydar.[8] The same general conceptualization occurs in Kathryn Babayan, who portrays Junayd much the same way as did Babinger nearly a century ago: the man who led the heterodox Turcoman of Anatolia in a rebellion.[9]

Other scholars, while acknowledging Junayd's political ambition, treated his religious beliefs as the reflection of folk Islam and not a consciously formulated ideology. Michel Mazzaoui, for instance, has noted that Junayd and Haydar were the first members of the Safavid family who were referred to by the chroniclers with the secular title 'sultan' as opposed to 'shaykh'.[10] He placed their recruiting success within the context of Ottoman centralization policies under Mehmed II, which were resented by Anatolian Turcoman who had long been the devoted followers of the order at Ardabil.[11] Hans Roemer believed that the conflict between Junayd and his more 'orthodox' uncle Ja'far was not a religious one, but was rather due to Junayd's militaristic tendencies.[12] Nevertheless, religion played a crucial role for the shaykh in recruiting his followers. Safavid agents, wrote Roemer, must have conducted propaganda in Anatolia, where simple Turcoman were attracted to miracle-working Sufis.[13] '[The Safavids] were highly esteemed—by the early Ottoman sultans, among others. How otherwise could one explain the ambitious plans and political aspirations of Junayd and Shaykh Haydar?'[14]

These two broad outlines of scholarly consensus underlie more recent studies as well. They are succinctly repeated in Andrew Newman's recent survey of the dynasty,[15] and are also accepted by Temur Aytberov, who has deciphered the newly discovered tomb of Shaykh Haydar and his brother in Dagestan by which he has confirmed the traditional death date of the Safavid leader.[16] Nor have they been rejected or nuanced by Kazuo Morimoto, who has recently published a chart dating to the 1460s claiming descent from the family of the Prophet Muhammad for the shaykhs of Ardabil (thus confirming the early proto-Shiite tendencies of Junayd).[17]

The above arguments, despite their many contributions, suffer from a number of problems. For one, much of our understanding of the early Safavids is too indebted to chronicles. Second, present-day scholars give primary, if not exclusive, causality to religious 'ideology'. Third, they presuppose the 'Great Man' version of history, whereby outstanding individuals are not the by-products of broad historical processes but are themselves agents that produce great historical events. Fourth, they posit Junayd and Haydar's religious and political ambitions as always already there and do not try to explain the particular historical reasons (other than personality) that might have pushed them on to the historical stage. Fifth, they often disregard the rhetorical nature of the polemics and apologetics directed at the events of the late fifteenth century. This chapter will revisit early Safavid history while steering clear of these methodological pitfalls. In order to avoid privileging narrative sources, other documents (such as royal letters and land-grant documents) will be analyzed in chronological order. However, the chronicles should not be completely ignored, and their place in the formation of the discourse on Safavid 'heresy' as well as the historical information contained in them will be investigated.

Death of Haydar

What is the earliest known contemporary reference to Safavid heresy? It occurs in a letter in Feridun Bey's famous anthology of diplomatic correspondence,[18] and it diverges from the modern scholarly consensus regarding the origins of the Safavid movement. This letter was dispatched by the Aqquyunlu ruler of western Iran and eastern Anatolia, Sultan Ya'qub, to the Ottoman Emperor Bayezid II. In it, Sultan Ya'qub informed his Ottoman counterpart that he had murdered Shaykh Haydar Safavi, Ya'qub's own cousin and brother-in-law, during a punitive skirmish in the Caucasus. It is true that on the surface, the letter appears to support the present-day conviction that Ya'qub disposed of Shaykh Haydar because of the latter's growing power and his heretical views, which he supposedly inherited from his maverick father Shaykh Junayd. However, a closer look reveals much more and indeed problematizes our modern viewpoint.

The document opens with a series of honorifics addressed to Bayezid, including *ghazi* in the path of God and *mujahid* for God's religion. Both terms are synonyms for holy warrior. This double designation of holy war is unusual in Ottoman–Aqquyunlu correspondence, at least based on the selection in Feridun Bey. Among the ten letters directed by Ya'qub or his father Uzun Hasan to the Ottoman court,[19] only one other greets the Sultan in Istanbul as a fighter for religion, and in that case with a singular *mujahid* in the path of God.[20] Why was Ya'qub so eager to emphasize this point?

The text then presumes to speak for Bayezid by stating that his excellency the *khudavandigar* (that is, the Ottoman sultan) surely knew that Ya'qub had been protecting what God had left in his charge by treading the straight path of the true law (*tariqa-i mustaqim-i shar'-i mubin*).[21] This is a curious statement. Obviously if Bayezid knew this to be the case, Ya'qub would not need to underscore it. What follows, however, clarifies the reason for Ya'qub's anxiety for establishing his religious credentials and proving his understanding of what it means to be a fighter for Islam.

Ya'qub stated that those who might betray the covenant between God and man would perforce be dealt with sternly. He went on to say that the head of the companions of darkness, Shaykh Haydar, although descending from the family of holy men (*awliya'*) and Sufis, had proven to be different than his predecessors and had begun to stray from the paths of his forerunners. He had brought infamy to those of a good name. By pretending to do *ghazw* in Georgia, he had attracted a crowd to himself through deceit and chicanery. But then he had started a *fitna* ('civil strife' with a religious connotation) due to his old enmity with a local Muslim ruler, the Shirvanshah. Haydar drove his nemesis into a fort and then began oppressing the Muslim inhabitants, killing men, women, and children. More disturbing still was that 'the signs of infidelity and deviation were manifested through their words and deeds'. The Aqquyunlu ruler, therefore, had no choice but to send an army after Haydar and put a violent end to his sedition.[22]

The contents of this apologetic letter diverge from the standard modern narrative of early Safavid history that is primarily based on the anti-Safavid chronicle of Fazl Allah Khunji Isfahani, the official historian of Ya'qub. Here Ya'qub, unlike his historian a few years later, designates Haydar, and not his father Junayd, as the originator of Safavid mischief and heresy. His language, however, would be mimicked by Fazl Allah who later claimed that it was Junayd who first strayed from the precedence of his holy ancestors, began to entertain political ambitions, and showed signs of rebellion.[23] Based on chronology alone, it is clear that the accusation of religious and political subversiveness was brought up against the Safavids as a justification for their suppression and then projected backwards. No doubt the Aqquyunlu had to explain their attack on a respectable Sufi shaykh who was engaged in a battle for Islam, and they did this by questioning both the religious credentials of the holy man and by denying his *ghaza*. But there is more evidence for this than mere chronology. The closing lines of Ya'qub's letter speak to this point. He writes,

Since that sect of darkness and that gathering of the dark were enemies of the prophet's law, foes of the 'Alid path (*tariqa-i murtazavi*), rebels (*khari-jiyan*) against government and religion, and mutineers against kingdom and the people ... the arrival of this blessed good news ought to cause an increase in the thanksgiving and prayers [of the Ottoman government].[24]

Ya'qub's choice of words is significant. By pairing the 'Alid path or *tariqa* (with the secondary connotation of a Sufi brotherhood such as the Safavids) with the holy law, he showed a simultaneous rever-ence for the Shi'a and the Sunni creeds, a trait he would have shared with the Timurids in the east. If Shaykh Haydar, like his son Isma'il, was indeed a staunch devotee of 'Ali ibn Abi Talib, then Ya'qub was here appropriating the voice of social protest, teaming it up with the 'orthodoxy' that the sultan was supposed to uphold. Referring to the followers of Haydar as Kharijites, a term used for people in Imam/ Caliph 'Ali's camp who rebelled against him and murdered him in the seventh century, is another attempt of a reversal by which he associates the Aqquyunlu with the true Shi'a and the Safavids with its opponents. Finally, at this point too, as in the beginning of the letter, Ya'qub felt obliged to tell the Ottomans how they should react to this news, thereby exposing his anxiety regarding the political implica-tions of his actions. But why did Ya'qub need to justify his actions to the Ottomans in the first place? When one untangles the complicated Ottoman–Aqquyunlu diplomatic relationship during the fifteenth century, more evidence emerges in support of the claims made above.

Mehmed II and Uzun Hasan

Politically, the Aqquyunlu principality in western Iran and eastern Anatolia shared many characteristics with its neighbours. Rapid consolidation by conquest and immediate fragmentation during suc-cession typified the political life of the Timurids and the Qaraquyunlu as well. Their most successful leader, Uzun Hasan, managed to defeat two of the most powerful monarchs of the day: Jahanshah Qaraquyunlu and Abu Sa'id Mirza, the Timurid. By 1471, however, the newly emerging Aqquyunlu state met its match when it clashed with the Ottoman Empire in eastern Anatolia. Besides its military conse-quences, this encounter had important ramifications for the role of religion in diplomacy and the discourse of legitimacy between the two polities.

Although it seems that Muslim potentates of the fifteenth century made war and peace with one another based on every reason except religious or 'ideological' ones, nevertheless, something resembling public opinion within Islamdom still mattered to these men. This is borne out by the attempts to justify major conflicts through religion. The battle between Uzun Hasan and Mehmed the Conqueror is one such example. Based on the letters preserved by Feridun Bey, the opinion of important religious men inside the Ottoman Empire was not entirely supportive of Sultan Mehmed. A curious letter to the sultan from Akşemseddin, Sultan Mehmed's spiritual adviser, bears out this assertion. Akşemseddin wrote to Mehmed that while initially he was sceptical, he had been convinced of Ottoman victory over the Aqquyunlu based on a number of dreams. One of these had been narrated to him as follows:

> I saw an assembly in which was the Prophet of God. On his right were Abu Bakr and 'Umar and on his left 'Ali and 'Uthman. In that assembly there was also a number of the blessed companions [of the prophet]. And I saw a number of the sublime holy men [*awliya'*] urge and plead with the Prophet of God for the victory of Hasan Beg over Sultan Mehmed, and it appeared that he accepted their pleas. Many of the companions also approved of it. Then three Good Men [*akhyar*] rose up and requested of him the victory of Sultan Mehmed over Hasan Beg, but he did not appear to accept their plea. However, they persevered in their request and earnestly persisted and repeated it. So the Prophet of God spoke to 'Ali and a long secret conversation took place between them. Then together they sat down and tarried a moment. Afterwards he uttered aloud all that was secret and 'Ali raised his hand, struck his thigh with it, and said in a loud voice three times, 'Sultan Mehmed has won over Hasan Beg'. I asked about the large crowd who had requested Hasan Beg's victory and it was said that they were the holy men of Konya and Karaman. And I also asked about the three who had requested Sultan Mehmed's victory, and it was said that they were Abu Ayyub Ansari, al-Shaykh al-'Arabi, and al-Sayyid al-Bukhari.[25]

This particular dream demonstrates much about the anxieties of the Ottomans prior to their encounter with Uzun Hasan. Although victory is assured to Sultan Mehmed, it is quite clear that the sheer number of the holy men in eastern Anatolia might have tipped the balance of religious legitimacy in favour of the Aqquyunlu. Even the pantheon of venerable figures from early Islamic history was initially disposed towards the adversary. Surely this was how the Ottomans perceived Muslim public opinion in Anatolia on the eve of their battle with another bona fide potentate of Islamdom.

The solution for the Ottomans was to assume the religious high ground with the Aqquyunlu as tensions escalated. They were further pressured into this position by a similar action on the part of Uzun

Hasan. In a letter to Mehmed II, the Aqquyunlu had stated that Muslim states should wage *ghaza* against non-Muslims and not fight each other, and had furthermore questioned the religious legality of certain Ottoman taxation practices.[26] In response Mehmed answered the first threatening letter of Uzun Hasan by stating: 'Our country is the abode of Islam. For generations, the lamp of our government has been lit with the oil of the *kafirs*' hearts. If you have violent intentions towards the people of Islam, then you are among the enemies of government and the *shari'a*. The same goes for those who aid and assist you.'[27] Here, the case for Ottoman authority is affirmed on the appeal to holy war, which Mehmed claims his ancestors had fought for generations. An Aqquyunlu invasion would thus amount to a betrayal of Islamdom and religious 'orthodoxy'. In another letter, Mehmed made a similar argument to his son Cem Sultan in Kastamonu, claiming that he attacked Uzun Hasan 'because it had become legally and rationally necessary to eliminate his evil from the abode of Islam, due to his having plundered the property, possession, wives, and children of Muslims'.[28]

This argument was subsequently expanded in Mehmed's correspondence with the Timurid ruler Sultan Husayn Bayqara. Not only were the Aqquyunlu enemies of Islam, thanks to their predatory actions towards Muslim lives and property, they had even gone so far to collude with Christian powers (Venice) against the Ottomans. The document is worth extensively quoting as it gives voice to the fullest expression of Mehmed's ideological position against Uzun Hasan. It reads as follows:

At the time when [Uzun Hasan] turned his attention and aggression toward the late Padshah Jahanshah Mirza and the martyred Khaqan Sultan Abu Sa'id, may their graves be fragrant, if only a small group of our victorious soldiers who had been commissioned to capture those borderlands had entered his kingdom in [Uzun Hasan's] absence and assailed it, then it is obvious in what state he would find himself. But since our worthy fathers and great ancestors were habituated to *ghaza* and jihad and were infatuated with elevating the word of God, and since the efforts of this glorious lineage has been concentrated only on fighting fiendish *kafirs* and *kafir* fiends, it seemed unmanly and not chivalrous to abandon the glorious precedent of our ancestors, which is in truth an obligation, and to set out after someone who is counted among the kings of Islam at a time when the bosom of his soul had become the target of enemy hands.[29]

[But now] it has become apparent that he has sent from everywhere letters to *kafirs* of every country, may the One Omnipotent God destroy them, and has prompted them to attack the lands of Islam, may the banners of religion be aloft therein forever. Many times have his emissaries and letters been captured and brought to our court. Although, with the help of

God the Most High and the goodness of his approbation, neither Islam nor Muslims will be harmed by it, it is still necessary to repel and stop him since the temptation of Satan does not ever cease.[30]

Thus the Ottomans claimed moral superiority over the Aqquyunlu based on their tradition of *ghaza* and jihad. The Aqquyunlu on the other hand showed themselves to be the enemies of Islam initially due to their attack on the Ottomans but then because of their conspiracy with the Venetians. Uzun Hasan's subsequent defeat cast a shadow on his dynasty's legitimacy. As John Woods has argued, 'The Battle of Başkent had demonstrated to the Muslim community that God had revoked His mandate from Uzun Hasan and designated a new champion.'[31] Following Uzun Hasan's defeat to Mehmed, many of his divine qualifications, such as the numerological explanation of his name as a sign of God's favour, were reinterpreted by chroniclers to refer to Mehmed.[32] Moreover, immediately after this debacle, we find the Aqquyunlu Sultan in the Caucasus, fighting a holy war. The primary goals would have included the need to gain quick booty, to engage his soldiers, to unite his emirs behind him, and to secure a victory to regain some of his lost prestige. However, against the background of the Ottoman rhetoric analysed above, it is not difficult to see the Georgian campaign as an attempt by Uzun Hasan to recover a bit of his damaged Islamic credentials which he had lost by joining a failed alliance with the Venetians against Sultan Mehmed II. A crucial detail in the description of later chroniclers strengthens this supposition. According to a sixteenth-century Safavid historian, after his defeat by Mehmed the Conqueror

Hasan Beg in the early months of 881 went to do *ghaza* in Georgia, and he took with him the *sayyids*, *ahali*, and shaykhs of his domain who held land grants (*soyurghals*). He conquered much of Georgia, took many slaves, and gave each of the *sayyids* and *ahali* a share of that booty. He returned to Tabriz in the same year.[33]

Raiding Georgia in the name of Islam and distributing the plunder among important religious men must have been intended to recuperate the tainted image of the Aqquyunlu. In the next section it will be argued that the same intent was at work as the successors of Uzun Hasan tried to make peace with the Ottoman Empire.

Ya'qub and Bayezid

Soon after the death of Uzun Hasan, his successors began their rapprochement with the Ottomans. The first evidence of this occurs in a letter, not reproduced by Feridun Bey, but one that is now at the Topkapı Palace, exchanged between Uzun Hasan's oldest son Khalil Allah and a certain Sinan Paşa.[34] This royal epistle is particularly significant because it posits *ghaza* and jihad as the key to their mutual friendship.

> From ancient times and for generations, a strong foundation and a solid groundwork of amity had existed between the two parties [Ottomans and the Aqquyunlu] so that nothing more excellent could have been imaginable. At a time when this sincere friend [Khalil Allah] had been absent from attendance upon His Majesty my father the Khaqan [Uzun Hasan], due to some accidental and silly matters that had been committed by the two parties, an event took place whose occurrence would not be reckoned possible by wise men. Then through the exchange of messengers, there has come to pass a simple alliance in the way of unity and friendship.[35] Henceforth the two parties will fire up *ghaza* and repel *kafir*s and idol-worshippers, thereby causing the strengthening of the religion of Islam.[36]

Here Khalil Allah distances himself from the Ottoman–Aqquyunlu war and downplays it. He expresses his interest in re-establishing diplomatic relations. What is particularly significant is that he attempts this by promising to match the Ottomans in their *ghaza* and jihad. By comparing this letter against those of Mehmed the Conqueror, who had claimed superiority through his holy wars and cast a shadow of doubt on the legitimacy of the Aqquyunlu, one can state that Khalil Allah and his court had internalized the Ottoman position towards them and were trying to distance themselves from it.

Following the overthrow of Khalil Allah by his younger brother Ya'qub, the policy of reconciliation continued. However, Ya'qub approached the matter with some hesitation, perhaps because he had to justify his rule in place of his older brother. He appealed to the ruler of Shirvan in the Caucasus to play the mediator between his court and Istanbul. The letter of Sultan Ya'qub to Shirvanshah Farrukhyasar speaks to this point.

> You had written that Paludeoğlu (?) has escaped and reached Ovacık on the frontiers of the well-protected domains [Aqquyunlu territory]; and that I should capture him and send him to Rum. Let me say openly that capturing him and sending him to Rum seems unlikely. I will however order that he be expelled from the aforementioned place. In your letter to the Sultan of Rum [Ottoman Sultan Mehmed (?) the Conqueror], you should write in such a way as to reassure him and set his mind at ease, seeing that there exists total unity between the two [of you].[37]

Ya'qub's request of Farrukhyasar did not fall on deaf ears since the Shirvanshah actually did write to the Ottoman court and fulfilled his role as mediator. In his letter to the Ottoman Sultan Bayezid II, Farrukhyasar wrote that he and Ya'qub owed obedience to the sultan because of Ottoman holy wars in the Balkans, which had been successful thanks to God's favour. Ya'qub Beg, embarrassed by the disobedience of his stubborn father toward the Ottomans, was now asking for forgiveness from the sultan on behalf of his family. He had asked Farrukhyasar to intercede on his behalf to re-establish diplomatic ties between the two.[38]

Judging by their subsequent exchange, these early gestures were successful, perhaps because Bayezid, who was busy dealing with the challenge of his brother Cem Sultan, would not have wanted to create another enemy on his eastern borders. However, what matters more to the present chapter is that the initial hostilities and later partnership between the Aqquyunlu and the Ottomans were established based on Ya'qub's acknowledgement of Ottoman superiority founded on Ottoman holy war in the Balkans. The Aqquyunlu in turn felt the need to constantly acknowledge this and at the same time defend their own tarnished Islamic image.

Thus, when Ya'qub attacked Shaykh Haydar while doing *ghaza* in the Caucasus, his actions, like those of his father Uzun Hasan, could be interpreted as aiding and abetting the enemies of Islam. He nervously defended his murder of the famous holy man by reassuring the Ottoman sultan that he still understood and respected *ghaza* (which was important to Istanbul), explained that Shaykh Haydar's campaigns were really not *ghaza* but attacks on Muslims, and that his beliefs verged on infidelity (as opposed to that of his ancestors, including his father Junayd).

With this in mind, we have no choice but to revisit the history of Haydar's father Junayd. If Junayd did not leave his home in Ardabil as a result of being exiled for seditious behaviour (as the documents above seem to suggest), then some other factor must have driven him away from home. It will be argued below that Junayd was most likely the victim of a new policy by the local Qaraquyunlu sultan, since this policy removed patronage from all but one member of the leading families in prominent shrine cities, which would include Ardabil.

Qaraquyunlu Land Policy

Qaraquyunlu land grants (*soyurghal*) were not just given to military commanders in exchange for loyalty and services rendered, but also to religious figures. In either case the recipient would be expected to have governing powers in the area while the locals would still have to provide soldiers for the king. For instance, a decree dated 17 September 1453 (13 Ramadan 857) issued to a Shaykh Dara'i grants the shaykh the area of Julfa and warns the prefects (*kalantaran*), chiefs (*kadkhudayan*), and the peasants (*ru'aya*) that Jahanshah has given their property and income (*mutavajjihat*) to the shaykh. They should now consider him their ruler (hakim) and head prefect (*darugha*), and they should obey him and also provide the army camp with soldiers and provision.[39] So here the recipient of the *soyurghal* is not simply being favoured or rewarded by the king but is also functioning as a government agent. It is worth noting that this individual is not a military commander, as was generally the case in the previous centuries, but a religious figure. In general, *soyurghals* to religious men provided them or their associated institution with tax immunity and not military governorship.[40] This change will prove of significance to Safavid history.

Another crucial development was that Jahanshah had begun directly intervening in the affairs of established and influential families in prominent shrine cities at the expense or exclusion of all but one member from the same family. A good case in point is the famous Shi'ite shrine in the city of Qum in central Iran. In fact the history of this institution parallels in some striking ways that of the Safavid shrine in Ardabil. Three decrees by the Qaraquyunlu and the Aqquyunlu help us trace these significant developments. There are almost verbatim copies of each other, with, however, some fundamental differences.

The first is dated 6 February 1463 (17 Jumada I, 867). It is issued by Jahanshah and gives the exclusive guardianship of the endowment of the Ma'suma Shrine of Qum to a certain Nizam al-Din Ahmad. The text describes how Nizam al-Din had brought documentation from earlier rulers such as Timur and Shahrukh showing that his family had been the sole guardians of the shrine for generations, and so Jahanshah affirmed his position exclusively and without a partner (*bidun-i musharikat-i ghayri*).[41] The same formula of exclusivity is used regarding the family (*bila mudakhilat va musharikat-i ghayr*). This terminology is certainly worth further analysis. Nizam al-Din's appearance before the king and request for guardianship without partners suggests that another claim could be made on the position. Otherwise what need would there be for a royal decree? Thus, a similar direct involvement of the royal court and its intervention in the Ardabil shrine, which we know happened in favour of Junayd's uncle Shaykh

Ja'far (see later), need not at all have been necessitated exclusively by perceived political danger from Shaykh Junayd, as later Safavid chronicles suggest.

But to return to Qum, some years later, following the defeat of Jahanshah by Uzun Hasan, the abovementioned decree was reissued by the new sultan, and it referenced and mimicked the original almost verbatim. However, here Uzun Hasan added another name to the document, giving the guardianship of the shrine to two individuals. Moreover, the economic powers of the guardians were extended to other buildings in the city, presumably to keep the original guardian appeased. All the Arabic honorifics are now in the dual form. The individuals named are Nizam al-Din Sultan Ahmad and Kamal al-Din 'Ata Allah. The phrase 'without partners' is taken out of the Jahanshahi text.[42]

This is also similar to what the Aqquyunlu were doing to the Safavids, picking a partner to share with the Qaraquyunlu-appointed (or -confirmed) leader, though we do not know whether they expanded their domains to other sites. Also crucial is that the title 'sultan' was added to Nizam al-Din's name (whereas it was missing from the Jahanshahi text). There is a similar development with the Safavids. As stated above, Shaykh Junayd and Haydar were the first members of the Safavid family who were referred to with the title of sultan. Safavid chroniclers and modern historians such as Mazzaoui make much of the addition of this 'secular' designation to Junayd and Haydar's names, assuming that it signals the shaykhs' quest for the throne of kings. However, based on the example of Qum, the title is not unique to the order in Ardabil and does not necessarily imply a claim to rule. It might have served to distinguish a more senior or higher claimant. If so, this would be how Junayd or Haydar would try differentiating themselves from their uncle Shaykh Ja'far, the Qaraquyunlu appointee.

Finally, under a later Aqquyunlu ruler, Sultan Alvand, the guardianship went back to one individual again. According to this third document, Nizam al-Din Ahmad came to the court and informed the king that his partner, Sayyid Kamal al-Din, had died and left no son behind. Therefore, the surviving guardian, who was now getting old, asked the sultan to transfer the guardianship to his son Sayyid Murshid al-Din Rashid al-Islam, and indeed the royal decree complied.[43] It is interesting to note that no investigation seems to have been undertaken to see if Nizam al-Din was telling the truth.

It is important to note here that the patterns detected at the shrine of Qum were not isolated actions but rather reflected a broader policy. A similar practice is at work in the management of Christian institutions. For instance, a decree by Jahanshah's wife Khatun Jan Begum issued 6 August 1462 (10 Zulqadeh 866) for Priest Matthew Katakius (?) appoints him as the head of the Armenians of Aghvan and allows him to fulfil administrative duties such as the appointment of priests, and so on.[44] However, under Ya'qub Aqquyunlu, a document from 1486–7 [AH 892] transmits his duties to two of his nephews, priests Simon Khalifah and Maradrun Mehrasia.[45] Here again we have evidence of dual appointments at a religious centre by the Aqquyunlu. What does all this mean for the Safavids? After the death of Junayd's father Shaykh Ibrahim, the Qaraquyunlu had begun politicizing important shrine cities and the holders of religious grants, giving support to one member of a particular family at the expense of other claimants. In that case, Shaykh Junayd was a victim of this loss of patronage and would have to go seek his fortunes elsewhere. It is time to revisit the narratives of early Safavid history and see how these findings allow for a modified reading of the commonly accepted version of events.

Alternatives

In light of the documentation analysed above, the origins of subversive political activity by the Safavids may now be presented in an amended fashion. The narrative sources for this early history fall into three categories. One set represents an official depiction initially commissioned by Shah Isma'il himself and propagated in the works of influential historians who were from the city of Herat with little direct knowledge of the events. These begin with Amini Haravi's official *Futuhat-i Shahi* and those who relied on him, such as Ghiyas al-Din Khvandamir, who penned *Habib al-Siyar*, Amir Mahmud b. Khvandamir, all the way down to Iskandar Beg Munshi. An alternative narrative is provided by historians who were more closely associated with Shah Tahmasp's capital city of Qazvin and were presumably in better contact with more individuals who were involved in the events. These include Ahmad Ghaffari's *Jahanara*, and especially Hasan Beg Rumlu's *Ahsan al-Tavarikh*. Finally, a third narrative with details about Shaykh Junayd's activities while in Anatolia is provided by the anonymous author who continued 'Aşıkpaşazade's *Tevarih-i Al-i Osman*. English language scholarship has relied heavily on the first tradition, but the other two should also be considered.[46]

The rise of Shaykh Ja'far's star at the shrine of Ardabil during the reign of Jahanshah was not an isolated event, nor even a reaction on the part of the Qaraquyunlu monarch to a mischievous Shaykh Junayd. Rather, here too, Jahanshah was implementing a policy similar to that of the shrine of Qum or the Christian institutions of Aghvan. By giving exclusive support to Ja'far, establishing a marriage alliance with him, and issuing *soyurghals* in his name, the Safavid order must have suddenly experienced a radical restructuring at the expense of most other members of the leading family, including Junayd. This hypothesis goes against the narrative of some Safavid sources dating back to the early official chronicle of Amini Haravi, who suggests that Jahanshah expelled Junayd because he feared the shaykh would cause the downfall of his kingdom,[47] an unlikely scenario given the power of the Qaraquyunlu at this point. Hasan Beg Rumlu's version is a bit more elaborate and diverges from Amini in this regard. According to his account, after Junayd's accession to the leadership of the order, Jahanshah wrote to Junayd's uncle Shaykh Ja'far (who was connected to the king through the marriage of his son to the king's daughter) and told him to exile Junayd from Ardabil.[48] The idea of Junayd's leadership of the order is improbable, since he was his father Shaykh Ibrahim's sixth son,[49] and he could not have ranked very high in the hierarchy of the order. But Hasan Beg's suggestion that Shaykh Ja'far was treated by Jahanshah as the order's leader is supported by contemporary documents that demonstrate a number of *soyurghals* made out to Shaykh Ja'far by the Qaraquyunlu ruler and his wife.[50]

Thus, it appears that a situation similar to what had happened in Qum and Aghvan took place in Ardabil also. In other words, here too royal power had intervened in the affairs of the religious institution and exclusively supported one member of the ruling family over others. It is certainly worth noting in this context that the exiled Junayd initially began his wanderings not in search of disciples but of a patron—a fact made necessary by the loss of former patronage. Thus, Junayd's first destination after his departure from home was the court of the most powerful monarch of the day in Anatolia—the Ottoman Sultan Murad II.[51] Failing to obtain Murad's backing, Junayd subsequently made his way to the Karamanid capital of Konya, that is, the domain of the second-most powerful monarch in Asia Minor. But here he did not go directly to the court instead stopping at the lodge of Shaykh Sadr al-Din Qunavi, where he got into trouble with its guardian Shaykh 'Abd al-Latif.[52] Anonymous/'Aşıkpaşazade suggests that Junayd ran afoul of the guardian in part because he did not show him the appropriate respect and did not meet with him for several days after his arrival there.[53] Later in an exchange between the two, Junayd made a comment about the interpretation of a Quranic chapter and 'Abd al-Latif seized the opportunity to denounce the Ardabil shaykh as a heretic.[54] It was a heated exchange, as people had to grab hold of each man and take him to his room.[55] The dubiousness of the accusation of heresy is further hinted at by anonymous/'Aşıkpaşazade who claims that Junayd's spiritual master (or teacher 'hoca') in Konya was none other than Mawlana Khayr al-Din, who later served as Mehmed the Conqueror's instructor—hardly a candidate who could be associated with heresy in the Ottoman domain.[56] Junayd left the lodge and went to Varsak province, and 'Abd al-Latif wrote to the Karamanid ruler Ibrahim Bey accusing Junayd of political and religious sedition.[57] Junayd then escaped to Syria, near Aleppo, and repaired an abandoned castle to reside in. However, in Aleppo, Junayd's behaviour was also considered haughty by the local notables, and it was only after an assembly was convened by the governor of Aleppo that three members of the Zayniya order[58] accused him of being a member of the heretical Musha'sha'a movement and of having abandoned the Friday prayer.[59] It is difficult to ascertain the truth of these accusations. 'Aşıkpaşazade claims that in Aleppo Junayd had begun attracting to himself other 'heterodox' groups such as the followers of Shaykh Badr al-Din (a religious man who almost forty years before had led an unsuccessful revolt in the Balkans).[60] Did he begin to entertain deviating positions after this or did suspicious contemporaries begin hurling the clichés of heresiography at him? It is worth noting that the sources do continue to hint at the jealousy of the various Sufi groups playing a role in Junayd's persecution.

Junayd and his followers were attacked by the order of the Mamluk Sultan and seventy of his followers were killed.[61] Thus, in the narrative of Junayd's wanderings in Anatolia, primarily based on 'Aşıkpaşazade's continuator, the shaykh's situation deteriorated at every point in his exile. He went from the Ottoman court to a respected Sufi lodge and thence to an abandoned castle. He was politely rejected by Murad II, chased by Ibrahim Bey Karamanoñlu, and attacked by the forces of the Mamluk Sultan. The supposedly all-important Safavid propaganda in Anatolia did not serve him until possibly the very end of these troubles, and as we have seen, even in Aleppo many of his supporters came not from a pre-existing Safavid network but from marginalized groups without a proper *tariqa* of their own.

All the same, even these followers did not avail him following his rout in Syria, and Junayd made his way with only his womenfolk to the Ottoman territory of Canik on the Black Sea coast. Here Junayd came

before Mehmed Bey, the Ottoman governor there, and gathered soldiers apparently with Mehmed Bey's approval to attack the Christian
city of Trabzon (*Canikte Mehmed Bey katına vardı, bir kaç bin kişi cem
oldu, Trabzona yürüdü*).[62] Who were these recruits? As stated before,
anonymous/'Aşıkpaşazade avers that Junayd had come to Canik alone
and without his followers. The Byzantine historian Chalkokondyles
says that the shaykh of Ardabil conscripted soldiers from the south,
east, the town of Samo, and some other towns.[63] Some members of
his army might have been Turcoman tribesmen as modern scholars
assume, but some clearly hailed from urban centres and others might
have been peasants or even soldiers in search of booty. What do we
know about the area from which Junayd recruited or about the recruitment practice of irregulars in the Ottoman military who depended
heavily on plunder for their livelihood? We know that starting in 1455,
the city of Tokat, which lay a short distance south of Canik, had begun
experiencing a period of population growth that was not matched by
grain production.[64] Would these peasants be willing to take up arms
to supplement their food shortage? Such an undertaking would not
be out of the ordinary since Ottoman peasants were at times required
to serve in the mounted auxiliaries units (*atlı*) that engaged in plunder
(the *akıncı*), as is suggested by a decree of Mehmed II in 1472 during
the preparations for his campaigns against Uzun Hasan.[65]

In any event, according to Chalkokondyles, Junayd made
great initial progress in this raid but suddenly withdrew. Anony-
mous/'Aşıkpaşazade states that Junayd's withdrawal had to do with
the fact that the Ottoman Beylerbeyi of Rum (Sivas) Hızır Ağa
attacked Trabzon and routed Junayd.[66] It seems possible that Junayd
was being used by the Ottomans here because Hızır Ağa then pressured the weakened Greek kingdom of Trabzon, the last remnant of
Byzantine power following the conquest of Constantinople, to submit
to Sultan Mehmed.[67]

Whatever the case may be, what is significant is that Junayd
had grown progressively desperate in his search for patronage, his
followers were coming from more and more marginal groups, and
he had shown himself capable of resorting to violence by recruiting
soldiers and leading them on a raid, albeit possibly with Ottoman
support. Failing to withstand an Ottoman army did not take away
from Junayd's demonstrated ability to recruit (a very useful skill in an
era of no professional armies), and this would have been among the
reasons that attracted the attention of another upstart monarch and a
rising star—the Aqquyunlu Uzun Hasan—who finally gave a home

to Junayd and even married his sister to him. Junayd stayed there for almost four years and then was sent back to Ardabil by Uzun Hasan.

Now, some Safavid sources state that upon Junayd's arrival at his family shrine, the Qaraquyunlu ruler Jahanshah became even more concerned and exiled the shaykh once again.[68] But this story is problematic. If Jahanshah were worried about the Safavid shaykh, why would he allow him back in the first place? An understanding of Aqquyunlu/ Qaraquyunlu politics during this period might solve our dilemma. We know that between 1456–7 and 1463, Jahanshah Qaraquyunlu was following a very cautious policy towards Uzun Hasan, almost one of appeasement.[69] However, while this might explain why Uzun Hasan was able to send Junayd back to Ardabil without Qaraquyunlu opposition, it still would not account for Jahanshah's decision to evict the shaykh once again. Perhaps Jahanshah's opposition was not directed at Junayd but was the indirect result of his continuous support of Shaykh Ja'far, Junayd's uncle, who was still the leader of the order in Ardabil and would probably not be too keen on sharing the leadership of the Safavid *tariqa* with his younger nephew. This is precisely the contention of Ahmad Ghaffari in his *Jahanara*, who writes that the shaykh had to leave due to the enmity of his scorpion-like family (*al-aqarib k'al-'aqarib*) and because Jahanshah had already made Shaykh Ja'far powerful over the order.[70]

Junayd's subsequent action would fit this explanation because we find him trying to raise money—through plunder. Junayd left for the outskirts of the city and gathered an army which he then led on a *ghaza* in the Caucasus. There, however, he fell afoul with the Shirvanshah Khalil Allah, and died in a battle against him. Why did Junayd's death not cause the same anxiety and concern as his son's years later? After all we possess no letter trying to justify the shaykh's death as we do with Ya'qub Aqquyunlu's epistle analysed earlier. Yet, a look at the chroniclers' explanations for Junayd's death might shed some light on this matter as both anonymous/'Aşıkpaşazade and Hasan Beg Rumlu present a defence of the Shirvanshah: according to anonymous/'Aşıkpaşazade, Khalil Allah took exception to Junayd's raid on the Circassians since they were poll tax–paying subjects of his kingdom.[71] According to Hasan Beg, Junayd's uncle Ja'far actually sent a letter stating that Junayd was a liar/imposter (*kazib*) and his leadership (*khilafat*) and propagation (*irshad*) were inauthentic and, therefore, should be suppressed.[72] Interestingly, at least in this version, Ja'far did not accuse Junayd of holding heretical views. Either way, both these legal excuses exonerate the Shirvanshah and moreover, the murder of Junayd could not be considered an affront to the respected Sufi family as Shaykh Ja'far was still alive and apparently even approved his nephew's death.

Following Junayd's fall in the Caucasus, the Safavid order experienced a period of internal calm. The political situation of the region, however, went through some drastic changes. The Aqquyunlu achieved two rapid and astonishing victories against the Qaraquyunlu (1467) and the Timurids (1469) but then suffered a dramatic setback at the hands of the Ottomans in 1473. Uzun Hasan himself died in 1478, and was succeeded by his son Khalil Allah, who was in turn overthrown by his younger brother Ya'qub in the same year. Junayd's son Haydar entered politics shortly after this. It must be noted that Uzun Hasan had raised his orphaned grandson in his court and then sent him off to Ardabil to his great uncle Shaykh Ja'far in 1470. Hinz believes that Uzun Hasan had 'forgiven' Ja'far's close relations with Aqquyunlu arch-enemies Jahanshah and the Timurid Abu Sa'id Mirza.[73] More likely, however, was that the position of Shaykh Ja'far as the respected head of the order was too secure for the new sultan to risk a confrontation. Instead we have the presence of two prominent figures in Ardabil. The practice of having two major candidates in the shrine, one from the previous era (Ja'far) and a new Aqquyunlu appointee (Junayd and then Haydar) would, moreover, resemble a similar policy at work in the shrine of Qum as well. The application of the title of 'sultan' to Junayd and Haydar in this period also parallels the developments in Qum and might suggest claims to superiority between the ruling pair at the shrine.

The events that led to Haydar's activities and eventual death in the Caucasus in 1488 include a series of *ghazas* undertaken by the young shaykh in 1483, 1486 (or 1487), and 1488. His first campaign was in part motivated by the very same reasons that had prompted his father. According to Hasan Beg Rumlu at least, Shaykh Ja'far began to make life difficult for Haydar who, nevertheless, could not muster the necessary forces to lead a campaign of plunder. In 1483, however, enough people gathered around him to make this possible.[74] Why did this finally occur? According to Hasan Beg, people came to him from Sham (Syria), Rum (Anatolia, especially around the Karamanid territory), and other countries.[75] This is an important phrase in Hasan Beg's narrative. Based on later Safavid history, we know of major tribal groups under Shah Isma'il and especially Shah Tahmasp, who are referred to as Rumlu or Shamlu. Hasan Beg does not mention these tribal forces nor does he refer to them by the term Qizilbash at this point. In fact, the first recorded mention of the word Shamlu does not occur until 1486 in an Aqquyunlu document.[76] It seems that the first group of Anatolians and Syrians who arrived in Ardabil to go to Georgia were disparate people on the move who may or may not have included pastoralists. It is also worth remembering that tribal names often evoke an eponymous ancestor (such as the Oghuz) or a limited region (such as the Mawsillu). The vast and more generic geography covered by the appellations Rumlu and Shamlu suggests the formation of new group identities among all sorts of displaced people in the late fifteenth century. But if Haydar's followers were not yet formed into tribes and included deracinated folks from Anatolia and Syria, why did they come in 1483 to join a Safavid raiding campaign and not in previous years as Hasan Beg states?

The Ottoman Empire by the time of Mehmed II's death (1481) was the only polity in western Anatolia that could lead *ghazas* against its Christian enemies. At the same time, the kingdom of Karaman too had been mostly incorporated into the Ottoman Empire. The death of Mehmed in 1481 suddenly led to a hiatus in Ottoman campaigns since his two sons—Cem, seated in the recently conquered Karaman (Rum proper), and Bayezid—began to fight over the succession. Perhaps this hiatus motivated some adventurers to temporarily seek their fortunes on an eastern *ghaza* in a 'non-state' enterprise. It is also possible that the battles between Bayezid and Cem left men from the defeated side (Karaman or Rum), who did not expect to be incorporated into the Ottoman army, to move east for new opportunities. A bit further south, in Syria (Sham) a few years back, the Aqquyunlu had defeated a Mamluk army and here too perhaps underpaid or unpaid soldiers could have found the idea of a *ghaza* not directed by the Aqquyunlu army attractive. Ottoman–Mamluk border conflicts also unfolded in the same region within the next couple of years and immediately afterwards we hear of Haydar's second and third *ghaza* in the Caucasus. Indeed, we know of instances of defection of the Karamnids to the Safavids. For instance, Şikâri (d. 1584) writes in his *Karamanid History* that after the death of Kasim Bey, the last of the Karamanid royal line, thousands of soldiers from the Karamanid principality joined Shah Isma'il due to their refusal to obey the Ottomans.[77] Of course the dates are off here because Kasim Bey actually died in 1483, and if the defections began following his death, we are in fact much closer to the final years of Haydar's activities.

Political reasons aside, socio-economic factors were also at work to encourage the defection of the Anatolian *sipahi* or at least their search for better prospects. Ottoman surveys in parts of the province of Karaman from the time of its conquest (beginning in 1468) till near the end of Bayezid II's reign (1501) suggest a gradual decline in the tax revenues by which the *sipahi* collected most of their income. Ironically this loss of revenue was due to the abandonment of pastoralism by some tribes and the shift to a commercial farming economy. This information provides a very strong case against the assumption of straightforward continuity of Anatolian tribes in the Safavid movement, especially if pastoralism is implied in that definition. The herding economy was actually on the decline in the very regions of Rum that supplied Haydar with his earliest newcomers.[78] If the patterns in Kayseri are any indication, the men would most likely be destitute soldiers who may or may not have taken to pastoralism to make a living. We must remember that a decline in the income of the *timar* or land grant would have affected not just the top commanders but numerous attendants and soldiers who were supposed to be in their employment.[79]

Whoever Haydar's recruits might have been, the uniformity established by their leader is quite significant. Haydar's soldiers are almost always called *ghazis* in the sources, not Sufis, Safavids, or even Qizilbash (except for Hasan Beg when referring to the final battle of Haydar). This means that they received a functional (that is, conscriptive) appellation as opposed to an ascriptive one. In other words, the group identity of Haydar's forces was meant to supercede tribal, *tariqa*, or regional affiliations, and their pay would derive not from the wealth of the Safavid shrine (to which at least early on Haydar had little access), but rather from the self-funded holy plunder.

Fifteenth-century Italian travellers emphasize the financial causes for Haydar's success. According to Caterino Zeno, 'Those incursions, in addition to the advantages he reaped from his booty, raised his reputation so high, that he soon had the support of all the chiefs of his faction, and having raised a large army marched on another similar invasion of Circassia.'[80] This is not to say that the devotion of the order's network of adepts was not important or that somehow financial and spiritual motivations are mutually exclusive. Rather, it was the victories and pay-offs of Haydar that allowed for the scale of recruiting that initially made him politically relevant within the Safavid movement itself, whose elite ('all the chiefs of his faction') had been convinced materially of his viability for leadership. So according to this scheme, the initial success of the shaykh and his itinerant core group attracted the attention of the important people in his order, who then joined him for further adventures. The later campaign in turn brought in more recruits with little direct connection with the shrine of Ardabil. Another anonymous Italian merchant writes, 'Secaidar [Shaykh Haydar], with an army of four or five thousand Suffaveans, was marching into Circassia, joined by numbers of volunteers in hopes of plunder.'[81] The Safavid movement was thus growing incrementally; soldiers were receiving good pay. By the time of Haydar's last march through the Caucasus, his army had swollen to a formidable size: '[People in the Caucasus] wished to bar [Haydar's] passage lest he should go on increasing his power, as he did every day on his march to Circassia, by being joined by such multitudes of volunteers for the sake of booty.'[82] The followers of Haydar thus included large numbers of people who did not belong to the order's network of devotees. It was, therefore, necessary to give cohesion to this motley crowd, and this cohesion involved the creation of a uniform.

Haydar's introduction of the uniform *Taj-i Haydari* (Haydarid Crown), the red headgear with twelve folds that earned his followers the derogatory designation of Qizilbash (redheads), was the hallmark of this uniformity. The twelve folds were meant to evoke 'Ali and his eleven descendants, but the colour red had a significance directed especially towards Ottoman military men: the Ottoman begs had given in the fifteenth century white headgear to the newly formed professional Janissary corps to distinguish them from the rest of the soldiers, which would include all the members of the Ottoman military such as the cavalry (*sipahi*), the irregulars, and the raiders (*akıncı*) who sometime wore red headgear.[83] In fact a resentment was developing between these soldiers and the 'slave' (*kul*) army of the sultan (the Janissary) during the mid-fifteenth century. Especially during the second reign of Mehmed II (1451–81), the *kul* army had begun to dominate over the local military elite in the empire.[84] Following Mehmed's death, the next two successions of the Ottoman throne were decided by a conflict between candidates who were supported by the Janissaries or other military groups. In both cases the Janissary candidate won (Bayezid II over his brother Cem Sultan and Selim I over his brother Korkut). Much of Haydar's activity took place during this period, and his use of the red cap is an obvious overture to the marginalized *sipahi* and *ghazi* groups of the Ottoman army. We may recall that some of these men did indeed bear the appellation of Rumlu, that is, those from Rum or Karaman, which was the seat of the defeated faction of Cem Sultan.

Now, while the Safavid cause was in part bolstered by immigrants from Anatolia, the sphere of Haydar's activity should also be made sense of within the local Aqquyunlu context. For one, we must keep in mind that in the reign of Sultan Ya'qub, close relatives of the Sultan were filling more important posts than before in Aqquyunlu history.[85] Haydar being the sultan's maternal cousin would have had much more leeway in this new administration. His attacks on the Muslim confederates of the Aqquyunlu and the Shirvanis (as opposed to Christian Circassians or Georgians), however, would have made it difficult for Ya'qub to tolerate his cousin's behaviour for long, not necessarily because of the friendship between the Aqquyunlu and the Shirvanis but, as seen above, because the Shirvanshah played an important role in Ya'qub's Ottoman policy. There is indeed some evidence that Farrukhyasar actually complained to Sultan Bayezid following Haydar's first *ghaza* in the Caucasus.[86]

Ya'qub finally summoned Haydar in 1487 after his second *ghaza* when Aqquyunlu emirs warned the sultan about the growing danger of his Safavid cousin.[87] The wording of Ya'qub's response to his statesmen is worth quoting: 'One cannot stain one's hand with the blood of a Muslim who has never shown rebellion. Nor can one destroy the house of kinship based on fears of possible evil intentions.'[88] Whether or not Ya'qub had actually said these words, it is important that the Aqquyunlu court knew Haydar's blood relations with the sultan, and his religious credentials would have made squashing him quite difficult. Instead, we are told, Ya'qub asked Haydar to swear an oath of loyalty.

The oath ceremony was presided over by the chief jurist 'Isa Savaji. The irony of this event lies in the fact that Qazi 'Isa was known for his championing of the *shari'a* and later undertook a vast financial reform of the empire in the name of Islamic law that hit hard the Turcoman emirs, a number of Sufis, the 'ulema, and their dependants.[89] Clearly he had not found fault with Haydar's 'orthodoxy' at this point. Following the oath, Haydar led his third and final *ghaza*, and this is what is generally referred to as Haydar's revolt that involved another attack on the territory of the Shirvanshahs. As John Woods has indicated, Ya'qub in part caused Haydar's rebellion because he wanted Haydar to reinforce a vanquished Aqquyunlu army on the borders of Georgia that never showed up, forcing Haydar and his men to devote their time in dangerous inactivity.[90] When Shirvanshah finally asked for help, Ya'qub sent his great emir Sulayman Bijan to deal with the Safavid *ghazis*.

The familial air of this conflict should not be overlooked. Ya'qub was married to Gawhar Sultan Khanum, the daughter of Shirvanshah

Farrukhyasar, as well as to Beg Jan Khatun, the daughter of Sulayman Beg Bijan.[91] Essentially, he was using his two fathers-in-law who were indispensable to him to get rid of his cousin who was threatening one of them. In this way, the break-up of the Aqquyunlu and their replacement by the Safavids resemble the contemporary fall of the Timurids to Shaybani Khan Uzbek, who was actually related to some of the Timurid princes and emirs.[92]

Haydar's death was no small matter, however, and the situation now was quite different than when Junayd was killed. Shaykh Ja'far does not seem to have been alive any more and Haydar was the actual head of the Safavid order. The ramifications of his murder in religious terms would have been highly negative. It is certainly relevant that before going to punish Haydar, Ya'qub spent some time at the Ardabil shrine.[93] The Shirvanshah too, before attacking Haydar, had asked permission from the 'ulema and Sufis of Shirvan.[94] In other words, both had to tread cautiously. Also, shortly after Haydar's death, Ya'qub decided to publicly wash his hands of the sin of alcoholism. The ban on drinking took place under the supervision of Qazi 'Isa less than a month after Haydar's death (16 July to 11 August 1488).[95] Whatever else these acts might have signified, their chronological proximity to Haydar's demise suggests that killing the shaykh of a respected Sufi order was politically quite awkward.

These actions, along with the letters to the Ottomans analysed earlier (justifying the act by denouncing the religious credential of Haydar), were all part of dealing with this problem. The charges against Haydar are of course foreshadowed by Ya'qub's defence of his cousin before making him swear an oath of loyalty. The accusation of rebellion and heresy were thus part of the attempt to justify an arbitrary political murder. It is interesting to note that the very same accusation was brought up against the champion of 'orthodoxy' Qazi 'Isa, who was arrested shortly after the death of his master Sultan Ya'qub by the Turcoman emirs and executed. The great emir Sufi Khalil charged the accused not with the confiscation of property but with believing in the ideas of incarnation and deviation and even called him a *zindiq* (Manichean)![96]

* * *

In sum, the earliest contemporary reference to Safavid heresy occurs in a text that tries to justify the killing of, not Junayd, but his son Haydar. In other words, the accusation of bad belief was not the cause but the result of the suppression of the early Safavids. The murderer of Haydar, the Aqquyunlu Sultan Ya'qub, developed these accusations in a letter to the Ottomans because of the sensitive relationship between the two states. Junayd, Haydar's father, and the originator of violent political activity, was the victim of Qaraquyunlu policy of intervening into the internal affairs of important shrines, which excluded all but one member of the family from the privileges associated with guardianship. Junayd's political adventurism was, therefore, the outcome and not the cause of his wanderings in Anatolia. Finally, the followers of Junayd and Haydar were not necessarily united by tribal bonds. Much of the behaviour of the two early Safavid leaders suggests an attempt to unify a diverse and disunited band of followers. The militant wing of the Safavid order was not already established but came about as a result of the exclusion of leaders not in the direct line of succession of the order. Without access to the vast landholdings of the shrine of Ardabil, and rejected by other potential patrons, Junayd and his son eventually set out for access to immovable property: plunder. Had their efforts not coincided with unintended consequences of Ottoman successes under Mehmed II, they would not have been able to recruit their military following and would probably not have made their mark on history.

Notes

1. Franz Babinger, 'Schejch Bedr ed-din, der Sohn des Richters von Simaw: Ein Beitrag zur Geschichte des Sektenwesens im altosmanischen Reich', *Islam* 11 (1921): pp. 1–106.
2. Walther Hinz, *Irans Aufstieg zum Nationalstaat im Fünfzehnten Jahrhundert* (Leipzig: De Gruyter, 1936), p. 22.
3. Hinz, *Irans Aufstieg zum Nationalstaat*, p. 23.
4. Hinz, *Irans Aufstieg zum Nationalstaat*, p. 73.
5. Roger Savory, *Iran under the Safavids* (Cambridge: Cambridge University Press, 1980), p. 16.
6. Savory, *Iran under the Safavids*, p. 18.
7. Savory, *Iran under the Safavids*, p. 18.
8. John Woods, *The Aqquyunlu: Clan, Confederation, Empire* (Salt Lake City: University of Utah Press, 1999), p. 142.
9. Kathryn Babayan, 'Jonayd', *EIr* (2009), available at www.iranicaonline.org/articles/jonayd, last accessed 21 July 2015.
10. Michel M. Mazzaoui, *The Origins of the Safawids: Šiʿism, Sufism, and the Ġulat* (Wiesbaden: F. Steiner, 1972), p. 72.
11. Mazzaoui, *The Origins of the Safawids*, p. 77.

12. H.R. Roemer, 'The Safavid Period', *Cambridge History of Iran*, eds. P. Jackson and L. Lockhart (Cambridge: Cambridge University Press, 1986), vol. 6, p. 201.

13. Roemer, 'The Safavid Period', p. 206.

14. Roemer, 'The Safavid Period', pp. 191–5.

15. Andrew Neman, *Safavid Iran: Rebirth of a Persian Empire* (London: I.B. Tauris, 2006), p. 10–11.

16. Aytberov Temur, 'The Newly Found Tomb-Stone of Sheikh Haydar the Safavid in Dagestan', *IrCaucasus* 13, no. 2 (2010): pp. 281–4.

17. Kazuo Morimoto, 'The Earliest 'Alid Genealogy for the Safavids: New Evidence for the Predynastic Claim to *Sayyid* Status', *IS* 43, no. 4 (2010): pp. 447–69.

18. Feridun Bey, *Münşeat es-Selatin* (Istanbul: Daru'-Tibaat el-Amire, 1848), vol. 1, pp. 302–4.

19. Bey, *Münşeat*, pp. 267, 268, 269, 271, 300, 302, 306, 308 (two letters), and 313.

20. Bey, *Münşeat*, p. 313.

21. Bey, *Münşeat*, p. 304.

22. Bey, *Münşeat*, pp. 302–3.

23. Fazl Allah Khunji Isfahani, *Tarikh-i 'Alamara-i Amını*, ed. M.A. 'Ashiq (Tehran: Miras-i Maktub, 2003), pp. 259–60.

24. Bey, *Münşeat*, p. 304.

25. Bey, *Münşeat*, pp. 273–4.

26. Woods, *Aqquyunlu*, p. 115.

27. Bey, *Münşeat*, vol. 1, pp. 271–2.

28. Bey, *Münşeat*, p. 276.

29. Bey, *Münşeat*, p. 277.

30. Bey, *Münşeat*, p. 278.

31. Woods, *Aqquyunlu*, p.120.

32. Woods, *Aqquyunlu*, p. 121.

33. Yahya b. 'Abd al-Latif Qazvini, *Lubb al-Tavarıkh*, ed. M. Muhaddis (Tehran: Anjuman-i Asar va Mafakhir-i Farhangi, 2007), p. 251.

34. *Beylerbeyi* of Anatolia according to L. Fekete in *Einführung in die Ppersische Paläographie* (Budapest: Akademia Kiado, 1977), p. 226.

35. Fekete, *Einführung in die Ppersische Paläographie*, p. 226.

36. Fekete, *Einführung in die Ppersische Paläographie*, p. 228.

37. Fekete, *Einführung in die Ppersische Paläographie*, p. 230.

38. Fekete, *Einführung in die Ppersische Paläographie*, pp. 236–8.

39. Mudarrisi Tabataba'i, *Farmanha-i Turkamanan-i Qaraquyunlu va Aqquyunlu* (Qum: Chapkhanah-i Hikmat, 1973), p. 25–6.

40. Bert Fragner, 'Social and Internal Economic Affairs', *The Cambridge History of Iran* (Cambridge: Cambridge University Press, 1986), vol. 6, *The Timurid and Safavid Periods*, ed. Peter Jackson, p. 510.

41. Fragner, 'Social and Internal Economic Affairs', p. 42.

42. Fragner, 'Social and Internal Economic Affairs', pp. 64, 65.

43. Fragner, 'Social and Internal Economic Affairs', p. 121–2.
44. Fragner, 'Social and Internal Economic Affairs', p. 36–7.
45. Fragner, 'Social and Internal Economic Affairs', pp. 92–3.
46. Ghiyas al-Din Khvandamir, *Habib al*-Siyar, ed. Muhammad Dabirsiyaqi (Tehran: Intisharat-i Khayyam, 2001), vol. 4, pp. 424–34. Amir Mahmud b. Khvandamir, *Iran dar Ruzgar-i Shah Ismail va Shah Tahmasp-i Safavi*, ed. Ghulamriza Tabataba'i (Tehran: Majmu'a- Intisharat-i Adabi va Tarikhi, 2001), pp. 59–72.
47. Amini Haravi, *Futuhat-i Shahi*, ed. M.R. Nasiri (Tehran: Anjuman-i Asar va Mafakhir-i Farhangi, 2004), p. 37.
48. Hasan Beg Rumlu, *Ahsan al-Tavarikh*, ed. A.H. Nava 'i (Tehran: Intisharat-i Asatir, 2005), vol. 2, p. 601.
49. Roemer, 'The Safavid Period', p. 205.
50. Ahmad Kasravi, *Shaykh Safi va Tabarash* (Tehran: Firdaws, 2000), pp. 58–9.
51. 'Aşıkpaşsazade, *Tevarih-i Al-i Osman*, ed. Ali Bey, reprint (Farnborough, England: Gregg International, 1970), p. 264.
52. 'Aşıkpaşsazade, *Tevarih-i Al-i Osman*, p. 243.
53. 'Aşıkpaşsazade, *Tevarih-i Al-i Osman*, pp. 264–5.
54. 'Aşıkpaşsazade, *Tevarih-i Al-i Osman*, p. 265.
55. 'Aşıkpaşsazade, *Tevarih-i Al-i Osman*, p. 265.
56. 'Aşıkpaşsazade, *Tevarih-i Al-i Osman*, p. 264.
57. 'Aşıkpaşsazade, *Tevarih-i Al-i Osman*, p. 265.
58. Hanna Sohrweide, 'Der Sieg der Safaviden in Persien und seine Rückwirkungen auf die Schiiten Anatoliens in 16: Jahrhundert', *Der Islam* 41 (1965): p. 119.
59. Muhammad 'Ali Ranjbar, *Musha'sha'ıyan: Mahiyat-i Fikri-Ijtima'i va Farayand Tahavullat-i Tarikhi* (Tehran: Mu'assasah-i Nashr-i Agah, 2003), pp. 94–5.
60. 'Aşıkpaşsazade, *Tevarih-i Al-i Osman*, p. 266.
61. 'Aşıkpaşsazade, *Tevarih-i Al-i Osman*, p. 266.
62. 'Aşıkpaşsazade, *Tevarih-i Al-i Osman*, p. 266.
63. Chalkokondyles, *Laonici Chalcocondylae Atheniensis Historiarum Libri Decem*, ed. Immanuel Bekker, (Bonn: Weber, 1843), p. 264.
64. Huri Islamoğlu, *State and Peasant in the Ottoman Empire: Agrarian Power Relations and Regional Economic Development in Ottoman Anatolia during the Sixteenth Century* (Leiden: Brill, 1994), pp. 149–50.
65. Heath Lowry, *The Nature of the Early Ottoman State* (Albany: State University of New York Press, 2003), pp. 51–4.
66. 'Aşıkpaşsazade, *Tevarih-i Al-i Osman*, pp. 266–7.
67. Hinz, *Irans Aufstieg zum Nationalstaat*, pp. 28–31.
68. Haravi, *Futuhat-i Shahi*, pp. 39.
69. Woods, *Aqquyunlu*, pp. 95–6.
70. Ghaffari, *Jahanara*, p. 261.
71. 'Aşıkpaşsazade, *Tevarih-i Al-i Osman*, p. 267.

72. Rumlu, *Ahsan al-Tavarikh*, p. 603.

73. Hinz, *Irans Aufstieg zum Nationalstaat*, p. 72.

74. Rumlu, *Ahsan al-Tavarikh*, pp. 859–60

75. Rumlu, *Ahsan al-Tavarikh* , pp. 859–60.

76. Woods, *Aqquyunlu*, p. 197.

77. Şikâri, *Karaman Oğullari Tarihi*, ed. Mesud Koman (Konya: Yeni Kitap Basımevi, 1946), pp. 206–8.

78. Nicoara Beldiceanu and Irène Beldiceanu-Steinherr, 'Recherches sur la province de Qaraman au XVIe Siècle: Étude et actes', *JESHO* 11, no. 1 (1968): p. 124 (facsimile of document)/pp. 70–1 (their translation).

79. Halil Inalcik, 'Ottoman Methods of Conquest' *SI*, no. 2 (1954): p. 121.

80. Charles Grey, ed and trans., *Narrative of Italian Travelers in Persia in the Fifteenth and the Sixteenth Centuries* (London: Hakluyt Society, 1873), vol. 2, p. 44.

81. Grey, *Narrative of Italian Travelers*, p. 185.

82. Grey, *Narrative of Italian Travelers*, p. 185.

83. James Reid, *Tribalism and Society in Islamic Iran* (Malibu, California: Undena), 1983, p. 21.

84. Inalcik, 'Ottomans Methods of Conquest', pp. 121–2.

85. Woods, *Aqquyunlu*, p. 132.

86. Woods, *Aqquyunlu*, p. 271n38.

87. Hinz, *Irans Aufstieg zum Nationalstaat*, p. 82.

88. Isfahani, *Tarikh-i 'Alamara-i Amını*, p. 271.

89. Vladimir Minorsky, 'The Aq-qoyunlu and Land Reforms (Turkmenica, 11)', *BSOAS* 17, no. 3 (1955): pp. 449–62.

90. Woods, *Aqquyunlu*, p. 142.

91. Qazvini, *Lubb al-Tavarıkh*, pp. 254–5.

92. Maria E. Subtelny, 'Babur's Rival Relations: A Study of Kinship and Conflict in 15th–16th Century Central Asia', *Islam* 66 (1989): pp. 102–18.

93. Hinz, *Irans Aufstieg zum Nationalstaat*, p. 86.

94. Hinz, *Irans Aufstieg zum Nationalstaat*, p. 86; Isfahani, *Tarikh-i 'Alamara-i Amını*, p. 282.

95. Isfahani, *Tarikh-i 'Alamara-i Amını*, p. 311.

96. Woods, *Aqquyunlu*, pp. 151–2.

INDEX

Names and subjects in the notes have not been indexed.

NOTES ON THE EDITOR AND CONTRIBUTORS

Editor

Ismail K. Poonawala is professor of Arabic and Islamic Studies at the University of California, Los Angeles. A specialist in Isma'ili studies, he is the author of *Biobibliography of Isma'ili Literature* (1977) and editor of several Isma'ili texts. He has also translated with annotations, Volume IX of Tabari's history, entitled *The Last Years of the Prophet* (1990) and *The Pillars of Islam*, 2 vols (2002, 2004).

Contributors

Ali Anooshahr is an associate professor of History at the University of California, Davis. His research focuses on comparative premodern Islamic history with a special emphasis on Indo-Persian culture. He is the author of *The Ghazi Sultans and the Frontiers of Islam: A Comparative Study of the Late Medieval and Early Modern Periods* (2009). He has also published several articles.

Clifford E. Bosworth was visiting professor at the Institute for Middle Eastern and Islamic Studies at the University of Exeter. He was a Fellow of the British Academy and an Honorary Member of the Hungarian Academy of Sciences. He was professor of Arabic Studies at Manchester University and was the British editor of *The Encyclopaedia of Islam*, second edition, and an editor of the UNESCO Collection of History of Civilizations of Central Asia.

Robert Dankoff is Professor Emeritus of Turkish and Islamic Studies at the University of Chicago. For several decades, he has been involved in editing, translating, and analysing the works of the seventeenth-century Ottoman traveller, Evliya Çelebi. His recent books include *An Ottoman Mentality: The World of Evliya Çelebi* (2004, 2006), [with Sooyong Kim] *An Ottoman Traveller: Selections from the Book of Travels of Evliya Çelebi* (2010), [with Nuran Tezcan] *Evliya Çelebi'nin Nil Haritası 'Dürr-i bî-misîl în ahbâr-ı Nîl'* (2011).

Peter B. Golden is Professor Emeritus of History, Turkish, and Middle Eastern Studies at Rutgers University. He is a specialist in the history of the Turkic nomads of medieval Eurasia. Among his publications are *Studies on the Peoples and Cultures of the Eurasian Steppes* in the series *Florilegium magistrorum historiae archaeologiaeque Antiquitatis et Medii Aevi* (2011), *Central Asia in World History* (2011), and *Turks and Khazars: Origins, Institutions and Interactions in Pre-Mongol Eurasia* in *Variorum Collected Studies Series* (2010).

Carole Hillenbrand is Professor Emerita of Islamic History at the University of Edinburgh, Corresponding Fellow of the Medieval Academy of America, and Honorary Life Fellow at Somerville College, Oxford. Her publications include *The Crusades: Islamic Perspectives* (1999) and *Turkish Myth and Muslim Symbol: The Battle of Manzikert* (2007). In 2005 she was awarded the King Faisal Prize for Islamic Studies, the first non-Muslim to be given this honour.

Robert Hillenbrand is a Professor Emeritus of Islamic Art at Edinburgh University, and currently professor of Islamic Art, St Andrews University. His nine books include the award-winning *Islamic Architecture: Form, Function and Meaning, Islamic Art and Architecture,* and most recently *The Sheikh Zayed Grand Mosque* and *The Islamic Arts of the Book.* He has edited ten books, written numerous articles, and held six visiting professorships. He was the Slade Professor of Art at Cambridge in 2008.

Sunil Kumar studies the culture, society, and politics of the Central Islamic Lands and its extensions into Afghanistan, and north India, specifically during the twelfth through the sixteenth centuries. He is currently writing the history of a Muslim urban centre in north India (thirteenth to sixteenth centuries), reading it largely from the perspective of micro-history. He is currently professor in the Department of

History, Delhi University, and has taught previously in LMU Munich, SOAS London, UC Berkeley, EHESS, and EPHE Paris. His authored monographs include *The Emergence of the Delhi Sultanate* (2007) and *The Present in Delhi's Past* (2010).

Gary Leiser is a retired US civil servant and specialist in the eastern Mediterranean world of the twelfth and thirteenth centuries. Among his publications are Questions and Answers for *Physicians: A Medieval Arabic Study Manual* (2004) and translations of the most important historical works of M.F. Köprülü, including, *The Origins of the Ottoman Empire* (1992), *Some Observations on the Influence of Byzantine Institutions on Ottoman Institutions* (1999), and *Early Mystics in Turkish Literature* with Robert Dankoff (2006).

Benedek Péri is associate professor in the Department of Turkic Studies, Eötvös Loránd University, Budapest, Hungary. His research focuses on the history of classical Turkish literary traditions (Ottoman, Azeri, Chagatay). He is the author of *Az indiai timuridák és a török nyelv: a török írás és szóbeliség a mogul-kori Indiában (Turkish Language and Literature in Mughal India,* 2005).

Francis Robinson is professor of the history of South Asia, Royal Holloway, University of London. Among his recent books are *Islam and the Muslim History in South Asia* (2000), *The 'Ulama of Farangi Mahall and Islamic Culture in South Asia* (2001), and *The Mughal Emperors and the Islamic Dynasties of India, Iran and Central Asia (1206–1925)* (2007). His primary research interest is Islam in South Asia, particularly religious change since 1800.

Svat Soucek is retired librarian at Princeton University. His research has focused, with Robert Dankoff, on Islamic Central Asia and Ottoman naval history. Among his publications are *Piri Reis and Ottoman Mapmaking after Columbus* (1996), *History of Inner Asia* (2000), and numerous articles, a select group of which has been reprinted as *Studies in Ottoman Naval History and Maritime Geography* (2008).